Date Due			

THE LIBERAL AWAKENING

(1815–1830)

Following his survey of England in 1815, Halévy describes in *The Liberal Awakening* the transition from glorious war to peace without plenty: the disillusionment of victory followed by the fear of revolution, economic crises, and democratic reform, which was finally to bear fruit in the reforms of 1830.

It is often held that for the past two centuries the established and traditional government of Britain has been party government—an idea that has been put into circulation by numerous superficial historical accounts. Halévy imparts to the reader his belief that such generalisations give a far from adequate picture of events. Canning, for example, did not hesitate to attack both parties when occasion demanded it. Robert Peel, another great statesman, twice 'betrayed' the party which regarded him as leader, and chafed with equal impatience against the rules which are usually seen as the immutable laws of British parliamentary government. As with persons, so with policies: thus it was the Whigs who proclaimed the virtues of Free Trade, but a Tory who translated the ideal into practice.

Halévy is essentially an historian of ideas rather than of events, and in *The Liberal Awakening* the genesis of the great social movements of today is clearly revealed.

A HISTORY OF THE ENGLISH PEOPLE
IN THE NINETEENTH CENTURY

A HISTORY OF THE ENGLISH PEOPLE IN THE NINETEENTH CENTURY

A HISTORY OF THE ENGLISH PEOPLE
IN THE NINETEENTH CENTURY — II

THE LIBERAL
AWAKENING

1815—1830

by

ELIE HALÉVY

Translated from the French by
E. I. WATKIN

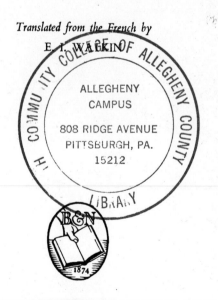

BARNES & NOBLE INC.

NEW YORK

Introduction

IN the first volume of this History of the English People in the Nineteenth Century, *England in 1815*, I traced in outline the political, economic, moral, and religious history of England during the troublous quarter of a century which began with the defeats of the War of American Independence and ended with Trafalgar and Waterloo. The volume was, in fact, rather a description than a history.

I depicted an England which under William Pitt and his successors was still in its general character very much what it had been under the hegemony of Lord Chatham, a country without officials and without police, where the executive was weaker than in any other country in Europe, and where the Justices of the Peace, members of the nobility and gentry, in whose hands the local government of England lay, were obliged to trust for the maintenance of order to the voluntary obedience of the people. Would new social conditions confirm or weaken this spirit of obedience? At first sight the observer would be inclined to reply that they must weaken it; for a revolution was taking place—the birth of the factory system based on the use of machinery. The practically unlimited output of the factories had called into existence a floating mass of workmen living from hand to mouth, attracted one year from the stable industry of the fields or the small workshop, to be thrown the next unemployed upon the streets of the large towns. Here surely was an army ready to wage a form of civil war inconceivable to the England which had made the revolutions of the seventeenth century.

It was then my task to study the moral, or to speak more accurately the religious, condition of the country. At first sight the religious institutions of England appeared to present the same spectacle of disorder and anarchy which the political constitution and the economic organization had displayed. Although the state Church enjoyed many privileges which would be intolerable today, nevertheless in the eighteenth century it was less autocratic, and occupied a humbler position than any Established Church in Europe. Both within and without her communion the Church of England was content to tolerate what we may call without exaggeration religious anarchy. But my investigations led me to the conclusion that, by the operation of one of the paradoxes of history, it was due indirectly to this anarchy that English institutions were after all so stable. For the imperturbable apathy of the Establishment left free scope to the often fanatical zeal of the Protestant sects. These sects were far from losing ground during that eighteenth century which a continental historian is inclined to regard as pre-eminently the century of rationalism; on the contrary, they were enormously strengthened by the birth and rapid growth of the great Methodist body. They offered an outlet by which the despair of the proletariat in times of hunger and misery could find relief, opposed a peaceful barrier to the spread of revolutionary ideas, and supplied the want of legal control by the sway of a despotic public opinion. Thus England was revealed as in very truth the country of self-government, the country which in the deepest sense—the moral and religious sense—of the phrase 'governs itself', instead of being governed by an external authority.

To sum up, if we would understand the gulf which separates the history of modern England from the contemporary history of the other European nations—and here, as a Frenchman, I am thinking particularly of my own country—we must, if my analysis is correct, be always on the alert to detect the silent influence exercised over the nation by these independent Churches of the lower middle class, an influence which their very number and diversity render it more difficult to define. These Free Churches created an atmosphere in which the two mighty watchwords, revolution and reaction, were emptied of their significance; for, on the one hand, the idea of a Church was not identified with that of a single Church which claimed the support of the State, and, on the other hand, when the people protested against abuses in the secular administration, it did not revolt at the same time against all spiritual discipline. In the first volume I attempted, in the light of this hypothesis, to explain what it was that enabled England to pass through the test of a long and terrible war without profound internal upheavals. I have now to relate how England, thanks to the institutions which I have described, endured successfully the test, in many respects a stern test also, of the return to the normal conditions of peace. To relate, not paint a picture; for events follow too quickly, one on the heels of another, to leave the historian leisure to linger on the road. Only at a later period, when the democratic and revolutionary movement seemed to have been finally defeated by the triumph of the pacifist and middle-class school of Free Trade, and when England, having attained at least a temporary equilibrium, ceased for a quarter of a century to have any history in the strict sense of the term, shall we be free to interrupt our narrative and return to description.

Since the publication of the first volume (published in Paris in 1913) ten years have elapsed. During that interval we have experienced another general war, which in many respects resembles the war from which England and Europe emerged in the summer of 1815. Certainly our war lasted a shorter time; but it raged with far greater intensity, destroyed more human lives, wasted more wealth, and its effect upon the history of mankind may well prove as revolutionary. Hence the present volume is perhaps more opportune in the date of its publication than would have been the case had it appeared earlier. No doubt the differences between the present situation and the situation a century ago are obvious. At that time England had not effected even the first of those democratic reforms which have transformed her political institutions during the past century, and the problems with which she is faced at present are entirely different from those which she had to settle then. Today a peacefully organized Labour Party constitutes a veritable State within the State. Then the Socialist creed was in its infancy. Today England shoulders the burden of taxation with a resignation—I might almost say a moral pride— no less intense than the enthusiastic determination with which she then refused to bear it. Moreover, if England occupies today a financial position far superior to that of a Europe ruined by the war, it must be added, on the other hand, that she has lost that enormous industrial superiority which she then enjoyed over the rest of the world, and that the United States of America are perhaps destined to take her place as arbiter of the balance of power among the nations. But the differences between present and past conditions provide food for very profitable reflections, and, when all has been said, the resemblances are striking. Today we may witness, and not in England alone, a world commercially out of gear, which presents the same financial difficulties, the same disturbance of the currency, the same anxiety to discover new markets, and the same disillusionment with victory. I remember the weary resignation with which in the early months of 1914, when engaged upon the first chapter of the present volume, I gave an account, only because it was my duty as an historian, of the inflationist theories of the Birmingham School which made so much noise in the fifteen years which followed Waterloo, and found it very hard to understand their attraction. But now, as I peruse my manuscripts and my proofs, I realize that the Utopias of a century ago are alive once more: the times of Thomas Attwood have returned.

But in other respects the ten years' delay has raised in my mind difficulties with which I must acquaint my readers before they begin this volume.

To all appearance for the past two centuries the established and traditional government of Great Britain has been party government. Two parties, we are told, the Whigs and the Tories, the Liberals and the Conservatives, have opposed, yet respected each other, both well aware that the existence of both is indispensable to the national welfare: for the one stands for progress, the other for order; the one represents the spirit of freedom, the other the principle of authority. I have no wish to deny that the historical reality does to a certain extent correspond with this conventional view. Assuredly England, for the reasons I have attempted to explain, is pre-eminently the country of compromise and toleration. But when this has been fully granted, it remains true that the current account of party government is superficial and crude. How large an element of fiction and self-deception is contained in the accepted view! There was, it is true, a period towards the end of the nineteenth century when two great men, disputing with each other the favour of the nation, at once leaders of a party and leaders of the people, bestowed an equal importance upon the two parties of which they were respectively at the head, and which succeeded to power according to a law of regular alternation. But had the political situation presented the same aspect at any time during the first half of the century? I cannot think so. Let us first consider individual politicians. Canning, the great statesman, was most certainly not a Whig. Was he, then, a Tory? In reality he had no love for either of the traditional parties, and before his death had pulverized both. Robert Peel, another great statesman, who twice betrayed the party which regarded him as its leader, chafed with equal impatience against those rules which they would have us regard as the immutable laws of British parliamentary government. After persons let us consider programmes. We can watch throughout the first half of the nineteenth century the slow progress of a definite programme of government which may be defined as unrestricted Free Trade. But although this programme finally became the monopoly of the Liberal Party, most certainly this had not always been the case. If Adam Smith was a Whig, he was the most sceptical of Whigs; and Fox, the leading Whig at the close of the eighteenth century, was an opponent of his doctrines. It was as the head of a Tory Cabinet that Lord Liverpool allied himself with the political economists, and his economic policy was opposed by the great families who constituted the general staff of the Whig forces. And even when the Whigs came into office their adoption of the Free Trade programme was bungling and half-hearted. When it was unanimous, it was obviously overdue, and on the eve of a General Election seemed no better than a move in the political game. And the honour of being the chief agent in translating the Free Trade ideal into practice was reserved for Robert Peel, the leader of the Conservative Party. All this surely is beyond dispute. Nevertheless, had I written my book ten years ago, I should probably have insisted on other aspects of the truth which seem less important today. For then, although many destructive agencies were already at work which justified gloomy predictions, the edifice of the two-party system appeared, on the surface at least, still intact. Since then we have watched a brilliant statesman adapt the tradition of Canning and Peel to the needs of a democratic age, break down the lines of party division, determine to be the leader, not of a party, but of the entire people, and invite the nation to follow him in discarding, as out-worn, the formula of party government. To myself and my readers I put the following question: Has the spectacle of the present clouded my vision of the past, or on the contrary, as I believe, has it enabled me to see the past more clearly as it really was?

On another matter also I may have failed to emancipate myself sufficiently from the anxieties of the present situation, and that is in my treatment of the relations between Great Britain and foreign Powers. I very soon found myself in the presence of Canning, that great Foreign Secretary, and to the best of my belief I have done full justice to his genius as an orator and a connoisseur of men. But I have been unable to see in him the great idealist, the hero of liberty, whose memory was revered by so many Englishmen fifty years ago. Am I mistaken in this? I have not, I believe, made a single assertion which I have failed to support by a fact or a document. Nevertheless, I would not deny the possibility that my estimate has been influenced by the events of contemporary history. I should like, in conclusion, to explain myself on this point.

Had I been contemporary of Canning, it is probable that, without troubling myself about the motives which inspired his policy, I should have rejoiced to watch him so successfully dividing, teasing, and flouting Governments so reactionary, so mean, and so mischievous that they were objects of scorn and hatred to every generous heart. And even if I had written ten years ago, I might possibly have pardoned Canning many of those dangerous decisions which were continually leading him to the brink of war. An entire phraseology was at my disposal then, to explain how war is often progress, movement, and life. But in the interval I have learnt what war means; therefore I feel an instinctive distrust of a statesman who made a career for himself out of diplomatic crises, and shone most brilliantly when the condition of the world was darkest. I prefer to a Canning—possibly more liberal, at least in his speeches, but certainly more bellicose—a Robert Peel, who was proud to call himself a Conservative, but was a far more resolute friend of peace. And I am even disposed to look with indulgence upon the fears which prevailed among the most timid section of the Tories, if only their effect was the prevention of war; nor can I resist the pleasure of quoting, when I meet them on my way, the words of the most reactionary and the most unpopular of Canning's Tory opponents: 'Men delude themselves by supposing that "war" consists wholly in a proclamation, a battle, a victory, and a triumph. Of the soldiers' widows and the soldiers' orphans after the fathers and husbands have fallen in the field of battle the survivors think not.' . . .

I desire to tender my thanks to the friends who have assisted me with their advice. Mr. Graham Wallas, Professor of Political Science at the University of London, was kind enough to read in manuscript the chapters of my third volume which treat of those earliest administrative reforms which followed the passage of the Reform Bill. M. Georges Dumas, Professor at the University of Paris, has given a more scientific character to my diagnosis of the mental disease which drove Lord Castlereagh to suicide. And I am under a very special obligation to M. Paul Vaucher, of the University of Paris, and Professor at London University, who, while the work was being printed, undertook at the British Museum the work of verifying, correcting, or completing doubtful statements and uncertain references.

Paris, 1923.   E. H.

Contents

PART I

THE YEARS OF LORD CASTLEREAGH
(1815-1822)

CHAPTER I

Fear of Revolution

I   THE DISILLUSIONMENT OF VICTORY

I

T HE long duel engaged between England on the one hand and revolutionary and imperial France on the other, between 'Carthage' and 'Rome', was at an end: 'Carthage' had vanquished 'Rome'. It was not only that England had definitely established her supremacy at sea—achieved ten years earlier by the victory of Trafalgar. Assisted by an alliance of all the Great Powers of Europe, she had also succeeded in frustrating the ambitions of France to extend her sway over the entire Continent. The Allied Armies entered Paris for the first time in 1814. When Napoleon's return from Elba offered a further challenge to the power of England, he merely furnished her with the opportunity to win her crowning victory. Wellington faced Napoleon on the battlefield, and Wellington was the conqueror. He was now in France in command of an army of thirty thousand men and, as the representative of England, was the arbiter of Europe. However slight the personal prestige of the two heads of the British Government—Lord Liverpool in the Lords and Lord Castlereagh in the Commons—there can be no doubt that when Parliament assembled on February 1, 1816, their position was to all appearance impregnable. The Whig Opposition suffered not only from numerical weakness, but from internal disunion. Those who for years past had supported the war policy of the Government were unwilling to renounce their share of the credit accruing from victory by making common cause with the small group who had consistently declared victory impossible, professed their admiration for Napoleon, and pressed for a peace. Nor was this all. Even those members of the Opposition who shared the rejoicing of the ministerialists at the victory of Waterloo were not united among themselves. The majority gave their unqualified approval to the treaties of Vienna. But a minority refused to recognize in the restoration of absolute monarchy in Spain and the return of the Bourbons to France the legitimate result of a war which had been, or ought to have been, waged on behalf of liberty. These dissensions in the Whig ranks had become so violent that Francis Horner prophesied a split;[1] and it was in fact prevented only by the complete indifference of public opinion to these questions of continental politics. The simple fact of victory was enough to put the Government in the right, all the Opposition groups without exception in the wrong. The House of Commons devoted a considerable time to discussion of the treaties of 1815. Brougham demanded that the terms of the mystical compact concluded in September by the Kings of Russia, Austria, and Prussia be communicated to the House. He also called for the communication of the treaty signed at Vienna in January 1815 between Austria, France, and Britain against Russia and Prussia. But to both demands Lord Castlereagh made an evasive reply, and Brougham did not press him. 'As to home politics,' he wrote to his friend Creevey, 'here we should make our main stand; and the ground is clearly retrenchment, in all ways, with ramifications into the Royal Family, property tax, jobs of all sorts, distresses of the landed interest, etc. In short, it is the richest mine in the world.'[2] Within a few months of Waterloo the economic disillusionment which always follows victory had begun to make itself felt. Perhaps these unexpected effects in the economic sphere would provide the Whig Opposition with a means of escape from the unpopularity under which it was suffering.

Among the malcontents the landlords uttered the loudest outcries, for their complaints had the greatest chance of being heard. In spite of the Corn Bill of 1815 the price of corn continued to fall. One excellent harvest was sufficient to effect a rapid fall of prices towards the end of the year. From 71s. 9d. in March the price of wheat had fallen in December to 55s. 9d., in January 1816 to 53s. 6d. The farmers had been encouraged by the war to

[1] Horner, Letter to the Duchess of Somerset, January 29, 1816; to J. A. Murray, February 27, 1816 (*Memoirs and Correspondence of Francis Horner*, vol. ii, pp. 290, 314).

[2] Brougham to Creevey, January 14, 1816 (*Creevey Papers*, vol. i, p. 248). Cf. Lord Grey to Brougham, December 16, 1816: '. . . of the execrable principle of these treaties . . . the public will take no heed. . . . But if the people can be made to understand that our triumphs have produced no security, that we must support a ruinous establishment in peace, to maintain our guaranty of the Bourbons—with the risk of a new war and all its consequences, if the French should again rise against them—I think it still possible that something may be done' (*Life and Times of Lord Brougham*, vol. ii, p. 300). Also Lord Holland to Francis Horner, January 10, 1817: 'It is through the unpopularity of the expenditure that we must get at the foreign system of politics, which, in my conscience, I think the cause of it' (*Memoirs and Correspondence of Francis Horner*, vol. ii, p. 396).

grow a constantly increasing quantity of corn, had become accustomed to invest their annual profits in their farms, and even to borrow further capital from the local banks. Since these banks were now no longer able to obtain from the farmers the interest on their loans, they were faced with failure, and were therefore compelled to require from the farmers not only their interest but the repayment of their capital. But what demands could the landlords, farmers, and country bankers put forward to avert total and immediate ruin?

It was impossible to ask for an extension of the protection given to cereals by the Act of 1815; for that Act prohibited the import of corn at a price below 80s. a quarter, and the present price barely exceeded 50s. The utmost they could ask was that the prohibition be made more stringent by repeating the clause which permitted the foreign importer to store his grain in British warehouses, though not to put it upon the market, or by extending the prohibition to certain other kinds of agricultural produce as well as corn, or possibly even that production should be encouraged by a system of bounties. Their chief grievance, however, was the taxation. They considered that even in war-time they had been taxed too heavily, since taxation had increased fivefold, whereas the price of wheat had merely doubled itself. But now, when the price of wheat had fallen almost by half, the burden was becoming intolerable, and would remain so until the Government consented to a thoroughgoing reduction of civil and military expenditure, and so long as it persisted blindly in a policy of redemption which ruined the producer in the interest of the bond-holder.[1] On this point they were in agreement with their adversaries of the previous winter, the manufacturers, who had opposed the Corn Law but who relished the Government's financial policy as little as themselves. Brougham, who had been lately returned to Parliament by the patronage of Lord Darlington, and whose victorious campaign on behalf of the repeal of the Order in Council had established his position as a successful agitator, united with Baring, Western, the City magnates, and the great landowners to demand a policy of radical retrenchment which involved an impracticable reduction of expenditure, and before

[1] See on the financial crisis the speeches of Western, H. of C., March 7, 1816 (*Parliamentary Debates*, vol. xxxiii, pp. 31 sqq.); also Brougham, H. of C., April 9, 1816 (ibid., pp. 1086 sqq.). Cf. an instructive letter from F. Horner to J. A. Murray, January 1816 (*Memoirs and Correspondence of Francis Horner*, vol. ii, pp. 287–8).

Parliament reassembled had set out the economic programme of the Opposition in the pages of the *Edinburgh Review*.[1]

The Prince Regent opened the session by a speech of which the tone was considered excessively optimistic. He spoke of the prosperity of manufactures and commerce and the excellent financial position; but industry was already suffering from a disease which would grow steadily worse. The recommencement of continental manufacture involved a decrease of British exports. War production was at an end, and the demand for the products of the metal foundries had therefore diminished. The wholesale disbandment of soldiers and sailors suddenly flooded the labour market with new hands, producing a general reduction of wages and widespread unemployment. To pass over these evils in silence, to be content with a passing admission that agriculture was not altogether prosperous, was a proof that the Government did not intend to pursue the financial policy demanded by public opinion.

2

On February 12 the Chancellor of the Exchequer, Vansittart, introduced his Budget. He maintained that a sudden reduction of the Army Estimates to the normal level of peace was impossible. Leaving out of consideration the thirty thousand men of the Army of Occupation whose cost was defrayed by France, and the twenty thousand soldiers of the Indian Army who were paid by the East India Company, he must provide for an army of twenty-five thousand in Great Britain, twenty-five thousand in Ireland, and forty-nine thousand in the Colonies—a total force of ninety-nine thousand, besides thirty-two thousand sailors. The cost of maintaining the Army and Navy on this footing he estimated at £29,000,000. Evidently he could not contemplate any serious reduction of the taxes. The only means to tide over the crisis was to avoid all loans, and retain the income tax imposed during the war, which he merely proposed to reduce from 10 to 5 per cent.

His proposals provoked an explosion of the general discontent. On the one hand the estimates for the Army and Navy were

[1] *Edinburgh Review*, October 1815, 'British Finance' (vol. xxv, pp. 541 sqq.). It would seem that this number did not actually appear before the second half of December. See the letters from Lord Grey to Brougham, December 16, 1815 (*Life and Times of Lord Brougham*, vol. ii, p. 300), and from Brougham to Creevey, January 14, 1816 (*Creevey Papers*, vol. i, p. 248).

denounced as extravagant and, as the members of the 'Mountain' and even many Whigs declared, a danger to the freedom of the nation. But the object of the most intense and most widespread attack was the income tax. The Cabinet was charged with a breach of their word, pledged on more than one occasion, in continuing the tax after the restoration of peace. Brougham and Baring prepared to set in motion a vast campaign of petitions against the maintenance of the tax. And on February 13, the day after Vansittart's speech, the City sent up to Parliament two petitions couched in the most emphatic terms. On the 26th the Chancellor of the Exchequer attempted to stop the petitioning by proposing that the tax should be put to the vote on the following day. But when Baring denounced the 'scandalous' haste and declared his intention to employ every possible method of parliamentary obstruction, Vansittart beat a retreat and postponed his motion for a week. During that week meetings multiplied throughout the country and petitions poured into the House. At first the Ministers, stunned by the violence of the attack, allowed their opponents to introduce their constituents' petitions and support them by long speeches without attempting a word in reply. Then, realizing the harm they were doing to themselves by their inaction, they attempted to criticize the petitions and found fault with the method by which they had been collected in a particular locality. But they received their death-blow when, on March 18, Sir William Curtis brought from the City a petition signed at a public meeting and bearing the names of twenty-two thousand shopkeepers, bankers, and merchants; a counter petition which they had not dared to produce had obtained no more than thirty-seven signatures. When the debate opened, it was in vain that Lord Castlereagh urged that the undertakings given in the past not to continue the tax in peace-time were not unconditional; that, since the House had already accepted the Government's estimates for the Army and Navy, they had not to determine whether the estimated amount should or should not be raised, but merely what was the best method of raising it, and that the only alternative was to continue the tax or borrow. After an animated but rapid debate, often interrupted by exclamations of impatience, 201 votes were given in favour of the tax, 238 against it. The Cabinet was defeated by a majority of thirty-seven.

On March 20 Vansittart admitted not a single but a double defeat. He informed the House that he abandoned not only the income tax but also the war tax on malt. Since the Commons had pronounced in favour of a loan, there was no particular reason why the produce of the malt tax should not be added to the loan, and this further remission seemed justified by the condition to which the agricultural crisis had reduced the country gentlemen. By his original remission of half the income tax Vansittart had relinquished £7,500,000 of revenue. Its total abolition, coupled with the abolition of the tax on malt, reduced the revenue by a further £10,000,000. How could the deficit be made good if the Government were to adhere to the strict principles laid down by Pitt and his successors in the matter of redemption? Vansittart finally carried a makeshift budget.

The Bank of England agreed to advance a loan of £3,000,000, provided it was authorized to increase its capital by a quarter, and the Treasury undertook to accept its notes for every kind of payment. And the Government also renewed £2,500,000 worth of Exchequer Bills which were falling due. A few exceptional sources of revenue, together with some departmental economies, rendered possible an apparent balance of the budget; but even the original plan of the budget had included a loan from the Bank of £6,000,000. £9,000,000, and £2,500,000 of Exchequer Bills brought the total loan to £11,500,000.

Thus the Cabinet which had concluded the treaties of 1815 emerged with discredit from this first session. To strengthen his position in the Commons, Lord Liverpool offered Canning Lord Buckinghamshire's place on the Board of Control. But this reappearance of Canning might with good reason be considered a further humiliation for Lord Castlereagh, the Leader of the Commons, thus driven to make terms with his former rival in order to maintain himself in power. The only consolation for their own weakness open to the Ministers was the obvious weakness of their opponents. The Opposition had secured without difficulty the rejection of the income tax, but when they attempted to follow up their success by a formal vote of censure on the Government, they failed to obtain a majority: indeed the Whigs could not even find a leader. The official leader of the Opposition, George Ponsonby, was universally regarded as a mere stop-gap. Brougham, though a man of great activity, who seized every opportunity to bring himself before the public, was too violent, too unstable, and too ill-provided with the necessary noble connections to have a serious claim to the position. Moreover, the economic situation during the prorogation of Parliament in May 1816 was in a state of rapid flux, and the Cabinet was compensated for its weakness in Parliament by the fact that over both parties alike there broke without warning a wave of popular discontent which swept the lower classes.

II   CRISIS AND AGITATION

I

In January the price of corn had fallen to its lowest level. It then rose steadily and by May had reached 76s. 4d. a quarter. The advance was stimulated first by the apprehension, then by the reality, of a bad harvest. The quarter which stood at 82s. 1d. in August reached in December 103s. Landlords and farmers exchanged discontent for satisfaction; but simultaneously a breach was opened between the farmers and their labourers. The latter united with the factory hands in a common revolt against the policy of dear bread. The continental market no longer sufficed to absorb the surplus of production, for it was in revolt against the dumping of British goods. In July the workers of Ghent made a bonfire of merchandize imported from Great Britain.[1] There resulted a fall in prices and wages, failures, unemployment, and finally a succession of disturbances among the labouring population such as 1815 had not witnessed.[2] The series opened in May with an outbreak of Luddism among the agricultural labourers, of which the principal seat was in the Eastern Counties. Beginning in Suffolk, in the neighbourhood of Bury St. Edmunds, it spread to Norwich, then to the district around Ely, and finally to Essex and the very outskirts of London. The agricultural labourers demanded the fixing of a price for corn and meat—2s. 6d. a bushel for corn, 4d. a pound for beef—set fire to barns, broke

[1] *Annual Register*, 1816, Chron. July 24.
[2] See for the crisis of 1816, J. A. Yates, *A Letter on the Distresses of the Country*; addressed to His Royal Highness the Duke of Kent, in consequence of his motion respecting the Revulsion of Trade and our sudden transition from a system of extensive war to a state of peace: while the supposed influence of our debt and taxes upon our manufactures and foreign trade is investigated, 1817. Also John Barton, *Observations on the Circumstances which influence the Condition of the Labouring Classes of Society*, 1817.

threshing machines, and armed with pikes and guns established in several localities a reign of terror. The magistrates summoned to their assistance first the yeomanry, then the regular troops. In Cambridgeshire, after a battle in which two rioters lost their lives, seventy-five labourers were brought to trial at the Assizes, twenty-four condemned to death, and five actually hanged.[1] Then the agitation spread to the manufacturing districts of the north and centre—to the weavers, hosiers, and colliers. On May 28 a strike began at Newcastle, caused by insufficient wages and the high price of bread.[2] In Shropshire and Staffordshire the workmen —not strikers but unemployed—perambulated the neighbouring towns, dragging carts full of coal and demanding public relief. Worcester, Coventry, Birmingham, Chester, Liverpool, Leicester, even the neighbourhood of London, witnessed these processions of unemployed.[3] October produced more serious disorders. At Walsall bakeries and mills were looted.[4] Strikes accompanied by violence broke out in two regions widely apart —in the collieries and iron foundries of South Wales and in the district around Glasgow.[5]

Thus vanished Brougham's dream of January, a coalition of the entire nation against a Cabinet held up to odium as a cabal of selfish tyrants. His victory in the matter of the income tax had proved barren. Once more all over the country the classes he had sought to unite were arrayed in mutual conflict, while a common terror of rebellion was restoring unity in the ranks of the governing class. What became of the prejudices entertained by the landed gentry against a standing army, when magistrates and yeomanry appealed for assistance to the local barracks? Where was the mutual dislike which divided the manufacturer from the aristocratic Justice of the Peace, when the latter was protecting the former against riot? And, on the other hand, the fury of the workers was directed against the possessing classes indiscriminately, whatever their political complexion, for they despaired of finding a friend among them. The proletariat regarded all the Members of a Parliament elected, as it then was, as equally interested in the maintenance of existing abuses, as belonging all

[1] Pellew, *Life of Lord Sidmouth*, vol. iii, pp. 145 sqq.; *Ann. Reg.*, 1816, Chron. May 9, 19, 22, 24, 27.
[2] *Ann. Reg.*, 1816, Chron. May 28.
[3] Ibid., July 5, 9. For the distress in Staffordshire, ibid., July 24.
[4] Ibid., October 30.   [5] Ibid., October 22, 28; *Examiner*, November 3, 1816.

alike to the class of the idle rich, who exploited the worker. A reform of the system of representation was, they believed, the indispensable preliminary to any other reform, economic or administrative.[1]

It was Sir Francis Burdett who first brought up again in Parliament the question of its 'radical' reform. Since 1812 the aged Major Cartwright and himself had agreed upon a concerted programme. Burdett accepted Cartwright's demand for equal constituencies and annual elections. Cartwright in return abandoned his demand for manhood suffrage, and contented himself with supporting Burdett's claim for the extension of the franchise to every ratepayer. To spread their propaganda they had founded a club, called the Hampden Club. Its object was twofold. It was intended, on the one hand (and this was Burdett's cherished project), to provide the reformers with a staff of leaders, of sufficiently respectable position to form the nucleus of a regular parliamentary party. Every member of the Club, therefore, must not only pay an annual subscription of £2, but must also prove that he was the owner or heir-presumptive of a landed estate whose rental value was not less than £300. And it was further intended (and this was Cartwright's contribution) to organize a mission throughout the country, and thus employ on behalf of parliamentary reform the methods which the Evangelicals and Methodists were employing so successfully to distribute Bibles and secure the abolition of the slave trade.

While the war lasted the Hampden Club barely managed to continue in existence. Its members were extremely few—a minute coterie composed of City politicians, such as Wood and Waithman, and eccentric members of the aristocracy like Lord Byron, Lord Cochrane, Sir W. Geary, and Charles Wolseley. But after the restoration of peace Cartwright was able to infuse new life into his propaganda. He secured one hundred and thirty thousand signatures to a petition which he drew up. The Secretary of the Club, Thomas Cleary, undertook a missionary campaign in Wales, and Cartwright himself toured Scotland, which was now beginning to awake from its political slumber. Both left behind them a number of local clubs to continue the work. It was the Hampden Club, or, to be more accurate, it was the indefatigable Major Cartwright, who secured the petitions which Sir Francis

[1] H. of C., April 30, May 8, 1816 (*Parl. Deb.*, vol. xxxiv, pp. 98, 369).

Burdett laid before the Commons in April and May.[1] Of course, Sir Francis achieved nothing, and even outside the House his efforts were scarcely better supported. A mere handful attended the meeting organized by the Hampden Club on June 15 to celebrate the sexcentenary of Magna Carta.[2] It was not until a month later, when the distress had increased in the manufacturing districts, that Burdett and the majority of his colleagues of the Hampden Club were not merely supported but swept headlong by the current of popular feeling.

In the year 1812, during a severe economic crisis, a group of philanthropists, among whom Wilberforce was the leading figure, had founded an Association for the Relief of the Manufacturing and Labouring Poor. This society, whose membership included laymen and clergy, politicians of every party, noblemen, bankers, and merchants, had rendered practical service by the relief works it had organized. In 1816 the situation was far graver. Wilberforce and his friends attempted to revive the Association of 1812. They obtained the support of many members of the aristocracy and the royal family, and to launch the new society convened a public meeting on July 29 at the City of London Tavern. The arrangements were excellent. The Duke of York took the chair, and the six resolutions were to be put to the meeting in turn by the Duke of Kent, the Duke of Cambridge, the Archbishop of Canterbury, the Duke of Rutland, Lord Manvers, and the Bishop of London. Wilberforce himself, now a national celebrity, was on the platform, and Vansittart also. But the public had not arrived with the peaceable dispositions which had been theirs at the period so recent, yet already so remote, when the war still continued, and it possessed that evening a leader of outstanding ability in the person of Lord Cochrane, the naval democrat, who had never forgiven society the condemnation which had excluded him from Parliament, and was sore, embittered, and ripe for revolution. In the uproar which ensued the organizers barely secured the passage of their six resolutions; and they were even compelled to modify the wording of the first. Then the Duke of York made his escape amid a storm of booing.[3] And in future the Association

---

[1] H. of C., April 30, May 8, 1816 (*Parl. Deb.*, vol. xxxiv, pp. 98, 369).

[2] A full Report of the Proceedings of the Meeting convened by the Hampden Club, which took place at the Freemasons' Tavern . . . on Saturday the 1st of June, 1816, upon the subject of Parliamentary Reform, 1816.

[3] *Cobbett's Weekly Political Register*, August 3, 1816, vol. xxxi, pp. 72 sqq. Cf. a letter

was never able to hold a meeting without interruption by some imitator of Lord Cochrane. It was a decisive moment in the history of the crisis through which England was passing. The conservative philanthropy, which owed its origin to the stimulus imparted by the Methodist revival, and by its obliteration of the lines dividing Whig and Tory, Church and Dissent, seemed to offer the surest remedy for civil strife, appeared at the moment to have been discredited. It seemed as if English politics would henceforth conform to the continental pattern, and that for the future there would exist in England, instead of the historic parties, only these two—the party of revolution and the party of counter-revolution.

A month after the riotous meeting in the London Tavern, the eight thousand liverymen of the City, after inflammatory speeches by a number of popular orators—Flower, Thompson, and above all the famous Henry Hunt—passed a series of resolutions, one of which demanded the reduction of taxation, the abolition of sinecures, and 'a reform of Parliament'.[1] A few days later a 'Committee of Public Safety', in which Bentham's friends, James Mill and Francis Place, took part, organized a public meeting at Westminster, at which Burdett and Lord Cochrane called for an organized campaign of petitions throughout the country, and proposed that delegates should be appointed, two for each district, to bring up the petitions to London in readiness for the opening of the session.[2]

His appeal met with an immediate response. There was not a vestige now of the apathy deplored so recently as June by the committee of the Hampden Club. Hampden clubs multiplied throughout the provinces, and their character was completely changed. Members were asked no longer for a subscription of £2 a year, but for a subscription of 1d. a week. In fact, the revolutionaries at the very time when they charged the Tory evangelicalism of Wilberforce with assisting the oppression of the people by drugging their just anger to sleep, borrowed from the popular evangelicalism of the sects its methods of organization,

from Francis Place to James Mill, August 2: 'No newspaper can describe the meeting at the City of London Tavern last Monday; many years have passed since I witnessed anything so exhilarating.' He continues with an account of the proceedings (British Museum, Add. MSS. 35, 152, pp. 199 sqq.).

[1] *Examiner*, August 25, 1816.

[2] Ibid., September 15, 1816. Also F. Place to James Mill, August 30, 1816 (British Museum, Add. MSS. 35, 152, f. 207 verso).

its trifling subscriptions, its open-air meetings, and its paid service of itinerant preachers, sent from town to town to spread the new doctrine.[1] The public to which this new propaganda was addressed were the factory hands who had no direct interest in Sir Francis Burdett's programme. That programme was accordingly abandoned; and a return was made to the original programme of Major Cartwright, the demand for manhood suffrage without restrictions of any kind.[2]

The districts in which the movement reached its peak can be accurately determined. Apart from a few isolated centres, such as Birmingham, whose manufactures had been especially threatened by the restoration of peace, and Norwich, which in May had been one of the strongholds of the rural agitation, they were the districts that had witnessed the worst Luddite outrages in 1812, those, namely, where the hand-loom weaver was endangered by the competition of the power loom, and where, therefore, the least economic crisis rendered his condition intolerable. In Nottinghamshire popular discontent had already in June found expression in acts of violence, acts of 'Luddism' in the strict sense of the term. The factory which Mr. Heathcote had just built at Loughborough had been reduced to a total wreck. When in August several workmen were tried on the charge of destroying the mill, the jury acquitted them amid the applause of the crowd and the judges were booed.[3] And it was at Nottingham that a mass meeting was held at the end of September which adopted resolutions whose wording served as a model for all the democratic meetings held in the provinces.[4] In Lancashire also the breakers of machinery proclaimed themselves democrats, signed petitions, and obtained signatures. A series of mass meetings held during the latter half of October in Liverpool, Manchester, Paisley, and Glasgow made a wide impression. It was estimated

[1] See on this point the tribute paid to the methods of the Bible Society by the *Courier*, no friend to the Evangelicals: 'It may be worthy of observation, and may furnish a subject for *curious* and serious disquisition to a reflecting mind, that the country is indebted to the *esprit de corps* of the above Society for the *magnificent* idea of producing by *small means great ends*, for creating *funds* and *fervour* in a *holy* cause by *penny* contributions' (January 22, 1817).

[2] See the text of Cartwright's Bill, *Pol. Reg.*, January 31, 1818 (vol. xxxiii, pp. 129 sqq.).

[3] *Examiner*, August 25, 1816. There is no mention of the incident in J. L. and B. Hammond, *The Skilled Labourer*, pp. 238 sqq., where the capital punishment of seven men found guilty of Luddism is related and the transportation of three others. For the frame-smashing in Nottinghamshire see *The Times*, October 12, 17, 19, 1816.

[4] *Pol. Reg.*, October 5, 1816 (vol. xxxi, pp. 324–5).

that one hundred and twenty thousand men had taken part in
three meetings held at Manchester, Paisley, and Glasgow.[1] We
may, if we like, term the movement a revival of Luddism; but
two features differentiated the new Luddism from the old. It
took the form of a political organization with a definite programme;[2] and the disaffected in the provinces now appeared to
be obeying the orders of the London revolutionaries.

2

In London a meeting of the Common Hall was held on
October 10 to protest against the Regent's refusal to receive in
due form the petition signed in August.[3] Eight days later, to
render their protest more efficacious, the Common Hall advised
the Common Council to re-elect Alderman Wood, in defiance
of the established custom, Lord Mayor for the second time.
Wood was in fact re-elected, and thus the year which followed
the conclusion of peace witnessed a revival of the old eighteenth-
century tradition of disorder.[4] On November 2 a meeting of the
Committee of the Hampden Club, over which Burdett presided,
resolved to draft a Bill for parliamentary reform, to be submitted
to the examination of the delegates from the provinces on their
arrival in London at the beginning of 1817. But Wood and
Burdett were no longer in control of the movement. As the
memories of victory grew fainter, Cobbett, the famous publicist,
recovered the popularity justly due to his talent as a journalist.
In November he hit upon the idea of evading the stamp duty by
publishing as a separate pamphlet one of the numbers of his
Political Register. It consisted of a lengthy address 'to the journeymen and labourers of England, Wales, Scotland, and Ireland'.[5]
He sold it at 2d. a copy, or 12s. 6d. a hundred. Its success was
enormous—forty-four thousand copies were sold. From November 16 onwards he published every week, after the regular issue
of his paper, a popular edition at 2d. a copy, on which no stamp
duty had been paid, and he announced his intention to continue

[1] *Pol. Reg.*, November 9, 1816 (vol. xxxi, p. 493).
[2] 'Luddism in a political form.' *Courier*, January 14, 1817.
[3] *Examiner*, October 13, 1816.
[4] Ibid., October 20, 1816.
[5] *Pol. Reg.*, November 2, 1816 (vol. xxxi, pp. 433 sqq.). For the price of this pamphlet
see ibid., November 23, 1816 (vol. xxxi, p. 529).

the publication 'until *the meeting of Parliament*, or, perhaps, until the reform *shall have actually taken place*'.[1] To win the support of his new public, a far wider body of readers, drawn from a lower social class, Cobbett changed his programme. Hitherto he had supported Sir Francis Burdett's programme. On November 23 he informed his readers that Major Cartwright had converted him to manhood suffrage.[2]

Major Cartwright? Was he telling the truth? On the contrary, for two or three years past, Cartwright had advocated the somewhat less radical programme of household suffrage. The man under whose banner Cobbett had tacitly ranged himself was the fanatical demagogue Henry Hunt, who for the past year had played the leading part at all meetings held in London. When the democrats of Westminster held their public meeting in September, they had been compelled to enter into preliminary negotiations with Hunt, as one power with another, to secure a pledge that he would moderate his language. In October he had disturbed the meeting of the Common Hall, and he presided at the mass meetings which, following the example of Nottinghamshire and Lancashire, London was organizing to approve and sign the petition to the Prince Regent.

The first open-air meeting was held at Spa Fields on November 15, and an enormous crowd attended. Henry Hunt made his appearance preceded by two men, one of whom carried a cap of liberty on the end of a pike, the other a tricolour flag, green, white, and red, the colours of the future British Republic. From the window of a public house he harangued the meeting. 'Everything,' he told his hearers, 'that concerned their subsistence or comfort was taxed. Was not their loaf taxed, was not beer taxed, were not their coats taxed, were not their shirts taxed, was not everything that they ate, drank, wore, and even said taxed? And these taxes appeared to be expended . . . in pensioning the fathers, the brothers, the mothers, the sisters, the cousins, and bastards of the boroughmongers . . . subsisting on the plunder wrung from their miseries.' And he advised his hearers to sign the petition 'before physical force' was 'applied'. Everything passed off peaceably, except for the looting of a few bakehouses in the evening, and the meeting adjourned till

[1] *Pol. Reg.*, November 16, 1816 (vol. xxxi, p. 497).
[2] Ibid., November 23, 1816 (vol. xxxi, p. 546).

December 2, after the resolution had been carried by acclamation.[1]

The meeting burlesqued the procedure adopted in August by the Corporation of London, and appointed Burdett and Hunt to deliver the resolution at Carlton House. Naturally Burdett did not go. But Hunt made it a point of honour to succeed where the shopkeepers of the City had failed, and place the petition in the hands of the Regent himself. He was turned away twice.[2] In these circumstances the meeting announced for December 2 became a meeting of protest against the insolent treatment of the petitioners by the Court.

As the appointed day approached popular excitement increased in the metropolis. On Monday, the 25th, a meeting was held at the Crown and Anchor of 'the friends of Lord Cochrane'. To punish his conduct in July their hero had been tried for his escape of the previous year and sentenced to a fine of £100. Refusing to pay he was sent back to prison, and his friends opened a subscription at 1d. a head to pay the £100 and set him at liberty. On Thursday, the 28th, a meeting of the Common Council declared in favour of reform, and invited the entire Kingdom to petition. On Friday, the 29th, a meeting of the Common Hall was held, which, in spite of an interruption by Hunt, confirmed the resolutions of the Common Council; and a philanthropic meeting held on the same day at Faringdon Without degenerated in defiance of its organizers into a meeting on behalf of reform.[3] December 2 was now close at hand, and the authorities were alarmed by the remembrance of the outbreak which had followed the meeting of November 15.

The meeting of December 2 began with every promise of brilliant success. A crowd larger than that of November 15 had gathered to hear Hunt; perhaps, indeed, it was larger and more excited than the organizers desired. As Burdett had been eclipsed by Hunt, Hunt was in turn eclipsed. Among the malcontents was a small group of revolutionaries called the Spenceans, from the name of their leader, Thomas Spence. They were not satisfied with political equality. They demanded equality of wealth to be obtained by the restoration of the land to the community. They

[1] *The Times*, November 16, 1816. Cf. H. Jephson, *The Platform, its Rise and Progress*, vol. i, pp. 383 sqq.
[2] *Examiner*, November 24, 1816.
[3] Ibid., December 1, 1816.

intervened in the proceedings of the Spa Fields meeting without any kind of previous understanding with Hunt. In obedience to the orders of their leaders, Preston and the two Watsons, they rushed suddenly on to the ground while the crowd was still waiting for Hunt to make his appearance. Seizing a cart, and displaying tricolour flags, they held a separate meeting in a corner while the mass meeting proceeded. Then, while Hunt was addressing the crowd, they left the meeting and, crossing Smithfield to Snow Hill, murdered a gunsmith, pillaged his shop, and so made their way into the City. The majority of the rioters consisted, we are informed, of disbanded sailors acquainted with the use of firearms. They paraded Cheapside from one end to the other, spreading terror by the shots which they fired as they passed. Finally, at the Mansion House the gates were barred upon a party of the rioters, who were thus surrounded and captured by a body of troops. The remainder fled eastward, apparently with the intention of seizing the armoury at the Tower, and looted other gunsmiths' shops. It was only with nightfall that peace was restored.

3

A committee of public safety, tricolour flags, caps of liberty, rioting by an armed mob—these were scenes from the French Revolution enacted by rebellious Londoners. The survivors of the political trials of 1793, at their annual November banquet, expressed their delight that the hour of vengeance was at hand.[1] But this noisy agitation in the French style provoked a sudden and violent change in public opinion. For the past two months the *Courier* and *The Times* had been harping on the danger of revolution, and insisting that it was impossible to allow these mass meetings to assemble for the organization of a political campaign if bloodshed were to be avoided. The riot of December 2 confirmed their warning; but the outcry was not confined to these Ministerial organs. There was not a single London daily that even pleaded extenuating circumstances on behalf of the organizers of the meetings. All contemporary witnesses agree on one point—namely, that the revolutionary agitation of 1816 was almost entirely confined to the lower orders, and that the members of the governing classes in favour of reform had steadily decreased

---

[1] *Examiner*, November 10, 1816.

from 1780 to 1792 and again from 1792 to 1816.[1] In August the London democrats had called upon the gentry of the provinces to hold county meetings. The latter had turned a deaf ear to their appeal; with the solitary exception of Cornwall[2] not a single county meeting was held during the following months. To be sure, the middle class, the manufacturers, merchants, and financiers, had many reasons to be dissatisfied with the Tory Government and the existing composition of Parliament. But their dislike of the Tories was nothing to their fear of an insurrection of the industrial and urban proletariat. If the great cities were given the franchise and used it to send to Parliament men such as Hunt and Cobbett, they would prefer to be governed by Lord Castlereagh and Vansittart. The rabble of shopkeepers who controlled the Common Hall of the City had drawn the Corporation of London into the agitation for reform. But this was a mere survival, the final manifestation of the traditional warfare between the City and the Court. We have depicted the irritation of the masses growing more intense every day towards the close of 1816; but the picture requires its complement. We must also depict the hostility which the agitation aroused among all those who possessed any property, and whose fear of the tax collector's demands was outweighed by their greater terror of the confiscations which a revolution would entail. No bookseller or innkeeper wished or dared to sell Cobbett's *Political Register*. Publicans who signed a petition or allowed signatures to be collected at their bar were threatened by the magistrates with the withdrawal of their licence.[3] A reign of terror was established throughout England by the nobility and middle class—a terror more formidable, though more silent, than the noisy demonstrations conducted by Hunt and Cobbett.

Lord Sidmouth kept in constant communication with the local magistrates. In several counties, where the danger of insurrection appeared particularly threatening, he invited the Lord-Lieutenants

---

[1] H. of C., February 24, 1817, Lord Castlereagh's speech (*Parl. Deb.*, vol. xxxv, p. 591). Cf. Southey to Lord Liverpool, March 19, 1817: 'The Spirit of Jacobinism which influenced men in my sphere of life four-and-twenty years ago (myself and men like me, among others) has disappeared from that class and sunk into the rabble, who would have torn me to pieces for holding those opinions then, and would tear me to pieces for renouncing them now' (C. D. Yonge, *Life and Administration of Robert Banks, Second Earl of Liverpool*, vol. ii, pp. 298–9).

[2] *Examiner*, November 10, 1816.

[3] H. of C., February 5, 1817, Lord Cochrane's speech (*Parl. Deb.*, vol. xxxv, p. 221).

to enrol special constables and prepare to call out the yeomanry. At his suggestion meetings were held, at which the magistrates carried motions calling upon the Government to restore order.[1] Encouraged by the influence in the Cabinet which the success of his methods had won, he had demanded six or seven months before, as a means of suppressing disturbances in Cambridgeshire, new legislation which should include the absolute prohibition of public meetings.[2] Would it not be good policy to gratify his and their desire? Instead of enduring an existence continually harassed by the financial problem, the Cabinet would see every section of the upper classes rally to their support. Nevertheless, his advice was rejected, and the Cabinet took no action. The ring-leaders of the riot on December 2 who had been arrested were released on bail, and all through December and January Preston and the two Watsons showed themselves with impunity in the London clubs.

What was the reason of this inaction? In the first place we must not forget how distasteful, almost humiliating, it was to an English statesman to have recourse within three years of Waterloo to special legislation for the maintenance of law and order. To be sure, the Government had obtained from Parliament in 1796 and in 1799 extraordinary measures to secure the public safety. But then the Government could plead in excuse the exceptional gravity of the situation, a war unprecedented in history, and urge that it would have performed only the half of its belligerent duties if, while fighting the French Jacobins abroad, it had failed to combat their allies at home. Apart from this exceptional case, the British Government had never employed since 1688 any methods to put down rebellion, save the ordinary process of the law. Never, except in Ireland. Had England, then, sunk to such degradation that it could be governed only by methods suitable to that semi-barbarous country? Peel, the Minister entrusted with the government of Ireland, did, in fact, complain in December that the unnecessary fuss made by the London Press over the events of December 2 made it more difficult for him to govern Ireland, and that its sole effect was to encourage the agitators on that side of the channel.[3]

[1] Pellew, *Life of Lord Sidmouth*, vol. iii, p. 166.
[2] Lord Sidmouth to Abbot, December 8, 1816 (ibid., vol. iii, p. 161).
[3] To Gregory, December 12, 1816: 'It will be thought by sensible and moderate men that the Government really wishes to magnify a mob into a rebellion, in order that a

Peel spoke of unnecessary fuss, and treated the London riots as contemptible; and his optimism was undoubtedly shared by the majority of his colleagues. Was not the spontaneous resistance offered by the entire body of the gentry and the middle class to the revolutionaries the best remedy for the evils which afflicted England? Since the public was willing to be its own police, why need the Government interfere? Already, in January, there was reason to hope that the disorder was abating. Though cases of Luddism occurred in Leicestershire,[1] tranquillity prevailed everywhere else; and there were symptoms which prognosticated the end of the crisis. When the Convention of Delegates, charged to collect before Parliament reassembled the petitions received from the capital and the provinces, petitions to which five hundred thousand signatures were appended, met in London on January 23, its debates betrayed considerable indecision, almost fear, among the members. Major Cartwright presided, but the convention had desired to have Sir Francis Burdett for its chairman, and only on his refusal had fallen back on Cartwright. A resolution in favour of manhood suffrage was adopted, but not without opposition. Cobbett changed his programme for the second time, and in deference to Burdett advocated household suffrage. His change of front involved him in a violent altercation with Hunt. Finally the meeting determined that their resolutions in the form in which they had been carried should be communicated to Burdett, who should be asked to introduce a Bill during the next session, which he should be at liberty to draft in whatever terms he pleased.[2]

But to these advances Burdett made no response. He hunted in Surrey first, then in Leicestershire. He went to visit his son, an officer in the Guards, who was ill at Brighton.[3] For he knew that the cause had been lost by the free-lances who had sought to annex it. He knew also that at Westminster, Place and his committee were in revolt against Hunt and Cobbett, and that, in the

tub may be thrown to the whale, the public attention diverted from economy, and a pretext made for maintaining the military.' To the Speaker, December 25, 1816: 'If the English papers will not magnify Watson to a Catiline and represent England to be in a state of confusion, I believe we shall have very little trouble here' (C. S. Parker, *Sir Robert Peel*, vol. i, pp. 236, 237). Cf. ibid., pp. 234, 235, Peel to J. Beckett, December 5, 1816.

[1] *Ann. Reg.*, 1817, Chron. January 27.
[2] See the account of the meeting in Bamford, *Passages in the Life of a Radical*, ed. 1893, vol. ii, pp. 20-1; also *Pol. Reg.*, February 22, 1817 (vol. xxxii, pp. 235-6).
[3] *Ann. Reg.*, 1817, Chron. January 27.

City Ward, Waithman and the 'patriots' of the Common Council, since in December they had at last succeeded in laying their grievances before the Regent, had separated themselves from the revolutionaries of the meetings, who roundly abused them in consequence. On the evening before January 16, when the Hampden Club held a meeting to prepare for the Convention of Delegates, Waithman and his friends held a rival meeting at the Freemasons' Tavern,[1] at which they founded, in opposition to the Hampden Club, a society of their own, which they called the Friends of Economy, Public Order, and Reform. Addressing the Common Council on the 24th, Waithman formally disavowed the tenets of universal suffrage and annual elections.[2]

4

The day fixed for the opening of the session arrived. Nothing in the official Press forecast extraordinary legislation. The speech from the Throne, prepared for reading at the opening of Parliament on January 28, admitted the existence of the crisis and the financial deficit, but was content 'to count upon the loyalty and good sense of the public to assist the Government to maintain order against the designs of the disaffected'. The Government opened a session which seemed destined to drag out as miserably as that of 1816 in a dreary struggle, renewed at every sitting, with the insoluble financial problems which had already confronted the Government during the previous year. Suddenly there occurred an unexpected and providential event. A large crowd had collected outside the Houses of Parliament to witness the arrival and departure of the important public personages and the Regent himself. The return of the Regent, who had driven to the House in the midst of a chilling silence, was greeted by an even worse welcome, for he was actually hissed. Just as he was re-entering the Palace a projectile passed through his coach. Two panes of glass were pierced. Had there been two bullets or only one? Was it a bullet at all, or merely a pebble? Whatever it was it was never found, and the question remained unsolved. But a violent panic took possession of Parliament; the members recalled the year 1795 when George III had been the object of a similar attempt.

[1] *Courier*, January 14, 23, 1817; *Examiner*, January 19, 1817.
[2] *Courier*, January 24, 25, 1817.

While Hunt, accompanied by the delegates from the provinces, made his way from Charing Cross to Palace Yard, and amid the huzzas of the crowd delivered to Lord Cochrane his pile of petitions in favour of reform, the Cabinet were engaged in a hurried meeting. Those who had been optimistic were frightened, those who had been alarmed took courage. After an invitation to the two Houses to pass an address of sympathy with the Prince Regent, they decided, as in 1795, to reply to the attempted assassination by tightening up the law.

When the address had been passed, the Government on February 5 placed on the table of either House the papers which Lord Sidmouth had collected, giving an account of the revolutionary plots of which the attempt of January 29 was the latest manifestation, and asked the Lords to appoint a secret committee of eleven peers to report upon them, and the Commons a similar committee of twenty-one members. The two committees were appointed, and reported on February 18 and 19. Their reports gave information of a plot formed to seize the Bank of England and the Tower, cause the Army to mutiny, and effect by armed force a Jacobin revolution in London. They denounced the communism of the Spenceans, and the attacks made upon the institution of private property. They laid stress upon the irreligious and blasphemous character of the revolutionary propaganda.[1] Eight days later Lord Castlereagh explained to the Commons the scope of the four Bills which, in the opinion of his colleagues and himself, were necessary for the restoration of order.[2] The first Bill suspended the Habeas Corpus Act until July 1: of the four Bills this met with the most opposition. Even *The Times*, which was by no means an organ of the opposition, and had all along asked for coercive legislation, protested that to suspend the Habeas Corpus Act, 'that great bulwark of our liberties, of our comforts, of our lives',[3] was to violate the Constitution itself. But, just because this Bill was the most debatable, the Cabinet hurried it through Parliament. On February 24, in the course of a single sitting, Lord Sidmouth introduced in the Lords, and carried by a majority of 150 to 35, the Habeas Corpus Suspension Act. On the 26th the measure was brought down to the Commons and passed on March

[1] See the text of the two reports, *Ann. Reg.*, 1817, pp. 6 sqq.
[2] H. of C., February 24, 1817, Lord Castlereagh's speech (*Parl. Deb.*, vol. xxxv, pp. 590 sqq.).
[3] *The Times*, February 26, 1817.

1.[1] Thus within a week the nation was faced with a *fait accompli*. The remaining Bills, which were of a more complex character, were brought forward by the Cabinet, not as novel legislation, but as the simple adaptation of existing laws to present conditions. An Act had been passed in 1796 to secure the personal safety of the King; it was only common sense to extend its provisions to the Regent. In 1797 Acts had been passed to repress attempts to incite the troops to mutiny. Why had these statutes been allowed to lapse? Moreover, the Act of 1799, which prohibited the federation of political associations, referred in several of its clauses to the Act of 1795, which had placed severe restrictions upon the right of public meeting. But the Act of 1795 was a temporary measure which had expired at the very date on which the Act of 1799 came into operation. Once already, in 1809, the Government had asked the Commons for permission to complete the imperfect statute of 1799. The Commons had refused the request:[2] would the House persist in that refusal when the grave abuses to which the right of meeting had given rise were so evident? Such were the three Bills which the Government now introduced in addition to the Habeas Corpus Suspension Act. The last of the three restored all the extremely stringent restrictions placed by the Act of 1798 upon the right of public meeting, contained a special clause which laid the Spencean group under the ban of the law, and declared illegal the device by which during the previous half-year the clubs had evaded the prohibition to federate—the election of delegates by a public meeting.

With a few trifling amendments the three Bills were passed without difficulty.[3] The Opposition never obtained above one hundred votes for any amendment they brought forward. At times the total number of members voting barely exceeded sixty. The Cabinet had deemed it politic to place the Duke of Bedford on the Committees of the Lords, in order thus to make the Whig aristocracy share the responsibility for these measures. The Duke pleaded ill-health as an excuse for refusal, and in this way without giving his support to the Government avoided open opposition. Even the *Morning Chronicle*, the leading organ of the Opposition, would hardly report the debates in full: Perry, the proprietor,

[1] 57 Geo. III, cap. 3.
[2] H. of C., May 18, June 9, 1809 (*Parl. Deb.*, vol. xiv, pp. 615 sqq., 987).
[3] 57 Geo. III, cap. 6, 7, 19.

was content to abuse the revolutionaries, whose activities had cost the Opposition the fruits of the parliamentary successes won during the previous session, and await better days in silence.[1] On March 25 the Lords passed the third reading of the last of the Government's Bills, the Seditious Meetings Bill. Two days later Lord Sidmouth dispatched to the Lord-Lieutenants a circular explaining the Act. After consultation with the Law Officers of the Crown, he asked them to instruct the Justices of the Peace in his name that every magistrate was empowered to arrest and to release only on bail any person found guilty of the public sale of blasphemous or seditious literature.[2] He thus took upon himself to interpret the law in a sense which extended beyond all precedent the jurisdiction of magistrates.

5

The counter-revolutionary terror which had prevailed since December increased in severity, and was now under the open patronage of Lord Sidmouth and his colleagues. No more public meetings were held, and the Hampden clubs disappeared. The City magistrates refused to sanction a debating society, on the ground that the Government desired to put a stop to all political discussion. The Cambridge Union Society was compelled to suspend its meetings, after ten years of active life, because its debates dealt with political questions, and because the Society happened to bear the same name as an association once founded by Major Cartwright. The same fate even befell societies whose object was purely scientific—the Literary Society of Manchester, the Academical Society of Oxford, the City Philosophical Society of London. A magistrate refused his sanction to a mineralogical society on the pretext that the study of mineralogy led to atheism.[3] 'The plains, or heights, or whatsoever they are, of Waterloo,'

[1] It is true that for some time Perry had been an object of distrust to the Opposition leaders. See, for instance, Brougham's letter to Lord Grey, March 14, 1816: 'His vile print. . . . He gives all advantages to the enemy, and makes Castlereagh appear to triumph, while he is lower than you can even fancy. The truth is, we have found that he has a Tory reporter as well as a Whig, and it is a mere chance that the truth is ever told' (*Life and Times of Lord Brougham*, vol. ii, pp. 310–11).

[2] Pellew, op. cit., vol. iii, p. 174.

[3] *Ann. Reg.*, 1817, Chron., p. 43; A. Prentice, *Historical Sketches and Personal Recollections of Manchester*, p. 112; H. of C., April 28, 1817 (*Parl. Deb.*, vol. xxxvi, pp. 17 sqq.), April 29, 1817 (ibid., vol. xxxvi, pp. 83 sqq.); Bentham, *Plan of Parliamentary Reform*, 1817, pp. 329, 335.

wrote Bentham, 'will one day be pointed to by the historian as the grave not only of French but of English liberties. Not of France alone, but of Britain with her, was the conquest consummated in the Netherlands. Whatsoever has been done and is doing in France will soon be done in Britain. Reader, would you wish to know the lot designed for you? Look to France, there you may behold it.'[1] In London the staff of the revolutionary army was breaking up. Hunt, to be sure, did not lay down his arms; to defend his position he had the services of a weekly whose first number appeared on the morrow of the re-opening of Parliament and the attempt on the Regent's life: it was called the *Black Dwarf*, and edited by T. J. Wooler. But he lost the favour of the public. For some time already his supporters had received notice of another meeting which he intended to hold at Spa Fields on February 12. The Government took its precautions, surrounded the place of meeting with soldiers, and arrested the rioters of the previous December. Everything passed off smoothly.[2] Hunt did not even dare to put in an appearance at a meeting of the electors of Westminster, which passed resolutions of a most moderate character.[3] A final meeting fixed for March 15 at Spa Fields could scarcely muster twenty persons. Where were the crowds of yesteryear? 'Bad news for St. Helena', was the triumphant exclamation of the *Courier*. 'Once more we feel that we possess a Government.'[4] Hunt found himself disowned by the Lord Mayor and the agitators of the City, disowned also by Sir Francis Burdett and the agitators of Westminster, and at loggerheads with Cobbett.[5] And when the news arrived of Cobbett's disappearance from the scene, the discomfiture of the revolutionaries was complete.

Almost ruined a year earlier, the incredible success of his *Register* had restored Cobbett to solvency. But the Cabinet was preparing to take its revenge by demanding the entire stamp duty he had failed to pay on the 2d. numbers. The amount due was fixed by report at £18,000. For Cobbett this meant ruin or prison. He travelled in secret to Liverpool and, leaving behind him a long

[1] Bentham, op. cit., 1817, p. iv. Written in May.
[2] *The Times*, February 11, 12, 1817; *Courier*, February 11, 1817.
[3] *Courier*, March 15, 1817.
[4] Ibid., March 24, 1817.
[5] *The Times*, January 25, 1817. See the attacks upon Cobbett in the *Black Dwarf*, January 29, 1817 (vol. i, p. 7), March 12, 1817 (vol. i, p. 112).

letter of farewell to his fellow countrymen,[1] sailed for America. There he found the democrats' paradise, a country where there was neither an Established Church nor a standing army, a republic of farmers where government and life were cheap. And 'No Wilberforces. Think of *that*!—no Wilberforces'.[2]

The provinces witnessed the same defeat of the campaign on behalf of reform. It is true that two revolutionary outbreaks marked the spring of 1817. But not only were they totally ineffective, they were exploited, and, in one instance at least, engineered by the Government to stimulate public alarm and justify their policy of coercion. The first of these took place in Lancashire. On March 3 a meeting was held at Manchester to protest against the suspension of the Habeas Corpus Act. The place of meeting was fixed a week ahead. Those who wished to take part in the demonstration were to come prepared for a long journey; for a solemn march to London was intended. The marchers were to make their way to Carlton House, bearing with them a petition in favour of reform. The organizers had revived a method first adopted by the starving miners of Staffordshire a year earlier. The miners had excited pity rather than fear. But the present demonstration was provided with a political programme, and for the past six months Hunt's violent language had been arousing the apprehensions of the middle class. A rumour got abroad that it was not a mere handful of Lancashire mill hands who were preparing for the march, but the entire proletariat of Lancashire and Yorkshire. Twenty-five thousand firearms, it was reported, were stored at Birmingham ready to be delivered to the marchers as they passed through.

The meeting was held. The 'Blanketeers' set out on the road— some in the direction of Stockport, others in the direction of Ashbourne, and others reached Derby. A few dragoons sufficed to disperse them, and the Government had made use of the meeting held on the 10th as an excuse to arrest the more dangerous leaders. The wildest tales gained currency. It was rumoured that the Lancashire weavers had formed a plot to take possession of Manchester, take the magistrates prisoner, open the gaols, fire the factories, and make the city a second Moscow.[3] Numerous

---

[1] *Mr. Cobbett's Taking Leave of His Countrymen.*
[2] *Pol. Reg.*, October 3, 1818 (vol. xxxiv, p. 216).
[3] Bamford, op. cit., ed. 1893, vol. i, p. 37.

arrests destroyed anything resembling a revolutionary organization that may have existed in Lancashire.

This was the very moment when the Seditious Meetings Bill was passed. The democratic societies, to which a public existence was henceforth denied, were driven underground and compelled to become secret societies, far more inclined than before to engage in conspiracy and plot acts of violence. At the beginning of May the reformers held secret meetings on the borders of Lancashire, Yorkshire, and Derbyshire to organize another march on London. This new scheme, unlike that of the Blanketeers, was of the nature of an armed rising. The conspirators were inspired by the wild aims attributed in the official Press to the demonstrations of March. The excitement continued throughout May, and on June 6, at Thornhill Lees, near Huddersfield, a meeting of delegates was held to make the final arrangements. But the police who were in touch with all the ramifications of the plot arrested the ring-leaders; and when, on the night of June 9, the revolutionaries made a show of carrying out their plan to raise Derbyshire and march on Nottingham, the attempt, like the Lancashire demonstration two months before, was a miserable fiasco. The Government had already obtained from the Lords the appointment of a new committee of inquiry; it reported on June 12, and recommended the suspension of Habeas Corpus for a further six months.[1]

Finally, the Cabinet secured an Act extending the suspension of the Habeas Corpus Act until March 1, 1818.[2] But the suspension provoked rather more opposition than on the previous occasion, and was followed by events which weakened the position of the Government. On June 14 the great Whig newspaper of York-shire, the *Leeds Mercury*, disclosed to its readers the fact that the conspiracy of the previous week had been fomented by a certain Oliver, who pretended to be an agent of the revolutionary clubs of London, but was in reality an *agent-provocateur* sent to the north by Lord Sidmouth. On the 17th Lord Fitzwilliam, the head of the Yorkshire Whigs, supported the revelations of the *Mercury* in a long open letter addressed to the Government. A few days later the revolutionaries accused of the December riot were brought to trial. The London juries were democratic and had

---

[1] For an account of these plots see Report of the Secret Committee, *Ann. Reg.*, 1817, pp. 65 sqq.; Bamford, op. cit., chap. v; A. Prentice, op. cit., chaps. vi and vii; J. L. and B. Hammond, op. cit., 1920, chap. xii.

[2] 57 Geo. III, cap. 55.

already given trouble to the Government by a number of acquittals.[1] It had come to light in the course of the debates that the accused owed their arrest to the denunciation of an accomplice named Castle, who had once been a spy in the pay of the police. Was he another Oliver? The attorney-general judged it prudent to drop the prosecution, and the accused were all acquitted.[2]

Then the provincial courts began to imitate the London jury. In Scotland Andrew Mackinley was acquitted on August 3.[3] In Yorkshire, on August 22, the jury acquitted the men accused of the June conspiracy.[4] In Ireland Roger O'Connor was acquitted, for it was proved that a perjured witness had fabricated against him a charge of highway robbery.[5] The sole defeat endured by the reformers during the second half of 1817 was the trial of the Derbyshire rioters. Delayed to the most opportune moment and skilfully engineered by the Government, it concluded in November with nineteen death sentences, of which three were carried out. This was the final episode of the drama.[6] The storm had blown over, and the ruling classes had recovered from their panic. Parliament had hardly reassembled in the following January when it repealed the Habeas Corpus Suspension Act of 1817.

The causes of the revolutionary movement, which during the previous winter and spring had aroused the fears of the gentry and middle class, were primarily and fundamentally economic. The workmen of the north and centre found themselves reduced to starvation by a trade depression, aggravated by the high cost of living. During the summer, however, the depression came to an end. The harvest did not belie its excellent prospects. The price of wheat, which in June had reached the figure of 111s. 6d. a quarter, fell steadily until in September it was 75s. a quarter. At the same time Lancashire and Yorkshire, the textile and iron-making districts, once more found a market for their goods, indeed could scarcely keep pace with the demand. The price of Consols rose, the 3 per cent stock, which in January had been at

[1] See Southey's complaints to Lord Liverpool, March 19, 1817, C. D. Yonge, op. cit., vol. ii, p. 299: 'If juries, either from fear or faction (as in Hooper's case the other day), give their verdict in the very face of facts, I beseech you, do not hesitate at using that vigour beyond the law which the exigence requires.'
[2] Ann. Reg., 1817, Chron. June 17.
[3] Examiner, August 3, 1817; Hone's Reformists' Register, August 9, 1817.
[4] Ann. Reg. 1817, Chron., pp. 72–3.
[5] Ibid., Chron., p. 203.
[6] See for the details of the trial J. L. and B. Hammond, op. cit., p. 366 sqq.

63, exceeded 83 in July and again in December. It was all very well for Ministers to make out that it was their measures of coercion which had nipped the rebellion in the bud. It was only to be expected that a revolutionary movement, which had been called into being by the economic crisis, should not survive its cause. If the agitators could no longer find workmen to attend their meetings, it was because they were no longer unemployed.

What, moreover, had been the demands put forward by the disaffected workmen? They desired a better standard of living, higher wages and lower prices. We should, therefore, have expected them to demand a minimum wage fixed by law or the repeal of the Corn Bill of 1815. But their programme had not been formulated by themselves; it had been received ready made from London. What, then, were the demands of the London revolutionaries, who dreamed of a general insurrection of the lower classes under their leadership? A reduction of the Army, and on this point they were at one with the workmen of the provinces. The suppression of sinecures and drastic retrenchment of the heavy Civil List, and the enormous salaries received by Ministers and highly placed functionaries. In this demand the working class was not so immediately interested, for the burden of taxation did not fall, at least not directly, on its shoulders. Finally the conquest of political power by means of manhood suffrage. This democratic programme, however, had not acquired a hold over the popular imagination. It was merely the programme of the London clubs, where the antiquated traditions of the eighteenth century still held sway, and where the atmosphere was steeped in the more recent memories of French Jacobinism. But just because it had been imported from France, the political philosophy of the clubs was out of harmony with the national temper.

6

When the committees in their January reports had called attention to the anti-religious character of the revolutionary propaganda, they showed their understanding both of psychology and political tactics; for the London democrats were, in fact, imbued with the anti-religious principles of the French republican, and their irreligion shocked British pietism. Bentham, who had just thrown down the gage to the triumphant Tories by declaring himself in favour of universal suffrage,[1] became, from the moment of Cobbett's flight, the acknowledged leader of the democrats. He was a theorist, freer than Cobbett from the vices of the demagogue, but also more detached from British prejudices. Nurtured in the ideas of the eighteenth century, and a disciple of Helvétius, the study of the problems of popular education which he had made for some years past in collaboration with James Mill had confirmed his anti-clericalism. At the very moment when Parliament passed a Bill which sought to reform the abuses of the Church by strengthening the disciplinary powers of the bishops, and was about to make a grant for the building of new churches to combat irreligion among the proletariat of the great manufacturing centres, Bentham devoted a bulky volume, entitled *Church of England Catechism Examined*, to a criticism of the Establishment and the exposition of a plan of church reform on democratic and economic principles. The clergy were to be elected by their parishioners, and their stipends very considerably reduced. He maintained the right of the State to disendow the Church, at least in part, and he sketched the lines on which the disendowment should be carried out. He then proceeded to the study of the Bible and wrote two further works: *Not Paul but Jesus*, a violent attack upon the Apostle as a fanatic and a clerical, and his *Analysis of the Influence of Natural Religion*, in which the object of his criticism is no longer merely the theology of St. Paul, nor even Christianity, but religion itself.[2]

Bentham shared this hostile attitude towards religion with Robert Owen, another reformer, who was indeed no democrat and whose economic doctrines would soon markedly diverge from his own. But Owen did but apply more thoroughly a philosophy common to both, and for the moment was glad to join forces with Bentham. Since 1812 he had been working hard to spread his principles both by speech and writing,[3] proclaiming

---

[1] *Plan of Parliamentary Reform*, Introduction (dated May 12, 1807), s. 8, 'Virtual Universality of Suffrage—Its Undangerousness' (pp. 101 sqq.). Bentham adds (p. 115): 'As to *absolutely universal suffrage*, though preferable to the others, I do not, nor ever should, advocate it. I should, nevertheless, as Earl Grey did once, "prefer it to the present system".' In 1818 he declared himself in favour of an unqualified system of universal suffrage, and drew up the twenty-six resolutions which, on June 2, Sir Francis Burdett laid before the House of Commons (*Parl. Deb.*, vol. xxxvii, pp. 1118 sqq.). See Halévy, *Formation du Radicalisme Philosophique*, vol. ii, pp. 208–9.

[2] See Halévy, op. cit., vol. ii, pp. 260 sqq.

[3] Mr. Owen's speech at a public dinner at which he presided, given to Joseph Lancaster at Glasgow in 1812 (*The Life of Robert Owen*, written by himself, vol. i, p. 245); 'A New

that the evils under which society suffered could be cured only by reforming the external conditions which make the individual what he is—that is, by changing his social environment. Ethics and religion were, so to speak, the original sin of humanity, for they were founded on the belief that the individual is responsible for his acts and can be reformed by exhortation and reproof. Other advocates of revolution were also at this juncture flaunting their hostility to religion, men of a widely different stamp from Bentham and Owen, namely, the romanticists of Byron's school. Byron himself published his *Manfred* in 1817, Shelley his *Alastor* in 1816, *The Revolt of Islam* in 1818, and *Prometheus Unbound* in 1820. Keats, a pagan, as convinced, if less aggressive than they, was flashing like a meteor across the firmament of British poetry. With these poets irreligion was a religion and contempt for morality a moral code. In London, Leigh Hunt had made the *Examiner* the common organ of all these enemies of Christianity; and although since the passing of the Coercion Acts he had turned his attention to the question of parliamentary reform, he did not relax his weekly campaign against theological fanaticism of every description—the fanaticism of the Spanish and French Catholics, of the Church of England, of the dissenting pietists whom he loathed so heartily.

More obscure, but equally worthy of our attention, were the pamphleteers of plebeian origin, who were spreading among the lower classes what they were pleased to term 'deism'. The first of these men to attract attention was William Hone with his *Late John Wilkes' Catechism*, *Sinecurists' Creed* and *Political Litany*. These pamphlets were at once parodies of the Anglican liturgy and satires directed against the Cabinet and its supporters. Hone conducted his defence before a jury for three entire days with such skill that he secured a triumphant acquittal. Others followed in his steps. Among them was Sherwin, a turnkey converted to deism by reading the works of Tom Paine, who at the age of eighteen became printer and editor of a *Political Register* devoted to the propagation of deism and republicanism. Another was Richard Carlile, who had been errand boy to an apothecary, a factory hand, a workman employed in printing *Sherwin's Register*, then an agent for the magazine, and finally its editor and owner.

View of Society; or Essays on the Principle of the Formation of the Human Character . . . 1813–14' (ibid., pp. 253 sqq.).

Its title was henceforward *Carlile's Political Register*. He was now the recognized deist bookseller. He published a new edition of Tom Paine's works, the *Principles of Nature* by Paine's American disciple, Elihu Palmer, and editions of Voltaire and Diderot. By his disinterestedness and his dislike of personal quarrels, he stood out above his entourage, who were violent demagogues and seemed to hate each other even more heartily than they hated the Regent, Cabinet, and Parliament.

Thus the conflict which had so long raged in France between traditional religion and the entire movement of modern thought was transferred to London. But although this propaganda made a great deal of noise, it was in reality very weak, even in the capital, and weaker still in the provinces. The Government had no difficulty in obtaining from Parliament the church building grant for which it asked.[1] England remained a deeply religious nation, and was probably becoming more religious every day. Therefore when the democrats wounded the susceptibilities of Anglican and Dissenter alike by language too frankly anti-Christian, they were employing the most unskilful tactics they could possibly have adopted. Public opinion treated the missionaries of secularism in a manner that differed widely with the individual, and the difference repays examination. Bentham and Owen were respectable members of the middle class who had won the esteem of a society in which philanthropy was the fashion by the zeal which they displayed, Bentham for the reform of the penal code and prison administration, Owen for the reform of the factory system. All that was asked of them was to keep their anti-religious convictions to themselves; and even when they persisted in publishing them, the public was content to ignore their extravagances. Owen, indeed, could count among his patrons noblemen and even princes of the blood. Bentham's friends endeavoured to dissuade him from publishing his anti-clerical pamphlets, and so far succeeded that he published them under a pseudonym. Byron and Shelley were in an altogether different position, for they had incurred the ban of society by the irregularity of their private life. Nevertheless, Byron's poetry still enjoyed the favour of the public, and John Murray, most respectable of publishers, continued to print the work of the poet while

---

[1] 58 Geo. III, cap. 45; 59 Geo. III, cap. 134; J. H. Overton, *English Church in XIXth Century*, pp. 150 sqq.

refusing his approbation to the thinker.[1] But the freethinkers of humbler origin were treated with far less consideration. They soon discovered that Hone's acquittal was no universal licence to print whatever they pleased. In 1817 began Carlile's long war with the courts, a war which became more unrelenting after January 1819.[2] Nor was it always the Government which set the law in motion. In 1819 the prosecutions were undertaken by the great middle class society for 'the Suppression of Vice', of which Wilberforce and his friends were at the head. They were having their revenge for the insults which they had suffered in 1816 at the City of London Tavern. While in France a Voltairean bourgeoisie chafed under the government of the Jesuits, in England a pietist middle class was persecuting Carlile.

III ECONOMIC QUESTIONS

I

Alike in its economic and in its political aspect the crisis of 1817 was now a thing of the past. If in Scotland both the populace and the middle class still denounced the scandalous system of representation which obtained in the royal burghs, in England, and even in London, the cause of parliamentary reform had lost its vitality. The Hampden Club meetings could scarcely muster one or two members.[3] 'Parliamentary reform,' wrote Hone, 'is not perhaps dead, but it is dying';[4] and although the leaders of the Opposition expressed in vague generalities their adherence to the principle of a gradual and moderate reform, they refused to treat reform as a question of practical urgency. Brougham, who in 1814 had desired to be the Benthamite candidate at Westminster, now refused any kind of alliance with the democrats.[5] Lord Grey, the erstwhile 'Jacobin' of 1792, retired to his distant

[1] The sole vengeance attempted by the English law against Byron was a refusal to protect his copyright, a clumsy revenge which hurt no one but Murray and assisted the cheap sale of the poet's works (E. Jacob, *Reports of Cases Argued and Determined in Chancery during the time of Lord Chancellor Eldon*, 1821, 1822, 1828, p. 474, note *a*).

[2] See the list of the earlier trials of Carlile in *The Republican*, No. I, August 27, 1819, pp. 14 sqq.

[3] *Proceedings of the Hampden Club*, June 1819. Cf. H. of C., February 27, 1817, Lord Cochrane's speech (*Parl. Deb.*, vol. xxxv, f. 762).

[4] *Reformists' Register*, February 17, 1817 (vol. i, p. 114).

[5] *Courier*, February 18, 1817. Th. Hodgskin to Francis Place, May 20, 1819 (British Museum, Add. MSS., 35, 153, 162).

estates in Northumberland, defended the House of Commons against the attacks made against its constitution, and warned the British public against the democratic peril.[1]

For the Opposition leaders perceived that the position of the Government, so badly shaken during the session of 1816, had been strengthened in the following year by the terror of revolution; and concluded that, if they were to succeed in weakening it again, political questions must be relegated to the background. Whig speakers accordingly found other themes. Romilly urged the reform of the criminal law,[2] Brougham pleaded the cause of primary education.[3] But it was financial questions which caused the greatest embarrassment to the Government. An opportunity to combine with their campaign for retrenchment an attack upon the royal family was doubly welcome to the Whigs. The Regent's daughter, the Princess Charlotte, died towards the end of 1817, a year after her marriage with Prince Leopold of Saxe-Coburg; her death left the Crown without a direct heir; and when the Regent's four brothers, who, though men of advanced years, were still bachelors, made haste to wed in hope of an heir, the enormous settlements for which they asked excited the indignation of Parliament. At the General Election of 1818 the Whigs reaped the reward of their prudent tactics. The election was hotly contested, and its result was a clear gain for the moderate Opposition.[4] If the split between the Whigs and the democrats enabled a Ministerialist to defeat Romilly in Westminster, the four City

---

[1] Speech at Newcastle, September 19, 1817: 'I am still a reformer, but with some modification of my former opinions: with more fear of the effect of sudden and inconsiderate changes, with a most complete conviction that to be successful reform must be gradual, and must be carefully limited to the necessity which has proved it to be wanting. . . . Of the House of Commons, as it at present exists, I am not unwilling to say that I think it is, with all its imperfections on its head, one of the best securities the people of this country ever had for the preservation of their freedom. Even now it is under the control of public opinion, to ensure the success of any wise and legal measures: even now the public voice may do much if it be directed to proper objects' (*Courier*, September 24, 1817).

[2] H. of C., February 25, 1818 (*Parl. Deb.*, vol. xxxvii, p. 610).

[3] For Brougham's campaign till 1818 see H. of C., May 21, 1816 (*Parl. Deb.*, vol. xxxiv, pp. 633 sqq.); May 22, 1817 (ibid., vol. xxxvi, pp. 822–3); May 8, 1818 (ibid., vol. xxxviii, p. 585); May 18, 1818 (ibid., vol. xxxviii, pp. 760 sqq.); June 3, 1818, Report from the Select Committee on the Education of the Lower Orders and Brougham's speech (ibid., vol. xxxviii, pp. 1207 sqq.). See also H. of C., April 13, 1818 (ibid., vol. xxxvii, pp. 1297–8); April 22, April 27, June 8, 1818 (ibid., vol. xxxviii, pp. 285, 336, 1294).

[4] Out of 380 constituencies, 115 were contested (Harriet Martineau, *History of the Thirty Years' Peace*, Book I, chap. xiv—ed. Bohn, 1877, vol. i, p. 252; Jephson, op. cit., vol. i, p. 441).

seats, on the other hand, were captured by the Opposition. The total Whig gain was estimated at about thirty seats.[1]

2

Between 1817 and 1819 the activity of the Whigs was concentrated upon the budget; circumstances made this inevitable. Both Parliament and people demanded retrenchment. To obtain their desire they had adopted a violent expedient in 1816. By suppressing the income tax they had made it impossible for the Treasury to defray current expenses. Every spring, therefore, the Chancellor of the Exchequer found himself faced by an insoluble problem.

In 1817 the Speech from the Throne recommended the state of the Treasury to the earnest consideration of Parliament, and undertook to effect all the economies in the Public Services compatible with the safety of the Empire. In 1816 the Army had cost £15,416,000, for 1817 the Government asked £9,080,000. The Navy had cost £9,516,000, for 1817 £6,000,000 was asked. The Artillery (ordnance) had cost £2,802,000, the estimate for 1817 was £1,221,000.[2] Moreover, Lord Castlereagh, on February 7, asked the Commons to appoint a committee to examine the condition of the public finances, and recommend any economies they might deem practicable. The Prince Regent set an example of patriotism by the voluntary renunciation of a fifth part of his income, a sum of £50,000, and the holders of Government offices were prepared, if Lord Castlereagh was to be believed, to dock their salaries by a sum equal to the amount of income tax to which they had been formerly liable.[3] On May 5 the committee brought in its first report. It recommended and immediately obtained the abolition of a number of important sinecures.[4]

Were these measures sufficient to avert the financial crisis? When the Ministers paraded so ostentatiously their intention to

[1] Their number rose from 140 to 173 (Spencer Walpole, *Life of Lord John Russell*, vol. i, p. 108).

[2] *An Account of the Total Annual Public Expenditure of Great Britain . . . for the year ended 5th January*, 1817. Account presented to the House of Commons respecting the Public Expenditure of Ireland for the year ended the 5th of January, 1817.

[3] H. of C., February 7, 1817 (*Parl. Deb.*, vol. xxxv, pp. 252 sqq.).

[4] First Report from the Select Committee appointed to inquire into and state the Income and Expenditure of the United Kingdom . . . and also to consider what further measures may be adopted for the Relief of the Country from any part of the said expenditure, without detriment to the Public Interest (sinecure offices).

carry through a policy of drastic retrenchment, their primary object it would appear was to prove the childish folly of such an expectation.[1] Since almost two-thirds of the public expenditure was taken up by the service of the National Debt, it was absurd to hope to balance the budget by economies effected in the remaining third. The expenditure for 1818 was estimated at £67,818,000, the revenue at £52,505,000, a deficit of £15,313,000.[2] This was roughly the amount which the income tax had produced. Was it the fault of the Ministry that the Commons had deprived it of this sum? It was also roughly the amount of the Sinking Fund; but by general consent the Sinking Fund was sacred. To balance the budget without the imposition of new taxes Vansittart proposed to issue bonds repayable at an early date, Irish Treasury Bills to an amount of £3,600,000, Exchequer Bills to an amount of £9,000,000. With the help of the revenue derived from a few exceptional sources, he was enabled to make good the deficit and balance the budget at the cost of a considerable increase in the Floating Debt. The panic aroused by the attempt against the Regent's life on January 29, and by the riots in Lancashire and Yorkshire, distracted attention from the financial problem. But, in spite of the revival of trade, it came up again in 1818. The expenditure on the Fighting Services fell, it is true, to £8,970,000; but if the estimates for the Navy and the Artillery were less than the actual expenditure of the previous year, they exceeded the estimates for 1817, reaching respectively the figure of £6,456,800 and £1,245,000.[3] Moreover, the sum of £400,000 was paid to Spain, as indemnity for the losses entailed upon her mercantile marine by the abolition of the slave trade, and £1,000,000 was allocated to the construction of new churches. The total expenditure for the coming year was estimated at about £67,350,000, the total receipts at about £52,500,000. There was always the same deficit of about £15,000,000, the amount of revenue lost by the abolition of the income tax. The Government made up the deficit by borrowing. The 3 per cent bonds were converted into 3½ per cent for all holders of the 3 per cents who paid 11 per cent

[1] H. of C., May 5, 1817, Lord Castlereagh's speech (*Parl. Deb.*, vol. xxxvi, p. 135).
[2] See Fourth Report from the Select Committee on Finance, June 5, 1817 (ibid., vol. xxxvi, p. ciii, n.).
[3] H. of C., April 20, 1818, Vansittart's speech. Actual expenditure for 1817: Army, £9,615,000; Navy, £6,473,000; Ordnance, £1,435,000 (Mr. Hume's Statement of the Actual Expenditure of the United Kingdom, as taken from the annual Finance Accounts, *Ann. Reg.*, App. to Chron. 1821, p. 283).

on the value of their holdings. It was a complicated form of loan, disguised as a loan for the consolidation of the floating debt to an amount of £27,000,000 worth of Exchequer Bills. By an innovation, which was the object of criticism in the Commons, the cost to the Treasury of this operation was charged upon the Sinking Fund, which cancelled previous debt to pay interest on the debt newly contracted. By this expedient the Government gained a year's respite. But when they came to prepare the budget for 1819, it became evident how impossible it was to go on in this way after four years of peace living from hand to mouth. If Vansittart raised a further loan of £12,000,000 on the usual terms, he was perfectly sincere when he explained that he did so only to meet certain exceptional demands on the Treasury—an arrangement which had been concluded with the Bank and the consolidation of a portion of the floating debt. He had still to make up the normal deficit on the annual budget, a deficit, as he stated, of £13,500,000. Since the Sinking Fund had risen to £15,500,000 for the year 1819, the financial situation might fairly be considered as a slight improvement on the position of the last few years, for the £15,500,000 was at least devoted to redemption of the old debt, and only a sum slightly inferior remained to be found. Nevertheless, it could be obtained only by departing from the principles of redemption laid down by Pitt. The Government had already embarked on this course in 1818, and during the debate Huskisson had made it plain that further steps must very soon be taken in the same direction.[1] In February he urged upon the Cabinet the absurdity and unreality of a financial policy which consisted in borrowing to redeem existing debt.[2] Vansittart yielded to his arguments and prepared a queer budget, which admitted the bankruptcy of Pitt's policy of redemption while making a show of preserving it inviolate.

He began by pointing out that a genuine redemption of the old debt must be effected, and consequently a genuine surplus in the annual budget devoted to that purpose, and therefore that a budget must be framed which would produce the surplus required. Since the annual Sinking Fund exceeded by £2,000,000 the sum of £13,500,000, which must be provided every year, if the deficit were to be made good, there was, therefore, according

[1] H. of C., April 20, 1818 (*Parl. Deb.*, vol. xxxviii, pp. 232–3).
[2] Huskisson to Lord Liverpool (C. D. Yonge, op. cit., vol. ii, p. 384).

to Vansittart, a real surplus of £2,000,000. He proposed that the normal surplus should not be allowed to fall below £5,000,000, and therefore that an additional £3,000,000 should be raised. Should it be raised by direct taxation? The income tax was more unpopular than ever: the *Edinburgh Review* had just laid down that public liberty was equally imperilled by 'an income tax', 'a large standing army', or 'the suspension of the Constitution'.[1] Vansittart obtained from Parliament the imposition of indirect taxes to the amount of £3,000,000. There was a general revision of the Customs duties, which involved a very substantial increase of the duty on wool, also higher taxes on tobacco, coffee, tea, cocoa, and pepper—their collection being transferred from the Customs to the Excise, and an increase of the Excise duty on malt and spirits.

The sum of £13,500,000 had still to be raised. By the employment of various expedients Vansittart was able to manage with £12,000,000. He borrowed that amount from the Sinking Fund, and declared his intention of borrowing annually from the same fund the sum needed to cover the deficit—provided £5,000,000 were devoted to the redemption of the outstanding debt. To be sure, Vansittart formed a very large Sinking Fund to pay off this new loan in obedience to the provisions of the Act of 1813; but it is equally certain that when he argued that in acting thus he was respecting the principles of redemption laid down by Pitt, he was talking nonsense. The annual contribution to the Sinking Fund was henceforward reduced to £5,000,000. 'The Ministers,' wrote Ricardo, 'considered the Commissioners as their trustees, accumulating money for their benefit, and of which they knew that they might dispose whenever they should consider that the urgency of the case required it. They seem to have made a tacit agreement with the Commissioners that they should accumulate £12,000,000 per annum at compound interest, while they themselves accumulated an equal amount of debt, also at compound interest. The facts are, indeed, no longer denied. In the last session of Parliament, for the first time, the delusion was acknowledged by Ministers.'[2]

Two years had passed since Ricardo had published his *Principles of Political Economy and Taxation*. He was now the master of a school of disciples, and his word carried great weight. But in

[1] *Edinburgh Review*, June 1818, 'State of Parties' (vol. xxx, p. 187).
[2] 'Essay on the Funding System' (*Works*, p. 544).

denouncing as dishonest the method employed by the Government to utilize the Sinking Fund for the creation of a further debt, he was far from demanding a return to Pitt's system of finance. He regarded it as now finally discredited,[1] and radically vicious, and declared his adhesion to Hamilton's thesis. Heroic measures were demanded if the debt were to be reduced, as seemed desirable, to its pre-war figure. There were some—for example, Cobbett, the demagogue, and MacCulloch, a young Scottish publicist and a friend of Ricardo[2]—who were even prepared to advocate the total or partial repudiation of the debt. Ricardo put forward a plan which amounted to the reimposition, in a far heavier form, of 'the Property Tax' which had been abolished in 1816 amid the acclamations of the entire nation. The measure he proposed for the rapid extinction of the debt was not an income tax, but a capital levy payable either in a lump sum or by a limited number of annual instalments.

3

The problem of the Poor Law was another question which engaged the attention of Parliament and the ruling classes. This problem also concerned taxation: for although the poor rate was a local, not a national, impost, its weight was none the less crushing; and the distress which afflicted the working classes made the burden heavier each year. The poor rate had risen from £5,418,846 in 1815 to £5,724,839 in 1816, £6,910,925 in 1817, and £7,870,801 in 1818. It fell most heavily on landed property, and the country gentlemen who filled the benches of the Commons were naturally anxious to shake off the load. Malthus had provided the malcontents with a theoretical justification. To guarantee the labourer a fixed standard of wages was, according to Malthus, to defy the laws of Nature, and give a promise which it was not in the power of the community to fulfil. Indeed, it would lead in the long run to the impoverishment of those it was

---

[1] For political as well as financial reasons. Ricardo to Trower, March 25, 1822: 'Of what use can it be to diminish the debt in time of peace, if you leave in the hands of Ministers a fund which experience shows will be used only for the purpose of ultimately further increasing the debt? While Ministers have this fund virtually at their disposal, they will on the slightest occasion be disposed for war. To keep them peaceable you must keep them poor.'

[2] An essay on the *Question of Reducing the Interest of the National Debt*, in which the justice and expediency of that measure are fully established, 1816.

intended to relieve; for it would encourage an imprudent birth-rate among the labouring class and thus, since the number of consumers would increase out of all proportion to the means of subsistence, a fall in wages would be produced by the attempt to maintain them at an artificial level. What use, asked Malthus, were Coercion Acts, if the cause of disorder—pauperism—were not attacked, and in turn the cause of pauperism, which was not, as the popular agitators insisted, the Government's extravagant expenditure, whether military or civil, nor even the amount of the debt, but the bad economics on which the Poor Law was based? Malthusian literature increased rapidly during these first years of peace. Curwen published his book on the Poor Laws.[1] The dissertation in which thirty years earlier Townshend had anticipated Malthus was republished.[2] Chalmers contributed two important and influential articles to the *Edinburgh Review*.[3] And the series was crowned by a fifth edition of the *Principle of Population*, provided with a triumphant preface and an additional chapter on the Poor Laws, in which Malthus attacked Cobbett and his supporters, whom he stigmatized as public poisoners.[4]

A further consideration, a consideration of political strategy, encouraged the Tory Cabinet to undertake the reform of the Poor Law. Malthus's doctrine was also Ricardo's, and had been adopted from the latter by Bentham, James Mill, and their fellow Utilitarians, who were all, like Ricardo himself, democrats. Thus the very men who denounced so vehemently the Government's financial policy, and called for a Parliament elected by manhood suffrage with a mandate to reduce the public expenditure to a minimum, agreed with Malthus, the opponent of democracy, that the taxation was not the cause of the distress under which the country suffered, and that even if the impossible could be realized and every tax abolished by a stroke of the pen, the misery and impoverishment of the masses would continue until the workers learnt to remove the true cause of their distress, the indiscriminate multiplication of the inhabitants of a territory

---

[1] *Sketch of a Plan for Bettering the Condition of the Labouring Classes of the Community and for Equalizing and Reducing the Amount of the Present Parochial Assessments*, 1817. Cf. his speech, H. of C., May 28, 1816 (*Parl. Deb.*, vol. xxxiv, pp. 871 sqq.).

[2] *A Dissertation on the Poor Laws*, by a Well-wisher to Mankind, 1817.

[3] *Edinburgh Review*, March 1817, 'Causes and Cure of Pauperism' (vol. xxviii, pp. 1 sqq.); February 1818 (vol. xxix, pp. 261 sqq.).

[4] *An Essay on the Principle of Population*, in three volumes, the fifth edition with important additions, 1817.

limited both in area and fertility. Surely it would be clever tactics if the Government could make the Malthusian democrats contradict themselves, while embroiling them with Cobbett and Hunt?

Already, in 1816, the landowners had made their complaints heard through the Board of Agriculture. The poor rate, they pointed out, fell exclusively on land, and the great manufacturers, who by throwing their hands on the street were making the cost of poor relief heavier, were exempt from the burden.[1] Parliament had responded to the wishes of the gentry by setting up a parliamentary committee, to inquire into the Poor Laws and their possible reform. Curwen, in the speech in which he moved the appointment of the committee, had suggested that the poor rate, levied exclusively on landed property, should be replaced by a parochial assessment, levied on every species of wealth, at a rate of 12 per cent on rents, 10 per cent on the interest of invested capital, inclusive of government stock, and $2\frac{1}{2}$ per cent on salaries.[2] Thus only a few weeks after the abolition of the Property Tax, Curwen the agriculturist and Ricardo the philosopher of industrialism, the former to meet the cost of poor relief, the latter to extinguish the National Debt, agreed in proposing the institution of a new impost of the same nature. Naturally, Curwen's proposal met with no response; but Curwen in his motion, Lord Castlereagh in a reply to Curwen in 1817,[3] and Sturges Bourne, the chairman of the committee in the report which concluded its labours,[4] were unanimous that even if it were impossible to get rid of the Poor Law altogether and thus realize Malthus's Utopian dream, a return must be made to the letter of Elizabeth's statute, and relief must no longer be granted to the able-bodied pauper, without providing some legal security that the recipient was not unemployed by his own choice. Three Bills were drafted by Sturges Bourne, and passed by the Commons.[5] Their object was

[1] 'Agricultural State of the Kingdom, being the Substance of the Replies to a Circular Letter sent by the Board of Agriculture' (*Ann. Reg.*, 1816, pp. 459 sqq., especially pp. 467 sqq.).

[2] H. of C., May 28, 1816 (*Parl. Deb.*, vol. xxxiv, pp. 884–5). In a speech delivered in 1817, Curwen again brought forward the same plan, but in a modified and optional form (H. of C., February 21, 1817, ibid., vol. xxxv, pp. 522 sqq.).

[3] H. of C., February 21, 1817 (ibid., vol. xxxv, pp. 522 sqq.).

[4] 'Report of the Select Committee of the House of Commons appointed to consider of the Poor Laws, 1817' (reproduced in its entirety in the *Ann. Reg.*, 1817, pp. 362 sqq.; see especially pp. 279 sqq.).

[5] 58 Geo. III, cap. 69 (Parish Vestry Act); 59 Geo. III, cap. 12 (Select Vestry Act); also a further statute 'to amend the Laws respecting the Settlement of the Poor', so far as regards renting settlement (59 Geo. III, cap. 50). Two of these Acts, and especially

twofold: (1) to reduce the discretionary powers to grant special relief which had been vested in the magistrates by recent legislation; (2) to strengthen the control of the landlords over the administration of the Poor Laws. It was to effect the latter purpose that a system of plural voting based on the amount of rates paid by each member replaced in the parish vestries the old system of voting by heads, that the new legislation encouraged the substitution of select vestries, representative bodies elected by the plural vote of the ratepayers, for the open vestries in which the parishioners governed themselves directly, and it was provided that the rates could no longer be raised above a fixed amount without the consent of a proportion of the ratepayers representative of two-thirds of the parish assessment. An attempt was made to render the administration of the Poor Law more regular by laying down rules for keeping minutes of the vestry meeting and accounts, and by encouraging the vestries or magistrates to appoint paid officials to be called assistant overseers. And, finally, the conditions under which the settlement was acquired which gave a pauper the right to relief from the parish were made more stringent.

4

All this went a very little way to satisfy the Malthusians. Nevertheless, whether as a result of the Sturges Bourne Acts, or because the economic position of labour had improved, the cost of the Poor Law steadily decreased from 1819 to 1824.[1] And was it, indeed, practicable to begin by more drastic measures? Would it be prudent, so soon after the passage of the Coercion Acts of 1817, to ask Parliament for a reform of the Poor Laws, which public opinion would regard as a final Coercion Act, aimed not only at the avowed enemies of the crown, the church, and property, but at the entire working class? The opponents of the Malthusian philosophy were still influential, both the Christians who regarded it as an outrage upon morality[2] and the democrats

the second, bear Sturges Bourne's name. For further details on the Sturges Bourne Acts see S. and B. Webb, *English Local Government from the Revolution to the Municipal Corporations Act*, vol. i, 'The Parish and the County', pp. 152 sqq.

[1] It was in 1818 that the amount of poor relief attained the figure which Sir George Nicholas terms its 'first maximum', £7,870,809; in 1824 it fell to his 'first minimum' of £5,736,900 (*History of the English Poor Law*, vol. ii, p. 466).

[2] John Weyland, *The Principles of Population and Production as they are affected by the Progress of Society*, 1816; James Grahame, *An Inquiry into the Principle of Population*: in-

in whose eyes it was a creed of selfish cruelty.[1] And the anti-Malthusians had just won an important adherent in the person of Owen, to whom the crisis of 1817 had revealed the deep gulf which on two important points divided him from Bentham and his disciples.

Owen had never cared for political democracy, and had made no secret of the loathing he felt for Cobbett and his fellow agitators. They, in turn, made him the object of the most violent attacks,[2] whereupon he proclaimed his abiding and implacable hostility to the entire democratic party. And, at the same moment, he perceived, as if in the light of a sudden inspiration, that his political economy had nothing in common with the economics of those more moderate and more practical utilitarians who followed Bentham. At a public meeting first, then in a memorial which he addressed in 1818 to the monarchs assembled at Aix-la-Chapelle, he refuted the doctrine of Malthus.[3] The prevalent poverty, he argued, was by no means to be explained by a growth of the population which exceeded the possible increase in the

cluding an exposition of the causes and the advantages of a tendency to exuberance of numbers in society, a defence of Poor Laws, and a critical and historical view of the doctrines and projects of the most celebrated legislators and writers relative to population, the poor and charitable establishments, 1816.

[1] G. Ensor, *An Inquiry Concerning the Population of Nations*, containing a refutation of Mr. Malthus's *Essay on Population*, 1818. Cf. *Gorgon*, June 6, 1818, and *Pol. Reg.*, May 8, 1819. The number entitled: To Parson Malthus, 'On the Rights of the Poor, and on the Cruelty Recommended by him to be Exercised towards the Poor'; also, September 11, 1819: To Henry Hunt, Esq., 'On the Workings of the Boroughmongers Relative to the Poor Laws' (vol. xxxiv, pp. 1019 sqq.; vol. xxxiv, pp. 97 sqq.).

[2] *Examiner*, August 4, 1816; ibid., September 1, 1816: 'Does Z found his particular hopes on the interview between Mr. Owen and the Emperor Alexander? We differ from him in our idea of both these great men, and augur as little from the want of power in the Manager of New Lanark as from the want of will in the Autocrat of all the Russias.' *Black Dwarf*, August 20, 1817: 'Mr. Owen's plan for the growth of paupers ... This land of "prosperity, wisdom, and freedom" is now occupied, in the consideration of a plan, which at first glance would seem better adapted for the meridian of Japan ... While the two Evanses are lingering in the gloom of a dungeon for being Spenceans, and although poor old Spence was persecuted until the hour of his death for his Spencean doctrines, behold, my friend, the vicissitudes of fortune. Mr. Owen with his Spencean plan advertises it through the country, convenes a public meeting to discuss it, and proposes the Ministers upon the committee to carry it into effect ! ! !' Cf. *Pol. Reg.*, January 10, 1818: 'We have been amused with a good-natured scheme of Mr. Owen for the relief of the poor. It seems to have been regarded, by some at least of our great folks, as a kind of Tub for the Whale; and in this way only can I account for the imposing manner in which he was enabled to bring it forward' (vol. xxxiii, p. 40).

[3] Address delivered at the City of London Tavern, August 21, 1817 (*Life of Robert Owen*, vol. i A., pp. 110–11). Also *Mémoire de M. Robert Owen, de New Lanark, en Écosse, adressé aux Souverains alliés, assemblés a Aix-la-Chapelle dans l'intérêt des classes ouvrières*, Frankfort, 1818. (The pamphlet appeared simultaneously in three languages—English, French, and German.) It is reprinted in the *Life of Robert Owen*, Supplementary Appendix, pp. 209 sqq.

means of subsistence. On the contrary, the great mechanical inventions, which marked the close of the eighteenth century and the rise of the factory system, proved that man's productive capacity had increased much more rapidly than the growth of population. In England the growth of production was now, he calculated, almost fifteen times what it had been before the war, whereas the population had increased only by a fifth. The poverty was due to the fact that the workman was denied a wage which enabled him to consume the entire product of the work he had performed with the aid of his machine. The difference went to the manufacturer, who exported the surplus to foreign markets. When the foreign markets were overstocked, a crisis resulted, the manufacturer failed, and the labourer was thrown out of work, and starved; evils due not to under-production but to a vicious distribution of wealth. Owen laid before the Poor Law Committee an elaborate scheme for the making use of the work-houses to reform the factory system. They would no longer be an instrument devised to make it difficult for the pauper to obtain relief by forcing upon him painful and unpleasant task work; henceforward they would be, to employ the words of Owen, 'villages of unity and mutual co-operation', where under Government control and with its financial assistance the inmates would enjoy all the advantages of the factory without the evils attached to the wage system.[1] Southey and Wordsworth, whom he visited at Keswick, gave him a sympathetic hearing.[2] And even after his attacks upon religion had alarmed the Tories, his Utopia was still the subject of a courteous debate in the Commons towards the close of 1819.[3] During the same year Parliament finally passed the Factory Bill, introduced in 1815 by Robert Peel at the instance of Owen. The measure was the achievement of over four years' effort and the slow labours of a committee of inquiry, and had been passed only with the help of the Evangelicals and after a preliminary defeat in the Lords. And how slight that achievement was! For the Act of 1819 restricted child labour to

[1] 'Report to the Committee of the Association for the Relief of the Manufacturing and Labouring Poor, referred to the Committee of the House of Commons on the Poor Laws, March 1817' (*Life of Robert Owen*, Supplementary Appendix, pp. 53 sqq.).
[2] Francis Place to James Mill, September 15, 1816: 'He set off to Southey and Wordsworth, and bespoke their good works.' 'Southey, as the story goes, is to say all manner of good things in his praise, and Wordsworth is not less captivated than Southey' (British Museum, Add. MSS., 35, 152 f., 214).
[3] H. of C., December 16, 1819 (*Parl. Deb.*, vol. xli, pp. 1189 sqq.).

twelve instead of the ten hours which Owen had desired; it did not apply to the entire textile industry, but only to cotton spinning, and the clause providing for the appointment of paid inspectors had been dropped.[1] Nevertheless, for all its timidity the Act was by no means without importance. The political economy of *laissez-faire* had suffered a defeat in the very year when, in the matter of the Poor Law, Parliament was apparently preparing to embrace it.

5

In short, the Government during the long crisis which followed the restoration of peace was faced with a choice between two policies. It could ally itself with the manufacturing middle class by adopting a programme of fiscal retrenchment and economic individualism, employ the language of liberty, and, on the plea of respecting the worker's freedom, refuse him its protection. But the interests of the country landlords, who composed the bulk of the Government's majority, were not identical with the manufacturers'. The landlords had carried the Corn Bill of 1815, which compelled the manufacturers to raise wages. And in 1817 they carried an increase in the import duty on wool, which dealt a severe blow to the cloth manufacture of Yorkshire. Parliament might, therefore, adopt a different attitude, resign itself to bear the expense of the Poor Law, develop the principle of paternal government implicit in the Tory doctrine, and pose as the protector of the workman against the plutocrat of the factory. In fact, it oscillated between the rival policies; but the former was plainly triumphant when, in 1819, by the restoration of specie payment, the school of Ricardo won a signal victory, and, moreover, at the very moment when Ricardo himself purchased a seat in the Commons.

The restoration of peace had, in fact, altered the character of this important problem, which had remained in suspense since 1812. Twice, in 1814 and again in 1815, without any appreciable change in the amount of currency, the prices of gold and silver had fallen almost to the level of the legal price. How, then, was it possible to maintain with Ricardo and Horner that the high price of the precious metals was due to the depreciation of the bank-note? Ricardo first, then Horner, had to admit that, on this

[1] 59 Geo. III, cap. 66.

point, their theory had not been borne out by the facts.[1] More-over, the Bank continued to insist that the suspension of specie payments was a temporary measure, and asserted that it was taking the necessary steps to make an abandonment of the arti-ficial currency possible, and in accordance with the bullionists' desire was restricting to the utmost of its power the number of notes in circulation. By these statements the Bank made new enemies in another camp. All those—and the agricultural interest above all—who suffered during a crisis from the fall of prices were disposed to ascribe the fall, and consequently the crisis itself, to the restriction of the currency. The restriction, they maintained, involved a universal breach of contract. Every creditor who had lent money before 1814 was receiving more than he had originally agreed to accept. And the bondholder in particular was receiving from the Government higher interest than that to which he was entitled by the terms of his loan. Thus the restriction of the currency injured the producer and benefited only the official and the bondholder. Sir John Sinclair pleaded the case of the agri-culturalist. An eccentric Tory banker of Birmingham, Thomas Attwood, went further. Arguing from the fact that the fall in prices benefited the idle consumer at the producer's expense, he arrived at the ridiculous conclusion that a general rise in the cost of living would encourage production in a society which on his hypothesis contained only producers. The population of England, whose numbers and industries were steadily increasing, was being crushed in the narrow frame of a currency which, if it increased at all, certainly did not keep pace with the people's needs. The State, he proposed, should issue sufficient notes to restore the prices which prevailed ten years earlier, and the issue must con-tinue until wages were 18s. a week, and the bank-rate 5 per cent. These measures would suffice to put an end to the crisis. He wrote in a clear and vigorous style, which disguised the web of sophis-tries of which his argument was composed. His pamphlets, pub-lished in 1816, 1817, and 1818, gained a wide hearing.[2]

[1] 'Proposals for an Economical and Secure Currency, 1816' (*Works*, p. 402). Cf. Ricardo to Trower, December 25, 1815; to Malthus, April 24, 1816.

[2] *The Remedy, or Thoughts on the Present Distresses*, 1816; 2nd ed., 1817. *Prosperity Restored, or Reflections on the Cause of the Public Distresses and the Only Means of Relieving Them*, 1817. *A Letter to the Right Honourable Nicholas Vansittart on the Creation of Money and on its Action upon National Prosperity*, 1817. *Observations on Currency, Population and Pauperism*, in two letters to Arthur Young, 1818. Cf. C. M. Wakefield, *Life of Thomas Attwood*, 1885.

Since the situation had changed since 1812, the Bank could be attacked only by new tactics. This did not escape Ricardo. Certainly, he continued to regard his arguments of 1809 as irrefutable, and to maintain that the depreciation of the bank-note was, if not the sole cause, certainly one of the causes of the unfavourable exchange. In a pamphlet which he published at the beginning of 1816,[1] he explained the practical measures necessary to replace the currency on a sound footing. The Bank of England must not be obliged to make specie payments. This would be to throw away by an act of folly the sole advantage gained by the suspension, that the public had learnt by experience that a paper currency properly regulated is preferable to the use of coin. That lesson must not be unlearnt now; but the Bank must be compelled to pay in ingots of gold and silver, each bar to be valued at a fixed price, for example, for the ingot of gold, £3 17s. an ounce. At the same time, to make impossible for the future the difficulties lately caused by the over-issue of the provincial banks, the principle of commercial freedom must be deliberately overruled and every private bank compelled, as a condition of trading, to deposit with the Treasury a fixed amount of Government securities and bonds. But these proposals were not the chief object of his publication. To those who can read between the lines, it reveals a change of front since the author developed, in 1809, his theory of international exchange to support the demand for a return to specie payment. Then he had accused the State of securing a hold over the Bank and using it as a means to exploit the public. Now a Member of Parliament, Pascoe Grenfell, was launching a violent campaign against the exorbitant profits made by the Bank under cover of the Act suspending specie payments, at the expense not only of the public but of the Government itself.[2] And even within the Bank a number of shareholders were in revolt against the insolent attitude which the directors adopted towards them, and the mystery in which, relying on the fact that their probity was incontestable, they systematically shrouded their policy.[3] To this

[1] 'Proposals for an Economical and Secure Currency, with Observations on the Profits of the Bank of England, 1816' (*Works*, pp. 391 sqq.).

[2] H. of C., February 13, 1816 (*Parl. Deb.*, vol. xxxii, p. 458); March 14, 1816 (ibid., vol. xxxiii, p. 264). For the collaboration between Ricardo and Grenfell see Ricardo to Malthus, September 10, 1815; another letter, undated, also addressed to Malthus, in September or October 1815; to Trower, March 9, 1816.

[3] 'Proposals for an Economical and Secure Currency, 1816' (*Works*, p. 429). Ricardo to Trower, February 5, 1816; Ricardo to Malthus, February 7, 1816.

double campaign Ricardo lent the weight of his authority. The Bank of England, urged the critics, is a joint-stock company. It enjoys the monopoly of issuing notes on the London Exchange. Its profits increase with the number of notes issued. It has, therefore, a direct interest in increasing the issue. Is the personal honesty of the directors a sufficient guarantee that, contrary to their immediate interest, they will restrict the issue of notes within reasonable limits? The Bank, moreover, is the medium through which the Government issues its treasury bonds and other stock. For every issue of bonds there is a corresponding issue of bank-notes, and further profit for the Bank. It is, therefore, to the interest of the Bank that the National Debt should increase, and the nation's loss is the Bank's profit. Further, the service of the Debt is in the hands of the Bank, and as the service extends with the growth of the Debt, the profit made by the Bank increases correspondingly. Here also the interest of this privileged corporation is in conflict with the interest of the public. But why should all this work, and especially the issue of bank-notes, be thus entrusted to a private company, equipped with a State monopoly? Why should it not be placed in the hands of a Government department managed by salaried officials? It is true the change cannot be effected immediately, for the Bank has taken advantage of the financial difficulties in which the war involved the Government to obtain an extension of its privileges until 1833; but at least an unwearied propaganda can prepare the public for the adoption of the new system at the earliest moment possible; and even while the contract remains in force, it is not impossible to obtain minor concessions from the Bank. Its directors are too well aware of the enormous value of their profits, the public knowledge of their extent, and the consequent danger of defying public opinion to refuse their consent to the concessions asked of them from time to time by the House of Commons. In 1808 they agreed to advance a loan of £3,000,000 without interest to continue until six months after the restoration of peace; and, again, in 1815 they concluded a new agreement postponing the date at which the loan should fall due until April 1816. When this agreement expires there is nothing to prevent Parliament from demanding more favourable terms.

Such was the theme of Grenfell's denunciation, which was supported by Ricardo. These complaints exerted such a powerful effect upon public opinion that the Cabinet felt obliged to give some satisfaction to popular feeling; but other forces were drawing the Ministers in the opposite direction. The country gentlemen were inclined, as we have seen, to complain of the restriction of the note issue; and the Chancellor of the Exchequer went in terror of the directors of the Bank, for he felt himself overpowered by the sheer weight of their expert knowledge and personal integrity. So in this sphere, as in every other, the Cabinet vacillated. It adopted a series of half-measures; and while nobody thanked the Ministers for what they did, everybody bore a grudge against them for what they failed to do.

6

In 1816 Ricardo believed, or affected to believe, that the coming session would witness the fixing of a date in the immediate future for the return to specie payments;[1] but when Parliament reassembled, the Government asked and obtained an Act prolonging the suspension until July 5, 1818. Horner even failed to get a clause inserted in the Act compelling the Bank to take the necessary steps to recommence specie payment on the expiration of this additional period.[2] As we already know, owing to the deficit occasioned by the abolition of the income tax, the Government far from being in a position to give orders to the Bank was obliged to ask it for a further advance, and to accept, in the face of Grenfell's protests, terms more unfavourable than those obtained in 1808: a loan of £6,000,000 at 4 per cent. Nevertheless, both the Ministers and the directors of the Bank made it clear that they had no intention to continue the suspension of specie payment in perpetuity. A provision of an old statute permitted the Bank to prepare for the termination of an artificial currency by the repayment in specie, after notice given to the Speaker, of notes whose value did not exceed £5; and in January 1817 the Bank availed itself of this provision.

In 1818 a settlement of the question appeared once more probable. The time had now arrived when, in default of a further postponement, the artificial currency would legally expire; also the date at which the loan of £6,000,000 was repayable. The country could now look back on three years' peace, and the

[1] 'Proposals for an Economical and Secure Currency' (*Works*, p. 404).
[2] H. of C., May 3, 1816 (*Parl. Deb.*, vol. xxxiv, pp. 243 sqq.).

speakers of the Opposition pressed home their demands. Nevertheless, the Government secured the postponement of specie payments for a year longer.[1] The directors had called the attention of the Cabinet to the dangers the change would involve. Encouraged by the success of the experiment which they had made in January 1817, they had undertaken a further risk in October, and had offered to repay all notes issued before January 1, 1817; but this time, they alleged, the experiment had turned out badly. In consequence of a bad harvest, the large sums of money required by wealthy Englishmen resident in France or Italy, and foreign loans on the London market, particularly the French loans of 1816 and 1817, almost all the specie paid by the Bank, to the value of about £2,600,000, had left England. Surely this drain upon British gold should not be encouraged. However, to prove that in spite of their fears it still kept in view the eventual restoration of specie payment, the Cabinet announced its intention to introduce a Bill dealing with private banks, which owed its inspiration to Ricardo's proposals. It was to come into force in 1820, a year after the date fixed for the return to specie payments. The Bill provided that every banker should deposit with the Commissioners of Amortization Government securities whose value must be double the value of their note issue, or treasury bonds equal in value to their note issue.[2] It does not appear, however, that the Bill was even introduced.

But when, at the opening of the session of 1819, the Government announced its intention to make a further postponement of specie payments till March 20, 1820, there was an explosion of public discontent. The Ministers beat a retreat and promised a preliminary inquiry by a parliamentary committee. Perhaps they hoped by the appointment of this committee to gain time and effect a compromise between the demands of the directors and the demands of public opinion. They contrived that the committee should be elected by ballot and manipulated the election so as in fact to choose its members.[3] They also contrived that the object of the committee should be defined more vaguely than the Opposition desired. But, if they really believed they could

[1] 58 Geo. III, cap. 37.
[2] H. of C., April 9, 1818, Vansittart's speech (*Parl. Deb.*, vol. xxxvii, pp. 1238 sqq.). Cf. H. of C., May 1, 1818, Tierney's speech (ibid., vol. xxxviii, pp. 453 sqq.).
[3] H. of C., January 25, 1819 (ibid., vol. xxxix, pp. 104–5); January 27, 1819 (ibid., vol. xxxix, pp. 132–3); February 2, 1819 (ibid., vol. xxxix, pp. 228–9).

postpone any longer the solution of the question, they were under a delusion.

The committee elected as its chairman Robert Peel. Still very young—he was born in 1788—he had been Secretary of State for Ireland at the conclusion of peace, but had resigned in 1818, and was thus at present in the position of a Minister without Portfolio, and everything pointed to him as the right person to discharge these exceptional functions. He was ambitious, and his ambition was fostered alike by the high estimate which all who came into contact with him formed of his cultivation, his knowledge of the business world, and his capacity for work, and by the predictions current in his entourage that, when he had attained the maturity of more advanced years, he, and no other, would be the future Prime Minister of a Tory Cabinet. His standing in Parliament had been raised still further when the University of Oxford chose him as one of her two representatives in acknowledgment of his unyielding attitude on the question of Catholic emancipation. He declared that his mind was perfectly open on the question of specie payment,[1] and if he must admit any bias in the matter, it was the bias which prevailed in Tory circles and was opposed to the doctrine of the bullionists;[2] but, as the work of the committee proceeded, it became more and more evident that the cause of the *status quo* was lost. When the directors gave evidence before the committee, they put up a very feeble defence. Their opponents' arguments went unanswered. Peel accepted the result, and in no hesitating terms made himself responsible for the victory of the thesis of specie payment. He was, no doubt, encouraged in this step by the publication of a pamphlet 'on the pernicious effects of a variable standard of value', dedicated to him by 'one of his constituents', his old Christ Church tutor, Copleston.[3] The pamphlet was a sign that if he declared in favour of the doctrine of Horner and Ricardo, Oxford would not disavow him. The year 1819 was a critical year in Peel's political career, and consequently in many respects a critical year in the parliamentary history of modern England. He now enjoyed the delightful experience of a

[1] Peel to the Rev. C. Lloyd (C. S. Parker, op. cit., vol. i, p. 292).

[2] Ibid., vol. i, p. 293: 'I voted with Van (Vansittart) in 1811; therefore if I was biased at all it was naturally in favour of a former opinion.'

[3] *A Letter to the Right Hon. Robert Peel . . . on the pernicious effects of a variable standard of value, especially as it regards the condition of the lower orders and of the poor laws.* By one of his Constituents, 1819. The title page bears for motto the French word, 'Laissez-nous faire'.

popularity of no ordinary kind. He did not speak the language of the Tory politician; but neither did he appear a deserter who had passed over to the Opposition. He was the umpire accepted by the nation to decide by his impartial verdict the dispute which divided the parties.

As a consequence of Peel's first report[1] a Bill was introduced and passed to prohibit the payment in cash of notes of low value.[2] This was necessary as a temporary measure, if, on the general resumption of specie payment, there was to be a sufficient amount of coin in the banks to meet the needs of the public. Peel followed this by a second report[3] which advised a further postponement of specie payment, but this time under entirely different conditions. Whatever a few sceptics might believe, the sole object of the postponement was to make better preparation for the return to normal conditions. Peel's Bill,[4] which passed both Houses, provided that the Bank should be obliged, as a first step, to pay gold ingots for notes to anyone who asked for them at a price of £4 1s. an ounce after February 1, 1820, of £3 17s. 10½d. an ounce after May 1, 1821, and cash payments must be resumed at the earliest two, at the latest three, years from the latter date. This was not altogether Ricardo's plan, though borrowed from it in part, and he lamented the final resumption of cash payments instead of the payment in ingots which he advocated. Neverthe-less, he felt himself entitled to acclaim the passage of the Bill as a personal victory, 'the triumph of science and truth over prejudice and error'.[5] And Cobbett also paid his characteristic tribute to the economist. 'I see,' he wrote, 'that they have adopted a scheme of one Ricardo (I wonder what countryman he is) who is, I believe, a converted Jew. At any rate, he has been a change-alley man for the last fifteen or twenty years. If the old Lord Chatham were now alive, he would speak with respect of the muckworm, as he called the change-alley people. Faith ! they are now become *everything*. Baring assists at the Congress of Sovereigns, and Ricardo regulates things at home.'[6]

[1] First Report from the Select Committee on the Expediency of the Bank resuming Cash Payments, April 5, 1819.

[2] 59 Geo. III, cap. 23.

[3] Second Report from the Select Committee on the Expediency of the Bank resuming Cash Payments, May 6, 1819.

[4] 59 Geo. III, cap. 49.   [5] Ricardo to Trower, May 28, 1819.

[6] *Pol. Reg.*, September 4, 1819 (vol. xxxv, p. 80): 'The Muckworm is no longer a creeping thing: it rears its head aloft, and makes the haughty Borough Lords sneak about in holes and corners.'

IV RENEWED AGITATION

I

The Opposition could claim the passage of Peel's Bill as a victory wrested from a reluctant Cabinet. Was it, therefore, within sight of the day when it would be called to office? In reality it remained weak, and was conscious of its weakness. It suffered heavy losses by Romilly's suicide and Horner's death, losses which were by no means supplied by Ricardo's entrance into Parliament. For Ricardo was an exponent of Benthamite radicalism, not a Whig. When Ponsonby died in July 1818, the Opposition had considerable difficulty in finding anyone to take his place. Neither his illustrious origin nor his personal talents could compensate for Lord John Russell's youth. For he was only twenty-seven and, moreover, of delicate health, shunned the fatigue of Parliamentary life, put in an appearance at Westminster only at rare intervals, and devoted his time to literary composition, both in prose and verse, and travel on the Continent. Tierney was finally chosen, after an interregnum of eighteen months, and the Government had little to fear from a man so old and so timid. Indeed, the choice is a striking evidence of the state of feeling among the Whigs, weakened by the anxiety with which they contemplated their own programme—Catholic emancipation, still as impossible as ever, and parliamentary reform for which their leaders felt less enthusiasm than ever after the violence of the agitators in 1817.

But the Whigs' embarrassment was not, however, as might have been expected, at their opponents' strength. The same bizarre situation continued to prevail—two rival parties equally weak, and equally aware of their weakness. The Ministers were possessed by a deep-rooted despondency, and awaited with resignation the fall which their Whig adversaries were too diffident to forecast, almost too timid to desire. Immediately after the General Election of 1818, Peel had resigned in accordance with the intention he had expressed to his colleagues several months earlier, and his defection was a danger signal.[1] When, at the end of 1818, on the final evacuation of French territory by the British army of occupation, Wellington joined the Cabinet as

[1] Croker to Peel, July 3, 1818 (C. S. Parker, op. cit., vol. i, p. 268).

Master General of the Ordnance, undoubtedly his entrance more than counteracted for the moment the bad impression caused by Peel's resignation. But he was careful to warn his colleagues that, if the Cabinet were thrown out, he would not be party to any attitude of 'factious opposition' towards their successors.[1] Lord Liverpool, the head of a Cabinet incapable of adopting a firm line of action on any of the leading questions of domestic politics, and content to carry on from day to day, asked himself the blunt question whether the Ministry were justified in remaining in office. By clinging to power, they were disgracing themselves 'personally', and became 'less capable every day of any real service to the country'.[2] But suddenly the situation of 1816 recurred, the Cabinet found itself faced with new economic difficulties, accompanied by a fresh outbreak of disorder, and the old Tory party might hope that once again the dread of revolution would place firmly in the saddle its two leaders, Lord Liverpool and Lord Castlereagh.

2

The year 1818 had been a year of somewhat abnormal prosperity, of speculation and over-production. The statistics of the raw material imported for the textile industries give some idea of this excessive activity. The imports of raw cotton and raw silk almost doubled between 1816 and 1818, the import of raw wool rose to three times its former figure.[3] This feverish production had not abated by October; never in the memory of man had so many vessels been seen in the port of Bristol.[4] But with the approach of winter the inevitable reaction set in, the market was glutted, prices fell, and the first failures were recorded from Manchester.[5] The present crisis was not so universal as that of 1816. The textile manufacture alone suffered severely, the mines

---

[1] Wellington to Lord Liverpool, November 1, 1818 (C. D. Yonge, op. cit., vol. ii, p. 378).

[2] Lord Liverpool to Lord Eldon, spring of 1819. 'After the defeats we have already experienced during this session, our remaining in office is a *positive* evil. It confounds all ideas of government in the minds of men. It disgraces us *personally*, and renders us less capable every day of being of any real service to the country, either now or hereafter. If, therefore, things are to remain as they are, I am quite clear that there is no advantage, in any way, in our being the persons to carry on the public service' (Lord Campbell, *Lives of the Lord Chancellors*, vol. vii, pp. 340–1).

[3] T. Tooke, *History of Prices*, vol. ii, pp. 61, 77.

[4] *Ann. Reg.*, 1818, Chron., p. 139.

[5] *Examiner*, December 6, 1818.

and iron foundries were entirely unaffected. Nor did it continue long. Already in July and August the prices both of raw materials and of manufactured goods had once more risen.[1] But if the economic crisis was milder and more brief, the political crisis to which it gave birth was more serious, and not only survived the former but actually grew more acute when it was already passing away. The violence of the outbreak is explained by the fact that for the past three years both the revolutionaries and the members of the ruling class had been preparing for the struggle. That the miners and ironworkers stood aloof from the agitation is not hard to understand, is indeed more easily explicable than their abstention in 1816. The crisis had left them untouched. It is more surprising to find that the centre of the political agitation was no longer the hosiery district—Nottinghamshire, Derbyshire, and Leicestershire. Here the programme put forward by the workers contained nothing of a political nature, but was confined to the old demand, a minimum wage, to be fixed either by voluntary agreement between masters and men, or by legislation. Robert Hall, the celebrated Baptist preacher, took part in the dispute and pleaded the cause of the stocking weavers.[2] The democrats' attitude was totally different. They had no liking for demands of this kind, which, they considered, made the workers forget that the real evil to be remedied, an evil from which the entire nation was suffering without distinction of class, was the enormous size of the National Debt, and the consequent load of taxation. Therefore, they maintained, the entire weight of the attack should be concentrated against the ruling oligarchy which alone was responsible for this financial misgovernment, by pressing the demand for a radical reform of the franchise.

This time it was in the districts to the north of Nottingham and Leicester, among the weavers of cloth, and, above all, among

[1] T. Tooke, op. cit., vol. ii, pp. 78–9. Perhaps Tooke exaggerates somewhat the speed of the recovery. See H. of L., November 30, 1819, Lord Lansdowne's speech (*Parl. Deb.*, vol. xli, pp. 418 sqq.); H. of C., 1819, Bennet's speech (ibid., vol. xli, pp. 890 sqq.); also the deliberately vague language of the speech from the Throne, November 23, 1819: 'Some depression continues to exist in certain branches of our manufactures' (ibid., vol. xli, pp. 2–3).

[2] An appeal to the public on the subject of the Framework Knitters' Fund, 1819. See also Cobbett's violent criticism of the workers' demands: 'To the Stocking Weavers of Leicestershire, Nottinghamshire, and Derbyshire. On the subject of their present turn out, and on the real causes of their distress' (*Pol. Reg.*, April 14, 1821, vol. xxxix, pp. 73 sqq.), and Robert Hall's answer, *A Reply to the objections advanced by Cobbett against the Framework Knitters' Friendly Society*, 1821.

the cotton spinners, that the propaganda was carried on in favour of this programme of radical opposition to the Government, at once a revolt against the taxation and an attempt to establish democracy. Far enough, evidently, from London. And this distance from London explains the long continued indifference which the Government displayed towards the movement. For in London everything was quiet, and the democratic party was falling to pieces. As late as February, Lord Castlereagh and the *Courier* maintained that the country was prosperous, and the Lancashire weavers held meetings to protest against their lie, or, if you will, their ignorance.[1] A strike of formidable proportions at Carlisle, caused by the reduction of wages, attracted in May and June the attention of the Government and the public.[2]

In Lancashire the agitation had been heralded by an unrest which had even preceded in the previous summer the commencement of the economic crisis. Two years earlier, when the cotton industry was passing through a period of depression, the spinners had consented to a reduction of wages. The mill-owners had, in turn, undertaken to restore the original rates as soon as the price of yarn recovered its former level. In 1818 they broke their promise, and the spinners replied in July by coming out on strike.[3] The strike lasted two months,[4] and was sufficiently grave to attract the notice of the London Press. The *Morning Chronicle* supported the strikers, *The Times* and the *Courier* denounced them. Towards the end of August, in the same district, the weavers went on strike in their turn. Though their wages had been slightly raised, they considered the advance miserably inadequate.[5] Even the miners

[1] *Manchester Observer*, February 20, March 7, March 20, 1819. For a general discussion of the conditions which prevailed among the working classes about this date see Bennet's interesting speech, H. of C., December 9, 1819 (*Parl. Deb.*, vol. xli, pp. 890 sqq.).

[2] *Ann. Reg.*, 1819, Chron., May 26, June 1, June 19. *Examiner*, February 14, May 16, June 6, 1819. H. of C., May 24, 1819. The presentation by Curwen of a petition of the Carlisle cotton weavers.

[3] See the Cotton Spinners' Address to the Public, *Ann. Reg.*, 1818, Chron., August 6; also the calculations made in an article in the *Gorgon* for September 12, 1818 (p. 134). According to this reckoning, the Manchester spinner received a net wage of 18s. 4d. *Examiner*, September 20, 1818, a letter signed H. Hudson and headed 'The Cotton Spinners and their Employers'. Seventeen thousand 'Spinners and Dyers' were on strike in Manchester at the beginning of August (*Gorgon*, August 1, 1818).

[4] *Ann. Reg.*, 1818, Chron., July 19, August 6, August 15.

[5] *Gorgon*, September 5, 1818; September 12, 1818: 'The Weavers are likewise in array against their masters. . . . Their present earnings are about 7s. a week; and they demand an advance of 7s. in the pound, which would raise their weekly wages to the enormous sum of 10s. 8d.'

prepared to throw in their lot with the strikers.[1] Lancashire seemed on the verge of a general strike.

But the movement failed. In September the spinners returned to work on the mill-owners' terms.[2] Indeed, they even signed individually a humiliating declaration in which they undertook never to enter into a combination to oppose the masters' interests.[3] The weavers, indeed, obtained a few advances, but these came far short of their demands.[4] At the end of two or three days nothing more was heard of the miners' strike. A few acts of violence accompanied the workers' defeat. On September 2, at Manchester, a large mill was attacked by several thousand workmen, fire was opened upon the crowd, several were wounded, and one killed.[5] On September 15, at Burnley, the mob rose and released from gaol the town crier, who had been imprisoned by the authorities for giving notice of a meeting organized by the weavers; it was only on the arrival, two days later, of the yeomanry from Manchester and Salford that the magistrates dared to assert their authority and restore order by arresting several ring-leaders.[6] But there was nothing about these isolated outbursts of violence which bore the least resemblance to a serious attempt at revolution. Only two years after the agitation of 1817 the events of these summer months seemed to prove that the programme of radical reform made no appeal whatever to the operatives of the cotton industry. It was in vain that a handful of agitators attempted to exploit the workers' distress and indignation in favour of their ideas; one of their number, a certain Baguley, was actually booed and beaten on August 24 by the Manchester weavers.[7] But in October, when the workers had been so ill-rewarded for having confined their demands strictly to the economic sphere, had not the moment arrived for the radical reformers to recover their hold over them? And now, at least, in December, when the distress of 1816 and 1817 had returned for the Lancashire operative,

[1] *Examiner*, August 30, 1818; *Gorgon*, September 5, 1818.
[2] *Examiner*, August 30, 1818; September 13, 1818.
[3] See the text of the declaration, *Gorgon*, September 26, 1818.
[4] *Ann. Reg.*, 1818, Chron., September 15, p. 123. *Gorgon*, September 26, 1818, p. 151: 'We learn from Manchester that the weavers have obtained a part of their demands; but immense numbers, twenty or thirty thousand, we are informed, are still standing out against their employers in various parts of Lancashire.'
[5] *Ann. Reg.*, 1818, Chron., September 2, p. 120.
[6] Ibid., September 22.
[7] *Examiner*, August 30, 1818. Baguley and two other agitators were tried and sentenced to two years' imprisonment (*Examiner*, September 13, 1818; *Medusa*, April 24, 1819).

the gathered discontent of the previous summer had prepared the soil for another revolutionary upheaval.

3

The January and February of 1819 did, in fact, witness mass meetings held in different towns of Lancashire, at Oldham, at Manchester, at Royton, and at Stockport, and attended by thousands. The resolutions passed at these meetings demanded the reform of the franchise and the repeal of the Corn Law.[1] This double programme reflects the dual character and origin of the movement which now began.

The demand for parliamentary reform was a revival of the old radical programme of 1816. And, as though to emphasize the relationship between the two movements, the famous orator of the 1816 meetings, Henry Hunt, dissatisfied with his reception by Sir Francis Burdett's group at Westminster, and sensing with the flair of the born demagogue that the strength of the democratic movement lay henceforward in the north, made his appearance at Manchester in the middle of January 1819, presided over a meeting and caused a riot in the theatre by refusing to stand up when the orchestra played 'God save the King'.[2] And while the agitators harangued, a work of silent organization proceeded.

The Hampden Clubs had disappeared in 1817. In 1818 we see their place taken by groups styling themselves Political Protestants. The first of these groups appears to have been formed at Hull,[3] and we hear of others in the course of the following year at York,[4] and at Newcastle and in the neighbouring towns.[5] The plan pursued by these societies was to open reading-rooms, where for a small subscription the members could read the latest newspapers, and while reading them, talk politics. In the words of their manifesto, they were formed 'for the purpose of protesting against the infringement of our indisputable right to real representation'.[6] And though the organizers were careful to define

---

[1] *Manchester Observer*: January 9, 1819, the meeting at Oldham; January 23, 1819, the meeting at Manchester; February 20, 1819, the meetings at Royton and Stockport.

[2] *Examiner*, January 31, 1819; A. Prentice, op. cit., p. 147.

[3] *Gorgon*, August 29, 1818.

[4] *Manchester Observer*, June 19, 1819.

[5] The *Briton*, November 13, 1819: 'The Loyal and Constitutional Declaration of the Political Protestants of Newcastle-upon-Tyne, Gateshead, Shields, Sunderland, and places adjacent.'

[6] *Black Dwarf*, August 11, 1819.

their 'Protestantism' in a sense strictly political, there is no doubt that at the back of their minds was the desire to associate their political Protestantism with the religious Protestantism embodied by the Nonconformist sects. They intended to model their democratic organizations on the pattern of the Free Churches.

Other groups came into existence in the autumn of 1818, which were almost wholly confined to Lancashire, and called themselves 'Unions'. The first union appears to have been formed at Stockport in October.[1] Its rules were approved by Cartwright, who had himself employed the term 'Union' six years earlier to designate the associations he had founded. We find societies of the same type at Manchester and Wigan in the summer of 1819.[2] At Stockport and Blackburn women scandalized the governing class by forming their independent associations.[3] What was the object of these unions? Like the Political Protestants they were small clubs open for the perusal and discussion of the newspapers. Sunday Schools were often attached to their reading-rooms.[4] 'Classes' of twelve members were held every week under the guidance of a leader chosen from themselves. In every town the classes were in turn grouped in sections, and the united sections governed by an elected committee, which met weekly to receive the subscriptions collected by the class leaders.[5] In June plans were made for a federation of these unions in a 'National Union', with a central fund and an assembly of delegates.[6] Cartwright always cherished the design of applying the methods of the Wesleyan mission to his democratic propaganda. Here the imitation was obvious. In his *Black Dwarf* Wooler pointed out that it was by their concerted action that the Methodists and their fellow Nonconformists had wrested tolera-

[1] *Liverpool Courier*, June 30, 1819.

[2] *Manchester Observer*, June 26, July 31, 1819. See also the Lord Advocate's speech, H. of C., December 9, 1819 (*Parl. Deb.*, vol. xli, pp. 923–4).

[3] *Ann. Reg.*, 1819, p. 104; *Pol. Reg.*, October 23, December 29, 1819; *The Times*, July 21, 1819.

[4] Francis Philips, *An Exposure of the Calumnies Circulated by the Enemies of Social Order, and Reiterated by their Abettors, against the Magistrates and the Yeomanry Cavalry of Manchester and Salford*, 1819, p. 9. *Notes and Observations, Critical and Explanatory, on the Papers Relative to the Internal State of the Country, recently presented to Parliament: to which is appended A Reply to Mr. Francis Philip's Exposure*. By a member of the Manchester Committee for relieving the sufferers of August 16, 1819 [J. E. Taylor], 1820, pp. 178–9. *Medusa*, September 11, 1819. See also the debates in Parliament quoted below, pp. 71 sqq., and A. Prentice, op. cit., pp. 116–17.

[5] See in *The Times* for July 21, 1819, the rules of the Female Union Society of Stockport.

[6] *Manchester Observer*, June 26, 1819; *Medusa*, July 10, 1819.

tion from the State and the Established Church; and this union was effected by their class meetings and other daily or weekly gatherings; and to encourage the reformers to follow their example he recalled the result of Lord Sidmouth's attempt in 1811 to restrict the supply of Nonconformist ministers.[1] 'Sidmouth was terrified by the unexpected opposition which he had raised. Like a child stung by a swarm of wasps, he fled, howling.'

But the resolutions adopted by the Lancashire mass meetings were not confined to the demand for parliamentary reform. They demanded also the repeal of the Corn Law of 1815. From October onwards, a vigorous campaign of petitions to this effect was carried on in the manufacturing districts. Every attempt was made to bring home to the people the crushing burden of the duties recently imposed. Every individual, it was explained, paid 6d. a day, or £9 12s. 6d. a year; every family with four children, £54 15s. a year; a population therefore of eighteen millions paid £164,250,000.[2] The question had been scarcely canvassed in 1816. The change is to be explained by the difference in the economic situation. If in 1816 the price of wheat had risen to 103s. the quarter, twelve months later it had fallen to 52s. 6d. To be sure, an attempt was made to prove that the Corn Bill was the cause of these wild fluctuations. But to bring forward such a charge was tantamount to maintaining that the Bill was ineffective, and had failed to fulfil its authors' intention. Now the entire situation was altered. Since the autumn of 1817 the price of wheat had remained stable at about 80s. the quarter, a price which to the consumer appeared exorbitant, but was in fact the price which the landlords in passing the Act of 1815 had desired to establish as the normal price. The Corn Bill now seemed a statute as effective as it was mischievous.

The manufacturers in favour of Free Trade had judged it prudent in 1816 to keep silence. But in 1818, and in the early part of 1819, the occasion seemed opportune to renew the alliance which in 1815 had been formed between the manufacturer and the worker to attack the monopoly enjoyed by the agricultural interest. To be sure, the manufacturers must first overcome the widespread dislike entertained for them by the working class. It

[1] *Black Dwarf*, January 26, 1820.
[2] *Examiner*, November 1, 1818. Cf. November 8, the article entitled 'On the Corn Bill, the Real Cause of the Present Depravity'.

was only yesterday that the democratic journalists were inveighing against the odious parvenus of the mill, devoid alike of education and heart, and were ready to invite the country gentlemen to save the worker from their systematic exploitation of his need.[1] And even now, as the mass meetings proceeded which they had at first encouraged, the manufacturers took alarm at the inflammatory language employed by many of the speakers. Nevertheless, a reconciliation was quite plainly in progress during the early days of 1819 between the more respectable element of the working class and the more progressive manufacturers.[2] This was evident not in Lancashire only but also in Yorkshire, where the millowners chafed under the new duties on wool. Almost everywhere the independent Press was making marked headway. Since the January of 1818 the Manchester Radicals had controlled an important weekly, *Wardle's Manchester Observer*. At Leeds Baines was making his *Leeds Mercury* a political organ of very decided views. In London Black, now editor of the *Morning Chronicle* and its future proprietor, was overcoming Perry's fears.

4

In June a series of mass meetings began, held regularly every Monday. On June 14 meetings took place at Glasgow, Ashton-under-Lyne, and on Hunslet Moor near Leeds. On June 21 there was a meeting at Manchester, a second meeting on Hunslet Moor, also meetings at Dewsbury and in several other towns in Lancashire and Yorkshire. The object of these demonstrations was perfectly legal—a petition to Parliament was drawn up asking for the reform of the franchise and the repeal of the Corn Law. But was it possible to avoid entirely imprudent behaviour and violent language? At the second meeting on Hunslet Moor, Baines, the respected proprietor of the *Leeds Mercury*, deplored

[1] *Gorgon*, August 8, 1818: 'We should consider the cause of Reform very much disgraced by such coadjutors. Independently, then, of these upstart *counterfeit gentlemen*, there would be a sufficiency of respectability, intellect and number, with the country gentlemen, the productive classes, and if the fundholders be *wise* they will not be excluded, to overwhelm *one* hundred of such contemptible oligarchies as that which tyrannizes in this country.' Cf. August 15: 'There are in Manchester a set of upstart scoundrels, who, without talents, education, or one gentlemanly quality, live in continual war with the lower classes.' August 29: 'A set of scoundrels domineer in the town of Leeds, in Yorkshire, who in point of *character* are exactly on a level with the Manchester *ruffians*. Proud, ignorant, and slavish, destitute of every noble and manly quality. They are a disgrace to human nature, the *mushroom gentry*.'
[2] A Prentice, op. cit., pp. 115 sqq.

the anti-religious tone of one of the speakers and the revolutionary language of the majority. He predicted, if these foolish methods were continued, a new suspension of Habeas Corpus, an increase of the Army, possibly even the establishment of a military dictatorship.[1] The Dissenters, pastors, and congregations alike found themselves in a position even more false than it had been in 1816 and 1817, for they were now more deeply compromised. If the revolutionary language of the agitators were allowed to pass without protest, the wealthy and socially respectable element in the congregation would be alienated. If, however, the minister protested, as he often did, the result was a counter-protest, articles in the papers, and demonstrations in the chapel.[2]

The indifference, indeed, with which throughout the closing weeks of the session Parliament treated the question of reform seemed to justify the revolutionary language talked at the meetings. Of what use was it to petition men who took no notice of the petitions? Just then the malcontents of Birmingham—for the movement was extending southward and had now reached Leicestershire, Nottinghamshire, and Warwickshire—conceived a highly original plan. What, they argued, was the grievance of which the large towns of the North and Midlands, Leeds, Manchester, and Birmingham, were complaining? Lack of representation. Why, then, should not these great centres brush aside the opposition of the men in power, hold an election, and send the men thus elected to London as their duly constituted representatives according to the spirit, if not the letter, of the Constitution?

On July 12 an enormous crowd assembled on New Hall Hill at Birmingham, fifty thousand if we can credit the claims of the organizers, twenty or twenty-five thousand according to the most moderate estimate. All the speakers were men of humble position:

[1] J. Waddington, *Congregational History*, 1800–1850, pp. 283 sqq.
[2] Ibid., 1800–1850, pp. 285–6. Letter from Mr. Alexander to his son, February 16, 1820: 'I am sorry that many of our good people have been caught in their traps, and have imbibed and manifested a spirit very opposite to that of the Gospel. . . . I thought it my duty, without dictating their political creed, to exhort them to patience and to peace. . . . I thought that I had done it charmingly, and that I had offended nobody, because I allowed that each had a right to choose his own political principles, only that, as Christians, they ought ever to maintain a Christian spirit. My hopes were disappointed. Almost all the weavers, the poorer part especially, were offended. White hats were instantly worn as flags of defiance.' (Hunt always wore a white hat.) 'One deacon threatened to resign, and, it appears, has resigned his office. Some of the hearers, and one member, have left the chapel; others, who have not left, are as cross and crooked as they can be.'

George Edmonds, a former schoolmaster, now the owner of a local newspaper devoted to the cause of reform, a pawnbroker, a cabinet-maker, a butcher, and two workers in an iron foundry. But the aged Cartwright had come down from London, and with him a journalist named Wooler. After a few short speeches a certain Sir Charles Wolseley, a democrat of good family, who had already taken part in the campaign of mass meetings, was elected by show of hands 'Legislatorial Attorney and Representative' of Birmingham. The crowd then dispersed in an orderly fashion and escorted the speakers home.[1]

Lord Sidmouth took up the challenge. Since Parliament adjourned the very week of the Birmingham meeting, there was no time at the moment to pass new Coercion Acts. But the existing legislation could be rigorously enforced, and already on July 7 the Home Secretary, only too pleased to yield to the demands of the gentry, had addressed a circular to the Lord-Lieutenants of the counties in which the disturbances had occurred calling upon them to adopt immediately all the measures necessary to preserve order, place themselves in communication with the magistrates, and keep the yeomanry everywhere in readiness to act. Sir Charles Wolseley and the principal organizers of the Birmingham meeting were brought to trial; and on July 30 a Royal proclamation denounced the speeches delivered at the meetings, impressed upon loyal subjects the duty of abstaining from every kind of seditious activity, and ordered the sheriffs and the magistrates to proceed against the fomenters of disturbance with the utmost rigour of the law.[2]

Lord Sidmouth's intervention was not without result. Leeds and Manchester were preparing to follow the example set by Birmingham. In consequence of the proclamation they abandoned their design. But the malcontents continued to hold mass meetings with the object, sanctioned by immemorial custom, of petitioning Parliament. When the meeting to be held at Manchester on August 9 for the election of a representative was abandoned, a public demonstration in favour of parliamentary reform was arranged for the 16th, over which Hunt would preside. In the interval the entire county was in a ferment of heated expectation. The mill hands engaged in mysterious drills, unarmed according

---

[1] Langford, *A Century of Birmingham Life*, vol. ii, pp. 420 sqq.
[2] *Ann. Reg.*, 1819, p. 105, and App. to Chron., p. 123.

to the Radical organs, armed according to the Tory Press. And their intention? To learn how to carry out without disorder the mass movements which would be involved when in their thousands, nay, in their tens of thousands, they assembled for a common demonstration. To prepare, replied the Tories, a violent revolution. Knots of workmen gathered in the streets of Manchester, hustled and insulted respectable citizens and their wives. The great day came. From all the towns of the neighbourhood, unarmed and in perfect order, with flags flying and drums beating, squadrons of workers marched into Manchester. Sixty thousand men and women had gathered in St. Peter's Fields when a carriage arrived containing Henry Hunt and his assistants, overpowered with delight at a spectacle more imposing than any they had yet witnessed. Scarcely had Hunt obtained silence and begun to speak when a platoon of cavalry was seen forcing its way through the crowd towards the platform. Surrounded and threatened by the masses who stood blocking their way, the cavalrymen drew their swords and struck out to right and left. A company of hussars hastened to their assistance. The crowd took to their heels, knocking one another down in their panic. Within ten minutes the place had been cleared. The banners which decked the platform were thrown into the gutter, and the demonstrators chased through the streets at the point of the sword. Eleven persons were killed, including two women, and several hundred wounded.[1]

A howl of execration arose throughout the length and breadth of England, and Lord Sidmouth did not mend matters by his letter of congratulation to the local authorities of Manchester. For the sanguinary affray of the 16th the revolutionaries invented a name which proved a master-stroke. The demonstration had been held in St. Peter's Fields. As Wellington had formerly defeated the foreigner at the battle of Waterloo, Lord Sidmouth could now point in triumph to his victory over his fellow countrymen at the battle of Peterloo.[2] The immediate result,

[1] In addition to the debate in Parliament, H. of C., November 29, 1819 (*Parl. Deb.*, vol. xli, pp. 357 sqq.), see the two works mentioned above, p. 60, by F. Philips and J. E. Taylor; also Prentice, op. cit., chaps. xi and xii (pp. 159 sqq.), and, further, the two most recent accounts—both the work of F. A. Bruton—*The Story of Peterloo*, written for the *Centenary*, August 16, 1919, and *Three Accounts of Peterloo by Eyewitnesses, Bishop Stanley, Lord Hylton, John Benjamin Smith, with Bishop Stanley's Evidence at the Trial*, 1921.

[2] The soubriquet 'Peterloo' appears as early as August 21 in the *Manchester Observer*.

therefore, of the Government's declaration of war against civil disorder was not to lessen but to intensify the agitation and the general tension.

On August 17 the report was current in Manchester that a body of men armed with pikes was marching upon the city. Panic was universal, the Cotton Exchange closed, and all traffic was forbidden in the streets.[1] On the 19th another fight took place between the troops and the mob. There were many wounded and two killed.[2] On the 23rd an explosion at a gunsmith's shop occasioned another panic: respectable citizens hurried to the nearest magistrate and demanded that the Riot Act should be read and the military summoned.[3] In London in July an enormous mass meeting had assembled in Smithfield, with Hunt in the chair, to demand manhood suffrage, annual elections, and voting by ballot.[4] But it was not until after Peterloo that the malcontents of the capital finally shook off their inertia. The Common Council, though its president was a Tory Lord Mayor, yielded to the pressure of public opinion and presented to the Regent a long memorial protesting against the events of August 16.[5] Sir Francis Burdett addressed to his constituents a violent letter denouncing the employment of armed force at Manchester, in which he threatened the King with the fate of James II.[6] Shortly before, he had been reconciled with Cartwright and Hunt. The latter, arrested on August 16 and released on bail, made a triumphal entry into London in September. Watson, Preston, and Thistlewood went out to Islington to receive him, surrounded by a crowd waving boughs of oak and laurel. Their numbers were reckoned by the democratic papers at two or even three hundred thousand.[7] New revolutionary newspapers began to appear; to the *Black Dwarf* and *Medusa* were now added the *Cap of Liberty*, the *Briton*, the *White Hat*, and Carlile's *Republican*. And the father of revolutionary journalism, Cobbett himself, emerged from his American retreat and made a theatrical return to his mother country. He landed at Liverpool, bearing in his hands the urn

[1] [J. E. Taylor], *Notes and Observations, Reply to Mr. Francis Philips*, pp. 188–9.
[2] *Ann. Reg.*, 1819, Chron. August 21.
[3] [J. E. Taylor], *Notes and Observations, a Reply to Mr. Francis Philips*, p. 189.
[4] *Morning Chronicle*, July 22, 1819. A second meeting after Peterloo, *Morning Chronicle*, August 26, 1819.
[5] *Ann. Reg.*, 1819, p. 110.
[6] The text can be found in the *Ann. Reg.*, 1820, App. to Chron., p. 899.
[7] *Cap of Liberty*, September 15, 1819.

which contained the ashes of Tom Paine.[1] Mass meetings of protest against the serious breach of law committed by the Lancashire magistrates on August 16 were widely held. They were not confined to Lancashire and Yorkshire; the agitation spread southward into the Midlands, and northward into Durham, Northumberland, and the Scottish Lowlands.[2] And the meetings were arranged according to a common plan, as was evident when on November 1, and again on November 15, simultaneous meetings, at which the same resolutions were passed, were held on the same day in all the large cities of Scotland.[3]

V THE SIX ACTS

I

Once more panic gripped the ruling classes. Once more, as in 1817, letters poured in to Lord Sidmouth from every shire, in which the magistrates called for rigorous measures to put down the agitation. It was useless to call attention to the orderly character of the meetings (there was no disturbance anywhere, except on one occasion at Paisley, when the ill-advised interference of the authorities provoked a riot).[4] For the peaceable behaviour of the revolutionaries was a proof that they were acting under the orders of some hidden authority.[5] The magistrates sent up denunciations of armies secretly enrolled, of the distribution of pikes. It was no longer, they said, a question of parliamentary reform. The aim of the Radicals, as they now began to be termed,[6] was not simply manhood suffrage and annual

---

[1] *Pol. Reg.*, November 13, 1819 (vol. xxxv, p. 382); December 4, 1819 (ibid., pp. 385 sqq.).

[2] The extent of the movement can perhaps be measured by the list of disturbed counties enumerated in Art. 8 of 60 Geo. III, cap. 2: Lancashire, Cheshire, West Riding of Yorkshire, Warwickshire, Staffordshire, Derbyshire, Leicestershire, Nottinghamshire, Cumberland, Westmorland, Northumberland, Durham, Renfrew, Lanark, the Counties of the Towns of Newcastle-upon-Tyne and Nottingham and of the City of Coventry.

[3] 'Papers Relative to the Internal State of the Country: Extract of a Letter from Sir John Byng to Lord Sidmouth, dated Pontefract, November 18, 1819' (*Parl. Deb.*, vol. xli, pp. 300–1); H. of C., December 9, 1819, speech by the Lord Advocate (ibid., vol. xli, pp. 925–6).

[4] *Morning Chronicle*, September 17, 1819.

[5] H. of C., December 9, 1819, The Lord Advocate's Speech (*Parl. Deb.*, vol. xli, pp. 925–6).

[6] Hitherto they had been known as reformers, or, to distinguish them from the advocates of a more moderate programme, radical reformers. Bentham had occasionally criticized the employment of the adjective 'radical' as capable of being misunderstood. 'Pull up a weed by the roots, there is an end of it' (MSS., Univ. Coll., No. 127). Was

Parliaments; they sought, by this or by any other means, to restore the land to the community and abolish private property. Lord Eldon and Lord Sidmouth shared these alarms[1] and managed, though not without some difficulty,[2] to infect their colleagues with their fears. Again, as in 1817, the Cabinet presented itself to the country as the defender of public order endangered by riot. The first measure adopted by the Government was to increase the Army by ten thousand. It then decided to convoke an extraordinary session of Parliament. The object of this step was twofold: first, to obtain parliamentary sanction for this additional levy of ten thousand troops, and not only did the Government secure the force for which it asked, but it was also empowered to raise two thousand additional marines, so as to free two thousand infantrymen more for the maintenance of order in the country;[3] secondly, to secure the passage of a series of Coercion Acts like those of 1817. Parliament met on November 23 and

the term 'radical' used as a noun before the events of 1819? A letter from Cartwright to T. Northmore, of August 18, 1817, contains the following sentence: 'The crisis, in my judgment, is very favourable for effecting a union with the *radicals* of the better among the Whigs, and I am meditating on means to promote it' (F. D. Cartwright, *Life and Correspondence of Major Cartwright*, vol. ii, p. 137). But is the letter dated correctly? Ought we not to read 1818 instead of 1817? There was no crisis in August 1817. As a noun 'radical' appears for the first time in *The Times* of August 16, 1819 (hitherto *The Times* had spoken of Ultra Reformers or Reformers); in the *Morning Chronicle* of September 27, in a quotation from the Tory organ, the *British Monitor*; in the *Courier* of August 27 (the Whigs, the Radicals, and the Moderates). It was first coined by the Tories as an offensive nickname for the revolutionary democrats. See Carlile, *The Republican*, April 21, 1820: ' I have often felt astonished at seeing individuals even fond of, and partial to, nicknames, such as Ribandmen in Ireland and Radicals in Great Britain. I am certain that the adoption and support of such terms have a tendency to bring a good cause into disrepute, and to prevent more discreet men from joining it. The name of Radical sprung up last year, and I feel astonished to see men embrace it, and adopt it as an anonymous signature to their communications. . . . The word Reformer stripped of its concomitants is all very well, but when we find the words Moderate, Thorough, and Radical applied to it, it becomes like a dead and useless weight on it, and creates opinions that would not have existed if those words had been kept out of sight and hearing.' Cf. *Pol. Reg.*, March 25, April 15, 1820 (vol. xxxvi, pp. 95, 323, 326). Bentham, in his *Radicalism not Dangerous* of 1820, employs the word *radicalists* (*Works*, ed. Bowring, vol. iii, pp. 605, 608, 609, 611).

[1] Lord Campbell, op. cit., vol. vii, p. 347. Lord Sidmouth to Lord Exmouth, August 15, 1819; to Lord Lascelles, October 15, 1819 (Pellew, op. cit., vol. iii, pp. 249, 280).

[2] Lord Eldon to Sir William Scott, shortly after August 16, 1819: 'Neither the Prince nor most of his Ministers seem to act as you think they should. He came here late on Thursday evening—rather night—and went off again to the Marquis of Hertford's, I believe—that he went there or elsewhere is certain. Eight out of fourteen Ministers, I believe, abroad—in that there is no harm: the other six are full as many as can usefully converse on any subject. So at least I think experience has taught me. Of the six, five are at their villas, and I alone am here. They come, however, daily; not that I can see that there is much use in it' (Lord Campbell, op. cit., vol. vii, pp. 345–6). Cf. *Letters of Dorothea, Princess Lieven, during her Residence in London*, p. 42, letter of October 5.

[3] H. of C., December 1, 1819 (*Parl. Deb.*, vol. xli, pp. 571 sqq.).

adjourned on December 29. Within little over a month all the measures introduced by the Government had been passed. They have gone down to history under the name of the 'Six Acts'.

Two of the six were intended to provide against the danger of an armed revolution. The first[1] prohibited every meeting or assembly for drilling or other military exercises. The instructors at any such meeting were liable to deportation for a term not exceeding seven years, or imprisonment for a term not exceeding two years. Those taking part in the drills were punishable by a maximum of two years' imprisonment. The Act was unobjectionable. Indeed, the fact that it was found necessary to pass it in 1819 proves how extraordinarily free the old political institutions of England were, had indeed pushed liberty to the bounds of anarchy. The second Act was more open to criticism;[2] for it restricted one of the traditional liberties of the individual Englishman—his right to bear arms. It empowered the magistrates, even beyond the limits of their ordinary jurisdiction, to seize arms dangerous to the public peace, to arrest their owners and release them only on bail, and, in search for arms, to enter private houses at any time of the day or night. The Ministers admitted that this statute, which they claimed to be a necessity and which was a weaker imitation of an Act passed against Luddism in 1812,[3] was an extraordinary measure. They asked that it should be passed as a statute of local application only, to be in force in the 'disturbed counties', of which a list was appended to the Act, with authority given to the King in Council to add or remove districts according to the needs of the moment. Moreover, the Act was a temporary measure, to remain in force only until March 25, 1822.

Another Bill dealt with the question of public meeting.[4] The Englishman enjoyed a traditional right to unrestricted liberty of public meeting. But this unlimited right, though possibly practicable in the small community which made the revolution of 1688, now presented dangers of a wholly novel kind, dangers which the last three months had made patent to everyone, when extended to the vast urban populations, the offspring of the factory system. A Radical agitator, named Thistlewood, had boasted at a meeting

[1] 60 Geo. III, cap. 1.
[2] 60 Geo. III, cap. 2.
[3] 52 Geo. III, cap. 162. See Lord Castlereagh's speech, H. of C., December 14, 1819, in which he compares the two Bills (*Parl. Deb.*, vol. xli, pp. 1133–4).
[4] 60 Geo. III, cap. 6.

that a thousand, ten thousand, a hundred thousand, even a million men had the right to assemble with or without banners, unarmed or armed, and that no magistrate had the right to interfere, unless an act of violence were committed.[1] If the law really was as Thistlewood stated, surely the necessity of amending it in the interest of the public safety was obvious. The number of persons who might take part in a public meeting must in future be restricted, and the organizers prevented from evading the provisions of the law by the device of simultaneous meetings. This was the double purpose of the Government, a purpose which it expected to attain by passing the voluminous statute consisting of forty clauses which, for the first time in English history, attempted to regulate the right of public meeting by a comprehensive code of legal restrictions. With the exception of certain specified meetings, such as the county meetings, the meetings held to elect Members of Parliament, and all meetings held with closed doors, it was henceforth illegal for anyone to attend a public meeting who was not a resident of the parish in which it was held, or at least the owner of real estate in the same county. The regulation would apply to all meetings of above fifty persons held with the object or on the pretext of discussing any grievance of a public character, any economic or professional matter, or any question which concerned Church or State. Meetings whose object was to alter the state of the law otherwise than by the authority of Parliament, or were calculated to excite hatred or contempt of the King, his heirs, the Government or the Constitution were absolutely prohibited. Full powers were conferred upon the magistrates to execute the statute, authorize or prohibit meetings, and arrest offenders, who were made liable to seven years' transportation. There followed a series of clauses which subjected to very strict regulation all places where, in return for payment, the public could hear lectures or take part in debates. A hundred pounds caution money must be deposited. When a licence was granted the magistrates would enjoy a permanent right of inspection; and the licence would be forfeited *ipso facto* by the delivery of speeches of a seditious, irreligious, or immoral tendency.

The remaining Bills restricted the freedom of the Press. One was an 'Act for the more effectual Prevention and Punishment

[1] H. of C., November 29, 1819, Lord Castlereagh's speech (*Parl. Deb.*, vol. xli, p. 384).

of blasphemous and seditious Libels'.[1] This statute, a very short
Act of four articles, gave the court, which had condemned any
such pamphlet, authority to order the immediate seizure of every
copy, even if an appeal had been lodged. For the second offence
it authorized the infliction of the penalties prescribed by English
law for high misdemeanours, or, at the discretion of the judge,
banishment for an unspecified number of years. It was clever
tactics to include sedition and blasphemy in the same category;
for there were large numbers both in the middle and in the
working class who were attracted by even a Radical programme
of parliamentary reform, but were shocked by the anti-Christian
character which the leaders of English Radicalism, aping the
French revolutionaries, had impressed upon the literature of the
movement.

Another statute, a measure of the first importance,[2] was
designed to render impossible for the future the device by which
Radical journalists had evaded the Press laws during the last two
or three years. Cobbett had given the numbers of his *Register* the
form of open letters addressed to a particular individual, which
commented freely on the affairs of the day, and had claimed that
his publications were therefore pamphlets, not the regular
numbers of a newspaper. Others had followed his example. The
device was now made illegal. All pamphlets containing political
news, or comment upon it, or dealing with any question of
Church or State, which, appeared at intervals of less than twenty-
six days, contained less than two leaves, and were sold for less
than 6d., would be subject to all the statutory dispositions to which
newspapers were subject. At the same time, the printer or editor
of every periodical publication was obliged to make himself
responsible for its contents by the deposit of a sum, fixed at £300
for the capital, £200 for the provinces. The powers conferred
upon the magistrates to put this Act into execution were defined
in plain and stringent terms.

The freedom of the Press was still further restricted by a sixth
Act,[3] which regulated procedure and was not intended as an
independent statute, but as a means of enforcing the other five.
It was aimed at the revolutionary journalists who for a year past
had eluded the utmost efforts of the prosecution by a skilful

[1] 60 Geo. III, cap. 8.   [2] 60 Geo. III, cap. 9.
[3] 60 Geo. III, cap. 4.

employment against their judges of the extreme laxity which marked judicial procedure in England. Carlile, for instance, had been prosecuted in December 1818, but English procedure was so complicated that the trial did not begin till the autumn of 1819, and Carlile had then secured a further postponement.[1] The new Act sought to render these delays impossible, by depriving the accused of the right to obtain automatically a postponement of the trial by demanding an imparlance, that is to say, a settlement of the case by amicable arrangement with the prosecutor.

2

The year which came to an end with this December of 1819 had everywhere proved an anxious year for the victors of 1815. In Germany, in consequence of plots among the university students and the assassination of Kotzebue, the German princes had met at the Carlsbad Conference, and, to facilitate the suppression of disorder, had drawn the bands of their federation tighter. In France the advances made by the ministers Dessoles and Decazes to the Liberals and Bonapartists had been the subject of conversations in London between Lord Castlereagh and the representatives of the Allied Powers. And England herself, as we have just seen, had her share, and more than her share, of the revolutionary agitation. 'You would have been horrified,' wrote Wellington to Pozzo di Borgo two days after the meeting of Parliament. 'Even those who know us best and are aware that what would be mortal to other nations is a trifle for us, were filled with alarm.' He continued, it is true, by informing his correspondent that the irreproachable attitude of the Commons had done much to reassure him. 'Our example,' he concluded, 'will do some good in France as well as in Germany, and we must hope that the world will escape the universal revolution which seemed to threaten us all.'[2] Nevertheless, from the standpoint of the orthodox Tory, the British Government had not won at the close of 1819 a victory comparable to that which it had gained at the opening of 1817.

[1] H. of C., November 30, 1819, Lord Grenville's speech (*Parl. Deb.*, vol. xli, pp. 505–6).
[2] November 25, 1819 (*Despatches Cont.*, vol. i, pp. 86–7): 'Vous auriez frémi. Même ceux qui nous connaissent le mieux et savent que ce qui serait mortel pour les autres ne compte pas pour nous ont eu terriblement peur. . . . Notre exemple rendre quelque service en France aussi bien qu'en Allemagne: et il faut espérer que le monde évitera la revolution générale qui paraissait nous menacer tous.'

Then the first acts of violence had been committed by the revolutionaries; now the first blood shed, on August 16, had been the workers'. Then the sole task before the Government was to overcome a revolutionary opposition outside Westminster—the Whigs, as a body, had felt themselves obliged to keep silence; now, on the contrary, the Whig Opposition, without waiting for Parliament to open, had returned whole-heartedly to its traditional procedure. A large number of county meetings, held under the patronage of the local aristocracy, had denounced the brutal conduct of the troops at Manchester. At one of these meetings, in Yorkshire, the Lord-Lieutenant, Lord Fitzwilliam, took the chair, for which he was deprived of his position. When Parliament assembled, the Opposition did not relax its hostility. Without even waiting for the introduction of the Six Acts, Lord Grey in the Lords and Tierney in the Commons called for an inquiry into the affray at Manchester, and Tierney's motion in the Commons secured 150 votes.[1] In view of the fact that Lord Grenville's group had left the Opposition and was giving its unreserved support to the policy of coercion,[2] the voting proved that the Whigs were a solid and imposing phalanx, which moreover maintained its unity unimpaired throughout the entire session.

The Whig orators denounced as at once unconstitutional and dangerous the increase in the Army only a few months after it had been found necessary to supply the financial deficit by voting new taxation to the amount of four millions, at a time when the revenue had diminished and the country was faced with a further

[1] H. of L., November 23, 1819; H. of C., November 23, 1819 (*Parl. Deb.*, vol. xli, pp. 4 sqq., pp. 67 sqq.). *Morning Chronicle*, November 26, 1819: 'A minority of one hundred and fifty on an Amendment to the Address on the first day of a Session is unexampled in the annals of Parliament.' *The Times*, November 26, 1819: 'The Ministers themselves never expected one hundred and fifty members would have voted for an amendment, which implied an opposition to an Address to the Throne, at the opening of a session of Parliament; and this rebuke, where generally they had form and precedent in their favour, will, we trust, induce them to be moderate in the demands which they mean to make upon public liberty, with the view, as they profess, to control disaffection.' See also the same journal, November 30: 'The nature of the new legislative measures . . . will appear from the proceedings in the two Houses of Parliament last night. We suspect that the division on the Address is the cause that they are less despotic than was intended and indeed threatened.'

[2] See H. of L., November 23, 1819, the Marquis of Buckingham's speech; November 30, Lord Grenville's speech. H. of C., November 24, 1819, Wynn's speech (*Parl. Deb.*, vol. xli, pp. 49–50, 448 sqq., 189 sqq.). Lord Nugent alone remained faithful to the Opposition. For his quarrel with his family see Rev. George Scobell, *A Letter to Lord Nugent in Answer to One from his Lordship to the Rev. Sir Geo. Lee, Bart., respecting the Catholic Claims*, 1820.

deficit, even if no additional expenditure were incurred. They expressed their belief that the true author of the measure was not Lord Liverpool, nor indeed any of his civilian colleagues, but Wellington, the soldier in the Cabinet, who perhaps was entertaining dreams of replacing the present form of government by a military dictatorship.[1] They proceeded to criticize the details, and often the principle, of the Six Bills introduced by the Government. Throughout the debate memories of the French Revolution were a favourite topic of discussion. Was the Government, asked the Tories, to imitate the weakness of Louis XVI and his ministers, and look on while the Throne and the Nobility perished, as they had perished in France? Were we to forget that it was religious infidelity and blasphemy which had brutalized the French character and given birth to the atrocities of the terror?[2] No, replied the Whigs, it was not weakness and tolerance which had destroyed the *ancien régime* in France, but a legitimate revolt against the tyranny of its laws. Freedom of the Press and freedom of public meeting were the safety valves which in England for over a century had prevented popular excitement exploding in rebellion.[3] And what need was there of legislation against anti-religious literature? The religious zeal which prevailed throughout the middle and lower classes could be trusted to treat such writings, had indeed already treated them, as they deserved. What justification could there be for hampering the far more effective propaganda of the Evangelicals against revolutionary principles by imposing a heavy tax on periodical publications?[4] The books in use in the Sunday schools controlled by the

[1] Brougham to Lord Grey, October 24, 1819 (*Life and Times of Lord Brougham*, vol. ii, pp. 347–9). For Wellington's militarism, a militarism confined to internal politics and devoid of any warlike tendencies, see his curious letter of April 19, 1819, to the Comte Decazes: 'En mon opinion la premiere affaire, la grande affaire, encore plus la seule affaire en France est que le Roi forme une armée qui lui soit réellement attachée et à sa famile royale. S'il s'agissait de guerre, je dirais une bonne armée, mais où est le fou qui pense à la guerre dans les circonstances actuelles de France et du monde? Non, l'essentiel de l'armée en France en tout temps a toujours été, et l'est surtout dans le moment actuel, qu'elle soit attachée au Roi' (*Despatches Cont.*, vol. i, pp. 55–6).—'In my opinion the most urgent, nay the sole, task before France today is the formation by the King of an army genuinely attached to himself and to the Royal Family. If there were any thought of war, I would add a strong army; but where can the lunatic be found who thinks of war in the present circumstances of France and the world? No, the essential characteristic of the French army has always been, and is today more than ever, its attachment to the Monarch.'

[2] H. of L., December 6, 1819, Lord Liverpool's speech (*Parl. Deb.*, vol. xli, p. 740).

[3] H. of C., November 29, 1819, Tierney's speech (ibid., vol. xli, p. 407); December 6, 1819, Perceval's speech (ibid., vol. xli, p. 798).

[4] H. of L., December 6, 1819, Lord Erskine's speech (ibid., vol. xli, pp. 707–8).

democratic Unions were perfectly orthodox, the religious instruction was given by Nonconformist ministers, and the lessons began with morning prayers and closed with night prayers.[1] In Manchester itself, the scene of the great meeting, new dissenting chapels were being built every year. Perhaps for the first time in a Parliament devoted to the Anglican Church, Methodism and even the old Nonconformist denominations were portrayed by numerous speakers as the strongest bulwark of English Society against the spread of Jacobinism.[2]

3

Nevertheless, sceptics were not wanting who doubted the sincerity of this opposition. The Radicals had no love for the Whigs, and made them the target of their sarcasms. At this very moment young Hobhouse, Byron's friend, was summoned before the bar of the Commons and committed to Newgate for a pamphlet he had just published in which he had used language derogatory to the House. But the pamphlet was directed entirely against the Whig Opposition.[3] There were even critics sufficiently malicious to insinuate that the Whig aristocracy was delighted to see the Tory Government shoulder the responsibility for it, and delighted also to play with the certainty of failure the noble part of an Opposition defending the cause of the people.[4] The charge

[1] H. of C., December 22, 1819, Brougham's speech (*Parl Deb.*, vol. xli, p. 1508).

[2] H. of C., December 9, 1819 (ibid., vol. xli, p. 920); December 21, 1819 (ibid., vol. xli, p. 1416). See in *The Times* a series of interesting articles attacking Carlile's antireligious propaganda but declaring any new legislation against it useless. The general disapprobation which it had already aroused was a sufficient security (November 2, 5, 6, 9, 10, and 17, 1819). It was immediately after this that the Tories began to display a certain sympathy with Wesleyanism. See Robert Southey, *The Life of Wesley, and the Rise and Progress of Methodism*, 1820; also a review of Southey's book in an article in the *Quarterly*, October 1820 (vol. xxiv, pp. 1 sqq.).

[3] *A Trifling Mistake in Thomas, Lord Erskine's recent Preface; Shortly noticed and respectfully corrected in a letter to His Lordship*. By the author of *The Defence of the People*, 1819. Cf. Hobhouse's earlier pamphlet, *A Defence of the People in Reply to Lord Erskine's two Defences of the Whigs*, 1819. See for this episode H. of C., December 9, 10, 13, 1819 (*Parl. Deb.*, vol. xli, pp. 917 sqq., 989 sqq., 1010; *Proceedings in the House of Commons and in the Court of King's Bench, relative to the author of the Trifling Mistake*, by John C. Hobhouse, Esq., 1820; also Lord Broughton (J. C. Hobhouse), *Recollections of a Long Life*, vol. ii, pp. 113 sqq.

[4] Brougham, *Political Philosophy*, vol. iii, chap. xxi, p. 184: 'In 1819 . . . many friends of popular rights were convinced that some check had become necessary, some regulation at least of such assemblages; and, among others, I well remember my friend Lord Hutchinson, when I complained of the Six Acts, saying that he thought the Whig party should be thankful they were out of office and that the odium of passing some such measure was, thrown off their shoulders upon those of their adversaries. "For, depend upon it," he said, "the right of meeting at all is in jeopardy from such assemblages—so numerous and so crowded".' Cf. M. de Caraman to M. Pasquier, January 7, 1820: 'The opposition was

deserves to be considered, but in our opinion must be considerably reduced. The proof that the Whigs' opposition to the Bills introduced by the Government was something more than an empty show, consists in the numerous and important amendments which were carried. To weaken Tory resistance the Whigs had recourse to the assistance of the 'saints'. Wilberforce and his friends were no less alarmed and, in some respects, more shocked than Lord Sidmouth or Lord Castlereagh by the democratic and antireligious propaganda. But they were anxious to keep on good terms with the Opposition, whose aid was indispensable to the success of their campaign against slavery.[1]

Not to mention the numerous modifications of detail introduced by Lord Castlereagh into his Bills to meet criticisms from the Opposition benches, three amendments, concerned with points of fundamental importance, were three victories won by the Opposition. The original draft of the Bill dealing with the Press had provided for the second offence the penalty of banishment or transportation at the judge's discretion. The Government was forced to abandon the penalty of transportation unless the banished journalist returned to the country without permission. The Bill against seditious assemblies prohibited in its original form all public meetings without distinction. It was a concession to Opposition demands that in its final form it did not apply to meetings held within closed doors.[2] Lord Castlereagh had introduced the Bill as a permanent measure applicable to the entire

nothing but a popular gesture with which the majority of the speakers would have dispensed, had they been sure of a majority' (Comte d'Antioche, *Chateaubriand, Ambassadeur à Londres*, p. 141).

[1] H. of C., December 6, 1819, speeches of Perceval and Wilberforce (*Parl. Deb.*, vol. xli, pp. 798 sqq.). Cf. Wilberforce to Stephen, October 18, 1819: 'I own—to you I may say it safely—that I am afraid of alienating the minds of all the Opposition and indisposing them to the support of our West India questions' (R. I. and S. Wilberforce, *Life of William Wilberforce*, vol. v, p. 36). Cf. his embarrassment when speaking of the Fitzwilliam incident. 'How shocking,' he writes to Z. Macaulay on October 9, 'are the resolutions of some of the meetings in the West Riding of Yorkshire! Yet the cause of the seditions being patronized by men of rank and influence may tend to rescue the multitude out of the hands of the Hunts and Thistlewoods.' Also to S. Roberts, November 6: 'I have had no intercourse with Government, but really arguments for the removal of Lord Fitzwilliam at once present themselves, though I will not pronounce whether the attendant evils may not be such as to countervail the good' (ibid., pp. 36. 37).

[2] H. of C., November 30, 1819, Brougham's speech (*Parl. Deb.*, vol. xli, p. 416); December 6, 1819, Lord Castlereagh's speech (ibid., vol. xli, p. 758). Cf. Mackintosh to Lord John Russell, January 12, 1820: 'The exception of meetings within doors is so important a mitigation (not to be found in the Acts of '95 and '99) that it may in time supply the means of defeating the whole restriction' (*Early Correspondence of Lord John Russell*, vol. i, pp. 210-11).

Kingdom. The Opposition had attempted to make it a temporary measure, and, like the statute providing for the confiscation of arms, applicable only to certain districts, and although it failed to secure the latter restriction, its efforts were so far successful that the Act was passed as an experimental measure to be in force only for a period of five years.[1] And finally, when the procedure Bill, which made it impossible to evade trial by postponement, came before the House of Lords, Lord Holland stated that he was prepared to vote for the Bill provided it were made bilateral, and put an end, at the same time, to the scandalous practice by which the Attorney-General was enabled, in the case of an *ex-officio* information, to protract indefinitely the interval between the information and the trial. The Lord Chancellor, Lord Eldon, expressed his agreement with the demand, and introduced into the Bill a clause limiting the interval to twelve months. When it passed the Lords the unusual spectacle was witnessed of an interchange of congratulations between Lord Eldon and Lord Holland.[2]

4

A further surrender on the part of the Cabinet marked this short session which Lord Liverpool and his colleagues had wished to devote exclusively to the passage of the Coercion Acts; and it was of no slight importance; for it concerned the original object of the meetings in the North, parliamentary reform. Though the middle-class inhabitants of the manufacturing towns were terrified by the turn which events had taken since August, and alarmed by the language of the Radicals, they were disquieted by the reflection that the Tories would take advantage of the situation to refuse to create the new constituencies which would give them the representation to which they were entitled. What attitude would the Whigs adopt to their demand for representation? Would they still continue their noncommittal attitude of 1817? Already, before the session opened, the *Morning Chronicle*[3] and the *Edinburgh Review*[4] called upon the party to change its tactics,

[1] H. of C., December 3, 1819, Tierney's speech (*Parl. Deb.*, vol. xli, p. 702); December 6, 1819, Lord Castlereagh's speech (ibid., vol. xli, p. 759).

[2] H. of L., December 13, 1819 (ibid., vol. xli, pp. 1008-9).

[3] *Morning Chronicle*, October 20, 1819 (which quotes *in extenso* a long article from the *Scotsman*).

[4] *Edinburgh Review*, October 1819, 'State of the Country' (vol. xxxii, p. 304).

and form a solid front on a programme of moderate reform. To bestow representation on the great towns of the North would, they urged, be far more efficacious than any Coercion Act in restoring tranquillity to the disturbed districts; and when Parliament assembled it was evident that this advice reflected a deep-seated necessity of the Whig position. Lord Grosvenor declared a reform of the suffrage indispensable.[1] Lambton, a wealthy mineowner, son-in-law of Lord Grey and Member for the County of Durham, announced his intention to introduce a Reform Bill in the course of the following session.[2] But it was Lord John Russell who took the decisive step.

As early as July Lord John had opposed to Sir Francis Burdett's radical programme an extremely moderate programme of his own, and declared his intention to lay it before the Commons during the following session.[3] Later, however, he was exasperated by the extravagance of the demands put forward by the popular leaders,[4] and in September displayed such lukewarmness in the cause of parliamentary reform that he disappointed his father, the Duke of Bedford, and his brothers, the Marquis of Tavistock and Lord William Russell.[5] He yielded, however, to his friends' entreaties,[6] and, although not very hopeful of the result,[7] in November, when Parliament was hastily summoned in extraordinary session, he kept the promise made in July. The borough of Grampound had just been convicted of corruption and the member thus returned, a Tory financier of Jewish origin named Sir Manasseh Lopez, had been sentenced to a fine of ten thousand pounds and two years' imprisonment.[8] On December 14 Lord John Russell

[1] H. of L., December 17, 1819 (*Parl. Deb.*, vol. xli, pp. 1266, 1276).

[2] H. of C., December 6, 1819 (ibid., vol. xli, p. 757).

[3] H. of C., July 6, 1819 (ibid., vol. xl, pp. 1516–17).

[4] H. of C., July 1, 1819 (ibid., vol. xl, p. 1496).

[5] Diary of T. Moore, September 4, 1819: 'Talked a good deal of politics. Lord John much more moderate in his opposition than the Duke and Lord Tavistock (Lord John Russell, *Memoirs of Thomas Moore*, vol. iii, p. 5).

[6] Mackintosh to Lord John Russell, October 14, 1819 (*Early Correspondence*, vol. i, p. 205). S. Allen to Lord John Russell, October 17, 1819 (Sp. Walpole, *Life of Lord John Russell*, vol. i, p. 116).

[7] Lord John Russell to Thomas Moore, December 14, 1819: '. . . I am going today to make a little motion for Reform. The violent will not care for it, and the other side will throw it out, and so my public attendance will cease for the present. There can be little doubt that in a few years, unless there is a sudden change of public opinion, the form of Government will be almost entirely changed . . .' (*Early Correspondence of Lord John Russell*, vol. i, p. 208).

[8] H. of C., April 2, 1819 (*Parl. Deb.*, vol. xxxix, pp. 1390 sqq.); May 17, 1819 (ibid., vol. xl, pp. 460 sqq.).

proposed that the borough in question should be deprived of the franchise, the penalty of disfranchisement enacted against any borough hereafter found guilty of similar practices, and the franchise thus forfeited transferred to some large town or thickly populated county. When he had finished his speech, Lord Castlereagh asked him to withdraw his motion, on his undertaking to leave the House at liberty, if it thought fit, to transfer to some large town the franchise of which Grampound had proved itself unworthy.[1] It is clear that dread of a revolution after the French pattern no longer, as in 1817, overcame all other considerations; far from it. On the contrary, the initiative taken in July by the populace of Birmingham, Leeds, and Manchester seemed to have begun already in December to bear fruit. Nor was it the Opposition alone which yielded to the popular pressure. It was no other than Lord Castlereagh himself who in the very midst of the debate upon the Six Acts surrendered, on one point at least, to the demands of the Radical meetings.

[1] H. of C., December 14, 1819 (*Parl. Deb.*, vol. xli, pp. 1110 sqq., 1118). John M. Cobbett to James P. Cobbett, December 30, 1819: 'They are in a monstrous stew here. Papa thinks Reform will be given by next spring by the Ministers themselves. Castlereagh has pledged himself to support one motion (Lord John Russell's) for Reform, and it will be, as they themselves very truly said the winter before last: if they are made to say A, they must say B' (Lewis Melville, *Life and Letters of William Cobbett*, vol. ii, p. 125).

CHAPTER II

The Awakening of Liberalism

I THE AFFAIR OF QUEEN CAROLINE

I

GEORGE III, the old, mad king, died in London on January 29, 1820. All the leading newspapers, without exception, while recounting the progress achieved by the nation under his reign, lamented his misfortunes and praised his virtues, and every word of eulogy was a satire, unconscious or intentional, on the vices of his successor. But there seemed no reason to expect that the accession of George IV would change in any way the political situation. The son of George III merely exchanged the title of Regent for that of King, and the question before the nation remained in February what it had been in January, namely, whether the contest begun in the previous year between Toryism and revolutionary Radicalism would continue or come to an end, and, if it should proceed, what the issue of the struggle would be?

There was no indication as yet that the situation in England, indeed in Europe generally, would become more tranquil. On February 13, at Paris, Louvel assassinated the Duke of Berry because 'the Bourbons are tyrants', and the Duke seemed 'destined to continue a family which was the hereditary enemy of France'. Ten days later the English public were startled by news of an equally sensational character which touched them more nearly. In the house in Cato Street which served as their rendezvous, a tiny group of conspirators were arrested as they were preparing to carry out an insane plot—the wholesale assassination of the Cabinet, which had been invited to dinner that evening at the house of one of their number, Lord Harrowby. The slaughter was to be followed by the seizure of sufficient cannon to overawe the populace, the occupation of the Bank, the establishment of a Provisional Government at the Mansion House, and the firing of London. Nine conspirators were arrested on the spot, and two who fled were taken a few hours later. The head of the gang was Thistlewood, who had been imprisoned for his share in the riot at Spa Fields in the winter of 1816, had been released in August 1819, and, as we have seen, had played a prominent part in the autumn meetings. Thus to all appearance the history of England had become indistinguishable from that of the Continent, oscillating between reaction and revolution.

Since these crimes aroused a wave of popular indignation, their immediate effect was not unfavourable to the party of order. In Paris Louvel's deed brought about the fall of the Decazes Cabinet and restored the extremists to power. In London Lord Sidmouth's police had taken no steps to nip the conspiracy in the bud. An *agent-provocateur* had supplied the plotters with arms, pointed out the most opportune time and place for their attempt, and in short drawn them into the ambush laid by the police.[1] But during this very winter, at the extremity of Southern Europe, the cause of the Holy Alliance suffered its first severe defeat. The army which King Ferdinand was preparing to dispatch to South America to suppress the rebellion of the Colonies revolted and demanded that the democratic Constitution of 1812 should be restored. At the beginning of March the King, like Louis XVI before him, surrendered to the insurgents, and swore to observe the Constitution of Cadiz. The moral effect produced in 1820 by the Spanish revolution can hardly be exaggerated. It was of this revolution that Byron was thinking when he called 1820 'the first year of freedom's second dawn'[2]; and it was the Spanish democrats who introduced into the political vocabulary of England, indeed of the whole of Europe, a new word. In opposition to the 'serviles', the partisans of absolute monarchy, they called themselves the 'Liberales'. It then became the habit among Tory polemical writers to dub the more thoroughgoing members of the Whig Opposition 'Liberales', Liberals, that is to say partisans of liberty after the pattern of Cadiz. In the long run the epithet was accepted by those against whom it had been directed, until it finally became the official designation of the revived and reconstituted Whigs.[3]

[1] H. of C., May 2, 9, 1820 (*Parl. Deb.*, new series, vol. i, pp. 54 sqq., 242 sqq.); also the complete report of the trial of the conspirators in the *Ann. Reg.*, 1820, App. to Chronicle, pp. 920 sqq. Cf. Lord Castlereagh to Metternich, May 6, 1820: 'Wherever the mischief in its labyrinth breaks forth, it presents little real danger, whilst it furnishes the means of making those salutary examples, which are so difficult whilst treason works in secrecy and does not disclose itself in overt acts' (*Memoirs and Correspondence of Lord Castlereagh*, vol. xii, p. 259).

[2] *Vision of Judgment*, vii.

[3] The term did not make a sudden appearance in the English political vocabulary like the term 'radical' at the end of 1819. This may appear strange at first sight, when it is considered that as an adjective 'liberal' was current in a laudatory sense (e.g. *liberal*

After the dramatic episode of February 24, popular agitation in England was quiescent for several weeks. Constitutional practice required a General Election within six months of the accession of a new monarch. Therefore the Cabinet decided to dissolve on February 28 the Parliament returned in 1818, and the entire month of March was occupied by the election of the new Parliament. Meetings necessary to make arrangements for an election had been expressly excepted from the provisions of the Act passed in November against 'seditious meetings'. The Radicals surely would take advantage of the opportunity thus provided to turn the election meetings into revolutionary demon-

measures, a *liberal* policy, *liberal* principles). The reason is that the noun had a foreign, a continental flavour. The Spanish word seems to have reached England about the beginning of 1816. See H. of C., February 15, 1816, Lord Castlereagh's speech. 'The "Liberales", who, though in a military point of view an anti-French party, were politically a French party of the very worst description. They had declared that they would not admit Ferdinand's right to the throne, unless he put his seal to the principles which they laid down, and among the rest to that of the sovereignty being in the people. The "Liberales" were a perfectly Jacobinical party, in point of principle' (*Parl. Deb.*, vol. xxxvii, p. 602). The term was introduced into French politics in 1819 (the members of the Opposition had hitherto been called 'Independents'. See De Vaulabelle, *Histoire des Deux Restaurations*, vol. v, p. 53). Indeed, when English writers used the term they continued for a considerable time to write it as a Spanish, Italian, or French word. See *Edinburgh Review*, March 1817: 'The Liberales are habitually sneered at (by Southey)' (vol. xxvii, p. 168). Brougham to Lord Grey, Geneva, August 27, 1817: 'My travelling companion' (an Italian) 'is a distinguished Liberale, of very high birth, who has just refused an arch-bishopric from principle' (*Life and Times of Lord Brougham*, vol. ii, p. 325). Sir Walter Scott's Diary, November 20, 1826: 'Canning Huskisson, and a mitigated party of Liberaux' (J. G. Lockhart, *Memoirs of the Life of Sir Walter Scott*, vol. iv, chap. xi). Occasionally we find writers beginning to give the word an English form, but only when speaking of Mediterranean and continental countries (F. Lamb to Lord Castlereagh, Munich, January 4, 1820, *Memoirs and Correspondence of Viscount Castlereagh*, vol. xii, p. 169; also *Ann. Reg.*, 1819, pp. 171, 172, 178; 1820, pp. 221, 239; 1821, Preface). We find it employed for the first time as the designation of an English party by the *Courier* in August 1819. See especially August 19: 'As we predicted, the *liberals* are beginning to ring their doleful changes upon the transactions that occurred at Manchester on Monday.' August 26: 'The *liberals* of course attribute this peaceable and orderly conduct to the lamblike and gentle dispositions of the Reformers themselves.' August 30: 'We have too high a respect for the noble qualities of British jurisprudence to imitate our *Liberals*.' But the term is used by an enemy to discredit those to whom he applies it. E. Ward, in a letter from Lisbon to Lord Castlereagh on September 28, 1821, writes (*Memoirs and Correspondence of Lord Castlereagh*, vol. xii, p. 438): 'The Cortes . . . are . . . a little afraid of England, and of England only. But they think the Liberal party is so strong amongst us that the Ministry, however they may love despotism and legitimacy, cannot act against them.' But Ward, writing from Lisbon, is obviously translating into English a Spanish or Portuguese word. It was in 1822 that Leigh Hunt, by the publication of a periodical entitled *The Liberal, or Verse and Prose from the South*, made the new term the semi-official designation of Byron's group. And the title of this publication, the tone of which is revolutionary in the extreme, and which drags in the mud the memory of Lord Castlereagh and King George III, is very significant. *Verse and Prose from the South* does not simply mean that the *Liberal* publishes articles written in Italy by Byron and Shelley, but is also intended to convey that the publication is animated by the spirit of the southern revolutions. For the later history of the word 'liberal', see vol. iii, part i, chap. iii, *sub finem*.

strations? Nothing of the sort happened. It was very long since a General Election had passed off so peaceably. The trial of Hunt and the other Radicals arrested at Peterloo in August 1819 began at York on March 16, three days after the return of the two members for that city. The judge asked one of the witnesses what difference he noticed between the scene he had witnessed in Manchester then and that of which he was the spectator at York now. 'The one,' replied the witness, 'looked like war and disturbance, and the other like merriment and rejoicing.'[1]

Did this mean the definite restoration of social peace within a few months of Peterloo? Not altogether. For the moment a condition prevailed of vague disquiet which eludes exact definition.

On the morning of April 5 the walls of Glasgow and the neighbouring towns were found placarded with a proclamation, signed by 'the committee for the organization of a provisional government', which called upon the people of England, Scotland, and Ireland to effect a revolution, warned the manufacturers to close their factories pending the establishment of the revolutionary government, and urged the soldiers to follow the example of the Spanish Army.[2] A proclamation of this kind might have been expected to herald a new period of disorder. But the general strike which followed nowhere degenerated into actual insurrection, unless indeed we are to regard as an incipient rebellion the ridiculous fiasco at Bonnymuir. A party of Radicals attacked in the open country ten hussars and ten cavalrymen of the Stirlingshire Yeomanry. Shots were exchanged. The rebels fled from the field leaving in the hands of the soldiers nineteen prisoners, five fowling pieces, and eighteen pikes.[3]

Nevertheless, with the sentence of two years' imprisonment passed upon Hunt, and the execution of Thistlewood and his accomplices, who astonished the middle class by the courage they

---

[1] 'The Trial of Henry Hunt . . . at the York Lent Assizes, 1820,' *Ann. Reg.*, 1820, p. 852). What was the result of the election? Unfavourable to the Government, according to Yonge (op. cit., vol. iii, pp. 48–9); favourable according to Harriet Martineau (*A History of the Thirty Years' Peace*, book ii, chap. iii, ed. 1877, vol. i, p. 349). Contemporary evidence is insufficient to decide. The *Courier*, a Tory organ, claimed a ministerial gain of eighteen or twenty seats; the *Morning Chronicle*, an Opposition paper, a gain of fifteen for its own party (*Morning Chronicle*, April 4, 12, 1820; *Courier*, April 11, 1820). See also the information, equally indecisive, sent to Charles Abbot (Lord Colchester) by his correspondents (*Diary of Lord Colchester*, vol. iii, pp. 124–6).
[2] See the text of the proclamation, *Pol. Reg.*, April 15, 1820 (vol. xxxvi, pp. 357 sqq.).
[3] *Ann. Reg.*, 1820, Chron., pp. 103 sqq.

displayed and the refusal of all save one to accept the ministrations of religion, the victory of the party of order was to all appearance complete. The lower classes were obviously intimidated: they lacked leaders and scented police plots everywhere. On the other hand, fights between soldiers and workmen still occurred at intervals in Lancashire.[1] In Yorkshire a rumour spread that the populace, armed with pikes and pistols, was preparing to rise.[2] Was it certain, after all, that the calm was more than superficial, and that the Six Acts were sufficient security against the future outbreak of agitations similar to those of 1816 and 1819?

2

Suddenly an unexpected incident occurred which re-kindled popular excitement, though in an entirely novel form. When in 1814 the Regent excluded the Princess of Wales from his Court, she revenged herself by launching a poisoned arrow at his head. She wrote to the Prince that for the present 'I waive my rights, but occasions may arise when I must appear in public and your Royal Highness must be present also. . . . Has your Royal Highness forgotten the approaching marriage of our daughter and the possibility of our coronation?'[3] From that day forward the Regent's mind was dominated by one idea, to obtain a divorce, and thus render impossible the reappearance of the woman he hated.

His intention was a source of great embarrassment to his Ministers, for the Royal divorce could not fail to cause a scandal. Only his incurable levity could have induced a man so unpopular as the Regent to expose himself and the entire Government to such a risk. If the Princess could be persuaded to leave England once more and bury herself on the Continent from the public eye and her husband's thoughts, would not the danger be averted or at least postponed? To negotiate with her the Ministers had recourse to Canning, very anxious just then to be reconciled with the Tories. Nor, indeed, did he find his task difficult. The necessity which the Princess experienced in London of keeping a constant guard over her words and actions was a heavy burden to her flighty temperament; and it was precisely their apprehen-

---

[1] *Ann Reg.*, 1820, p. 126.   [2] Ibid., p. 128.
[3] Brougham to Lord Grey, May 1814 (*Life and Times of Lord Brougham*, vol. ii, pp. 223 sqq.).

sion of the indiscretions she would commit abroad which troubled her regular advisers, Brougham at their head. But it was in vain that they opposed the plan suggested by Canning. The utmost Brougham could obtain when she left England in November 1814, was that it should be given out that she intended only a brief visit to the Continent, and that she should maintain her entire household at Kensington Palace as though she expected to return almost immediately.[1] Her concession amounted to nothing. In Italy, where she established herself, she found freedom and happiness. She forgot England, and at once ugly rumours spread about her private life. Three years passed by. When, in 1816, Princess Charlotte married Prince Leopold of Saxe-Cobourg, her mother was not informed of the wedding, and when, a year later, the girl died, she was not informed of her death. But it would be impossible to treat the death of George III and her husband's coronation as the marriage and death of Princess Charlotte had been treated. When the Regent's wife became Queen of England, she could not be kept in ignorance of the change in her position sufficiently long to prevent her return to the country. More insistently than ever the Regent urged his Ministers to obtain for him the divorce on which his heart was set.

They continued to plead the necessity for prudence, and no Minister was more alarmed at the prospect of a divorce than the 'Keeper of the King's Conscience', the Chancellor, Lord Eldon. But there were other influences working in secret against the Cabinet and flattering the Regent's whim. Sir John Leach, the Vice-Chancellor, seems to have conceived the hope that by adopting this course he might some day supplant his superior. He even went so far as to circulate in the Press a report of Lord Eldon's resignation.[2] Finally Lord Liverpool yielded and allowed the Regent to send to Italy a Secret Commission of Inquiry. But the Cabinet obtained from him a preliminary undertaking that when the Commission had reported, however damning the

---

[1] Brougham to the Princess of Wales, July 30, 1814; to Lord Grey, August 9, 1814 (*Life and Times of Lord Brougham*, vol. ii, pp. 253 sqq., 257-9). After the publication of these letters in which he is seen struggling, in 1814, against Canning's influence over the Princess, he wrote (ibid., pp. 352-3): '. . . Among the advisers of her going abroad was Canning. This he owned in the House of Commons, in the debate of 1820, upon her return. *Neither Whitbread nor I were at all aware of it.*' It is clear how little reliance can be placed on Brougham's statements when they are not confirmed by contemporary evidence.

[2] Lord Campbell, op. cit., vol. vii, p. 330.

evidence which they collected might prove, he would treat the question of proceedings against his wife as open for further consideration; and in any case the dispatch of the Commission did not bind the Cabinet to any particular course of action.

The inquiry lasted about six months, and on July 10, 1819, the commissioners sent a report to London on Princess Caroline's misconduct which fulfilled the Regent's utmost hopes.[1] But when the report was dispatched, the small circle acquainted for the past month with the progress of the inquiry, still a secret from the general public, had been filled with alarm. On June 14 Brougham had approached Lord Hutchinson, an old friend of the Princess and an intimate friend of the Regent, to propose a compromise. An amicable separation would be arranged between husband and wife. The future Queen would renounce her claim to be crowned, and in return receive an annuity for life and a title in keeping with her position—for example, Duchess of Cornwall.[2] The Cabinet supported Brougham's proposals, and pointed out to the Regent the great difficulties a judicial process would involve. Should the case be brought before the Church Courts? The proceedings would drag on for years. Or should Parliament be asked to decide it? The legality of the procedure was doubtful and it would be politically dangerous. Or should the Princess be tried for high treason? When the charge was of such extreme gravity, English law exacted overwhelming proofs of guilt, and could they be certain of sufficient evidence?[3]

3

The Regent, however, proved obdurate, and, to make matters worse, the Princess displayed a desire to revisit England. She informed Lord Liverpool and Brougham of her design. The latter, in alarm, prevailed upon her to postpone her intended return. But when the report spread through Europe that the old King's death was imminent, she could restrain herself no longer and travelled homeward as far as Marseilles. It required another letter from Brougham to decide her to retrace her steps and return to Italy, in a state of intense anger at her chilly reception by the

[1] See the documents quoted in C. D. Yonge, op. cit., vol. iii, p. 11 n.
[2] Ibid., vol. iii, pp. 15–16.
[3] Minutes of Cabinet, June 17, July 24, 1819 (ibid., vol. iii, pp. 17, 19 sqq.).

French authorities.[1] George III died on January 29. For several days the Regent had been suffering from a severe cold. As a result of two very tiring days, January 30 and 31, his cold developed into pneumonia. On the night of the 31st he was in danger of death, and the doctors did not pronounce him out of danger until February 10. During his illness his inveterate hatred of his wife became an obsession. He determined that her name should not be inserted together with his own in the Anglican Prayer Book. He determined she should never be crowned by his side. He determined to obtain an immediate divorce whatever the cost. And in the critical situation through which England and Europe were passing the Ministers were compelled to waste entire days discussing with their sovereign this contemptible and sordid domestic squabble.

On February 11 the Cabinet laid before the King a long note drawn up at a meeting held the evening before. The Ministers, basing their objections on the advice tendered by the law officers of the Crown, explained the great difficulty of a judicial process. Granted that the suit could be brought before the House of Lords without previous consultation with the ecclesiastical authorities, the wife possessed the right to prove negligence or ill-treatment on the part of her husband, and, if the Queen decided to make use of her right, it was obvious how damaging the result might be. Moreover, the law required that the proceedings should be public. Possibly permission might be granted, for reasons of State, to hold them within closed doors; and it might even be found possible to prevent, or at least suspend until the close of the suit, the publication of the evidence. But this privacy would itself produce a very bad impression: a flood of speeches, motions, and petitions would inevitably be let loose in Parliament and in the country, with the worst possible effect on public opinion. It would be more prudent to abandon the divorce. Since the annuity granted to the Princess of Wales in virtue of the agreement made in 1814 expired with the death of George III, it might surely be possible to reach a settlement with her by which, in return for a continuation of the annuity for life, the Queen would consent to live abroad and even accept the omission of her name from the Prayer Book.[2] The overtures made by Brougham in

[1] Letter from Princess Caroline, March 16, 1820 (*Ann. Reg.*, 1820, p. 131).
[2] Minute of Cabinet, February 10, 1820 (C. D. Yonge, op. cit., vol. iii, pp. 25 sqq.).

1819 gave reason to hope that she would consent to an arrangement of this kind. If she refused, then, and not before, it would be time to think of a divorce.

The King, egged on by his doctor Knighton, and advised by Sir John Leach, would not hear of compromise. Even when on February 12 the Privy Council gave orders that henceforward Anglicans would offer their prayers not for the King and Queen but for 'the King and all the Royal Family', he was still unsatisfied, and replied to the note of his Cabinet by a note drawn up in very skilful terms. He criticized the opinions given by Lord Eldon, the Attorney-General, and the Solicitor-General. He declared himself ready to defy public feeling to obtain his just right. He objected to the terms of the proposed arrangement. To accept it would, he said, be to surrender the opportunity he now possessed to prove beyond cavil the Queen's guilt, and leave hanging in perpetuity over his head the threat of her sudden return whenever it was to the interest of a political group to make use of her. And at the same time he told Lord Liverpool that, if the Cabinet refused to comply with his will, he would get rid of them, and, if he were unable to find obedient Ministers in England, would retire to Hanover.[1] Those who on January 30 had not ascribed any political importance to the accession of George IV had been rudely undeceived. For twenty-four hours the Cabinet regarded itself as dismissed, and the papers were discussing the formation of its successor.[2]

But the King was very quickly made to understand that he would not be able to find in any quarter Ministers prepared to be the instruments of his whims; and his threat of retirement to Hanover was a piece of silly bluff which no one could take seriously. On the 14th the Ministers, still in office, reaffirmed in a second note the position they had adopted on the 11th, with the proviso that if 'the Princess' should after all carry out her project of returning to England, further measures must be adopted to meet the novel situation thus created.[3] On the 17th the King yielded to the pressure of his Cabinet. Perhaps he counted, and not without reason, on his wife's folly to give him his revenge. The funeral of George III took place the same day, and on the

[1] C. D. Yonge, op. cit., vol. iii, p. 24. Lord Castlereagh to Lord Stewart, February 13, 1820 (*Memoirs and Correspondence of Lord Castlereagh*, vol. xii, pp. 210 sqq.).

[2] *Star*, February 16, 1820; *Greville Memoirs*, February 20, 1820.

[3] Minute of Cabinet, February 14, 1820 (C. D. Yonge, op. cit., vol. iii, pp. 38 sqq.).

following day Parliament met. The object of the session was merely to dispatch urgent business, and receive the formal announcement of dissolution. Nevertheless, the question of the Queen was raised. Joseph Hume, a Radical member, asked whether the Queen would continue to receive the annuity of £3,000 guaranteed to her until the death of George III, and Lord Castlereagh, in a brief reply, gave the assurance that her interests would receive due consideration. On the 21st Hume again interposed in the debate to deplore the treatment accorded to the Queen. Why had no address of condolence and congratulation been passed to her as well as to her husband? Was she to continue to live abroad supporting herself by alms? Was her fate no concern of Parliament? Tierney, as the official spokesman of the Whigs, adopted an attitude of absolute neutrality in the quarrel between the King and Queen, either because he shared the views of certain members of the Whig aristocracy and hoped to witness a public scandal which would damage the Court and the Tories,[1] or, as is more probable, because he wished to prepare for a possible change of government by winning the King's favour.[2] So long as the Queen had not purged herself of the misconduct of which public report accused her, Parliament, Tierney declared, was not justified in voting her any sum out of the national revenue. But why should the country remain in the dark as to the truth of the charges made? The omission from the Prayer Book of all mention of her was not enough. There must be a public inquiry.[3] Brougham spoke after Tierney, and his language was far more guarded. He refused to take any notice of current gossip, or any alleged inquiries. Prudence and moderation had never been more needed. There was no place here for party spirit.[4] Parliament was then dissolved and for several days the Cato Street conspiracy diverted public attention from the Queen.

[1] Lord Grey to Brougham, August 25, 1819: 'I have always doubted the reality of the Princess's intention to come home, and what you say confirms me in the opinion of its being a mere bravado. Her business, which in any circumstances must be disagreeable enough to all who cannot avoid taking some part in it, would have become much more so by her arrival in England. I should, however, have felt some hesitation in taking upon myself the responsibility of advising her not to come; for if she had done so, and played all her game, I am convinced she would have beaten the Prince and his foolish adviser Leach out of the field' (*Life and Times of Lord Brougham*, vol. iii, pp. 341–2).
[2] Wilberforce's Diary, April 27, 1820: 'There has been a flirtation between Tierney and the King' (R. I. and S. Wilberforce, *Life of William Wilberforce*, vol. v, p. 54).
[3] H. of C., February 21, 1820 (*Parl. Deb.*, vol. xli, pp. 1623 sqq.).
[4] H. of C., February 21, 1820 (ibid., vol. xli, pp. 1627–8).

4

It was now the Queen's turn to take the offensive. In April the London Press published the open letter which she addressed to the British public. In this letter she complained of the slights put upon her by all the Courts of Europe at the instigation of the English Court. She claimed from Lord Liverpool and Lord Castlereagh the honours due to a Queen of England. She gave orders that a palace in London should be placed at her disposal; for she intended to arrive shortly. 'England is my real home, to which I shall immediately fly.'[1] The rumour spread that she was already on the way and would reach Dover that very night. The Cabinet saw itself compelled to make up its mind at once upon the attitude it would adopt.

At this juncture the Ministers happened to be again at loggerheads with their sovereign. In truth, they had never ceased quarrelling since his accession. The Ministers asked each other whether the King did not suffer from an hereditary taint, were not mad like his father. No sooner had he ascended the throne than he took possession of the entire personal property of the late monarch, his jewels and the jewels of Queen Charlotte and Queen Caroline, and Lord Liverpool and his colleagues, dreading his violent temper, had not dared to object. He was now demanding an increase in his Civil List. He was dissatisfied with the List which his Cabinet intended to lay before Parliament, though it was strictly in accordance with precedent. This time fear of the Commons outweighed with the Ministers fear of the Royal anger. They were firm, and the King gave way.[2] And just then the Queen's manifesto brought up again the question of the divorce. After their long delay the Ministers at last decided to approach Brougham.

On April 15 Lord Liverpool asked him to transmit to the Queen the following proposals. She would receive during her life an annuity of £50,000 on condition she never set foot in England, took a title other than that of Queen of England, and renounced her claim to the position and privileges of a Queen consort.[3] Brougham accepted the commission and concealed the fact that

[1] *Ann. Reg.*, 1820, pp. 129 sqq.
[2] C. D. Yonge, op. cit., vol. iii, pp. 48–9. *Greville Memoirs*, the beginning of 1823.
[3] Lord Hutchinson to Brougham, June 4, 1820 (*Life and Times of Lord Brougham*, vol. ii, pp. 359–60); C. D. Yonge, op. cit., vol. iii, p. 53.

he had even less influence over the Queen than Lord Liverpool or Lord Eldon had over the King. The Ministers would indeed have been astonished had they known that he had never dared to inform the Queen of the letter he had written a year earlier to Lord Hutchinson; and he had good reason to believe that she would now be even less amenable than in 1819. Alderman Wood, the Radical politician of the City, merchant draper and purveyor by appointment to the Queen, had been the object of violent attacks during the election by the candidates of the Court. He took his revenge by entering into correspondence with the Queen and urging her to make a stand. Brougham was afraid of the Queen and Alderman Wood. He kept Lord Liverpool's letter in his pocket and awaited events.

The Queen set out on her journey home. On May 9 she was at Geneva. There she was joined by James Brougham, who had been sent by his brother to attempt to open her eyes to the evidence collected two years before by the Commission of Inquiry, and press upon her a prudent course. But she wished to see Brougham himself, and sent a courier to ask him for a meeting. He stipulated that they should meet in a French town as near to England as possible, for his time was taken up by parliamentary business. The Queen agreed to meet him at Saint-Omer on the 30th, and immediately continued her journey. At Montbard in Burgundy she was met by Alderman Wood, who was accompanied by Lady Anne Hamilton, formerly her maid of honour. Would she really cross the Channel? In London men betted on the chances of her arrival.[1] The King awaited her coming with unconcern; it would give him his divorce. For the moment his entire interest was engrossed in arranging even to the most minute details the gorgeous ceremonial of his coronation. If the peeresses took no part in the ceremony, the celebration would lose much of its splendour. But what justification could there be for their presence if the Queen were not crowned with the King? This was the grave problem which occupied the attention of George IV and his Cabinet.

The Queen's courier, sent to fix the meeting with Brougham for the 30th, did not reach London till the 31st, and the same day Lord Liverpool received a message from the Queen demanding the dispatch of a Royal yacht to convey her from Calais to Dover

[1] Lord Eldon to his daughter, May 29, 1820 (Lord Campbell, op. cit., vol. vii, p. 360).

on June 3. He wrote off at once to Brougham to press upon him the fulfilment of his engagement. Brougham could no longer evade compliance, and on June 2 set out for France. Lord Hutchinson accompanied him as the representative of the King and Cabinet.

On June 3 Brougham and Lord Hutchinson arrived at Saint-Omer. The Queen gave them both the impression that she was determined to come to London at whatever cost. Brougham dared not tell her that she was asked to renounce the title of Queen. He prevailed upon Lord Hutchinson to abstain from threats at the outset, and upon the Queen to defer her decision for a day or two. Then, when Lord Hutchinson lost patience, he thought it more prudent to leave the negotiations to him. The entire proceedings on the afternoon of June 3 were confined to an interchange of letters. Lord Hutchinson wrote to the Queen at 4 o'clock, an hour later the Queen replied in a note of three lines that 'it was quite impossible for her to listen to such a proposition', and left immediately for Calais.[1] She sailed the same evening at 11 o'clock and landed at Dover the following day at 1 o'clock in the afternoon, 'Count' Bergami, her chamberlain, and, according to public report, her lover, had left her at Saint-Omer; Alderman Wood accompanied her to England.

5

The Queen's arrival in England was the signal for an extraordinary attack of public hysteria which raged for months. When she set foot on land she was greeted by a salute from the cannon of the fort, and the huzzas of the entire population. The horses were taken from her carriage, and she was drawn to her hotel in triumphal procession preceded by flags and trumpets. Next morning there was a triumphal departure from Dover, in the evening a triumphal entrance into Canterbury. The same welcome accompanied her to London. Young men on horseback escorted her carriage, the church bells rang full peals. At Canterbury the officers of a cavalry regiment came in uniform to salute her. At Chatham she was received by surpliced clergymen. When she reached the suburbs of London the weather, hitherto rainy, became fine. The carriage was open and the Queen, accompanied

[1] For the negotiations between Lord Liverpool and Brougham and the interview at Saint-Omer, see the documents published by C. D. Yonge, op. cit., vol. iii, pp. 54 sqq.

by Alderman Wood, made her entrance bowing to the vast crowds. When she had crossed the Thames and entered Westminster the crowd set itself in motion and formed an immense cortège behind her. The procession passed in front of Carlton House and the sentry presented arms. She stopped at the gate of Alderman Wood's house in Mayfair, which he had placed at her disposal. The crowd gathered beneath the windows hustling and pelting all passers-by who refused to salute. Bills affixed to every wall in the City ordered the inhabitants to make an illumination in honour of the Queen, and the mob perambulated the West End streets smashing the windows of houses which displayed no lights. Lord Sidmouth and the Marquis of Hertford were among the many who had their windows broken that night. After two Cabinet councils the Government communicated to the House a Royal message which placed at the disposal of the representatives of the nation 'certain papers respecting the conduct of Her Majesty since her departure from this Kingdom', and asked the House of Lords to appoint a secret committee to consider whether there were sufficient grounds on which to commence judicial proceedings against the Queen, and, if so, what form they should take.[1] It was now very late in the day to prevent the trial from going forward. Nevertheless, two final attempts were made to obtain an amicable settlement.

The first of these was of a more or less secret and informal nature. In the entourage of the King, as in that of the Queen, hesitation and conflicting counsels continued to prevail. The Ministers knew that they were detested by the King, whose mind Leach was still poisoning against them and who held over their heads the threat of dismissal. Brougham, on the other hand, had been proved guilty of keeping back from the Queen the commission with which the Cabinet had entrusted him on April 15, and she, encouraged by Wood, loaded him with abuse. On June 15 a final meeting was arranged between the Duke of Wellington and Lord Castlereagh on the one side, and Brougham and Denman, the counsel employed by the Queen, on the other, with a view to devise a settlement acceptable to both parties. But the Queen's representatives began by demanding that her

---

[1] H. of L., June 6, 1820; H. of C., June 6, 1820 (*Parl. Deb.*, N.S., vol, i, pp. 870–1). H. of L., June 7, 1820 (ibid., vol. i, pp. 886 sqq.). The Government asked the Commons as well as the Lords to appoint a secret committee, but the project lapsed during the final attempts at a settlement.

name should be reintroduced into the Prayer Book, and the English representatives abroad should officially notify her Royal status to the foreign Courts. On the second point the King offered a compromise, which she refused; on the first he was obdurate. The negotiations were broken off.[1]

The second attempt was of a more formal character. After an understanding with the Queen's counsel, Wilberforce, in his naïve pride, entertained the belief that his moral influence was sufficient to settle the dispute. On June 14 four representatives of the Commons presented themselves in Court dress at the Queen's lodging. They were Wilberforce, Stuart Wortley, Sir J. Acland, and Banks. She received them courteously, but with considerable haughtiness. She listened to an address in which she was assured that should she shrink from the scandal of a judicial inquiry nobody would construe her action as an implicit confession of guilt but would regard it as the decision most becoming her own modesty, the dignity of the Crown, and the interests of the country. When the reading was finished she turned to Brougham. He had helped to arrange the interview,[2] and for his pains had been disavowed and abused by the Queen and denounced as a traitor by the Radical Press. Now he must undergo the humiliation of reading the Queen's reply. It was brief and a flat refusal. When Wilberforce and his colleagues left the house they were obliged to make a headlong rush into the first of the carriages which had brought them to escape the shower of stones which greeted their exit.[3]

6

Since a settlement was impossible, the secret committee of the Lords began its work, taking no notice of the Queen's formal demand for a public inquiry. On July 4 the committee reported to

[1] *Ann. Reg.*, 1820, p. 127. Cf. C. D. Yonge, op. cit., vol. iii, p. 53.
[2] Wilberforce to Sam. Roberts, June or July 1820: '. . . In fact I had every reason to believe Her Majesty would have acquiesced, but for circumstances which I would rather state to you in person than by letter. Give me credit, however, for not assuring you on light grounds that the Queen's chief law officer recommended that acquiescence' (R. I. and S. Wilberforce, op. cit., vol. v, p. 64).
[3] For Wilberforce's intervention, see H. of C., June 22, 1820 (*Parl. Deb.*, N.S., vol. i, pp. 1213 sqq.). Even Wilberforce had been carried away by the current of public sympathy for the Queen. See his Diary for June 6: 'She approaches wisely, because boldly. . . . How deeply interested all are; indeed, I feel it myself about her! One can't help admiring her spirit, though I fear she has been very profligate' (R. I. and S. Wilberforce, op. cit., vol. v, p. 55).

the effect that the charge brought against the Queen, of 'an adulterous connection with a foreigner originally in her service in a menial capacity', rested on the concordant testimony of a large number of witnesses drawn from every rank of Society. The following day Lord Liverpool brought in a Bill of Pains and Penalties[1] depriving Queen Caroline of her Royal title and dissolving the marriage. An interval of six weeks followed, during which the Queen's presence continued to excite in the London streets the same scenes of noisy enthusiasm as on her first arrival. A mob of loafers was permanently stationed in Portland Street, where she now had her lodging. From time to time shouts were raised of 'Queen! Queen!' and from time to time she would acknowledge her admirers by appearing on her balcony by the side of Alderman Wood, bowing and retiring.[2] When her carriage drove up to the door the crowd became thicker. She came out between two lines of spectators, and drove round Hyde Park amid a crush of vehicles, hustling throngs of pedestrians, huzzas for herself, hisses for the King.[3] Finally the Government placed a country house at her disposal in the vicinity of London—Brandenburgh House, situated on the banks of the Thames. August 3, the day on which she left London for her new residence in a carriage drawn by four horses, was another day of triumph.[4] Meanwhile the King had been compelled to postpone his coronation 'for divers weighty reasons', according to the official proclamation.[5]

At last the date fixed for the opening of the trial arrived. A stout barrier which, as it proceeded, had to be further strengthened to keep out the mob which sought to force an entrance, transformed the approach to Westminster Hall into a trenched camp, garrisoned, since the troops from the neighbouring barracks were deemed an insufficient protection, by a large number of regiments

---

[1] Blackstone, *Commentaries on the Laws of England*, iv, 256. 'The high court of *parliament* . . . is the supreme court in the Kingdom, not only for the making, but also for the execution of laws, by the trial of great and enormous offenders, whether lords or commoners, in the method of parliamentary impeachment. As for Acts of Parliament to attain particular persons of treason or felony, or to inflict pains and penalties, beyond or contrary to the common law, to serve a special purpose, I speak not of them; being to all intents and purposes new laws, made *pro re nata*, and by no means an execution of such as are already in being.'

[2] Wilberforce to Hannah More, July 21, 1820 (R. I. and S. Wilberforce, op. cit., vol. v, p. 72).

[3] *Ann. Reg.*, 1820, Chron., July 3, 9.

[4] Ibid., August 3.

[5] Ibid., July 12.

drafted from the provinces. In the vicinity by the riverside were the lodgings of the witnesses brought from Italy at the charge of the prosecution. Their arrival at Dover and in London, a month earlier, had occasioned such violent outbursts of popular hostility that complicated devices had been employed to conceal their presence until the day when they were to give their evidence. The Queen had taken up her residence in St. James's Square, close to the Houses of Parliament. In the small hours of August 17 the crowds began to gather along the route from St. James's Square to Westminster. As the peers passed by, those who belonged to the popular party were cheered, the others were booed. For the first, but by no means for the last time, Wellington was hissed by the crowd.[1]

About 10 o'clock in the morning the Queen left St. James's Square, drawn slowly by six horses amid the acclamations of the spectators. During the first two days of the trial she listened to the speeches of her counsel, Brougham and Denman. They were but the skirmishing of the advance-guard. The defence warned the prosecution that they possessed the right of 'recrimination' against the plaintiff and reserved the liberty to employ it, should it be in their client's interest to do so. On August 19 the Attorney-General, Sir Robert Gifford, opened the case for the prosecution.

He told the story of the Queen's private life since her departure from England in 1814. In the October of that year at Milan she had engaged as her courier an Italian named Bergami, formerly the valet of General Pino. On her arrival at Naples on November 8 she had changed the usual arrangement of her apartments. She had dismissed from her bedchamber a certain William Austin, who had occasioned much talk in 1806, and installed Bergami in a room next her own. The Attorney-General fixed upon the night of November 9 for the beginning of her adulterous connection with Bergami. He went on to describe the wandering life led by the Queen in Italy, Germany, Tunis, and Palestine. Bergami, a companion ever more inseparable, slept in a room adjoining her own, and on board ship shared her cabin. He depicted him taking his meals with the Princess, accompanying her to balls where the scantiness of her attire shocked a country by no means inclined to be prudish and occasionally even led to her expulsion from the room, and indulging in obscene amuse-

[1] *Creevey Papers*, vol. i, pp. 306–7.

ments in the company of the Queen and a eunuch whom she had brought back from the East. Then he related how he had gradually got rid of the Queen's English attendants, had installed his sister, under the bogus title of Countess Oldi, as her maid of honour, not to speak of his mother 'Donna Livia', and his daughter 'Princess' Victorine—in all ten members of his family. And upon himself he had bestowed the position of Chamberlain to the Queen, with the imposing title of Knight of Malta, Grand Master of the Order of Saint Caroline, and Baron della Francina.

The Attorney-General had just concluded his accusation on Monday, the 21st, when the sound of drums and trumpets announced the Queen's arrival. Brougham and Denman had contrived that she should make her appearance exactly at the right moment. She had escaped the humiliation of listening in person to the Attorney-General's speech. And, crushing though the accusation might well have seemed in its accumulated mass of evidence, was that evidence after all so conclusive when the witnesses came forward individually to be cross-examined by the defence? The Peers heard the testimony of a long series of witnesses—Swiss, Germans, and above all Italians, men and women of every conceivable profession—sailors, a mason, a notary, large numbers of domestic servants, hotel servants, and valets dismissed from the Queen's service. As the days passed it became clear that the prosecution was making no progress. The Press reported with greedy interest every detail of the trial. For a fortnight the entire population of England wallowed in obscenity. The papers favourable to the Queen—they were the vast majority, and *The Times* was at their head—attacked this rabble of bought spies, and held up to contempt their Italian jargon, their slips of memory, their treachery, their lies. No doubt the Queen's reputation was left under a cloud. But what did the British public care for that? It thought only of satisfying its grudge against a King universally detested, who was sufficiently ill-advised, when the scandals of his own life were common knowledge, to drag into publicity this bedchamber gossip with no other object except the gratification of getting rid of his wife.

On September 7 the Solicitor-General resumed the prosecution. On the 8th the Lords granted the defence three weeks' postponement in which to collect any witnesses they might desire to summon. On September 7 the Queen made a State progress by water from one end of the Port of London to the other.[1] On the 13th 5,000 sailors walked in procession to pay their respects to her.[2] On the 30th twenty Italians who came to give evidence on her behalf were received with public honours at Dover and in London.[3] On October 3 the trial reopened.

The proceedings began with a long speech for the defence by Brougham, which occupied two sittings. He was not content with criticizing in detail the evidence for the prosecution. He caused a sensation by reading a letter written by the Prince of Wales to his wife in 1796, in which he gave her her entire liberty and promised never to ask for the resumption of marital relations, even if their daughter's death should deprive him of an heir. After writing such a letter and using his own liberty in the fashion which was notorious, with what face, asked the speaker, did he now seek a divorce after twenty-five years had elapsed? He concluded with an eloquent appeal to the patriotism, prudence, and pity of the British Peerage. The evidence for the defence followed. Taken as a whole it was unsavoury and unconvincing. But what of that? The King's conduct remained unpardonable; and it was against the King that Denman aimed the final speech for the defence, in which he related the story of Nero and Octavia. He told of Octavia's acquittal at the first trial amid the plaudits of the people, of her condemnation secured by Nero at a second trial, of her banishment, and of her mysterious death by dagger or poison.[4] Meanwhile the popular manifestations in the Queen's honour had redoubled and gave proof of more skilful organization. Not a week passed without a procession of forty or fifty thousand men marching in military formation along Piccadilly, headed by a band and displaying banners.[5] When the Attorney-General had replied, the Peers were invited to express their opinion individually before the Bill was taken to the second

---

[1] *Ann. Reg.*, 1820, Chron., p. 403.   [2] Ibid., pp. 414–15.

[3] Ibid., pp. 44–5.

[4] H. of L., October 24, 1820 (*Parl. Deb.*, N.S., vol. iii, pp. 1087–8). Denman's philippic achieved a great success and served as the theme of satirical caricatures. 'Nero Vindicated, with a wood engraving by Brawston, depicting the tyrant arrayed in all his glory. *Nero Vanquished*, embellished with an elegant wood engraving, portraying the fallen condition of the Modern Nero. *State Caterpillars*, with eighteen correct wood engravings, coloured, with appropriate mottoes selected for each, and original descriptive poetry, comprising King Nero, Sneaking Derry, Doctor Circular, Lord Liveapuddle, Old Bags, Duke of Villainton,' etc.

[5] Creevey to Miss Ord, October 24, 26, 30 (*Creevey Papers*, vol. i, pp. 332, 334); *Pol. Reg.*, November 11, 1820 (vol. xxxvii, p. 1135).

reading. It was only what everybody expected when the leaders of the Opposition, headed by Lord Grey, either expressed their belief in the Queen's innocence, or declared that her guilt had not been sufficiently established by the evidence. More significant were the verdicts given by Peers who had not identified themselves so closely with the contending parties. Lord Harewood 'wished he was as clear as to the perfect innocence of the Queen as he was as to the impolicy of passing this Bill'.[1] 'No noble Lord,' declared Lord Ellenborough, 'ought to vote for the second reading of the Bill who did not think that the Queen was guilty; but they would allow him to add that it was not necessary for all those who might vote against the second reading of the Bill to think that Her Majesty was innocent.'[2] Lord Clifford considered that the Queen had been guilty, if not of adultery, at least of extremely immodest behaviour, but he could not forget that her conduct might possibly have been different if the King had treated her differently, and he expressed his intention to vote against the second reading.[3] The Queen felt that the hour of victory was at hand.

On October 25 she informed the public that after the 30th she would receive no more addresses.[4] By this step she withdrew herself from the popular enthusiasm and was rewarded by visits from the Duke of Sussex, Prince Leopold of Saxe-Coburg, and Lord and Lady Fitzwilliam.[5] On November 2, in consequence of unfavourable reports, she announced her intention to appear at the bar of the Lords to read a protest. She abandoned the design on the following day on an unconvincing pretext—in reality, no doubt, because her friends were once more entertaining hopes of an immediate triumph. When the Bill passed the second reading by a narrow but sufficient majority of twenty-eight votes, she caused the protest to be read by Lord Dacre. It asserted her entire innocence. The decisive moment had now arrived when the clauses must be debated and the Bill put to the third reading. That the House of Lords, and not the ecclesiastical courts, should pass the Bill in the first instance was a usurpation by the Temporality of the preroga-

[1] H. of L., November 3, 1820 (*Parl. Deb.*, N.S., vol. iii, p. 1539).
[2] H. of L., November 4, 1820 (ibid., p. 1621).
[3] H. of L., November 6, 1820 (ibid., pp. 1675–6).
[4] *Pol. Reg.*, November 11, 1820 (vol. xxxvii, p. 1138).
[5] *The Times*, October 27, 28, 1820. *Letters of Dorothea, Princess Lieven, during her Residence in London*, p. 48.

tive of the Spirituality to which the Archbishop of York declared that he could never assent. He had voted against the second reading, and he demanded, as the only terms on which he could vote for the third, that the clause declaring the marriage dissolved should be expunged from the Bill. The Bishops supported him, but not the leaders of the Opposition, who realized that the amendment would facilitate the passage of the Bill. The divorce clause was therefore carried by the large majority of 129 against 72 Tory votes. The result was that the Bill, with the Opposition and the Bishops voting against it, passed the third reading by a majority of only nine votes—108 to 99. Lord Liverpool then rose, admitted that it was impossible with so small a majority to take the Bill, though passed by the Lords, to the Commons, and asked that the discussion be adjourned for six months—that is to say, in parliamentary terminology, that the matter should be dropped. And that very day, to avoid embarrassing debates, Parliament was hurriedly prorogued till January 23. In the House of Commons the session closed amid scenes of indescribable disorder.

7

When the Queen left Westminster her passage was saluted not only by the applause of the crowd, but by the soldiers who set down their arms to join in the clapping. For three successive nights London was illuminated, and the discredited witnesses Rastelli, Majocchi, and la Demont were burnt in effigy. Lord Grey, who had spoken on the Queen's behalf, enjoyed a triumphal reception when he returned to his estates; the Marquis of Buckingham, on the other hand, and the Bishop of Llandaff, were mobbed by a hostile crowd for having voted against her. On November 29, in the midst of a vast concourse of spectators, the Queen drove to St. Paul's to return public thanks, and a few days later the King received an address from the City demanding 'the immediate dismissal of those unworthy Ministers, the contrivers and conductors of so foul a conspiracy'.[1] This was indeed a complete misrepresentation of their attitude. They had been forced into the proceedings in spite of themselves, and now when, as they had foreseen, the divorce had not been secured, their relations with

---

[1] *Ann. Reg.*, 1820, Chron., December 10.

their sovereign were worse than ever. They publicly expressed their contempt for the King, and he in turn regarded them as traitors and plotted their downfall. Nor did Parliament thank them for braving at last the King's anger, after they had yielded for months to his caprice. In 1819 Lord Grey had hoped, in the interest of the Whigs, that the Queen would return. His calculations now seemed to have been verified. Her return had indeed proved disastrous to the Tories.[1] To all appearances the Ministry was doomed, and a serious defection weakened it still further. For a year past Canning had gone his own way apart from his colleagues. When the Queen's name had been omitted from the Prayer Book he had made it clear that, in his opinion, by taking this step the Cabinet abandoned the intention of a public trial. After her return he had stated in the House of Commons that he personally would never take his place among her accusers, and he had supported Wilberforce's attempt at a settlement with all the influence at his command. When the trial was inevitable he had offered his resignation, and had only withdrawn it at the King's special request and on the understanding that he would take no part in the proceedings. And he spent the entire period of the trial abroad, travelling on the Continent. In December he resigned, and his resignation, both in itself and in the circumstances in which it was made, was a far more serious blow to the Cabinet than Peel's resignation two years before.

But was the country faced with nothing more serious than a Cabinet crisis? Did not the events of the last few months present the appearance of an incipient revolution? When the Queen replied to the countless addresses which poured in to her from London and the provinces, her answers had at first been marked by great caution, and she had been careful not to turn the defence of her honour into a political question. But as time went on her language became less guarded, and she identified her cause with the cause of imperilled freedom. It was common knowledge that Cobbett now composed her replies.[2] Every day the London Press did its utmost to hold up the King to hatred and contempt, and

---

[1] *Pol. Reg.*, December 30, 1820 (vol. xxxvii, p. 1643): 'No man now calls himself a Tory.'

[2] Until July 15 Cobbett had criticized very severely the Queen's addresses: he ascribed them to Brougham and blamed their timidity. Suddenly his tone changes; for he himself is now the writer of the addresses. See, for example, *Pol. Reg.*, June 24, 1820 (vol. xxxvi, pp. 1034–6), and July 8, 1820 (vol. xxxvi, pp. 1115–16). Cf. Lewis Melville, *Life and Letters of William Cobbett*, vol. i, pp. 148 sqq., 163 sqq.

the Government dared not apply the Press laws, which they had made more stringent in 1819, and bring the journalists to trial. Nor did the Ministers dare to apply the statutes against seditious assemblies, though London, during the entire summer, had been the theatre of popular demonstrations comparable to that witnessed at Manchester on August 16, 1819.[1] There had been the same crowds, the same military discipline among the demonstrators. Could the Government count on the troops to put down an insurrection? Wellington felt uneasy about the *moral* of the Army.[2] On June 15 an attempted mutiny at a barracks at Charing Cross had provoked a sympathetic riot. Could Nonconformity be trusted to exert as usual a sobering influence upon the lower classes? The Evangelicals throughout all the sects had themselves lost their heads. Even among the Wesleyans, usually so loyal to the Established Government and who continued to use the forms of the Anglican liturgy, ministers disobeyed the orders of Conference and persisted in praying for the Queen.[3] Alarm reigned in many noble families, not all adherents of the Tory party. The Duke of Bedford, one of the most decided leaders of the Whigs, told his son, the Marquis of Tavistock, in July that 'the British monarchy was at an end'.[4] It was a long time before Tory fears could be allayed. When Chateaubriand, later appointed French Ambassador in London, was praising to Lord Liverpool the stability of British institutions, the Prime Minister answered:

[1] Creevey to Miss Ord, October 26, 1820 (*Creevey Papers*, vol. i, p. 332). Cf. November 11, 1820 (ibid., vol. ii, p. 341).

[2] Memorandum to the Earl of Liverpool respecting the State of the Guards, June 1820 (*Despatches Cont.*, vol. i, pp. 127 sqq.). See also a more confident letter of July 31. Wellington had been reassured by the information he received about the Regular Army: 'It is upon them, I have every reason to believe, that the Queen and her advisers have principally relied. It was a great point to get the King to the review with his arm in a sling' (ibid. vol. ii, p. 141). But see, on the other hand, the alarmist letter of September 17 from Sir Herbert Taylor to Wellington: '. . . Whether from a sense of his own increased importance which the soldier has acquired during the late war, or from being influenced to a certain extent by the latitude of opinion and observation upon public questions which has been assumed by the lower classes: grievances, whether real or supposed, are brought forward and urged in a more decided tone than heretofore. . . . What was formerly a representation, made respectfully, with a view to obtain explanation, has in many instances become a remonstrance or complaint of injustice done, often tumultuously urged. To what this may lead in time, God knows' (ibid., vol. i, pp. 146–7). Cf. Croker to Lord Melville, June 16, 1820 (*Croker Papers*, vol. i, pp. 175–6); Wilberforce's Diary, June 9, June 22, 1820 (R. I. and S. Wilberforce, op. cit., vol. v, pp. 56, 60); also the document reprinted *Pol. Reg.*, July 8, 1820 (vol. xxxvi, pp. 1246 sqq.).

[3] *The Times*, February 28, March 2, 1821; T. P. Bunting, *The Life of Jabez Bunting, D.D.*, with notices of contemporary persons and events, vol. i, pp. 178–9.

[4] Diary of C. J. Hobhouse, July 23, 1820 (Lord Broughton's *Recollections of a Long Life*, vol. ii, p. 129).

'What can be stable with these enormous towns? One serious insurrection in London and all is lost.'[1]

But others were more sceptical. Brougham, the Queen's dubious advocate, exasperated a Liberal friend by telling him that the affair was nothing but a passing wave of popular feeling and, like the scandal of the Duke of York and Mrs. Clarke, would be quickly forgotten.[2] Many symptoms confirmed this reassuring diagnosis. It was all very well for Cobbett to be the Queen's adviser and compose her addresses. He had to face the fact that, as a result of the Stamp Duty Act, his *Register* had scarcely any readers.[3] Hunt had been in prison since the spring. On August 3 at the Warwickshire Assizes an entire group of Radicals received sentence, among them Cartwright and the journalist Wooler.[4] And public attention was so entirely engrossed by the approaching trial of the Queen that their condemnation passed almost unnoticed. On August 16, while a vast procession stretching without a gap from Hyde Park Corner to Hammersmith went to pay its respects to the Queen,[5] scarcely a thousand could be brought together in Manchester to celebrate amid universal indifference the anniversary of Peterloo.[6] The ferment of 1820 veiled the decline of the Radical movement. The deaths of Princess Charlotte and George III had been mourned by a sorrowing nation, and the British public now gave another proof of its ingrained devotion to monarchy even in its attack upon George IV, by dropping the cause of manhood suffrage to display its sympathy with a persecuted Queen. The Radical agitators found themselves relegated to the background. Once more it was the Whig leaders who

---

[1] *Mémoires d'Outre-Tombe*, 2 partie, livre ix (ed. Biré, vol. iv, p. 279).

[2] Creevey to Miss Ord, January 17, 1820 (*Creevey Papers*, vol. ii, p. 2). Lord Eldon, though opposed to the trial, was never alarmed. See his letter to his daughter, June 1820: 'The lower orders here are all Queen's folks; few of the middling or higher orders, except the profligate, or those who are endeavouring to acquire power through mischief. . . . There is certainly an inclination to disquiet among the lower orders; but it is so well watched, that there is no great cause for uneasiness on that account' (H. Twiss, *The Public and Private Life of Lord Eldon*, vol. ii, pp. 372–3).

[3] 'An Account of all the Weekly Newspapers published in London on Saturdays and Sundays. . . . The most violent of the Opposition Press stands higher in 1819 than in 1820. . . . The *Champion*, which in 1819 consumed 64,100 of stamps, in 1820 takes only 36,934. *Cobbett's Register* disappears from the list; *Duckett's Dispatch* drops from a duty of £300 to £2 5s. 6d.; the *Englishman* decreases from 199,525 to 173,800; the *Examiner* differs from 205,000 to 194,500; the *Independent Whig* from 50,405 to 4,694; and *Wooler's Gazette* from 101,415 in 1819 to 77,850 in the following year' (*Ann. Reg.*, 1820, Antiquities, etc., pp. 720–1).

[4] Ibid., App. to Chron., pp. 958 sqq.

[5] Ibid., Chron., August 16.

[6] Ibid., August 16.

received the applause of the crowd. Lord John Russell, more clear-sighted than his father, the Duke of Bedford, considered that 'the Queen's business' had 'done a great deal of good in renewing the old and natural alliance between the Whigs and the people and weakening the influence of the Radicals with the latter'.[1]

8

When Parliament reassembled in January 1821 the question whether the abandonment of the prosecution did not involve the restoration of the Queen's name to the Prayer Book was raised by numerous petitions and formed the subject of three debates in the Commons. On the first occasion the Government carried the day by 310 votes to 209, on the second by 324 to 178, on the third by 298 to 178, in spite of a speech by Wilberforce in the Queen's favour. Then the Queen, who in November had given a solemn pledge that she would refuse every offer of money so long as her name was not mentioned in the services of the Church, yielded and accepted an annuity of £50,000 voted by both Houses. So far as Parliament was concerned the affair of the Queen was concluded; and that public opinion also regarded it as settled was evident in July, when, after the long delay, the gorgeous ceremony of the coronation took place at last. In vain the Queen drove to Westminster Abbey and demanded her rightful place by the King's side. She was sent from door to door, and finally turned back amid an indifferent crowd, from which she received very few cheers and many hoots.

In August, to the King's great relief, she died, carried off by a rapid illness, and her funeral was the occasion of a final riot. It had been arranged that the funeral train, on leaving Hammersmith, should skirt the capital by the northern suburbs on its way to Harwich, where the body was to be embarked for Germany. But the plan did not succeed in preventing the seditious demonstrations which were feared. The crowd compelled the procession to change its route. It was in vain that in Hyde Park the cavalry escorting the funeral drew their swords, and the infantry fired their rifles, causing two deaths and many wounds. The triumph of the Londoners over the Court was crowned by the passage of

[1] Tom Moore's Diary, November 24, 1820 (*Memoirs of Thomas Moore*, vol. iii, p. 172).

the hearse throughout the entire City. This, however, was the final scene. When on September 1 Croker returned from Ireland, where George IV, whom he had accompanied, had been received with applause, he found the capital 'more quiet, *in fact*, than it looks in *the newspapers*'.[1] 'The tranquillity which obtains in London and generally throughout England,' wrote, in October, M. de Caraman, the French Chargé d'Affaires, 'allows us to count the present time among the fortunate periods which have no history and are therefore all the more precious to humanity.'[2] England had recovered its mental balance. The Wesleyan body, which for the first time in its history had suffered a setback in 1820, losing nearly five thousand of its adherents in Great Britain,[3] more than recovered its losses in 1821.[4] Popular enthusiasm had returned to its traditional form, religious not revolutionary. Lancashire, Cumberland, and Cornwall were the theatre of successful revivals.[5] In Cornwall in 1823 there were two thousand conversions in a single fortnight.[6]

What was the reason of this calm after the agitations of 1819 and 1820? It was evidently due to the recovery of trade. The economic had given place to a political crisis, and the noisy farce of 1820 had but masked the failure of the political agitation when the industrial depression had passed away. Already in May a Member of Parliament, a Glasgow manufacturer named Kirkman Finlay, had the pleasure of calling attention to the flourishing condition of trade and manufacture, the rise in wages, and the spectacle of the workers 'coming back by degrees from that delusion and infatuation into which their own folly had plunged them, and which, had they persevered in it, must have worked their destruction'.[7] The crisis had been the consequence of over-production, and the day was bound to come when supply and demand would correspond once more. It had now arrived and its arrival had been hastened by the opening of new markets. Except among the iron foundries and at Birmingham, where the crisis began at

---

[1] *Croker Papers*, vol. i. p. 208.

[2] Caraman to Pasquier, October 2, 1821 (Comte d'Antioche, *Chateaubriand, Ambassadeur à Londres*, p. 189).

[3] *Minutes of Methodist Conferences*, vol. v, p. 126: '191,217 members in Great Britain —that is to say, 4,688 less than in the previous year.'

[4] Ibid., vol. v, p. 230: '200,354 members. Gain: 9,137.'

[5] G. Smith, *History of Wesleyan Methodism*, vol. iii, pp. 65, 72–3.

[6] A Stevens, *History of Methodism*, vol. iii, pp. 225–6.

[7] H. of C., May 16, 1820 (*Parl. Deb.*, N.S., vol. i, p. 428).

the very moment that it came to an end elsewhere,[1] there was no more unemployment, and the workers found themselves secure from starvation. All prices dropped except the price of labour, and the revenue from taxation in 1820 and 1821 exceeded the estimates of the budget. The official statistics show a parallel rise in the value of exports. From £42,702,000 for 1818, it had fallen in 1819 to £33,534,000. It rose in 1820 to £38,394,000, in 1821 to £40,832,000, in 1822 to £44,243,000. Was England heading for another crisis such as had followed the boom of 1818? Men were glad to reject the gloomy foreboding and place their faith in the economists, who considered the crises of 1817 and 1819 temporary phenomena due to the transition from a state of war to a state of peace, and believed that after five years of peace the worst difficulties had been surmounted. Thus the farther the year 1815 is left behind, the greater the danger of revolution becomes on the Continent, where it is due to ideal factors, the less it becomes in England, where its causes are of the material order. We must not, however, conclude that this decline of revolutionary Radicalism had any tendency to strengthen the Cabinet. On the contrary, it might be said to have lost its *raison d'être*. And since the Ministers were unpopular with the lower classes since 1817 and 1819, discredited by their repeated changes of front and final retreat in 1820, and moreover at variance with the Court, the Whigs, inspired with a double measure of joy and hope, pressed their attacks vigorously home. The problem before the Cabinet was to discover the best tactics with which to repel their assaults.

II THE POLICY OF REFORM

I

On June 28, 1820, during an interval in the Queen's trial, Brougham brought before Parliament an entire scheme of primary education. The system which he desired to erect rested in part on the Justices of the Peace. They were to be empowered to order at Quarter Sessions, on the request of two of their body or of a certain number of householders, that a school should be

---

[1] *Ann. Reg.*, 1821, p. 69. Tooke, *History of Prices*, vol. ii, p. 78 n. H. of C., February 8, 1821, 'Trade of Birmingham: Petition of the Merchants' (*Parl. Deb.*, N.S., vol. iv, pp. 523 sqq.).

opened in a particular parish. The cost of purchasing the land and building the school would be borne by the State; Brougham estimated that its total amount would not exceed £850,000 for the whole of England. The education given in these schools would not be free: the children would be charged a minimum fee of 2d., a maximum of 4d. a week. But these charges would not meet the cost of upkeep and the magistrates would be authorized to add a school rate to the rates already chargeable. The other pillar of Brougham's system was the clergy of the Establishment. No one could be admitted as a candidate for the position of schoolmaster who was not a churchman and moreover provided with a recommendation by a clergyman. He must then be elected by the body of ratepayers, but his election would not be valid until it had been confirmed by the parson of the parish. The latter would enjoy a permanent right to inspect the school, a right also given to the bishop, who moreover would have power to dismiss the schoolmaster. The instruction was to be religious but not dogmatic. The last provision aroused the distrust of the Anglican clergy, to whom it was inconceivable that there could be any effective religious instruction which was not dogmatic. At the same time the Dissenters were in arms against Brougham's proposals, which, they considered, gave the Anglicans a monopoly of primary education to the detriment of Nonconformity. The project was never even discussed. The Queen's trial absorbed the attention of the public, and demanded every moment of Brougham's time. It is doubtful whether Brougham introduced the motion with any other intention than to deliver a sensational speech. Nevertheless, the plan of a system of primary education established by the State for the benefit of poor children had been brought for the first time before Parliament, and moreover, in its most comprehensive form.[1]

Mackintosh, continuing the work of Romilly, pressed for the mitigation of the Penal Code. In fact, his first successful attempts in this direction dated from 1819. It was in that year that he had obtained from the Commons the appointment of a committee 'to consider of so much of the criminal laws as relates to Capital

[1] H. of C., June 28, 1820 (*Parl. Deb.*, N.S., vol. ii, pp. 49 sqq.). See in the *Edinburgh Review* for August, 1820, 'The New Plan of Education for England' (vol. xxxiv, pp. 214 sqq.), a defence of Brougham's scheme against Nonconformist criticism; also, for the protest of the Dissenters, the *Eclectic Review*, March 1821, 'Observations on Mr. Brougham's Bill' (vol. xv, pp. 193 sqq.).

Punishment in Felonies'.[1] When in 1820 the committee presented its first report Mackintosh sought to give effect to its recommendations by introducing into the Commons six Bills, three of which were finally accepted by the Lords.[2] The first of the three repealed the statute which punished with death every theft from a shop the value of which exceeded five shillings.[3] The second repealed a number of obsolete statutes which made capital a number of purely technical offences.[4] The third substituted deportation for the death penalty in the case of certain grave crimes.[5] The Chancellor, Lord Eldon, who had opposed an obstinate resistance to the Bills introduced by Romilly, now showed for the first time symptoms of weariness, and gave way on several points. In 1821 Mackintosh was not so successful. The three Bills thrown out in 1820 again failed to pass either the Lords or the Commons.[6] The current of opinion in Parliament, hitherto favourable, was apparently checked for a time by the arguments with which, in 1819, Lord Castlereagh and Lord Sidmouth had opposed the reform of the Penal Code.[7] Before reducing the number of 'capital felonies', they had urged, Parliament would do well to review the entire system of 'secondary penalties' and devise some punishment other than the death penalty which would have a deterrent effect upon the criminal. Deportation to Australia had lost all its terrors. To be deported was simply to emigrate at the expense of the Government to a better climate, and emigration was becoming increasingly popular with the working class.

When Peel returned to the Cabinet as Home Secretary just before the session of 1822 opened, he showed that he regarded the arguments put forward by Lord Castlereagh and Lord Sidmouth as serious objections, not mere excuses for delay. He tried the experiment of deporting a number of criminals to Bermuda instead of to Australia, to be employed there on public works of urgent necessity.[8] He announced his intention to proceed im-

[1] H. of C., March 2, 1819 (*Parl. Deb.*, vol. xxxix, pp. 777 sqq.).
[2] H. of C., May 9, 1820 (ibid., N.S., vol. i, pp. 227 sqq.).
[3] 1 Geo. IV, cap. 117.   [4] 1 Geo. IV, cap. 116.
[5] 1 Geo. IV, cap. 115.
[6] An Act was, however, passed abolishing the death penalty in Ireland for certain cases of fraudulent bankruptcy (1 and 2 Geo. IV, cap. 40).
[7] H. of L.,February 25, 1819, Lord Sidmouth's speech (*Parl. Deb.*, vol. xxxix, pp. 615 sqq.). H. of C., March 1, 1819, Lord Castlereagh's speech (ibid., vol. xxxix, pp. 740 sqq.).
[8] H. of C., June 4, 1822 (ibid., N.S., vol. vii, pp. 803–4); S. and B. Webb, *English Local Government*, vol. vi, 'English Prisons under Local Government', p. 45 n.

mediately with the reform of the prison system, which had been prepared by the labours of three parliamentary committees.[1] To secure the certain punishment and, if possible, the prevention, of crime he proposed to supply England, and London first of all, with the police force still entirely wanting. In accents of evident sincerity he explained that in proposing the establishment of such a force he harboured no secret design to provide political reaction with a weapon.[2] Moreover, he promised that if in 1823 Mackintosh introduced Bills with the object of reducing the number of capital felonies he would not refuse them his sympathetic consideration. Mackintosh, however, was not satisfied with these promises, however encouraging they might be. He obtained from the Commons a formal engagement, passed by 117 votes to 101, 'at an early period of the next session of Parliament to take into their most serious consideration the means of increasing the efficacy of the criminal laws, by abating their undue rigour'.[3]

2

But then as always economic problems were the questions which held the interest of Parliament and public; and no sooner had trade recovered than the perpetual conflict of interests which divided the manufacturer and the agriculturalist reappeared in an exceptionally acute form. If after 1820 the condition of the worker was more tolerable than it had been for years previously, this was due in part to the sudden and rapid fall in the cost of foodstuffs. The price of wheat, which in January 1819 had exceeded 80s. the quarter, had slowly given way as the year proceeded. In December it stood at 65s. 10d., had fallen to 63s. 2d.

---

[1] H. of C., June 4, 1822 (*Parl. Deb.*, N.S., vol. vii, pp. 803–4). See 'Report from the Select Committee appointed to consider the expediency of erecting a Penitentiary House or Penitentiary Houses under Acts 34 and 19, Geo. III . . . and who were instructed to inquire into the effects which have been produced by the Punishment of Transportation to New South Wales, and of Imprisonment on board the Hulks', 1810–11. Second Report, 1810–11. Third Report, 1812.

[2] Ibid.: 'God forbid that he should mean to countenance a system of espionage, but a vigorous preventive police, consistent with the free principles of our free Constitution, was an object which he did not despair of seeing accomplished' (*Parl. Deb.*, N.S., vol. vii, p. 803). Cf. H. of C., March 14, 1822: It was his intention to obtain for the capital 'as perfect a system of police as was consistent with the character of our free country' (ibid., N.S., vol. vi, p. 1166).

[3] H. of C., June 4, 1822 (ibid., N.S., vol. vii, pp. 790 sqq.). It should be added that in the course of the session a Bill was passed which had been introduced by an advanced Whig to render the Criminal Code more complete, providing penalties for certain offences hitherto overlooked.

by the middle of January 1820, and rose again in April until it almost reached 74s. Then the crash began. In December the price of wheat was 54s. the quarter, and in the opening months of 1821 it fell below that figure, in May and July it was under 52s., and in December it was 46s. 2d. In January 1822 the price of wheat was under 46s., on June 22 it was 43s. 10d. On June 29 and July 6 it was 42s. 6d. Once more the labourer's prosperity was the ruin of the farmer and the landlord. The landowners, however, were the class which had long been accustomed to regard its economic and political supremacy as indispensable to the welfare of the nation, and for the past three years had been engaged in organizing a powerful body, called the Agricultural Association, for the defence of its interests. A certain George Webb Hall made use of the Association to start throughout the country districts a formidable agitation, conducted by the traditional methods of county meetings and petitions; and as the price of wheat fell it grew noisier.[1] What, then, were the demands put forward by the discontented country gentlemen? First and foremost that the burden of taxation should be lightened. In apportioning the amount taken by the State, the manufacturer and the bond-holder, so they maintained, were favoured at their expense; all, indeed, were overtaxed, but all were not equally overtaxed. In 1820 one speaker in Parliament attempted to show that a third part of the expenditure of the average Englishman was absorbed by taxation, whereas the landlord was taxed to the amount of eight-fifteenths, or over half his income.[2] If the speaker used the word 'taxes' in the strict sense, his estimate will not bear scrutiny, but if he included under this denomination every kind of public burden it may quite well have been correct. For the tithe which supported the clergy of the Establishment was levied exclusively on landed property. Hence, to the delight of the Radicals, the country gentlemen, for all their attachment to the Church, now began to raise the question of the tithe. The cost of the Poor Law also fell most heavily on land, although the manufacturers, by

[1] *The Times*, November 8, 1819. H. of C., May 30, 1820, speeches of Robinson and Baring (*Parl. Deb.*, N.S., vol. i, pp. 612, 659). *Pol. Reg.*, December 15, 1821 (vol. xl, pp. 1409 sqq.); December 4, 1824 (vol. lii, p. 589). The text of the petition will be found in a pamphlet entitled *Observations on the Report of the Select Committee of the House of Commons*, to whom the several petitions complaining of the depressed state of the agriculture of the United Kingdom were referred in the session of 1821, by George Webb Hall, Chairman of the General Committee of Management for the Petitioners, 1821.

[2] H. of L., May 16, 1820, Lord Stanhope's speech (*Parl. Deb.*, N.S., vol. i, p. 405).

creating a proletariat of factory labour, were responsible for the enormous increase of pauperism. Curwen therefore brought up again his proposal to replace the existing poor rate by a general rate to be levied on every species of income whether derived from real or personal estate.[1] Moreover, at every debate upon the budget the country gentlemen were loud in their demands for a reduction of taxes, especially those directly levied upon agriculture, the malt tax, and the tax on horses used for agricultural purposes. In vain did the Cabinet point out the folly of these proposals. To abolish any tax which happened to be objectionable to a certain number of taxpayers was simply to distract public attention from the really grave financial problem of the National Debt. Peace, it was true, had lasted for five years; but nobody believed that it could last much longer, since the outbreak of revolution on the Continent seemed to presage a new series of wars.[2] How then could England meet the cost of a war, when it came, if the country were already saddled with a debt of over eight hundred millions? To which their critics replied that without touching the Sinking Fund civil and military expenditure could be reduced to the figure, according to some of the speakers, of four million.[3] Towards the close of 1819 their terror of revolution had driven the gentry to vote in haste an increase of the standing army, now in 1820 their fear of imminent financial ruin drove them to demand drastic cuts in the military and naval expenditure.

But the reduction of taxation, as Ricardo pointed out, did not reach the source of the evil. For it could not prevent the fall in the price of corn, and if the sole causes of this fall were the exceptional harvest of 1820, whose yield exceeded the average by a third, and the importation of Irish corn, a novel phenomenon of rapid growth, non-existent in 1818, in 1821 exceeding a million

[1] H. of C., May 30, 1820, Curwen's speech (*Parl. Deb.*, N.S., vol. i, p. 670).

[2] H. of C., July 2, 1821, Lord Grosvenor's speech: 'We were now in the seventh year of peace; and, allowing for the common chances of war, we might not be further than as many more from renewed hostilities' (ibid., N.S., vol. v, p. 1471). *The Times*, November 19, 1821: ' With 875 millions st(erling) of debt, bearing an interest between 30 and 40 millions per annum, it would be ridiculous to take pains about proving the necessity of retrenchment. That debt or interest, at the present amount of the Sinking Fund, would receive no very sensible diminution within less than twenty years. Yet who can promise us a general peace of half or one quarter of twenty years, and, taxed as we now are even beyond what we can bear, by what miracle can the means of encountering an enemy be provided?'

[3] H. of C., June 27, 1821, Joseph Hume's speech (*Parl. Deb.*, N.S., vol. v, p. 1351).

quarters,[1] it was evident that no legislation could provide a remedy. Nevertheless, the agriculturalists persisted in their belief that it was in the power of the legislator to raise the price of corn —a feat which could be accomplished, according to them, by one of two methods.

The price of corn might be raised directly by the imposition of new duties. It is certainly hard to understand how the agricultural community could still continue in 1821 to expect a cure for their sufferings from a revision of the tariffs; for the Act of 1815 had set up a double system for the control of imported cereals. Importation was absolutely forbidden when prices fell below a certain figure (80s. a quarter for wheat);[2] it was permitted free of duty whenever this level was exceeded. It was therefore under a system of absolute prohibition that the corn grower in 1820 witnessed the fall of prices. But this fact did not save the Act of 1815 from the agriculturalists' criticism. They maintained that the sudden change from absolute prohibition to absolute freedom of importation encouraged speculation and caused artificial fluctuations in the price of wheat when it approached 80s. They therefore demanded the establishment of a sliding scale by which wheat might be imported below the price of 80s. on payment of a heavy duty, and might not be admitted, even above that price, except on payment of a duty, though a lighter one. And at the same time they called for measures more immediately effective. They asked for an increase of the duty on oats.[3] They criticized the official prices, which were based, according to them, on a faulty system of calculation, were in excess of the real prices, and therefore, in spite of their low figure, gave too favourable a picture of the economic situation. They objected to the right permanently enjoyed by the foreign grower, whatever the price of corn might be, if not to sell his corn in England, at least to store it in British warehouses; for, they explained, the presence of this wheat in bond had an unfavourable effect on prices. They even insinuated that possibly some of it found its way onto the market. They also asked that the State should advance them loans

[1] Tooke, op. cit., vol. ii, pp. 82–4.
[2] The Corn Law of 1815, like all the later statutes of the kind, fixed a different price for each of the six cereals: corn, oats, barley, rye, peas, and beans. To simplify our narrative here, and wherever throughout these volumes we shall speak of the Corn Laws, we shall only take into account the standard fixed for wheat; for it was upon the price of wheat that the controversy hinged.
[3] H. of C., March 7, 1821, Sir E. Knatchbull's speech (*Parl. Deb.*, N.S., vol. iv, p. 1144).

on the security of corn deposited in government warehouses. Later, when the period of surplus production and low prices had passed, their corn would be returned on payment to the State of the capital and interest of the loan. They asked, further, that to relieve the glut in the home market a bounty should be given for the export of cereals.

Moreover, Parliament could employ another more indirect method to effect a rise in the price of cereals, indeed of prices generally, namely, a depreciation of the currency. The Bank of England had not availed itself of the two years' postponement granted by the Act of 1819, but had restored without restriction specie payment in May 1821.[1] Opponents of the artificial currency had always claimed that its result had been the depreciation of the bank-note. Accordingly they expected that the return to specie payment would result in a restriction of the currency. When, therefore, the return of gold coins to circulation was accompanied by a general fall of prices, of manufactured articles as well as of cereals, it seemed reasonable to ascribe the fall to a diminution in the amount of currency (whether notes or coin). The country gentlemen were attracted by Attwood's theory, and urged that the Bank should take steps to effect an inflation of the paper currency, to continue until corn rose once more to 80s. And they found another scheme submitted just then to the House of Lords by Lord Stanhope equally attractive. That nobleman proposed what he called 'the equitable adjustment of all debts'. According to him, every debt contracted under the system of artificial currency, beginning with the National Debt, ought to be reduced in exact proportion to the increase in the value of money since it had been contracted.[2] The more moderate critics did not ask for the repeal of the Act of 1819, but were content to propose that one of its clauses should be amended so as to permit the country banks to continue after 1823 the issue of notes for sums not exceeding five pounds. Baring, moreover, though he did not himself belong to the class of country gentlemen, brought forward a proposal which seemed calculated to afford them a partial satisfaction. He objected to the abandonment by the Government

[1] 1 and 2 Geo. IV, cap. 26, 27.
[2] H. of L., February 21, 1822 (*Parl. Deb.*, N.S., vol. vi, pp. 555–6). Ellice claimed to be the originator of the proposal (H. of C., April 3, 1822, ibid., vol. vi, pp. 1439 sqq.). Cf. H. of C., February 5, May 7, 1822, Sir Francis Burdett's speech (ibid., vol. vi, pp. 28–9, 407 sqq.).

of the old double standard in favour of a gold standard: according to him bimetallism would have placed the currency on a broader basis.[1]

3

Such were the claims, muddleheaded but none the less insistent, made by the agriculturalists. They did not constitute a strictly defined parliamentary group. They were simply a very large body of members, which not only comprised the entire representation of the counties, but even included many representatives of the boroughs. Nor can we identify them with either of the two historic parties. Equally with the Tory the Whig aristocracy was an aristocracy of great landowners, and there was a Whig, as well as a Tory, gentry. The camp of the country gentlemen, nicknamed by their opponents the 'Jolterheads', contained not only Tories, such as Sir Edward Knatchbull and Sir Thomas Lethbridge, but Whigs, such as Coke and Western. Indeed, if we regard more closely the leaders of both parties, we may possibly conclude that in 1820 the Whig leaders were more favourable than the Tory to the claims of the agriculturalists. Lord Liverpool in the Lords frankly expressed his opinion that legislation was powerless to remedy the evils of which the agriculturalists complained,[2] and that, though the landlord and farmer might suffer, the low price of foodstuffs was a boon to the working class.[3] In the Commons Lord Castlereagh spoke in the same sense,[4] and, turning towards Ricardo, asked him if he would kindly give the country gentlemen the instruction in political economy of which they stood so sorely in need.[5] Outside the Cabinet Huskisson employed all his energy to refute in speech after speech the agriculturalists' arguments,[6] and Peel, who had been the object of their unremitting attack since the passage of the Act of 1819 which bore his name, returned to the Cabinet towards the end of

[1] H of C., March 19, 20, 1821 (*Parl. Deb.*, N.S., vol. iv, pp. 1327–8, pp. 1516–17).
[2] H. of L., May 16, 1820 (ibid., vol. i, pp. 417 sqq.). Cf. the same date (ibid., p. 394): 'In political economy far more danger was to be apprehended from doing too much than from not interfering at all.'
[3] H. of L., July 2, 1821 (ibid., vol. v, p. 1469). For a full exposition of Lord Liverpool's views on economics see his important speech of Feb. 26, 1822 (ibid., vol. vi, pp. 682 sqq.).
[4] H. of C., May 31, 1820 (ibid., vol. i, p. 729); February 5, 1821 (ibid., vol. vi, p. 361).
[5] H. of C., April 3, 1822 (ibid., vol. vi, p. 1453). Lord Castlereagh quoted Ricardo again during the same sitting (ibid., p. 1457).
[6] See especially H. of C., February 15, 1822 (ibid., pp. 417 sqq.).

December 1821. On the other hand, there were several members of the Whig Opposition who, like Lord Grey, were convinced advocates of a thoroughgoing system of Protection in the farmer's interest. Throughout these two or three sessions Brougham took care that all his actions and speeches were such as to procure him the good will of the country gentlemen.[1] But perhaps the most significant proof of this attitude among the Whigs is a letter which Lord John Russell, the model of Whig orthodoxy, addressed in January 1822 to his constituents, the gentry and farmers of Huntingdonshire. After an opening passage of pleasantries which seemed to imply that the writer accepted the thesis of equitable adjustment, he proceeded to denounce the party which in the name of the so-called science of political economy 'aimed at substituting the cereals of Poland and Russia for English cereals', and refused to see 'the difference between an agricultural and a manufacturing population in everything that concerned the morals, discipline, energy, and tranquillity of the nation'. It is true he advised the agriculturalists not to demand the amendment of the Act of 1815; but only from motives of prudence, to escape falling into a trap—for they were far from sure that any new statute they might obtain would be in conformity with their wishes. The Cabinet was at the mercy of every breeze of public opinion, and appeared to be in collusion with the political economists. 'Political economy is now the fashion: and the farmers of England are likely, if they do not keep a good look-out, to be the victims.'[2]

4

The struggle lasted three sessions. Three times the agriculturalists demanded the appointment of a committee to investigate the causes of their distress and recommend the measures so urgently necessary for their relief. Each time they obtained the committee for which they asked; but the first year the Cabinet succeeded in

[1] H. of C., May 30, 1820 (Parl. Deb., N.S., vol. i, p. 683); July 3, 1821 (ibid., vol. v, pp. 1503–4); May 8, 1822 (ibid., vol. vii, pp. 449 sqq.). Cf. Ann. Reg., 1822, p. 98.
[2] The Times, January 18, 1822. For Ricardo's bitter comments upon this stupid manifesto see his letter to Trower, January 25, 1822. Sub finem, also on Protection to Agriculture, Section IX (Works, p. 489). For the attitude of the Whig Party in general, and of Lord John Russell in particular, see the debates, H. of C., June 14, 1822 (Parl. Deb., N.S., vol. vii, p. 1078 sqq., especially pp. 1081–2, for the passage of arms between Lord Castlereagh and Lord John Russell).

confining the scope of the inquiry within narrow limits. The committee was merely to investigate the method by which the official prices were fixed. The second year the composition of the committee was such as to defeat the agriculturalists' hopes. Huskisson and Ricardo were members—it was on this committee that they became personally acquainted; and it was Huskisson who drew up the report. It was not until the appointment of the third committee in 1822 that the Government realized the necessity of doing something to satisfy the country gentlemen.[1] When we consider the results secured by their efforts, extending over three years, it is easy to understand why their campaign was more successful on some occasions, less successful on others.

The financial dispute between the supporters and opponents of 'Peel's Bill' presented a paradoxical aspect to those who remembered the earlier struggle of war-time. Then the supporters of an artificial currency were prepared even to fly in the face of facts and deny that the bank-note had depreciated; and the bullionists, on the other hand, had demanded a return to specie payment in order, by restricting the currency, to raise the pound note to the level of the gold sovereign. Now it was the advocates of an artificial currency who attributed the fall of prices to the restricted circulation of paper money, consequent upon the return to specie payment, and who therefore turned their old arguments against the bullionists, and called for a return to the artificial currency in order to raise prices. The bullionists replied by denying that the operation of the Act of 1819 had to any considerable extent restricted the circulation of paper money: Ricardo called attention to the fact that even in 1819 the value of the pound note was not more than 5 per cent below the value of the gold sovereign.[2] Indeed, the new law could not have been enforced so easily, had it not merely sanctioned a return to normal conditions, which was already taking place before the Act was passed. It was, moreover, quite possible that Thomas Tooke was right, and that by 1822

[1] For the conditions under which the three committees of 1820, 1821, and 1822 were appointed, did their work, and reported, see the excellent account by Spencer Walpole, *History of England*, vol. ii, pp. 102 sqq. For the work of the committee of 1821 and the friendship formed during its labours between Huskisson and Ricardo, see Ricardo, letters to Trower, April 21, July 4, August 22, 1821; to MacCulloch, March 23, April 25, June 18, July 6, 1821. The report of this committee is the work of Huskisson. For the work of the second committee see, further, *Quarterly Review*, July 1821, 'Report . . . on the State of Agriculture' (vol. xxv, pp. 466 sqq.).

[2] 'On Protection to Agriculture', 1822 (*Works*, p. 467); H. of C., June 11, 1823 (*Parl. Deb.*, N.S., vol. ix, p. 851).

the currency, far from being restricted, had actually increased.[1] Under these conditions to go back on Peel's Bill was out of the question. Nevertheless in 1822 a concession was made to the advocates of inflation. An Act was passed continuing until 1833 the licence given to the provincial banks to issue notes of a low denomination.[2]

The question of the Corn Law had also assumed at this juncture a paradoxical aspect. We should have been surprised to find the Free Traders choosing this particular moment to demand a modification of the Act of 1815; for in spite of the statute which sought to fix at 80s. the normal price of corn, the actual price had fallen to a level of about 42s., and it was the agriculturalists who complained. We are, however, far more surprised to see the agriculturalists themselves calling for a reinforcement of the Act of 1815; for the Act prohibited the importation of foreign cereals, at the prices then obtaining—and what more rigorous protection could the farmers desire? But we have just seen what their grievance was. Finally the Cabinet and House of Commons agreed to repeal the Act of 1815, which when the price of wheat was in the neighbourhood of 80s. admitted no graduated transition between absolute prohibition of importation and Free Trade.

The proposal to impose a fixed duty on imported corn, either immediately or at a future date, at once or by degrees, was brought forward by several members: some, Protectionists, who desired an almost prohibitive tariff—others, Free Traders, who wished to restrict the duty to the amount required to balance the excessive imposts upon British agriculture. Ricardo proposed that the tariff should be fixed at the small sum of 10s.[3] Finally, however, in conformity with the recommendations of the committee and the provisions of the Bill introduced by the Government, the principle of a sliding scale was accepted. The new statute enacted that when the price of wheat in the home market exceeded 70s. a duty of 12s. should be levied on imported corn. Above 80s. the duty would be 5s. And it would be reduced to the merely

[1] *History of Prices*, vol. ii, pp. 95 sqq.

[2] 2 and 3 Geo. IV, cap. 70. The Government attempted on this occasion to strike a bargain with the Bank of England that, in return for a prolongation of its monopoly, it should permit the establishment of joint-stock banks in the provinces; but the negotiations broke down. See H. of C., April 29, 1822, Lord Castlereagh's speech (*Parl. Deb.*, N.S., vol. vii, pp. 160–2; H. D. Macleod, *Theory and Practice of Banking*, vol. ii, pp. 228–9).

[3] 'On Protection to Agriculture', 1822 (*Works*, p. 480).

nominal figure of 1s. when the price in the home market exceeded 85s.[1] What did the measure amount to? Did the permission to import corn when the price was 70s. instead of 80s. constitute a victory for Free Trade?—or did the tariff imposed render the concession nugatory? And did the substance of the new statute consist in the provision which raised to 85s. the price at which importation became practically free? Whatever the answer to these questions, it would not be discovered until many years had elapsed; for it was laid down in the opening words of the Act that it was not to come into force until the price of wheat had once more reached the figure of 80s. envisaged by the Act of 1815. The Cabinet had, in fact, given a purely formal satisfaction to the country gentlemen, which they had the sense to accept. The Bill was passed in July amid a universal indifference, which contrasts strangely with the heated debates upon the agrarian question during the early weeks of the session.[2]

5

In the matter of inflation and agricultural protection the country gentlemen had obtained very slight satisfaction. When, on the other hand, it was a question of reform in the public finances, of lightening the burden of taxation and cutting down expenditure, their attack was irresistible. A reduction of the Civil List and general retrenchment were items which had figured on the programme of every Opposition candidate at the election of 1820;[3] and what programme could possess more attraction for the public? Joseph Hume, a friend of Bentham and James Mill, who made a speciality of picking the budget to pieces every year, clause by clause, became the most popular figure in Parliament, as the result of an important speech which he delivered in the House of Commons in 1821, in which he subjected every item of the

[1] 2 and 3 Geo. IV, cap. 60.

[2] *The Times*, July 11, 1822: 'The Corn Bill was read a third time yesterday in the House of Lords. We mention this merely for the curiosity of the thing—that an expedient which a few months back was regarded with so much silly confidence in one class of men, and which gave rise to such superfluous apprehensions in every other, should now be almost universally forgotten while yet on its road through Parliament. For our part, we rejoice that the Bill is what it is—that the principles and intentions are so completely defeated by its practical insignificance,' etc. etc.

[3] See the electioneering pamphlet then published by Creevey, *A Guide to the Electors of Great Britain upon the Accession of a New King, and the Immediate Prospect of a New Parliament*, 1820.

military and civil expenditure to close scrutiny, and demanded that it should be reduced to the figure of 1792, the last year of peace.[1] Joseph Hume was a member of the tiny group known at Westminster as the 'Mountain'. On this occasion he had the support of the country gentlemen. There was no longer a stable majority in the House. The Ministry was either actually defeated or only averted defeat by a bare majority. But it preferred submission to resignation.

Hume in 1821 obtained the appointment of a committee to discover more economical methods of collecting the taxes;[2] and the Treasury decided to reduce, as far as possible, all salaries to the level of 1797.[3] In 1822 the entire system of retiring pensions was revised. In future they would be provided without cost to the taxpayer out of a fund to be obtained by deductions from the salaries paid to officials in active service.[4] The Civil Service Estimates were reduced from £2,100,000 in the budget of 1820 to £1,900,000 in the budget of 1821 and £1,700,000 in the budget of 1822. The Estimates for the Army and Navy were proportionately reduced. The Army Estimates, which had reached in 1820 a maximum of £9,422,000, fell to £8,750,000 in 1821 and £7,925,000 in 1822. The Naval Estimates, which had also attained in 1820 the maximum figure of £6,586,000, fell to £6,177,000 in 1821 and £5,480,000 in 1822.[5] Public expenditure was reduced. The economic situation improved. In 1821 the revenue from taxation exceeded the estimated amount. The value of the funds rose uninterruptedly, and since in October the 5 per cents exceeded 110, the Government was able at the opening of 1822 to convert them into 4 per cents, which represented an annual saving to the Treasury of £1,230,000. But the problem of the National Debt was as far as ever from solution.

On the one hand, for every economy effected, and for every

---

[1] H. of C., June 27, 1821 (*Parl. Deb.*, N.S., vol. v, pp. 134–5 sqq.).

[2] H. of C., March 23, 1821 (ibid., vol. iv, pp. 1401 sqq.). Hume had already, on July 4, 1820, attempted in vain to secure this inquiry (ibid., vol. ii, pp. 476 sqq.).

[3] H. of C., February 12, 1830, Dawson's speech (ibid., vol. xxii, pp. 452, 453).

[4] 2 and 3 Geo. IV, cap. 11 B, amending 50 Geo. III, cap. 117. H. of C., March 11, 1822, Vansittart's speech (ibid., vol. vi, pp. 1015 sqq.).

[5] These figures represent the expenditure estimated in the budget. The actual expenditure was as follows: 1819, Army, £9,451,000; Navy, £6,396,000; Artillery, £1,538,000: Total, £17,385,000 (the maximum). 1820, Army, £8,926,000; Navy, £6,388,000; Artillery, £4,402,000: Total, £19,716,000. 1821, Army, £8,933,000; Navy, £5,944,000; Artillery, £1,338,000: Total, £16,215,000. 1822, Army, £7,699,000; Navy, £5,194,000; Artillery £1,008,000: Total, £13,901,000 (*An Account of the Public Expenditure of the United Kingdom for the Year . . .*).

increase of revenue, Parliament demanded a corresponding reduction of taxes. Western was within an ace of obtaining in 1821 the abolition of the additional duties on malt, imposed in 1819, and Curwen with Brougham's assistance carried against the Government the abolition of the tax on horses used for agricultural purposes. In 1822 Vansittart judged it prudent to avoid a defeat by anticipating the demands of the country gentlemen. Not only did he abandon the duty on malt, a loss of £1,500,000; he also lowered the duty on salt from 15s. to 2s. the bushel, which meant that, unless consumption increased, the revenue it brought in would fall from £1,500,000 to a mere £200,000. He reduced by half the tax on leather, and abolished the duty levied on the vessels of the Merchant Service in proportion to their tonnage, the 'tonnage' duty, also the Irish window tax. The total revenue he abandoned in this budget of 1822 amounted to £3,500,000.

On the other hand, even if these taxes had not been abandoned, it would have been extremely difficult to carry out a policy of genuine redemption. From what source could the marvellous increase of revenue be expected which was required to supply the loss of about £15,000,000 when the income tax was abolished in 1816? The Chancellor of the Exchequer continued to struggle with the same difficulties and to have recourse to the same shifts. In 1820 the Government issued a loan of £5,000,000 bearing a nominal interest of 3 per cent, a real interest of about $4\frac{1}{2}$ per cent. In 1820 and 1821 £440,000 was raised by a lottery; and the Government still continued to patronize the method termed in their curious phraseology 'a loan from the Sinking Fund'—a method so complicated that already in 1819 it had been the object of sharp criticism by Members of Parliament. By these means the Treasury raised £12,000,000 in 1820, £13,000,000 in 1821, and £7,500,000 in 1822. Then Vansittart made a categorical statement of his intention to adopt new methods in the next session, and promised what he called 'a general revision of the Sinking Fund'.[1] By this phrase he obviously meant the restriction for the future of the sum devoted every year to the Sinking Fund out of the annual surplus—a surplus which since 1817 the Treasury had attempted to fix at the figure of £5,000,000 per annum.[2] He

[1] H. of C., July 1, 1822 (*Parl. Deb.*, N.S., vol. vii, p. 1417).

[2] See Vansittart's speech, H. of C., February 21, 1822 (ibid., vol. vi, pp. 606–7); February 26, 1822 (ibid., vol. vi, p. 864); also Ricardo's endorsement of his declarations, H. of C., July 1, 1822 (ibid., vol. vii, p. 1428). Some of his critics ascribed to Vansittart

had evidently taken Huskisson's advice, and was prepared to effect a reform demanded by the nation. But the nation could place little trust in his capacity to accomplish it. His budget of 1822 exasperated public opinion by its extraordinary complication. But his critics were mistaken when they denounced him as a financial Machiavelli and charged him with deliberately complicating his budget to conceal the rotten state of the national finances. His weakness was his bad conscience. Compelled by his colleagues to sacrifice the system of redemption introduced by William Pitt, he did clumsily what he did against the grain.

6

When they were defending Peel's Bill against the attack of the agricultural interest and struggling to prevent the country gentlemen from tightening the Corn Law of 1815, the political economists were on the defensive. In the campaign for retrenchment and a reduction of taxation agriculturalists and economists joined in a common offensive. But the economists had the courage to undertake, unaided by the agriculturalists, a further campaign against particular monopolies, and with the connivance of the Tory Cabinet their campaign was crowned with success. With the connivance did I say? This may well be an understatement. It could be maintained without much exaggeration that it was the Ministers who opened the attack. In December 1819, while the debates upon the Six Acts were still proceeding, a petition was laid upon the table of the House signed by eighty London merchants, asking Parliament to take into consideration the difficulties with which industry and trade had to contend and the best remedies to apply. The number of signatories was not large, and when a member categorically charged Lord Castlereagh with having engineered the petition in order to divert to economic questions public opinion dangerously excited over the question of parliamentary reform, the charge went unanswered.[1] The petition led to nothing; but Parliament was scarcely prorogued before Thomas Tooke, an economist and a friend of

the intention of altering the arrangements by which the Sinking Fund increased at compound interest (*Parl. Deb.*, N.S., vol. vi, pp. 680, 864–5), and, although he protested against this interpretation of his words, it remains true that Lord Liverpool had declared the matter an open question (H. of C., February 26, 1822, ibid., vol. vi, p. 713).

[1] See the debates, H. of C., December 24, 1819 (ibid., vol. xli, pp. 1569 sqq.).

Ricardo, acting in concert with Lord Liverpool,[1] took up the matter afresh and secured the signatures of a very large number of London merchants to a new petition, which Baring presented to the House of Commons on May 8, 1820.

The petition was couched in terms calculated to impress the imagination. It was confined to a plain statement of principle in fifteen articles. It maintained that 'the maxim of buying in the cheapest market and selling in the dearest, which regulates every merchant in his individual dealings, is strictly applicable as the best rule for the trade of the whole nation'; that 'a policy founded on these principles would render the commerce of the world an interchange of mutual advantages, and diffuse an increase of wealth and enjoyment among the inhabitants of each State', and that the most efficacious means by which Great Britain could make other nations abandon 'the protective or restrictive system' was to be the first to set the example of following the 'most liberal' policy.[2] Ricardo was delighted to see the English merchants adopt the doctrines of Adam Smith, though he deplored the fact that it had required more than half a century to convert them.[3] The truth was that British trade no longer needed the duties and regulations which had formerly proved so efficient a protection of its infancy. Manufacturers and merchants now found them an obstacle to their propaganda when they attempted to convert the English agriculturalist and the foreign manufacturer to Free Trade. They were met by the rejoinder, 'Why should we adopt Free Trade and not you?' ·Petitions were also presented from Birmingham, Glasgow, Manchester, and Liverpool.[4]

The Ministers replied with the utmost cordiality to the Members who presented or supported these petitions. Indeed, was it not they who in the first place had encouraged, possibly even invited, the entire agitation? Robinson, the President of the Board

---

[1] T. Tooke, op. cit., vol. vi, pp. 331 sqq. The Petition of the Merchants of London in 1820, in favour of Free Trade, with a statement of some circumstances connected with its origin and presentation. See especially pp. 338 and 340, also p. 342: 'It will be clear, I think, from the narrative which I have now given, that whatever effect or success might attend the Merchants' Petition of 1820 was due principally to the favour with which its doctrines were regarded by Lord Liverpool and a portion of his Cabinet. There was nothing connected with the preparation or presentation of the Petition which could be construed into pressure on the Government; and the simple truth is that the Government were at that time far more sincere and resolute Free Traders than the Merchants of London.'

[2] See the complete text of the petition, Ann. Reg., 1820, App. to Chron., pp. 770-3.

[3] H. of C., May 8, 1820 (Parl. Deb., N.S., vol. i, p. 191).

[4] H. of C., May 12, 19, October 17, 1820 (ibid., pp. 333, 424, 478, 748 sqq.).

of Trade, replying to Baring in the House of Commons,[1] and Lord Liverpool replying to Lord Lansdowne in the House of Lords,[2] declared themselves, with the necessary reservations, in favour of Free Trade: Robinson's language was particularly explicit.[3] Two committees of inquiry were appointed—one by the House of Lords in 1820, the other by the House of Commons in 1821. When the appointment of the second committee was moved in the Commons, it was Wallace, the Vice-President of the Board of Trade, who made the motion. He apologized for his action to Baring, who in the ordinary course should have been the mover. It had, he explained, been judged advisable that the motion should be made by a member of the Government; for the 'Ministers wished to prove to the House and the country that the consent which had been given, on the part of the Government, to the formation of a committee of this nature, was not a forced or reluctant consent'.[4]

Wallace and his colleagues were not slow to afford practical proofs of their intention to give the policy of the Board of Trade a liberal character. This opening stage of the struggle for Free Trade was carried on between the merchants and the shipowners. If it were intended to make England 'the great emporium and the great mart of the world'[5] the desire to attract the vessels of every nation to British ports might easily involve damage to the shipowners' immediate interests. A statute of 1810[6] had replied to the continental blockade by encouraging with a very heavy Preferential Tariff the import of Canadian timber as against timber from Norway and the Baltic. This measure of colonial protection profited the shipowners, inasmuch as the greater distance between Canada and Liverpool, as compared with the distance between Norway and Leith or Hull, put more money into their pockets;

[1] H. of C., May 8, 1820 (*Parl. Deb.*, N.S., vol. i, pp. 182 sqq.).
[2] H. of L., May 26, 1820 (ibid., pp. 565 sqq.).
[3] H. of C., May 8, 1820: 'The Hon. Member had done him the honour to pay him some compliments, to which he did not conceive himself entitled; but he must say neither did he conceive himself or his colleagues deserving of the qualification which was tacked to them, namely, that he and those with whom he had the honour of acting had a sort of pathetic feeling, and went on from year to year, looking more to their offices than to the interests of the people. He might have felt differently on this question, and he admitted that he did feel differently from some others with whom he acted, but on questions of this nature, and particularly on that of the transit duties, he met with more opposition from the other side than from his own side of the House' (ibid., vol. i, p. 183).
[4] H. of C., February 6, 1821 (ibid., vol. iv, p. 425).
[5] H. of C., July 18, 1820 (ibid., vol. ii, p. 457).
[6] 50 Geo. III, cap. 77.

and they were ready with arguments of a patriotic nature in favour of these long voyages—an excellent school, they pointed out, for sailors.[1] An Act of 1821, too timid to satisfy Ricardo and his friends, but sufficient to excite the shipowners' wrath, reduced the preference hitherto given to Canadian timber.[2] A simultaneous attack was made upon the venerable system of the Navigation Laws which since the seventeenth century had for a century and a half protected the English Mercantile Marine against foreign competition. Five important Bills[3] were passed in 1822, almost without debate, and without putting a single clause to the vote.

The Ministers were no revolutionaries; nor could there be any question of demolishing at a single blow the entire fabric of the Navigation Laws, by which no goods might be imported into England which were not carried either by a British vessel or a vessel belonging to the nation importing. But, without attacking its principle, this legislation might be less rigorously applied. In the first place, a great work of simplification was undertaken. Over two hundred antiquated statutes, often contradictory, a labyrinth which could be threaded only by the legal antiquary, were repealed at a stroke. In the second place, the unqualified refusal, in force since the seventeenth century, to permit Dutch ships to land in England, was abandoned, and this step, in conjunction with the simultaneous abolition of certain protective measures specially directed against the commerce of Prussia and Russia, had the effect of placing all the nations of Europe on an equal footing as regards their commercial relations with England; and all the European nations alike benefited from the liberal spirit which inspired the new legislation. In future for an article to be admitted into England from a foreign port it need not have been produced in the country from which it was exported. Whatever its place of origin, European or otherwise, it might be imported into England provided the vessel on which it was shipped belonged to the port in question.

In virtue of an agreement concluded in 1816 the United States had secured complete reciprocity of treatment for British vessels in American ports and American vessels in British ports. But they

---

[1] H. of C., February 9, March 29, 1821, Marryat's speech (*Parl. Deb.*, N.S., vol. iv, pp. 550, 1508).
[2] 1 and 2 Geo. IV, cap. 37, completed and amended by 1 and 2 Geo. IV, cap. 84, ss. 1–4.
[3] 3 Geo. IV, cap. 41, 42, 43, 44, 45.

had failed to get this reciprocity extended to their commerce with the British Colonies in America. American goods, though their importation had been permitted since 1805, could be imported only in British vessels. The United States had made reprisal by a law which closed American ports to British vessels from the Colonies and thus totally destroyed the American trade of the latter. The Colonies complained to the Home Government, and it did not turn a deaf ear. The ports of the British American Colonies were opened to vessels from the United States.

But the United States did not constitute the whole of the New World. South America, of which the greater portion was nominally subject to Spain, had been for several years past in a state of rebellion. The Act of 1805,[1] which had permitted the importation of goods from Spanish America to the English Colonies, had mentioned 'Colonies belonging to or under the dominion of any foreign European sovereign or State'. Now when Spanish dominion over the countries across the Atlantic was scarcely more than a name, the new statute[2] ignored the sovereignty of Spain and spoke simply of 'any foreign country in the Continent of North or South America, or any foreign island in the West Indies'; and England wished to encourage these South American States, whose trade with her Colonies she was thus fostering, to trade also directly with herself. Hitherto their goods could reach Europe only indirectly through the Spanish market. In future South American produce might be shipped directly to England either on English or native vessels.

Nor could the English Colonies be refused this freedom to trade with the entire world which the nations of South America had just conquered by armed rebellion and which England by her new legislation was inviting them to use to the full. Certainly they were not granted all the rights of an independent State. England retained for herself the monopoly of importing manufactured articles, and, unless it were to an American port, their raw materials could be exported only on British vessels. Nevertheless, the Colonies now obtained for the first time the right to export all their produce directly to Africa and Europe.

[1] 45 Geo. III, cap. 57.   [2] 3 Geo. IV, cap. 44.

III FOREIGN AND DOMESTIC POLITICS

I

So far as South America was concerned the new statute amounted to a recognition of the independence—the economic independence, at least—of the colonies in rebellion against Spain.[1] In this acknowledgment England's commercial policy joined hands with her foreign policy. Three democratic republics had been set up, at Buenos Aires, in Chile, and in Colombia, and this revival of Jacobin principles cannot, we may be sure, have been very agreeable to the English Cabinet. The British Government had attempted to mediate between Spain and her Colonies, and would perhaps have favoured the plan of establishing monarchies in South America governed by Bourbon princes, if France had not espoused it so warmly that the Cabinet shrank from encouraging a possible revival of the eighteenth-century Bourbon Family Compact. In this matter, however, the Ministers were obliged to do violence to their political preferences and shape their policy in conformity with public opinion, which under the combined influence of several different motives was enthusiastic in support of the new republics.

Ever since 1815 England had been sending out her swarms over the entire Globe. Noblemen and members of the middle class had betaken themselves to Paris or Italy to enjoy cheaper living, lighter taxation, a better climate, and more abundant pleasures. Unemployed labourers left England to find work on the virgin soil of North America, South Africa, and Oceania; and the revolutions which were breaking out wellnigh throughout the entire world afforded to all who were goaded by the spirit of adventure and found a life of peace insipid the opportunity to come forward as the sworn champions of liberty. In Paris Sir Robert Wilson aided La Vallette to escape: at Ravenna Byron came into conflict with the Austrian police. But South America offered these knights-errant the most glorious adventures. Lord Cochrane was in command of the Chilean Fleet, Commodore Browne commanded the Fleet of the Republic of La Plata stationed before Buenos Aires. In Venezuela General MacGregor

---

[1] For the policy pursued by Lord Castlereagh in regard to the Spanish Colonies see C. K. Webster, 'Castlereagh and the Spanish Colonies', Ap. *English Historical Review*, January 1912, October 1915 (vol. xxvii, pp. 78 sqq.; vol. xxx, pp. 631 sqq.).

passed from battle to battle, and General English was at the head of an Anglo-German corps of three hundred men. It was estimated that more than ten thousand men sailed from the Irish ports in 1819 'to fight against the cause of despotism in South America', and that one brigade alone contained over fifteen hundred who had fought at Waterloo.[1] In deference to Spanish complaints the English Government was obliged to amend the old Foreign Enlistment Act; for this statute, which forbade in principle the enlistment of Englishmen in a foreign army, did not apply to the case of colonies in revolt against their mother country. But, although the amending Bill was carried, the warmth displayed by the Opposition, which was headed by Mackintosh, showed how deeply the cause of the South American Colonies had engaged English sympathies.[2]

The sympathy of Englishmen went out to peoples who had adopted representative institutions and were struggling against a despotic Government. Nor could the English fail to experience an instinctive pleasure when they saw Spain lose her transatlantic Colonies as England had herself lost the greater part of her Colonies in North America. The opponents of slavery, to whose cause the Evangelical party had lent an enormous accession of strength, entertained great hopes from the liberation of the Spanish Colonies. For the countries now achieving independence were the last to which slaves were still sent from Africa, and they would no doubt be more willing than Spain or Portugal to follow the advice of the British Government, by discouraging the slave trade and even abolishing the institution of slavery. Wilberforce, who here, as elsewhere, occupied a position on the border-line between orthodox Toryism and Liberal principles, warmly supported the cause of the Spanish Colonies. Finally, and this was perhaps the weightiest consideration, their independence was in the interest of British commerce: in South America there had been opened providentially a market for English goods, which was believed to be of an almost incalculable size—people spoke of a population of twenty millions—at the very time when the nations of a Europe which had returned to the normal conditions of peace were excluding British trade by heavy tariffs or even by absolute prohibition.

[1] *Examiner*, May 23, 1819.
[2] 59 Geo. III, cap. 69. See Mackintosh's speech, H. of C., May 12, 1819 (*Parl. Deb.*, vol. xl, pp. 365 sqq.).

The events which were taking place in South America directed the attention of the British public to questions of foreign policy. We have already seen how in the opening months of 1820 the army at Cadiz, instead of embarking for South America to re-establish there the authority of the Crown, had mutinied, restored in Spain the Constitution of 1812, and compelled Ferdinand to accept it. Thus the South American question was complicated by a Spanish question, and democratic principles gained once more a foothold in Europe.

From Spain they spread to Naples, where a mutiny among the troops copied exactly the mutiny in Spain. On July 7 the Duke of Calabria, King Ferdinand's eldest son, and invested by him with the office of Vicar-General of the Kingdom, solemnly accepted the 'Spanish Constitution'. Then towards the end of August the Portuguese Army followed the example of the Spanish. Here the insurrection presented a peculiar character; for it was the rebellion of Portugal against a Government settled for the past thirteen years in Brazil and against the English general, Lord Beresford, who commanded the army and governed the country in the name of the absent monarch. In November the Junto, set up as a provisional Government, adopted with certain modifications the Spanish Constitution. Rome and Piedmont witnessed abortive attempts at rebellion. In Greece the entire Morea, under the leadership of Ypsilanti, shook off the yoke of the Sultan.[1]

A year earlier, alarmed by the growth of revolutionary opinions in Germany, the three great absolutist Powers had met at Carlsbad to deliberate on the best means of checking the movement; but today outside the boundaries of the German Empire the entire south of Europe had become Jacobin—and the situation was marked by a feature even more serious. The sole instrument available to suppress revolution was the army; but the revolutions in Spain, Naples, and Portugal had actually been the work of the army. In what country of Europe could the Government any longer be confident of its soldiers? While Wellington was

---

[1] See the curious sketch of the European situation drawn by *The Times*, March 17, 1821: 'Let us coast the European Continent from Stockholm downwards. Sweden has a representative government; Norway, the same; in England, according to a foreign secretary, "freedom is only a habit"; Flanders has a Constitution by solemn compact; Spain is almost unanimous in the love, and now safe, we trust, in the possession, of her liberty; Portugal, Piedmont, Naples, three-fourths of Europe, are actually free—three-fourths of Europe are in that grand and proud condition which the remaining fourth has attempted to proscribe as rebels to its supreme and self-constituted authority.'

concerned, as we saw above, at the spirit of insubordination which prevailed in the British Army, French soldiers were plotting against the Government,[1] a mutiny broke out in Russia, and many people expected that the Prussian Army would shortly proclaim a Constitution.[2] In the circumstances it is incredible that Machiavellian designs entertained by Alexander upon the Ottoman Empire, by Metternich to annex Italy, and by Louis XVIII to annex Savoy and extend French influence in Spain, can have played any considerable part in their deliberations. The memories of the general war of the peoples against their kings were hardly twenty years old. No wonder the rulers were frightened now. The Emperor of Russia, the Emperor of Austria, and the Crown Prince of Prussia, at a conference held at Troppau on November 20, 1820, invited Ferdinand of Naples to confer with them at Laybach. They hoped to deliver him from the oppressive surveillance in which he was held by his rebel subjects, possibly even from execution. Once the royal persons were safe, an Austrian army would invade the Kingdom of Naples to restore order. The English and French Ambassadors to the Court of Vienna attended the Conference at Troppau. They were officially charged to communicate to their Governments the decisions taken by the three Allied Powers, and to request at least their diplomatic, if not their military, support. What would be the answer of the English Government?

2

It had been obvious since 1815 that the peculiar geographical position of Great Britain, together with the unique character of her political institutions, would oblige her Foreign Office to adopt an independent policy unlike that of any continental

[1] Cobbett wrote in the *Political Register* for July 29, 1820: 'In order to avoid coming too close, is there anyone, in his senses, who thinks that France can remain for a year without a second revolution?' (vol. xxxvii, p. 76).

[2] *Morning Chronicle*, July 1, 1821. The Hon. F. Lamb to Lord Castlereagh, March 24 1821 (*Memoirs and Correspondence of Lord Castlereagh*, vol xx, pp. 374–5). For a long time past the supporters of monarchy had felt anxious about Prussia. See Lord Castlereagh to Rose, December 28, 1815: '. . . With all that partiality and a grateful admiration of the conduct of that nation and its armies in the war, I fairly own that I look with considerable anxiety to the tendency of their politics. There certainly at this moment exists a great fermentation in all orders of the State; very free notions of government, if not principles actually revolutionary, are prevalent, and the Army is by no means subordinate to the civil authorities. It is impossible to say where these impulses may stop, when they find a representative system in which they may develop' (ibid., vol. xi, p. 106).

Government. 'In the present state of Europe,' wrote Lord Castlereagh on December 28, 1815, to Rose, the British representative accredited to the Czar, 'it is the province of Great Britain to turn the confidence she has inspired to the account of peace, by exercising a conciliatory influence between the Powers, rather than put herself at the head of any combination of Courts to keep others in check. Your safest course at present will be to keep quiet.' And he concluded by using the phrase which would shortly be current in the language of European diplomacy: 'It is not my wish to encourage, on the part of this country, an unnecessary interference in the ordinary affairs of the Continent.'[1] This letter was written at the moment when the British Cabinet refused to authorize the Prince Regent to affix his signature to the mystical pact known as the Holy Alliance, on the ground that the constitution did not permit the head of the executive to conclude a treaty with a foreign monarch on his personal responsibility. Nevertheless, when Lord Castlereagh recommended to his agent a policy of quiet and non-intervention, he was not inspired by fear of committing British Liberalism to the cause of the great continental despots; for Alexander had quarrelled with Metternich and was supporting the French and German Liberals against him. Castlereagh refused to take sides in the dispute.

When the Congress of Aix-la-Chapelle was held in October 1818, to arrange the evacuation of French territory, admit the King of France into the Alliance, and at the same time take measures to safeguard his dynasty against republican or Bonapartist attacks, Castlereagh, who represented England at the Congress, perceived that a reconciliation was imminent between the Emperors of Austria and Russia. Delighted at a *rapprochement* which in his opinion was likely to preserve the peace of Europe, he ceased to advocate a policy of isolation and expressed the wish that the system of conferences between the sovereigns of Europe to discuss the affairs of the Continent might be developed to the utmost, that the congresses might become a regular institution and be held periodically. 'It is satisfactory to observe,' he wrote to Lord Liverpool, 'how little embarrassment and how much solid good grow out of these reunions, which sound so terrible at a distance. It really appears to me to be a new discovery in the

[1] To Rose, December 28, 1815 (*Memoirs and Correspondence of Lord Castlereagh*, vol. xi, pp. 104 sqq.).

European government, at once extinguishing the cobwebs with which diplomacy obscures the horizon, bringing the whole bearing of the system into its true light, and giving to the counsels of the great Powers the efficiency, almost the simplicity, of a single State.'[1] It was his colleagues in London who took alarm and recalled him to a juster sense of English feeling on the subject.[2] He retreated, and British foreign policy returned to the attitude of 'isolation' adapted to an 'insular' nation.

The mere fact, however, of the understanding between Alexander and Metternich sufficed to give the policy of non-intervention a more markedly 'liberal' character than it had possessed between 1815 and 1818. The continental policy to which Castlereagh henceforward refused to be a partner was the policy of the two Emperors who had made a compact to interfere in the domestic affairs of the European States to suppress revolutionary Liberalism. Of such intervention Castlereagh disapproved in principle, not only in Germany[3] but even in France,[4] where, it might seem, the English Government was bound by an express undertaking to protect the reigning dynasty. In support of his attitude he invoked two arguments. He pointed out that intervention would stimulate revolutionary feeling, once more, as in 1792, confused with patriotism, and thus make it more dangerous. It would therefore do more harm than good. And he argued from the political institutions of his country. The English Government could not associate itself with the policy of Austria and Prussia unless it first obtained the sanction of Parliament; but it was extremely doubtful whether it would emerge victorious from the debate; and, even if it did secure a majority, the debates, which would certainly not lack warmth, would have a most deplorable effect upon the public opinion of Europe.[5]

[1] To Lord Liverpool, October 20, 1818 (*Memoirs and Correspondence of Lord Castlereagh*, vol. xii, pp. 54–5).
[2] Lord Bathurst to Lord Castlereagh, October 20, 1818 (ibid., vol. xii, pp. 55 sqq.). W. A. Phillips (*The Confederation of Europe*, pp. 166 sqq.) underestimates the divergence of opinion between Castlereagh and his colleagues.
[3] Lord Castlereagh to Sir Charles Stuart, February 4, 1820: 'In the present instance nothing had passed but a consultation between two of the Allied Powers *not German*, whether there is any ground for *the Allies* (which would include France) to interfere in German affairs. This Government has discouraged such interference' (*Memoirs and Correspondence of Lord Castlereagh*, vol. xii, p. 210).
[4] Lord Castlereagh to Lord Stewart, January 14, 1821 (ibid., vol. xii, pp. 185–6).
[5] Lord Castlereagh to Lord Stewart, January 14, 1820: 'The character of our government is such as to compel us to adopt a more guarded attitude than other countries in our dealings with foreign Powers' (the original is in French) (ibid., vol. xii, pp. 189–90).

When, therefore, the Spanish question arose, the allied sove-reigns were not surprised to receive in May 1820 a secret com-munication from the English Government opposing in advance any project of collective intervention. Castlereagh appealed to the opinions expressed by Wellington, who of all men had the most thorough acquaintance with Spanish conditions, and Sir Henry Wellesley, the British Ambassador at Madrid, in support of his contention that intervention in any shape or form would aggravate the revolutionary peril in Spain and, far from protect-ing, endanger Ferdinand's life. Even the meeting of a conference would be a dangerous gesture and impart to the Alliance a novel character which would not be agreeable to England. The Alliance had been concluded to free Europe from the dominion of France. It was never intended to become 'a union for the government of the world, or for the superintendence of the internal affairs of other States'.[1] Nevertheless, a conference was held at Troppau. The Allies decided upon armed intervention, and communicated their decision to the English Government. The continental Press published broadcast the fact of the communication. Then Castlereagh made up his mind that the time had come to publish to the world the opposition between the English standpoint and that of the continental Powers. On January 19, 1821, when only a year had elapsed since by obtaining from Parliament the Six Acts he had appeared to identify himself with the reactionary policy of the Great Powers, he laid down for the first time in a public document the principle of non-intervention. He pro-nounced the decision taken by the three sovereigns directly opposed to the fundamental laws of the United Kingdom, and inadmissible from the point of view of international law. Though he expressed his disapproval of the manner in which the Nea-politan revolution had been effected, he did not admit that there was any ground for intervention; but though he disapproved of Austrian intervention, he was not prepared to take action to prevent it, provided, of course, the allied sovereigns did not attempt annexations which would upset the territorial arrange-ments of Europe, as established by the treaties of 1815.[2]

To George Rose, January 15, 1820: '. . . Our Allies must recollect that we have a Parlia-ment to manage, and it is essential to their interest not to have angry discussions on continental politics provoked' (*Mems. and Corresp. of Lord Castlereagh*, vol. xii, p. 175).

[1] See the text of the secret communiqué, *Ann. Reg.*, 1823, p. 93.

[2] Circular Dispatch to His Majesty's Missions at Foreign Courts relative to the Dis-

3

These declarations were calculated to give considerable satisfaction to the friends of a Liberal policy. Nevertheless, when Parliament reassembled it was evident that the Opposition was not yet satisfied. Throughout the entire session Castlereagh's foreign policy was the subject of protracted and stormy debates. The Opposition speakers refused to believe that English neutrality was sincere. If the Government were honest in their professions of neutrality, why had they allowed six weeks to elapse after the allied sovereigns had informed them of the decisions taken at Troppau before they issued their reply? Why during the interval had they placed a man-of-war at Ferdinand's disposal in which to leave Naples and accept the invitation of the three monarchs? And why did Lord Castlereagh employ such ambiguous language, always ready to palliate, even to justify the actions of the Austrian Government, always speaking of the Carbonari with irony or disapproval? Party spirit exploited the rumours current in regard to the Conference of Troppau. According to the Tories an Englishman had reported to the Emperor Alexander an utterance of Tierney's promising, if the Whigs were returned to power, to set Napoleon at liberty. The rumour assumed so definite a shape that Tierney found it worth his while to make a formal disclaimer of the words put into his mouth,[1] and Napoleon's death came at an opportune moment to release the Whigs from the prospect of the difficult problem which they must solve if ever they returned to office. And the Whigs in turn had their own tales to tell of the proceedings at Troppau. The allied monarchs, they declared, had discussed the attitude to be adopted if the Whigs, the *Liberales* and *Carbonari* of England, defeated the Tory Government. Ought they to declare war, or would it be better to put England in quarantine, as a nation infected by the plague? To alarm British patriotism, the Whigs predicted, as a consequence of the principles laid down at Troppau, the landing of foreign troops and a Russian army encamped in Hyde Park.[2]

cussions at Troppau and Laybach, H. of C., February 1, 1821 (*Parl. Deb.*, N.S., vol. iv, pp. 283 sqq.).
[1] H. of C., February 21, 1821, speeches of Robinson and Tierney (ibid., vol. iv, pp. 889–90).
[2] H. of C., March 20, 1821, Sir Robert Wilson's speech (ibid., vol. iv, pp. 1350 sqq.). H. of C., February 21, 1821, Mackintosh's speech (ibid., vol. iv, pp. 837 sqq.); May 4, 1821, Hutchinson's speech (ibid., vol. iv, pp. 510 sqq.).

What were the intentions of the Opposition leaders when they criticized Castlereagh's foreign policy? Evidently they were not content with a passive policy of non-intervention; they desired active intervention in favour of the revolutionaries. Ever since the conclusion of the treaties of 1815 the Whig publicists had never ceased to denounce them as a violation of the lofty ideals for which the Allies had claimed to be fighting. The sacred principle of national independence had been outraged by the Russian annexation of Finland, the Swedish annexation of Norway, the Prussian annexation of a part of Saxony, the enforced union of Genoa with the Kingdom of Sardinia and of Belgium with the Netherlands, and by the extension of Hanoverian territory. And however difficult it might be to repair the wrongs then committed, England must return to her traditional office as the protector of small nations against the Great Powers. In 1819 young Lord John Russell, in *A Letter to Lord Holland on Foreign Politics*, had attempted to resuscitate the old Whig doctrine of the Balance of Power. He contrasted that system which, according to him, had 'governed the wars and treaties of Europe from the fifteenth century to the year 1818', 'with the system of the Holy Alliance'—a system 'of general and mutual guaranty of all the Governments now subsisting on the Continent'. He declared the former far preferable to the latter, which contained no 'principle of self-recovery', and provided no security against the preponderance of a particular State or the violation of a nation's rights. Possibly other Powers had benefited by the institution of 'an Amphictyonic Council'; England, at all events, who once held in her hands the balance of power, had most certainly lost her place of honour.[1]

But in the golden age of Whiggery and the Balance of Power war had been the instrument by which England had preserved her prestige unimpaired, and it was as a justification for war that the Balance of Power was now advocated by Lord John. One of the arguments he employed in defence of the traditional creed was the impossibility of conceiving a court of arbitration capable of settling international disputes.[2] Could Liberals, in fact, accept the arbitration of the Tribunal of Kings in session at Aix-la-

[1] *A Letter to the Right Honourable Lord Holland on Foreign Politics*, ed. 4, 1831, pp. 2, 46–7.
[2] *Memoirs of the Affairs of Europe from the Peace of Utrecht*, 1824, p. 23.

Chapelle, Troppau, and Laybach.[1] Thus the real issue debated in the House of Commons between Castlereagh and the Opposition was the choice between peace and war. The Opposition refused to accept the policy of non-intervention as it had been applied in Italy. The Whigs would have desired the dispatch of a formal remonstrance to Austria, which, coming from England, would have possessed sufficient weight to prevent Austrian intervention. If, however, it had produced no effect, would the Opposition have been prepared to advocate war? At the very time when the Government was endeavouring to gratify its desires by reducing each year the naval and military expenditure, would it have sought to force upon the Government a foreign policy which involved the increase of that expenditure?[2] The question is not easy to answer. The Opposition speakers in the Commons refused to admit that a more energetic diplomacy would necessarily lead to war. But in the House of Lords, where the enthusiasts for the Balance of Power were farther removed from the control of public opinion, they spoke more frankly. 'He sincerely hoped,' declared Lord Grey, 'that peace would not be interrupted; but he was much more anxious that the honour of the country should be preserved unstained.'[3] And, according to Lord Holland: 'The question was not at present one of peace or war, but whether Government were not called on to state the reasons of their conduct, which had been misrepresented by Austria. If such an explanation should lead to a war, he would lament the circumstances; but from the fear of such an event he would not abstain from vindicating the honour of the country.'[4]

4

In the meanwhile the Austrian Army invaded the Kingdom of Naples and, assisted by the popular apathy, restored despotic

[1] Nevertheless, we should not overlook the modest beginnings of pacifism as an ethical and political principle. On June 14, 1816, 'a Society' was founded 'for the Promotion of Permanent and Universal Peace', which published pamphlets and formed affiliated societies. To judge by the list of members, it included orthodox Nonconformists, Unitarians (Sir John Bowring), Quakers (William Allen), and convinced freethinkers (Bentham). Cf. John Sheppard, *An Inquiry on the Duty of Christians with Respect to War; including an Examination of the Principle of the London and American Peace Societies*, in a series of letters, 1820. See also on the Society *The Times*, August 17, 1825, and on Sheppard's book, *Eclectic Review*, October 1820, Art. III (N.S., vol. xiv, pp. 236 sqq.).

[2] H. of C., May 4, 1821, Lord Castlereagh's speech (*Parl. Deb.*, N.S., vol. v, pp. 515 sqq.).

[3] H. of L., January 23, 1821 (ibid., vol. iv, p. 10).

[4] H. of L., March 2, 1821 (ibid., vol. iv, p. 1063).

government. When in the rear of the invading Austrians the army mutinied in Piedmont and compelled the proclamation at Turin of the Spanish Constitution, Austrian troops, acting in conjunction with a Russian force, suppressed the Piedmontese revolution as they had suppressed the Neapolitan. On May 12 the Allied Governments met again in congress, and addressed from Laybach to their diplomatic representatives a long circular letter in which they declared that 'useful or necessary changes in legislation, and in the administration of States, ought only to emanate from the free will and the intelligent and well-weighed conviction of those whom God had rendered responsible for power', and that it was incumbent upon the Allies to take whatever action might be necessary to prevent any violation of this fundamental principle.[1] Without British help they had won the victory. Dumbfounded by this sudden collapse of the revolutionary movement in the South of Europe, the Opposition kept silence.

In the debate upon the Address from the Throne which opened the session of 1822, not a word was uttered on foreign politics. During the session an animated debate took place on the subject of the Alien Act, which must be periodically renewed, and which conferred upon the British Government special powers of police supervision over foreigners domiciled in England and in particular political refugees.[2] These refugees had fled to London from Metternich's police; were they to be hunted down even there and the English police placed at the service of Austria? Isolated if impassioned protests were raised by Mackintosh, Hume, Sir Robert Wilson, and Wilberforce against the atrocities committed by the Turk in repressing the Greek insurgents and, moreover, committed under the very eyes of England's unheeding repre-

---

[1] See the full text of the letter, *Ann. Reg.* 1821, App. to Chron., pp. 599 sqq.

[2] 2 and 3 Geo. IV, cap. 97. See the speeches of Robert Peel, June 5, 1822; Mackintosh, June 14, 1822; and of Hobhouse, July 1, 1822 (*Parl. Deb.*, N.S., vol vii, pp. 805 sqq., 1092 sqq., 1433 sqq.). Cf. 43 Geo. III, cap. 155; 54 Geo. III, cap. 155; 55 Geo. III, cap. 54; 56 Geo. III, cap. 86; 58 Geo. III, cap. 96. When, in 1818, Lord Castlereagh asked Parliament to renew the Alien Act for two years, he pointed out how extremely mild its application had been. In six years only nine aliens had been deported (H. of C., May 5, 1818, ibid., vol. xxxviii, p. 523). And the number of foreigners resident in England, which exceeded twenty-five thousand in 1822, was increasing every year (H. of C., June 5, 1822, Robert Peel's speech, ibid., N.S., vol. vii, p. 806). When Peel was at the Home Office he did not expel a single foreigner under the provisions of the Act (H. of C., April 20, 1826, Robert Peel's speech, ibid., N.S., vol. xv, p. 499). Renewed once more in 1824 (5 Geo. IV, cap. 37), the Alien Act was replaced in 1826 by a simple Registration Act passed as a permanent measure (7 Geo. IV, cap. 54).

sentatives.[1] But these protests found no response. Public opinion would not make it a grievance against the Government that they had prevented war between Turkey and Russia, even though it were at the price of Greek independence. 'Fear of Russia,' wrote Chateaubriand, the French Ambassador in London, 'has made the whole of England Turk.'[2] At the other end of the Mediterranean, in Spain, the situation continued to give cause for anxiety. There was an entire group in the entourage of Louis XVIII who advocated French intervention, and it was not easy to see how, when the Congress of the Great Powers met in the following autumn at Verona, Castlereagh would be able to prevent an intervention dreaded by all Englishmen irrespective of party. To be sure England had at her disposal an instrument with which she could take her revenge for the humiliating diplomatic defeats to which she must submit in Europe, and the Cabinet seemed to be moved by a half-conscious instinct of retaliation when, on the occasion of the reform of the Navigation Acts, it took the first steps towards recognizing the independence of the Spanish Colonies. But it should not have cloaked the decision in silence and obscurity, as though it were nothing more than a concession made by the politicians to the interests of commerce. In short, Castlereagh's policy in every step he took was fatal to the national honour. England, which in 1814 and 1815 had settled the terms of European peace, now abandoned the control of Europe to the great Continental Powers. But the public discontent was at once exasperated and paralysed by the lack of any alternative to the policy of non-intervention laid down by Castlereagh in January 1821.

The reason is now clear why the Opposition, throughout the session of 1822, left the problems of foreign policy in the background and devoted all its energies to economic questions; and why their attitude on questions of foreign politics was of necessity marked by increasing caution. How could they possibly in the same breath press upon the Government undertakings of a military nature and demand the reduction of expenditure upon the Army and Navy? Further, it was only by an alliance with the country gentlemen that the Whigs believed it possible before the close of

[1] H. of C., July 15, 1822 (*Parl. Deb.*, N.S., vol. vii, pp. 1649 sqq.).
[2] Chateaubriand to Montmorency, July 19, 1822 (Comte d'Antioche, *Chateaubriand, Ambassadeur à Londres*, p. 293).

the session to place the Government in a minority and produce a Cabinet crisis; and the country gentlemen, the jolterheads, could not be persuaded to interest themselves in the revolutions of Madrid, Naples, and Piedmont. We must not, however, conclude that the rise in the price of money, the fall in the price of corn, taxation and the Sinking Fund occupied the entire attention of Parliament during this session. The House of Commons continued to discuss the well-worn theme of Catholic emancipation, which since the beginning of the century had been a source of never-ending difficulties, and the equally venerable question of parliamentary reform, which had revived the moment peace had been concluded, and on two occasions had seemed to arouse the passionate enthusiasm of the masses. During the years which followed the death of George III parliamentary circles cherished the illusion, warranted it would seem by the weakness of the Tories, that both these problems were on the eve of a settlement in conformity with Liberal ideals.

5

Although the question of Catholic emancipation affected a handful of English Catholics, it was substantially an Irish question; and the condition of Ireland was as disgraceful as ever. When after Waterloo peace was restored for the second time, Peel, who for six years ruled Ireland in the spirit of a stern parent, obtained from Parliament as a remedy for the prevailing disorder two extraordinary measures. One was a Police Act, which authorized the Lord-Lieutenant to raise in any country in which disaffection was rife a body of armed police, to be maintained at the expense of the county.[1] The other was an Insurrection Act, which empowered him to establish in a particular district a modified system of martial law, and in particular to forbid the inhabitants to leave their houses without a special permit before sunrise or after sunset.[2] In 1818 Peel considered that order had been sufficiently restored, and did not ask for a renewal of the Insurrection Act. But towards the end of 1819, at the very time when the British Parliament was passing the Six Acts, disorders broke out afresh in the country districts of Ireland. The Government hesitated for some time before taking active measures, and was

[1] 54 Geo. III, cap. 31.
[2] 54 Geo. III, cap. 180.

content to dispatch reinforcements to Ireland without asking Parliament to pass any special legislation. Castlereagh had always favoured a policy of conciliation in Ireland,[1] and Peel, who two years before had resigned the position of Secretary of State for Ireland, was no longer present to force his hand. But towards the end of 1821 the agrarian disorders became so serious that, when the session of 1822 opened, Parliament passed a new Insurrection Act[2] and suspended Habeas Corpus.[3] More efficacious than legislation to alleviate, if not altogether to cure, the disorder, was a famine which broke out in Ireland in the spring. From banditti the Irish peasants became beggars; and English charity in no stinted measure came to their assistance.

There was, however, no direct connection between this unrest among the lower classes and the Catholic question. It is true that the lower classes in Ireland were Catholic, and therefore predisposed to lend a ready ear to their priests when they explained their sufferings as the effects of Protestant persecution. The tithes payable by the small tenants to the Protestant clergy were naturally odious to them—a fact of which the English Government was so fully sensible that in 1822 it dealt with the question for the first time and carried an Act which made it possible for any tithe-payer who might wish to do so to commute his tithe.[4] But it would be false to regard the tithe as the real cause of the troubles of Ireland, or to treat the disturbances as in any true sense a religious struggle. 'The disturbances,' declared Robert Peel, 'which now prevailed, had no precise or definite cause. They seemed to be the effect of a general confederacy in crime ... a systematic opposition to all laws.'[5] The radical cause of the disorders was the inequitable distribution[6] of property. 'If their

---

[1] Peel to Lord Whitworth, July 7, 1814. Peel, acting in concert with Lord Sidmouth was obliged to overcome the opposition of Lord Liverpool and Lord Castlereagh (certainly the opposition of the former was more pronounced than that of the latter) before the Cabinet would consent to introduce the Insurrection Act (C. S. Parker, *Sir Robert Peel*, vol. i, pp. 146–8). Cf. H. of C., June 28, 1820, Lord Castlereagh's speech (*Parl. Deb.*, N.S., vol. ii, pp. 91 sqq.). 'Castlereagh made a Whig speech,' wrote Hobhouse that night in his Diary.

[2] 3 Geo. IV, cap. 1. Continued until August 1, 1823, by 3 Geo. IV, cap. 80.

[3] 3 Geo. IV, cap. 2. See also 3 Geo. IV, cap. 3, 4.

[4] 3 Geo. IV, cap. 125.

[5] H. of C., April 26, 1816 (*Parl. Deb.*, vol. xxxii, p. 27).

[6] See Sir Robert Peel's reflections in his letter to S. Beckett, December 5, 1816: 'Distress in this country has a different effect—almost a contrary effect—from what it has in England. Sheer wickedness and depravity are the chief causes of our crimes and turbulence, and I am satisfied that severe distress would rather tend to diminish than to increase them' (Parker, op. cit., vol. i, p. 235).

lordships,' said Lord Liverpool, 'looked at the different proclamations, handbills, notices which had been sent forth in the disturbed parts of Ireland, though they would sometimes find religious difference mentioned (and that in a slight degree) they would hardly perceive any notice taken of the Government. . . . It was an insurrection against property, and not against the government of the country.'[1] The insurrection possessed neither definite programme nor recognized leaders. The lack of interest in Catholic emancipation displayed by the lower classes in Ireland is proved by a significant fact. Since 1793 Irish Catholics, though incapable of election to Parliament, had possessed, unlike their English brethren, the right of suffrage, and the electorate in the Irish counties was far more democratic than in the English. There was, therefore, nothing to prevent the Irish Catholics from uniting to return members pledged to their cause. But these slaves, though continually in revolt, remained slaves nevertheless, and continued to vote in their masses for the candidates selected by the landlords. Therefore the question of emancipation, even when the disturbances in Ireland were at their height, was, generally speaking, fought above the heads of the Irish proletariat.

The restoration of peace was unfavourable to the cause of emancipation; for its supporters belonged for the most part to the group which had opposed the war and despaired of a successful issue. In consequence the old Tory party, which had supported the war through thick and thin, reaped the benefit of the victory. Moreover, we have already seen the disastrous effect on public opinion produced by the action of the ultramontanes—that is to say, of the majority of Irish Catholics—in 1813, when they threw over Grattan, the untiring advocate of the Catholic cause, at the very moment when he believed the battle had been won.[2] Ultramontanes and cisalpines continued to quarrel, to their mutual enfeeblement and the Protestants' delight. The Parliament of 1812, which had been favourable to the Catholic claims while the war lasted, became hostile as soon as it was over. There was a majority of thirty-one against the Catholics in 1816, of twenty-four in 1817.

A small majority to be sure; and it was also remarked that all the leading statesmen in the Commons, on the Government as

[1] H. of C., June 14, 1822 (*Parl. Deb.*, N.S., vol. vii, pp. 1060-1).
[2] See vol. i, pp. 485 sqq.

well as on the Opposition benches, were in favour of Catholic emancipation. On this matter Castlereagh had always been in agreement with Canning. The solitary exception was Peel. Charged with the responsibility for the government of Ireland, he had conceived a loathing for the Irish. In 1814 he expressed the wish that the Insurrection Act might become part of the permanent law of Ireland,[1] and in 1816 avowed his conviction that 'an honest despotic government' was 'by far the fittest government for the country'.[2] He regarded the Irish as semi-savages, and ascribed their barbarism to 'the pernicious influence of the religion they profess'.[3] It was his personal intervention in the debates of 1816 and 1817 which secured the small majorities in favour of the 'Protestant' cause.[4] The University of Oxford showed its gratitude by choosing Peel henceforward as its representative. Nevertheless, Peel did not oppose the passage in 1817 of an Act which threw open to Catholics even the highest commands in the Army and Navy.[5] This was the reform for which ten years before the Whigs had attempted in vain to secure the assent of George III, who had dismissed the Cabinet and replaced it by a Tory Ministry. Now under a Tory Government the Bill which was introduced in the Lords passed the Commons without a single voice being raised in opposition.

6

Peel resigned his seat in the Cabinet. A new Parliament was elected. In 1819 a motion in favour of Catholic emancipation was rejected in the Commons by the insignificant majority of two votes.[6] Then George III died, and a persistent rumour got abroad that the change of monarch would be favourable to the cause of Catholic emancipation. George IV was hardly on the

[1] To the Speaker, Abbott, September 30, 1814 (C. S. Parker, op. cit., vol. i, p. 135).
[2] To Gregory, September 30, 1816 (ibid., vol. i, p. 215).
[3] To Speaker Abbott, December 25, 1816 (ibid., vol. i, p. 236). He continues: 'It is quite impossible for anyone to witness the remorselessness with which crimes are committed here, the almost total annihilation of the agency of conscience as a preventive of crime, and the universal contempt in which the obligation of any but an illegal oath is held by the mass of the people, without being satisfied that the prevailing religion of Ireland operates as an impediment rather than an aid to the ends of the Civil Government.'
[4] See the interesting accounts of these two parliamentary battles, given by Peel himself. To Lord Whitworth, May 25, 1816 (ibid., p. 226); also May 10, 181 (ibid., p. 247).
[5] 57 Geo. III, cap. 92.
[6] H. of C., May 3, 1819 (Parl. Deb., vol. xl, pp. 6 sqq.).

throne when he entered into negotiations with Lord Wellesley, who had always been a supporter of emancipation. Surely this was a sign of the King's wish to make him Prime Minister? A sign also that King George did not feel himself bound in conscience to carry out the wishes of his dead father? That he was returning to the convictions of his youth? The King, whose sole desire was the divorce, allowed reports to circulate calculated to conciliate the sympathies of the Opposition and free him from dependence upon his Cabinet. When he visited Ireland in 1821 he enjoyed a triumphal reception. Moreover, the events taking place on the Continent supplied the advocates of emancipation with fresh arguments. They were now in a position to press the orthodox Tories to explain why they showed such distrust of the Catholic Church in England, when everywhere else their sympathies were with the supporters of the Church[1] against the partisans of revolution. Moreover, it was ridiculous to be afraid of the Catholic Church at a time when throughout Latin Europe the Jacobins, Liberales, and Carbonari seemed on the verge of triumph, and rebellion was breaking out even in the Papal States.[2] 'We doubt much,' wrote *The Times*, 'whether in half a century from hence there will be any such person as a Pope of Rome.'

It was the question of Catholic emancipation which for an entire year made the re-constitution of the Cabinet, inevitable after Canning's resignation, a matter of peculiar difficulty. The Prime Minister was anxious for Canning to re-enter the Cabinet; but he failed to overcome the obstinate refusal of King George, who could not forgive him his independent action in the matter of the divorce, and he finally consented to go to India as Governor-General. And at the same time Peel accepted the position left vacant by Lord Sidmouth at the Home Office. Peel's political character presented two strangely contrasted aspects. In all economic questions he was a thoroughgoing Liberal—in which respect, indeed, he did not differ from Lord Liverpool and Lord Castlereagh, who were in alliance with the political economists against a coalition of the Whigs and the country gentlemen; but in the matter of Catholic emancipation his Toryism was far more orthodox than Castlereagh's. Therefore, when Canning consented

---

[1] [The 'clericals' of a later date, then termed in France the parti prêtre.—Trs.]
[2] *The Times*, April 2, 1821.

to go to India, and Peel returned to the Cabinet, the Protestant party won a double victory.

Lord Liverpool, however, though personally opposed to emancipation, read the situation too well not to understand that some compensation must be given to the Catholics. When the Six Acts were passed, and again on the occasion of the Queen's trial, the Grenvilles had broken with the Whigs, and had loudly proclaimed their allegiance to the party of Order and the Court. They deserved and demanded their reward. It was not refused. The Marquis of Buckingham was created Duke of Buckingham; Henry Wynn was sent as British Ambassador to the Swiss Cantons; Charles Wynn replaced Canning at the Board of Control. The Grenvilles, however, had always been in favour of emancipation; and a more significant step was taken when the Marquis of Wellesley, a supporter of emancipation, was made Lord-Lieutenant of Ireland. He refused to work with Saurin, the Irish Attorney-General, who was an ultra-Protestant, and obtained his removal to make way for Plunket, who since 1815 had been the recognized advocate of the Catholics in the Commons, and had made it his business to introduce almost every year a motion in favour of their claims.

In 1821 Plunket introduced in the Commons two measures of Catholic emancipation. The first of these Bills opened to Catholics all offices in the United Kingdom except those of Lord Chancellor and Lord-Lieutenant of Ireland. They were exempted from making the declaration, hitherto demanded, against Transubstantiation; and the terms of the old Oath of Supremacy, which repudiated all allegiance, temporal or spiritual, to a foreign Power, were so modified that a Catholic could take it without violating his conscience. The second Bill, on the other hand, sought to reassure public opinion by exacting a number of guarantees from the Catholic clergy. The Government was given the right of veto on the appointment of bishops, and an oath of allegiance was required from all Catholic priests. The two Bills were finally combined in one measure which the Commons passed, rejecting every amendment brought forward. But the English ultramontanes led by Milner and the entire Irish clergy had not been slow to express their opposition to the proposed guarantees, although they had been approved by Rome. It was impossible to defend a Bill rejected by the very people on whose behalf it had been framed. The House of Lords threw it out. The following year Plunket, now a member of the Cabinet, showed no disposition to re-introduce his Bill of the past session, pleading that he was under no obligation to introduce it annually, and that the political situation rendered its introduction during the present session inopportune.[1] Canning, who had not yet left for India, then came forward and brought in a Bill of more modest scope. The previous year Catholic peers had been allowed to take part in the Coronation. Canning proposed that henceforward they should be admitted to the duties as well as to the ceremonial of their Order. There were not above half a dozen Catholic peers. Neither Church nor State could be subverted by so modest a reform. But the adversaries of emancipation were quick to see the danger to their cause which lurked in Canning's manoeuvre. Once the principle was admitted that Catholics might sit in one of the two Houses of Parliament, it would be impossible to exclude them for long from the other. Moreover, Canning's Bill did not accompany this measure of partial emancipation with guarantees against Papal interference in the domestic affairs of the country. If it were carried, it would be difficult to supply them later.[2] Passed by the Commons, the Bill was thrown out by the Lords. The problem was not easy to settle. Nevertheless, the fact remains that on the question of emancipation the two Houses were in open conflict, and nobody could doubt that at no very distant date the will of the Commons must prevail. As early as 1819 the most ardent of the anti-Catholics, Peel, had realized that it would be impossible to hold the position for long, only swearing to offer 'a very unavailing, but a most sincere and uncompromising, resistance to a measure which will . . . establish Roman Catholic ascendency in Ireland'.[3] When in 1821 he spoke against Plunket's Bills, everyone remarked the despondent tone of his speech. He admitted that on this accursed question there was only a choice between two evils. He claimed credit for having dissuaded the Protestants from further exciting public feeling by opposing the Catholic petitions with counter petitions, and

[1] H. of C., March 29, 1822 (*Parl. Deb.*, N.S., vol. vi, pp. 1387-8).
[2] H. of C., April 30, 1822, Robert Peel's speech (ibid., vol. vii, p. 259); May 10, 1822, Wetherell's speech (ibid., vol. vii, pp. 476 sqq.).
[3] To Gregory, February 15, 1819 (Parker, op. cit., vol. i, p. 297). This letter was written the day after the sitting at which the anti-Catholics only obtained in the Commons a majority of two.

promised that if Parliament should decide to pass the measure, he would do everything in his power to make the nation accept it.[1] The same note of despair was sounded in his speech of 1822, in which he declared that he would not relax his opposition to the measure because he foresaw the probability of its ultimate success. He apprehended that it was in the true spirit of the Constitution that members of that House should maintain their opinions to the last, notwithstanding overwhelming majorities against them?[2] He seemed to anticipate that the Ministry would fall and the Whigs take office to carry through the inevitable emancipation.[3] He resigned himself to the prospect, was even glad to leave to the Whigs the responsibility for a reform which in his opinion was dangerous, and which, whatever the enlightened might think, continued to inspire the mass of the English people with the deepest misgivings.

IV PARLIAMENTARY REFORM

I

It fared with parliamentary reform as it had fared with Catholic emancipation. In 1817, after the first popular demonstration in its favour, a demonstration which presented the appearance of a rebellion, both parties agreed in refusing to contemplate any reform of the franchise. In 1819 men's ideas had changed. Even Lord Castlereagh, in his reply to a motion by Lord John Russell in favour of reform, admitted that some satisfaction must be given to the middle-class population of the great manufacturing centres. The revolutions in southern Europe followed, and for several weeks it seemed as though Portugal, Spain, and the different States of which Italy was composed were about to become representative democracies. It was a great encouragement for the English Radicals. 'Can we resist,' Peel asked his correspondent

---

[1] H. of C., February 28, 1821 (*Parl. Deb.*, N.S., vol. iv, pp. 989–90, 1003–4). 'I thought Peel tame and feeble,' Ricardo wrote to Trower on March 2; and writing on April 21 to the same correspondent, he said: 'The Catholic Bill is lost. I am sorry for it, though I cannot but think that it is only delayed.'

[2] H. of C., May 10, 1822 (ibid., vol. vii, p. 507).

[3] C. W. Wynn to the Duke of Buckingham, May 15, 1822 (*Memoirs of the Court of George IV*, vol. i, p. 326). Cf. Ricardo's words in a letter to Trower of November 26, 1820, on the subject of a possible Whig Ministry: 'We may probably find men who will remove the disabilities from the Roman Catholics, and make some amendments in our criminal laws, but this will be all.'

Croker—'I mean not next session or the session after that—but can we resist for seven years Reform in Parliament? Will not—remote as is the scene—will not recent events in Spain diminish the probability of such resistance?' And to avert the peril which threatened from the Radicals he suggested that Tories and Whigs should combine to carry out a programme of moderate reform.[1] Then things took another turn. It was now the country gentlemen who were in revolt. They saw that the House of Commons would not accede to their wishes; the Committee of Inquiry appointed in 1821 had proved hostile, and its report, which had been drawn up by Huskisson, was influenced by Ricardo's economic theories. Controlling, as they did, the county electorate, by universal consent the soundest portion of the entire electorate of the country, they began to ask themselves why the majority of the representatives of the boroughs opposed their demands; and came to the conclusion that it must be ascribed to the gross corruption of the borough electors, which made them tools of the Ministers, the large manufacturers, and the financiers. Therefore, they concluded, a reform of the representation which would disfranchise the rotten boroughs could not fail to promote their interests. The county meetings, which were very widely held during the early months of 1822, were not content with asking for the protection of the landed interest, or for some measure of partial bankruptcy; they also declared for parliamentary reform. Simultaneously petitions were being circulated asking for the release of Henry Hunt, who had now been two years in prison, and the petitioners took the opportunity to demand a reform of the franchise. The agitation was perfectly legal, was unaccompanied by any violent demonstrations, and universal suffrage made no part of its programme. It invited, therefore, the sympathy of the moderate reformers.

In the session of 1820 Lord John Russell, appealing to the words spoken by Castlereagh the previous December, proposed that the borough of Grampound should be disfranchised and its seats transferred to Leeds; and that in the new borough the suffrage should be conferred upon every occupier of a house whose annual rental was not less than five pounds. It was estimated that the

[1] Robert Peel to Croker, March 23, 1820 (*Croker Papers*, vol. i, p. 170). For seven years? Seven years was the utmost period for which a Parliament might legally continue in existence. Peel, that is to say, believed that the Parliament elected in 1820 would be compelled to undertake the reform of the franchise.

population of the proposed borough of Leeds, which beside the town itself would comprise ten villages, was seventy thousand, that of these seventy thousand about twenty-eight thousand were adult males, and that of these twenty-eight thousand about eight thousand would become electors if Lord John's Bill were passed.[1] Thus the principle of moderate parliamentary reform was definitely submitted to the legislature, embodied in a particular instance. The hostility of the Tories was instantly aroused, and Castlereagh himself beat a hasty retreat. The Tories complained that Lord John had made the property qualification for the vote in his new borough too low, and urged that it should be raised to ten or even to twenty pounds. On what principle, moreover, should the qualification be made? Why not grant the franchise at once to every ratepayer? And was not this the radical defect of Lord John's proposal—that the creation of a new borough necessitated the creation of a new franchise?[2] They even went so far as to maintain that by creating a new borough Parliament would exceed its powers and infringe the Royal Prerogative. Were they, then, to return to the traditional procedure and absorb the borough of Grampound in the adjacent hundred? This was in fact Canning's proposal;[3] but it could not be disputed that the county of Cornwall, to which Grampound belonged, possessed, with its twenty-one boroughs, far more than its fair representation. So long as its members were strangers to the county, financiers who purchased their seats in the open market, the evil was more tolerable, for the corruption of the system redressed its inequity. If, however, by the enlargement of its electorate Grampound ceased to be a rotten borough, the inequitable distribution of seats under the existing system would become too glaring.[4] Castlereagh proposed a compromise, which on Lord Liverpool's initiative was accepted in principle by the House of Lords. The seats taken from Grampound were given not to a new borough

[1] H. of C., May 9, 19, 1820, Lord John Russell's speech (*Parl. Deb.*, N.S., vol. i, pp. 237 sqq., 480 sqq.).
[2] See the debates, H. of C., March 5, 19, 1820 (ibid., vol. iv, pp. 1077 sqq., 1338 sqq.).
[3] H. of C., May 19, 1820 (ibid., vol. i, pp. 504 sqq.). The hundreds were small territorial divisions believed to date from the reign of Alfred. In theory ten families of freeholders constituted a tything, and ten tythings a hundred (Blackstone, *Comm.* 1, 115). The limits of the electoral borough would therefore, if this procedure were adopted, be extended to the limits of the hundred within which it lay, and within the constituency thus formed the franchise would belong, as in the counties, to the forty-shilling freeholders.
[4] H. of L., May 10, 1820, Lord Liverpool's speech (*Parl. Deb.*, N.S., vol. v, pp. 630–1).

but to the enormous county of Yorkshire. At the last election eighteen thousand electors had voted in Yorkshire. In future they would return four instead of two members.[1] Lord John and his friends accepted the amendment, while reserving the right to claim later separate representation for Leeds or any other large town. But it was evident that public opinion would not be satisfied with such tinkering with the existing franchise. Not only did the Radical members such as Lambton persist in putting forward demands very similar to those made at the meetings of 1817, triennial if not annual parliaments and household in place of manhood suffrage; the Whig aristocracy, encouraged by the signs of yielding displayed by the Tory ranks, took concerted action and sought to devise a scheme of general reform on which they could all agree.

In a series of county meetings which followed immediately the conclusion of the Queen's trial, the Duke of Bedford, Lord Holland, and Lord Grey urged the necessity of reforming the system of representation.[2] Of these three politicians it was the Duke of Bedford who committed himself most definitely in his public utterances; but even Lord Grey appeared to regret the timidity he had shown in 1817. In a letter to Lord Holland, he stated that in his opinion Lord John Russell's motion was not altogether satisfactory. Lord John, he thought, had limited too narrowly the scope of the reform; and writing a few months later to the same correspondent, he expressed his belief that the time for half-measures had passed by, if the demands of public opinion were to be satisfied.[3] A year later the intellectual leaders of the party entered the arena. Lord John Russell, at once the representative of a great family and a publicist, asked the Commons to institute an inquiry into the question of reform.[4] In the pages of the *Edinburgh Review* Mackintosh drew up an entire scheme of

[1] 1 and 2 Geo. IV, cap 47.

[2] Their speeches were inserted by Cobbett in his *Political Register*, January 20, 1821 (vol. xxxviii, pp. 146 sqq.). J. C. Hobhouse, Diary, January 23, 1821: 'Lord Milton owned to me that Reform was gaining ground in his mind. Indeed, I never saw so great a change as to Reform in my life' (Lord Broughton's *Recollections of a Long Life*, vol. ii, p. 140).

[3] Lord Grey to Lord Holland, December 26, 1819; April 23, 1820 (G. M. Trevelyan, *Lord Grey of the Reform Bill*, p. 372). He seems, however, to have been still doubtful how far he should consider himself obliged to introduce a Reform Bill, should he ever become Prime Minister. See Lord Grey's speech to the Northumberland meeting (*Pol. Reg.*, January 20, 1821, vol. xxxviii, p. 151); also J. C. Hobhouse, Diary, December 7, 1820 (Lord Broughton, op. cit., vol. ii, p. 139).

[4] H. of C., May 9, 1821 (*Parl. Deb.*, N.S., vol. v, p. 604). The motion was only rejected by 155 votes to 124, the Tory attendance at the sitting being very poor.

'moderate' reform to serve as the party programme.[1] The schemes propounded respectively in Lord John's speech and in Mackintosh's article follow the same lines. A more speedy procedure must be adopted in future to disfranchise the boroughs which were notoriously corrupt and transfer their seats to towns important for their wealth and large population. According to Mackintosh's estimate there were in all twenty of these. But when the session of 1822 opened Lord John suddenly adopted a bolder line of action. He asked for the immediate addition to the House of Commons of a hundred new seats. Of these hundred additional members sixty would be county representatives, the remaining forty would represent manufacturing centres at present without a representative; and he pointed out that the franchise in these new boroughs need not be uniform. If objection were taken to this sudden increase in the number of seats, the hundred boroughs which under the present system had the smallest electorate might be deprived of half their representation and for the future return only one member instead of two.[2] It was plainly no longer a question of giving the Grampound Bill a general application but of a reform on a very large scale, which, if entitled to be called 'moderate' because it did not include manhood suffrage, was nevertheless 'radical' in comparison with any measure of reform hitherto acceptable to the Whig party as a whole.

What was the explanation of this sudden boldness? It was due beyond question to the apparent conversion *en masse* of the county meetings—that is to say, of the country squires—to the cause of Reform; and the same reason explains the undemocratic tone which pervaded Lord John's speech, his eulogy of the revolutions effected in the past by aristocracies, the expulsion of the Tarquins and of the Stuarts, his appeal not to the Whigs alone, but to the 'influence of a united aristocracy', and more especially to the Tory members of the House of Commons, his emphatic tributes to the county electorate, and the preponderance given to the counties in the measure itself. It seemed to him a favourable opportunity

---

[1] *Edinburgh Review*, November 1820, 'Parliamentary Reform', an article occasioned by Lord John Russell's speech of December 14, 1819 (vol. xxxi, p. 199). Though the number is dated November 1820, it did not appear till the beginning of 1821, being held up for Mackintosh's article (Lord John Russell to Thomas Moore, January 7–8, 1821, *Early Correspondence of Lord John Russell*, vol. i, p. 217).

[2] H. of C., April 25, 1822 (*Parl. Deb.*, N.S., vol. vii, pp. 52 sqq.). 'This was a great step for him', was the comment of J. C. Hobhouse (Lord Broughton) in his Diary, April 25 (Lord Broughton, op. cit., vol. ii, p. 183).

to attempt the formation of a sort of country party which under the leadership of the great Whig families would support his policy in opposition to the Court party, and the temporary estrangement between the Court party and the Court itself was a further encouragement to the project. If these were indeed the hopes entertained by Lord John,[1] he was quickly undeceived. His motion could muster no more than 164 votes against 269 for the Government. The Tory gentry had remained loyal to the Cabinet. But one thing at least had been achieved: for the first time the Whigs had presented a solid front in support of a concrete measure of Reform, and at any time the fortunes of the parliamentary war might place them in power. This consideration explains the tone of the great speech in which Canning opposed Lord John's motion. It is instructive to compare it with the speech which Peel would shortly deliver against the Catholic Bill introduced by Canning himself. Both speeches, dealing with different questions, display the same determination and the same uneasiness: 'If the noble lord shall persevere—and if his perseverance shall be successful—and if the results of that success shall be such as I cannot help apprehending—his be the triumph to have precipitated those results, be mine the consolation that to the utmost and the latest of my power I have opposed them.'[2]

2

The labours of the session continued until August 6, and, when Parliament was prorogued after six months of unremitting warfare against the Government. it was evident that the new strategy of the Opposition, its attempted alliance with the country gentlemen, had not obtained the victory it had been designed to achieve. In adopting it had the leaders of the Opposition, who were themselves great landlords, sought to promote the interests of their class? Or had they merely pursued an immediate political advantage, hoping to place the Ministers in the minority in a

[1] Did he entertain much hope? Consider the pessimism of his language in his letter to Moore of February 26: 'The country is flat and poor and dispirited, the country gentlemen base and servile, and these Ministers have really established themselves in such a way that it will require King and Country to unite very strongly to turn them out' (*Early Correspondence of Lord John Russell*, vol. i, p. 223). A year earlier, in his *Essay on the History of the English Government and Constitution from the Reign of Henry VII to the Present Time*, his remarks on the question of Reform are extremely cautious and by no means such as to make the reader anticipate his bold scheme of 1822.

[2] H. of C., April 25, 1822 (*Parl. Deb.*, N.S, vol. vii, p. 136).

House where the country gentlemen were in a majority? Whatever their motive, they had failed. The vast majority of the country gentlemen had remained faithful to the Government; and, on the other hand, the Whigs had alienated the political economists and the manufacturers at the very moment when the self-esteem of these powerful groups was flattered by the sight of Lord Liverpool, Robinson, and Wallace shaping the commercial policy of the Kingdom in accordance with their wishes. The session of 1822, on which the Whigs had built such high hopes, had proved after all as disappointing as those which had gone before it.

In 1820 they had expected the Queen's trial to produce revolutionary changes, or, at the very least, a Cabinet crisis. But the Ministers were still in office—possibly, it was surmised, for life. As Brougham had foretold, the affair of the Queen had been forgotten as completely as the earlier scandal of the Duke of York and his mistress. In 1821 the Whigs had hoped to exploit the revolutions of southern Europe against the Government; but in 1822 their silence seemed an admission that Lord Castlereagh's policy of non-intervention was, after all, the wiser course; and now, when their attempt to form an alliance with the country gentlemen had proved so barren, could they still hope that they would be able to overthrow the Government in the near future on the question of Catholic emancipation or of parliamentary reform? It was a very doubtful prospect.

Every speaker in the House agreed that these questions were being debated in an atmosphere of unruffled calm, even, according to some, of apathy. In Ireland the Catholic Board which O'Connell had directed in his youth had ceased since 1819 to keep him in the public view, the atrocious crimes committed in the Irish country districts had nothing to do with the Catholic question, and the agitation on behalf of parliamentary reform at the county meetings was, after all, more or less superficial, as though engineered rather than spontaneous; for since unemployment had ceased in the factories and foodstuffs were cheap, it was no longer sustained by a wave of popular discontent like those which had moved the proletariat of the large towns in 1816 and 1819. The spring had not passed before it was completely dead. 'Seize so favourable an opportunity,' urged the advocates of reform, 'to settle two grave problems with the calm deliberation they require, and do not wait until they must be settled in a hurry under the threat of revolution.' 'What good purpose,' replied their adversaries, 'is served by effecting reforms for which there is no urgent demand?' The latter argument was weaker than the former, but it was better adapted to win the suffrages of a legislature.

The Opposition, therefore, was as remote from office as ever. Did this mean that the prestige of the Government stood higher? Certainly not. 'There is no serious or genuine fear of revolution. Neither the politicians nor the public believe in its possibility. But there is a widespread feeling that the old tenets, whether of the Government or the Opposition, are outworn, and in every direction search is being made for that new creed which everyone believes to be necessary, but no one possesses. The result is that the Cabinet is very strong and the official Opposition very weak, yet the Cabinet is the object of general attack and the Opposition is very strong in the country.' These remarks of a foreign observer describe excellently the political situation.[1] Never, indeed, had the Cabinet been more unpopular than at present, and of its members no one was more disliked than the Leader of the Commons, Lord Castlereagh: and his unpopularity, in some respects unaccountable, is all the more significant.

It is unaccountable in the first place because Castlereagh was by no means the most reactionary of the Ministers. The straitest sect of Toryism was represented in the Cabinet by Lord Eldon, Lord Sidmouth, and after 1818 by Wellington, and Castlereagh was responsible for the Coercion Acts only inasmuch as he had yielded, often after considerable hesitation, to their pressure. And if he is to bear the blame for Vansittart's blunders he ought in justice to receive credit for the steady support which he gave in Parliament to the Liberal economics of Robinson and Wallace; and in the matter of Catholic emancipation and the government of Ireland he had been, since Canning's resignation, the head of the Liberal section of the Cabinet. On the question of parliamentary reform, he was less obstinate in defence of the existing system than Canning; and even the Opposition could not help admitting that he had dissociated the foreign policy of Great

---

[1] Guizot to Madame Guizot, June 17, 1822 (*Lettres de M. Guizot à sa famille et à ses amis*, p. 41). Guizot here repeats the impressions received by young Victor de Broglie, who had just visited England.

Britain from the policy of the absolutist Powers. Why, then, was he so unpopular?

One reason was that the most reactionary Ministers sat in the House of Lords. There they were led by Lord Liverpool, a prudent statesman who hardly attracted public notice, and the only Opposition they had to face was the moderate and courteous criticism of Lord Lansdowne. In the House of Commons Castlereagh, in his capacity as leader, was exposed to the blows aimed at the policy of the Government by the most active members of the Opposition—Lord John Russell, Mackintosh, Brougham, Hobhouse, and Sir Francis Burdett. Further, at every congress which the allied sovereigns had held since 1814 to discuss the affairs of Europe, it was Castlereagh who sat as the representative of England by the side of the Emperor of Russia, the Emperor of Austria, and the King of Prussia. Too modest and too anxious for the maintenance of peace to quarrel flatly with the rulers in concert with whom he regularly worked, possibly even flattered by his admission to their intimacy, he failed, where England's foreign policy was concerned, to speak the energetic language which would have stirred and delighted public opinion. He was, moreover, a poor speaker, and his jargon and rigmarole, which had become a byword, made him the laughing-stock of Members of Parliament and journalists.[1] To attacks and jibes he opposed an attitude of silent disdain which was ascribed to haughtiness,[2] though it was perhaps only a form of nervousness. But were his enemies sincere when they taxed him with pride? They knew that he was harmless, and it was for that very reason that they

[1] *The Times*, February 18, 1822: 'Lord Londonderry's speech of Friday night presented one of the most singular specimens of eloquence ever heard within the walls of the House of Commons or read out of them—"Principles of relief vivifying and fructifying"; "A company making new strides, and taking fresh dimensions of prosperity"; "The proposal to repeal taxes to a great extent went to contradict the great causes of nature"; "It was delusive and dangerous to say that distress arose from taxation, and not from Providence and the great principles of Nature"; and "There was no distress in this country that could not be removed by a due application of the principles of resurrection." These and many other expressions excited bursts of laughter, so that if the subject itself was painful in an extraordinary degree, the manner in which it was treated by His Lordship excited much merriment.' Cf. Byron, *Don Juan*, Canto IX, xlviii, xlix. [We have continued to speak of Lord Castlereagh for the sake of convenience, but by his father's death on May 31, 1822, Lord Castlereagh had become Marquis of Londonderry.]

[2] H. of C., February 21, 1821, Mackintosh's speech: 'The noble lord, whose peculiar character it was to remain calm and undisturbed through every discussion, however it might personally or politically relate to him, would not induce him (Sir J. M.) to suppose that he felt uninterested at that moment, for he rather thought that this silence was the result of agitation on the part of the noble lord' (*Parl. Deb.*, N.S., vol. iv, p. 845).

fastened upon him as their victim. His unpopularity, therefore, was at once unmerited, and well deserved. The statesman deserves to be judged severely who can neither make himself feared nor loved.

Penetrated in every fibre with disgust, Castlereagh longed to retire from political life. He said so to his friends; and on one occasion, speaking in the House, he threatened to resign. When Parliament was prorogued, his colleagues and even the King were frightened by a gloom which threatened melancholia. His attention easily wandered, he became lost in reverie, and trembled at the slightest sound. This heavy melancholia, which so often ends with suicide, was known on the Continent in the eighteenth century as *le mal anglais*, the English disease, and since the century opened *le mal anglais* had made two important victims among the politicians of its native country—Whitbread in 1815, Romilly in 1818. An even more important figure was now to be added to the list. On August 12, at his country seat at North Cray, Lord Castlereagh cut his throat with a penknife.

The death of this conscientious administrator and prudent and peace-loving diplomatist was hailed by the entire body of Liberals and revolutionaries both in England and on the Continent as if it had been the death of a tyrant. The violent end of the man who had been one of the principal signatories of the Peace of 1815 was regarded as an event almost more important in the annals of European liberty than the revolutions in Spain and Italy two years before. As befitted his position, Castlereagh received a public funeral, but when his coffin was being carried by the bearers into Westminster Abbey a group among the crowd of interested spectators greeted the disappearance of the Prime Minister with noisy cheering.

PART II

THE DECOMPOSITION OF THE TORY PARTY
(1822–1830)

CHAPTER I

The Hegemony of Canning

I CANNING'S POLICY

I

ONE man was marked out by his brilliant genius to succeed Castlereagh. That man was Canning; but he was the object of universal distrust and dislike. The older Whigs, the contemporaries of Lord Grey, remembered that when still a young man he had entered public life as the protégé of their party—that he had since betrayed the Whigs, placed his talent as a writer at the service of the Tories, and in the pages of his *Anti-Jacobin* had overwhelmed the Whigs with his sarcasms. It was by these tactics that he had won the confidence of Pitt, who had made a wealthy match for him and had appeared to regard him as the future heir of his policy. Nor, on the other hand, could the Tories forget that after Pitt's death he had betrayed them in turn, had been in opposition from 1809 to 1812, and had conspired with the Whigs to drive them from office. He had then dismissed his group of followers, had accepted after Napoleon's defeat an embassy for which he was paid on the most munificent scale, and had finally returned to the Cabinet as President of the Board of Control—in other words, as Minister for India.

Too restless, however, to restrict himself to his official duties, he had intervened with his usual brilliance in the debates, and when the Six Acts were passed his sarcastic tongue had inflicted many a wound upon the democrats and the Whigs. After this, for the second time he had deserted the Cabinet, had refused to act with his colleagues in the matter of the Queen's divorce, and had resigned. He had not, indeed, gone over to the camp of the Opposition, but had exasperated the Whigs by his zealous support of the Tory policy. On April 17, 1821, Hobhouse, himself the victim of an insulting allusion by Canning, undertook to avenge all who had suffered like himself. In a long diatribe, which was heard by a silent and delighted House, he denounced Canning as a sophist, a rhetorician, and a political adventurer, who might perhaps be tolerated by a Parliament corruptly elected, but was doomed to disappear the moment the system of representation had been reformed and in a purified House of Commons there was no longer room for 'talents without character'.[1] Canning, aware that he had alienated both the public and the Court, and was now left without support from any quarter, relinquished his personal ambitions and consented to go to India as Governor. There, he expected, would end in exile a career already long and apparently a failure. He was then fifty-two. 'Canning,' wrote Lord John Russell, echoing the verdict of Hobhouse, 'is, I suppose, to bury himself in India: he is a fool for his pains, but it is a fine moral on the value of character in this country.'[2] And from the Tory benches Lord Eldon had referred 'to the right honourable gentleman whom he wished very well whatever part of the world he might go to'.[3]

When Castlereagh disappeared so unexpectedly from the scene, Canning had not yet sailed for India. He saw at once that the Ministers would be unable to dispense with his services, and let it be plainly understood that he would consent to join the Cabinet only if he were given Castlereagh's entire inheritance, the Foreign Office, together with the management of the House of Commons.[4] The King, however, supported in this by Lord Eldon and several other orthodox Tories, would not hear of Canning either as Foreign Secretary or as Leader of the Commons. He offered the position of Leader to Peel. Wellington, a Minister in the Upper House, would take the Foreign Office.[5] Unlike Canning, Peel could be relied upon to oppose Catholic emancipation. It was for that reason that the University of Oxford had chosen him rather than Canning for her representative. Moreover,

[1] *Parl. Deb.*, N.S., vol. v, pp. 425–6.

[2] To Thomas Moore, January 1822 (Sp. Walpole, *Life of Lord John Russell*, vol. i, p. 127 n.). Sp. Walpole compares with this passage another taken from Lord John's *Memoirs of the Affairs of Europe*: 'It is the character of party, especially in England, to ask for the assistance of a man of talent, but to follow the guidance of men of character.' But it is with Hobhouse's speech, delivered before Lord John Russell's letter, that both passages should be compared.

[3] H. of L., June 21, 1822 (*Parl. Deb.*, N.S., vol. vii, p. 1232). These 'good-byes' were probably the fashion in Tory circles, for a week earlier Lord Manners had written to Peel: 'I trust the House of Lords will deal with the measure as it deserves, and give the author of the Bill a good dressing for not suffering the country, for one year at least, to be exempt from the fever. He is a terribly restless, ambitious, and treacherous fellow, and I heartily wish him a prosperous voyage and a permanent residence in India' (C. S. Parker, op. cit., vol. i, p. 314).

[4] Canning to Morley, August 26, 1822 (A. G. Stapleton, *George Canning and his Times*, p. 362).

[5] C. D. Yonge, op. cit., vol. iii, pp. 195 sqq.; C. S. Parker, op. cit., vol. i, pp. 320, 327 sqq.

the fashion in which he had governed Ireland for six years, the part he had since taken in effecting the return to specie payment, and the talent he had displayed during the past months at the Home Office, seemed in the opinion of many to designate him in spite of his youth, for he was only thirty-four, as a future Prime Minister. Lord Liverpool, though strongly in favour of Canning, would perhaps have yielded to Tory pressure, if Peel had consented to join the intrigue. He had, however, the modesty or the wisdom to decline. He refused to consider it a slight to serve under Canning, his senior by twenty years;[1] and as for Wellington, he had long been of opinion that to strengthen the Government Canning's adhesion must be obtained at whatever cost.[2]

Though the King's repugnance was very strong—for he had not forgotten the Queen's trial—he yielded on September 8. In a letter which he wrote to Liverpool, to be shown to Canning, he declared that 'the highest ornament of his crown' was 'the power of extending grace and favour to a subject who may have incurred his displeasure'.[3] At first Canning was recalcitrant—he would not admit that he stood in any need of forgiveness; but he was soon brought to a more reasonable point of view when it was pointed out to him that all his wishes would be simultaneously gratified by the Foreign Office together with the leadership of the Commons. He accepted, and soon, like the adroit courtier that he was, reconciled himself with George IV by appointing as his private secretary Lord Francis Conyngham, a son of the King's mistress, who in consequence of a quarrel with Peel had done much during the early days of September to forward his rival pretensions.[4]

There was no question in this case of a re-constitution of the Cabinet in the strict sense. Since Canning was completely

[1] Peel to Lord Liverpool, August 20, 1882 (C. S. Parker, op. cit., vol. i, p. 320); to the Speaker (Manners Sutton), September 2, 1822 (ibid., p. 332). Cf. H. of C., May 1, 1827, Peel's speech (*Parl. Deb.*, N.S., vol. xvii, p. 403).

[2] C. Wynn to the Duke of Buckingham, July 15, 1822 (Duke of Buckingham, *Memoirs of the Court of George IV*, vol. i, p. 350). C. W. Wynn to the Duke of Buckingham, August 20, 1822 (ibid., p. 365); September 3, 1822 (ibid., p. 372). Wellington to the King, September 7, 1822 (*Dispatches, Cont.*, vol. i, pp. 274–6), Memorandum shown to Lady Londonderry upon appointing Mr. Canning to Office, September 7, 1822 (ibid., vol. i, pp. 277–8). Cf. Sir Henry Lytton Bulwer (*Historical Characters*, p. 324) for an account of the decisive interview between Wellington and the King.

[3] Greville Memoirs, November 16, 1822 (C. S. Yonge, op. cit., vol. iii, p. 200).

[4] Lord Brougham, *Recollections of a Long Life*, vol. ii, p. 13. Miss Maria Copley to Creevey, January 12, 1823: 'Lord F. Conyngham's appointment gives great disgust, and I don't wonder at it. Lord Alvanley calls him *Canningham*. The King is quite delighted with his Secretary of State, and was seen the other day at the Pavilion walking about with his arm round Canning's neck' (*Creevey Papers*, vol. ii, p. 59).

isolated, he had no staff of subordinates whose claims must be satisfied. The Grenvilles, indeed, made an attempt to secure recognition of their services in supporting with all the weight of their interest Canning's candidature for the succession of Lord Castlereagh; but Canning himself opposed their intrigues.[1] There was only one man whose advancement he desired; for Huskisson he asked the Board of Control, that is to say the India Office, with a seat in the Cabinet. But if Huskisson had acquired considerable influence in Parliament during the last two or three years, he had also incurred the hostility of the country gentlemen by opposing their demands. He was not given the Board of Control. Even in the following January, when Lord Liverpool decided to get rid of Vansittart, whose incapacity was notorious, and replace him at the Exchequer by Robinson, Huskisson did not immediately succeed the latter at the Board of Trade; and when in April he did become President of the Board, he was still excluded from the Cabinet. Canning was not yet sufficiently powerful to satisfy his aspirations and defy the opposition of the Tory gentry in the Commons.

In truth, when he entered upon his new office he found his position far from easy. Though the Tories accepted his collaboration, they submitted with ill grace. They paid homage to his gifts of oratory, 'which everywhere, but especially in free Governments, covers a multitude of sins',[2] but distrusted his ability to replace Castlereagh as a practical politician. Among the Whigs and 'Liberals' hatred of Canning had become a deepseated habit, and at first they uttered their sentiments freely in the party organs. The *Edinburgh Review* protested against this new 'experiment', to which the patience of the country was subjected.[3] The *Examiner* described Canning as 'vain, intriguing, restless, mean, faithless, and unprincipled'.[4] *The Times* refused to see in him anything but an orator, fertile in witty sayings, but entirely destitute of the qualities which make the true statesman.[5] But whereas the distrust of the Tories was destined to increase as time

[1] Duke of Buckingham, *Memoirs of the Court of George IV*, vol. i, pp. 379 sqq.

[2] *Ann. Reg.*, 1822, p. 183.

[3] *Edinburgh Review*, November 1822, 'Mr. Canning and Reform' (vol. xxxvii, p. 407).

[4] *Examiner*, September 15, 1822.

[5] September 2, 6, 13, 16: '. . . A hired advocate, retained to palliate the weaknesses and transgressions of a party, the great majority of whose members he excels in the use of speech.' '. . . The apologist of bad measures, not the author of good ones.' '. . . Mr. Canning is indeed a fit agent or associate for the Holy Alliance.' '. . . The unfortunate

went on, the hostility of the Opposition subsided very rapidly. A few weeks, or rather a few days, had scarcely elapsed since Canning's appointment, when the report went round, a report which had been cleverly spread by his supporters, that the substitution of Canning for Castlereagh was equivalent to a change of Government.[1] The *Morning Chronicle* of October 2, in an article otherwise guarded in tone and which still made many reservations,[2] went so far as to promise Canning 'the glorious title of liberator of Europe' if he had the courage to resist the Emperor of Russia, as he had formerly resisted the tyranny of Napoleon; and the energetic intervention of the Foreign Office in October on behalf of John Bowring, a friend of Bentham's, who was harried at Boulogne by the police of Louis XVIII, justified the hopes of the *Chronicle*, and was a gesture which attracted the attention of Liberals on both sides of the Channel.[3] In a very short time the name of Canning became an object of execration at the Faubourg St.-Germain and Metternich's Chancellery at Vienna. In Milan the Carbonari believed that English foreign policy was now conducted by a 'Radical'.[4]

2

What in reality was Canning's political creed? He had never been a Radical—was anything in the world rather than a Radical. Time and again both to the House of Commons and his constituents at Liverpool[5] he had explained the reasons which led him

Country Gentlemen, reduced as they are to beggary, must expect from that rooted foe to innovation no shadow of relief or assistance.'

[1] *Greville Memoirs*, November 24, 1822.

[2] 'Mr. Canning is no favourite of ours. We like him less than many of his political coadjutors, perhaps because his personal talents point him out as the *Champion* of principles which we abhor. . . . Mr. Canning has some character. . . . He does not blink an awkward question, but glories in his own shame. . . . He is downright in the expression of his miserable opinions, and pursues his rash resolves with inveterate obstinacy. . . .' And after suggesting to Canning the task which he was now in a position to accomplish as the liberator of Europe, the article added: 'In sober sadness we fear that he is not equal to the task.'

[3] For the affair see H. of C., February 27, 1823 (*Parl. Deb.*, N.S., vol. viii, pp. 289 sqq.).

[4] H. of C., April 28, 1823, Hobhouse's speech (ibid., p. 1345).

[5] See Canning's speech to his Liverpool constituents of March 18, 1820, after his re-election (*Speeches*, vol. vi, pp. 369 sqq.). See especially pp. 387–8: 'I will take away a franchise because it has been practically abused, not because I am at all prepared to inquire into the origin or to discuss the utility of all such franchises, any more than I mean to inquire, gentlemen, into your titles to your estates. Disfranchising Grampound (if that is to be so), I mean to save Old Sarum.' See, further, his speech of August 30, 1822, addressed to the same audience, when he still intended to sail for India (ibid., vol. vi, pp. 393 sqq.).

to oppose any reform, thoroughgoing or moderate, of the English representative system. It was not that he was blind to its anomalies and corruption; but was it worth while to reform these vices at the possible cost of destroying the delicate balance of the Constitution which had kept it safely in the *via media* between absolute monarchy and Jacobin revolution, and had rendered it, after a trial of over a century, the model of every free Government? If the credit of the House of Commons was low, if revolutionary Radicalism had apparently been gaining ground, the reason was that unskilful Ministers had lost touch with public opinion, and had thus withdrawn from vital contact with the national mind the Parliament of which they were the mouthpiece. 'The true way,' the *Edinburgh Review* had written in 1819, 'to silence the cry for annual parliaments is *for septennial parliaments to do their duty*; the grand antidote against a rage for universal suffrage is for those who have been elected by a limited class of constituents to act as if they considered themselves charged equally with the interests of all.'[1] When these lines were published Canning was very far from following their advice. Hoping probably to receive promotion in the Cabinet,[2] he had identified himself heart and soul with the most thoroughpaced reactionaries. But that was three years ago, and circumstances had changed since 1819. He was convinced that it was now possible, by following a policy of freedom, to reconcile the country with Parliament, and be at the same time a popular statesman and Leader of the Commons.

What exactly did he understand by this policy of freedom? Catholic emancipation? This was a matter on which his settled convictions diverged from those of the majority of his party. But it was also a matter on which the majority of the Tories claimed, not without reason, to represent the majority of the nation. Would he, on his return to the Cabinet, insist on the necessity of dealing with this thorny question without further delay? In the important speech which he delivered at Liverpool on August 30, fifteen days after Castlereagh's suicide, he made a point of reassuring the Tories by declaring himself ready to accept

---

[1] *Edinburgh Review*, October 1819, 'State of the Country' (vol. xxxii, p. 299).

[2] Several months before the passing of the Six Acts Grenville had written, on January 31, 1819: 'She (Lady Bathurst) said that Canning's conduct had been so good towards them (the Ministers), they were anxious to put him in some more considerable office.'

what he termed 'a liberal compromise'.[1] As Foreign Secretary his immediate sphere was the foreign policy of England, and he did not forget that it was by their foreign policy that both the Pitts had acquired their fame as great statesmen. We should, therefore, pay special attention to the terms in which, in this same speech of August 30, he laid down the principles by which his foreign policy would be governed. There was to be no intervention in the struggle everywhere in progress between democracy on the one hand and monarchy and aristocracy on the other. Thanks to the excellence of her institutions England, 'praised be God for it', was not interested in these conflicts. She must not support either party, content to be an onlooker, eventually perhaps umpire of the contest. But surely this policy of nonintervention, of isolation in regard to the great Continental Powers, was the very policy which the Tory Government had avowedly pursued for the past two years. Did not the Liberals, whose good will Canning sought to conciliate, expect from him a more active policy? To these questions it is difficult to return a categorical reply. Our own answer will appear gradually as we proceed with our narrative. For the moment let us be satisfied with inquiring what forecast of Canning's policy his past conduct would have suggested in this autumn of 1822. When he had broken with the Tories and joined the Whigs in an intrigue against them, it was to insist upon a more active intervention in Spain, to redress the violation of her national liberty. The occasion, in his opinion, had demanded that in the interest of England, France should hear the language of freedom fearlessly spoken, whereas the Ministers, obsessed by the memory of 1793, persisted in employing the language of legitimacy. In other words, the historic bellicose tradition of the eighteenth-century Whigs must be renewed. There was every indication that he would attempt to revive in 1820, against the Holy Alliance, the policy he had urged in 1809 against Napoleon. But in the interval he had returned to the Tories, and, with the lack of restraint characteristic of so many great orators, had spoken a very different language. In 1819 he had vehemently denounced the proposal, advocated by the Whigs, to repeal the Foreign Enlistment Bill.[2]

[1] *Speeches*, vol. vi, p. 398.
[2] H. of C., June 10, 1819 (*Parl. Deb.*, vol. xl, pp. 1103 sqq.); June 14, 1819. If we are to believe Greville, Canning's speech did not prove very effective.

In March 1821, when he was no longer in the Cabinet, he had come to the assistance of his former colleagues and, replying to Sir Robert Wilson's criticisms, had identified himself with their Neapolitan policy. To the demand that England should return to the policy of Queen Elizabeth and, throughout Europe, support the democrats against the Holy Alliance, as Elizabeth had supported the Protestants against the Catholic Church, Canning had made the cynical reply that Elizabeth had assisted the Protestants only when the interest of England demanded that she should do so, that at the very time when she was encouraging the Huguenots she had concluded the Treaty of Blois, and within a few months of Saint Bartholomew had agreed to be godmother to a child of Charles IX.[1] Canning, as we shall presently see, never ceased to employ this language of unashamed patriotic selfishness.

Moreover, in the March of 1821 Liverpool's Government had already broken with the great continental Powers. Indeed, it would be no easy task, if we were to confine ourselves to the actual course of diplomacy, to point out any new departure in the foreign policy of the country after Lord Castlereagh's suicide. But Castlereagh had adopted this attitude of isolation in face of the Holy Alliance only under the pressure of public opinion, half-heartedly and almost apologetically. Canning had the skill to make the most of the new policy, and practised it ostentatiously. Its pursuit meant that England began to make common cause, were it but passively, with the democratic parties against which the Holy Alliance declared war in whatever country they seized the reins of power. Canning did not share Castlereagh's fear of this qualified union and passive assistance, because he had more confidence than Castlereagh in the power of resistance possessed by English institutions, was less afraid that his country might catch the infection of continental Jacobinism. Moreover, to prevent the Cabinet from being divided by public dissensions he was obliged to emphasize again and again, with perfect sincerity, but more loudly perhaps than he would have desired, the contempt he entertained for democratic principles. He seemed to himself, he said, to be walking on a razor's edge. Throughout four sessions he managed to keep his balance, not to engage in war and yet

[1] H. of C., March 20, 1821 (*Parl. Deb.* N.S., vol. iv, p. 1372). See ibid., p. 1376, Mackintosh's protests against the speech with which Canning had amused the House: 'It would really seem as if he occasionally retired from the Government in order to have an opportunity of eulogizing its councils with a greater appearance of disinterested impartiality.'

earn something of the glory which had been possessed by the great War Ministers, the Elder and the Younger Pitt, give the English Liberals and the entire world the impression that his policy was inspired by a new spirit, and satisfy the Tories that it was identical with the policy whose principles had been laid down by Castlereagh. It had never been in Castlereagh's power to perform such miracles; but a poet had succeeded the man of prose.[1]

II SPAIN AND SOUTH AMERICA

I

We must not expect the proceedings of the Congress of Verona to reveal Canning's foreign policy taking shape immediately on his arrival at the Foreign Office. Indeed, if he had possessed the leisure and the power to adopt the course he thought best, England would not even have been represented at the Congress. For several weeks before Canning entered the Cabinet, Wellington had been deputed to take Castlereagh's place at Verona. The instructions which he brought with him were signed by Lord

[1] Certain of Canning's apologists have adopted another line to glorify their hero. According to them it was he who was responsible for the new direction taken by the foreign policy of England after 1818, and, above all, after 1820. Certainly we are not prepared to deny that at the Congress of Aix-la-Chapelle Canning was distinguished among all his colleagues by the insistence with which he demanded that England should dissociate herself from the Holy Alliance (see Lord Bathurst to Lord Castlereagh, October 20, 1818, *Letters of Lord Castlereagh*, vol. xii, pp. 55 sqq.). Without going so far as to suggest with Stapleton (*Political Life of Mr. Canning*, p. 140 n.) that the confidential note of May 5, 1820, was drawn up in part, perhaps even entirely, by Canning (in fact, the conjecture has been disproved by C. K. Webster, *The Foreign Policy of Castlereagh*, 1815, 1822, p. 245), we are ready to grant that between 1818 and 1820 he worked in close collaboration with the Foreign Office. But did his advice meet with opposition from his colleagues or from Castlereagh himself? The very letter from Lord Bathurst to which we have just referred proves that in 1818 Canning's views on these matters were in agreement with those of so uncompromising a Tory as Lord Sidmouth. See, on the other hand, the disconsolate letter written to him by Castlereagh when he left the Cabinet at the end of 1820: 'The unanimity of sentiment which has prevailed in the Cabinet upon our general policy, internal and external, makes it additionally painful that a single question should have led to a result so prejudicial as your leaving the Government must be, under any circumstances, to the public service. . . . As the individual member of the Government who must feel your loss the most seriously, both in the House of Commons and in the business of the Foreign Office, I will not refrain from expressing my disappointment'—December 19, 1820 (A. G. Stapleton, *George Canning and his Times*, p. 319). Further, did Canning after his retirement continue to work hand in glove with Castlereagh? The supposition would explain the zeal with which he defended, in the spirit described in the text, Castlereagh's Neapolitan policy against the attacks of the Whigs. But this argument is fatal to the liberal defence of Canning. Why, we are compelled to ask, did the Whigs in 1821 criticize so bitterly Castlereagh's policy and Canning's speech?

Bathurst, not by Canning,[1] and his position was too eminent and Canning's advent too recent for it to be possible to regard him as merely the agent of the latter.

Three matters engaged the attention of the Congress.

First of all, to wind up the affairs of Italy. His instructions forbade the British representative to interfere. Nevertheless, the decisions reached were such as he desired. For the Austrian Government reduced by half its army of occupation at Naples and began the evacuation of Piedmont, undertaking to complete the operation within nine months. No doubt Metternich's policy was determined by the fear that the French Government might reply to the Austrian occupation of Piedmont by a French occupation of Savoy. French intervention in the Congresses of the Holy Alliance did more to weaken the Alliance than the new attitude of isolation adopted by the British Government.

Then there was the Eastern question. The Greek rebellion was making progress and diplomatic relations had not been restored between Russia and the Porte. At the moment the matter in dispute between them was the measures which the Sultan had just adopted to prevent Greek sailors trading with the Russian ports on the Black Sea under the flag of the Powers to which the passage of the Dardanelles was guaranteed by treaty. Canning instructed Wellington to support the Sultan against the Emperor. Wellington refused to obey, and Lord Liverpool approved his refusal. If Canning had gained his point and England had attached herself to the Sultan's cause, and adopted a separate policy from that pursued by the other Powers, a severe blow would have been dealt to the cause of Greek independence.[2]

And, finally, there was the Spanish question. On this point Lord Liverpool, Canning, and Wellington were in entire agreement, and English public opinion in entire agreement with them. The nation was unanimous in the determination that the French Government should not, under the plea of freeing King Ferdinand

---

[1] H. W. V. Temperley, *Life of Canning*, p. 153.

[2] Wellington to Canning, October 4, 1822 (Wellington, *Despatches, Cont.*, vol. i, p. 353); also Lord Liverpool's letters to Canning, October 21, 24, 1822 (C. D. Yonge, op. cit., vol. iii, pp. 246–7). Stapleton (*Political Life of Mr. Canning*, vol. i, p. 205) passes rapidly over Canning's mistake (?), throws the blame of it upon the English Ambassador at Constantinople, Lord Strangford, and in his account of subsequent events makes his readers believe that Wellington merely carried out Canning's instructions instead of correcting them (ibid., vol. ii, pp. 377–8). Temperley (op. cit., p. 208) increases the confusion of Stapleton's account.

from his bondage to the Revolutionary Government, renew the ambitious design cherished by Louis XIV and Napoleon—the veiled annexation of Spain and the fusion in one great Latin monarchy of France, Spain, and all the Spanish Colonies in the New World. Wellington's task at Verona was rendered easier by the fact that Metternich shared his apprehensions in regard to the policy of France. The dispositions shown by the Emperor of Russia were, it is true, less satisfactory. He offered Louis XVIII the services of a Russian army of one hundred and fifty thousand men; but the French Government shrank from accepting assistance so humiliating to its prestige. Wellington left the Continental Powers to their quarrels, and when they decided to confine their joint action in the matter of Spain to the delivery of notes of protest, to be followed eventually by the recall of their representatives, he warned them that England would not participate even in this diplomatic intervention, their ambassador would deliver no note, and would remain at Madrid after his colleagues' departure to assist the cause of peace by every means at his disposal.

It was in Paris that English diplomacy won, a few days later, a genuine victory. The constitutional army in Spain had just defeated the insurgents of the northern provinces. French public opinion was increasingly hostile to war; the Cabinet itself was divided, and the Prime Minister, M. de Villèle, in favour of peace. After a visit from Wellington, on his way home from Verona to London, de Villèle dismissed his Minister for Foreign Affairs, M. de Montmorency, who was a partisan of war. He replaced him by M. de Chateaubriand, who before he went to Verona as the representative of France had been Ambassador in London, was a friend of Canning, and seemed destined to restore the good understanding between France and England after its momentary eclipse. Thus at the end of December the danger of military intervention in Spain had apparently diminished. Therefore England learnt with consternation at the end of January of the warlike speech with which Louis XVIII opened the session of the Chamber. There was 'little hope of preserving peace'. 'A hundred thousand French troops under the command of a prince of the blood' were 'ready to march'. 'Ferdinand VII must be free to give his people the institutions of which he was the sole legitimate fountain', 'from that moment hostilities would cease'.

2

Parliament was opened on February 4, exactly eight days after the French Chamber. The Speech from the Throne had been already drawn up when Louis XVIII pronounced his speech. It was decided to alter the text and suppress a phrase in which the King explicitly stated his determination to remain neutral;[1] and the words in which he declared himself opposed to all intervention in Spain, and ready at any time to tender his good offices 'to prevent the calamity of a war between France and Spain', seemed so plain that the Government secured the unanimous support of Parliament. Lord Liverpool, in the Upper House, took the Spanish Constitution under the protection of England, and adopted a bellicose attitude.[2] In the House of Commons Brougham substituted for the amendment to the Royal speech which he had intended to put forward, a lengthy and impassioned diatribe against the Holy Alliance and the Bourbons, which was received with loud applause.[3] Canning was absent, for his return to the Cabinet necessitated his re-election and it had not yet taken place. But from the triumphant letter he had written, only a few days earlier, to his friend, Sir Charles Bagot, we may conclude what he thought of the events which were taking place. 'Villèle is a Minister of thirty years ago—no revolutionary scoundrel, but constitutionally hating England, as Choiseul and Vergennes used to hate us—and so things are getting back to a wholesome state again. Every nation for itself and God for us all. Only bid your Emperor (the Emperor of Russia) be quiet, for the time for Areopagus and the like of that is gone by.'[4]

Until the Easter adjournment the House of Commons presented the unwonted spectacle of apparent unanimity. The older Tories kept up their hostility to Canning and pretended to regard Peel

---

[1] H. of C., April 28, 1823, Hobhouse's speech: 'Rumour said that the Foreign Secretary had prevailed over his brother Ministers in procuring the omission of the words "strict neutrality" in H.M.'s speech' (*Parl. Deb.*, N.S., vol. viii, p. 1346).

[2] H. of L., February 4, 1823 (ibid., N.S., vol. viii, pp. 29 sqq.).

[3] H. of C., February 4, 1823 (ibid., N.S., vol. viii, pp. 4–5 sqq.).

[4] Canning to Sir Charles Bagot, January 3 (?), 1823 (A. G. Stapleton, *George Canning and his Times*), pp. 369–70). Seven months later he wrote to J. H. Frere (August 8): 'I do not deny that I had an itch for war with France and that a little provocation might have scratched it into an eruption' (G. Festing, *John Hookham Frere and his Friends*, p. 257).

[5] Creevey to Miss Ord, February 14, 1823: 'People in office are in loud and undisguised hostility to him. . . . I never saw such a contrast as between the manners of ministerial men even to him, and what it used to be to Castlereagh' (*Creevey Papers*, vol. ii, p. 63).

as their real leader.[1] But the intensity of the anti-Bourbon feeling obliged them to silence. The attitude of the old Whigs was equally reserved: but the young Liberals, delighted to find themselves in harmony with the feeling of the nation, were loud in their professions of satisfaction with the policy pursued by the Government, and by this means sought to make capital for themselves out of Canning's popularity. Brougham, who had constituted himself the unofficial Leader of the Opposition, became reconciled with Canning and preached prudence to any of his followers who might have embarrassed the Cabinet or himself by an inopportune motion.[2] On February 21, when the Government proposed that the Navy should be increased from twenty-one to twenty-five thousand men, he declared the proposed increase insufficient and assured the Ministers that if they judged preparations on a larger scale necessary they would have the support both of the House and the nation. Canning found himself compelled to moderate this excessive zeal,[3] as he was obliged three days later to decline the embarrassing compliments showered upon him by Sir Robert Wilson and Hobhouse, who made a point of distinguishing between the present policy of the Government and what they termed the policy of the 'late ministry'.[4] He protested that the Tory policy had undergone no change since Castlereagh's death, but was careful to add before resuming his seat that the Ministers had been greatly assisted in carrying on the government of the country by the indulgence—he would not say

[1] Creevey to Miss Ord, April 28, 1823: ' Ward met me . . . yesterday . . . his talk was . . . that Canning with all his talents and superiority had no support—that Peel had all the Tories and Canning no one of any party with him' (*Creevey Papers*, vol. ii, pp. 68–9).

[2] H. of C., February 12, 1823 (*Parl. Deb.*, N.S., vol. viii, pp. 115–16). Cf. Miss Maria Copley to Creevey, March 6, 1823: 'A still more difficult riddle for me to solve is your friend, Mr. Brougham. Why does he make such love to Canning? Why is he in none of your divisions? Why is he in astonishment at the small demand of Ministers? Is it catalepsy? All your good humour and civility make the debates very flat.' See also Creevey's reply, March 11. According to him, Brougham was aiming at a seat in the Cabinet (ibid., vol. ii, pp. 64 sqq.).

[3] H. of C., February 21, 1823: 'The present state of Europe is one in which the discussions in this House can produce no greater effect than has been already produced by preceding discussions, but on which they may possibly do harm' (*Parl. Deb.*, N.S., vol. viii, p. 193).

[4] H. of C., February 24, 1823, Hobhouse's speech: 'He would be understood to speak of the present and not the late Ministry; for, if the same language had been held at Troppau and Laybach, as he had reason to believe had been held at Verona, we should not now have been placed in the emergency of having to choose between the consideration of those difficulties and dangers which beset them at home and the maintenance of the independence of Europe and the liberties of mankind at large' (ibid., vol. viii, p. 340).

the unexpected indulgence—which the House had displayed in their regard. For two months the Commons refrained from embarrassing the Government by a debate on the Spanish question. Immediately before Parliament adjourned, two members who were not leaders of the official Opposition asked both Houses to pass a vote of no confidence.[1] It was a waste of time; they did not obtain a hearing. Parliament looked to the Ministry to prevent the French Army entering Spain.

When Parliament reassembled on April 9 the position had changed. Three days earlier the French Army had crossed the Bidassoa and begun its march upon Madrid. It was a rebuff to Canning's diplomacy. But what had in fact been his policy during the previous six months? The documents published by the Government in support of their conduct were badly received by the Liberals. For they revealed the fact that in September Canning had instructed Wellington to state 'frankly and peremptorily' that, 'come what may', England would not participate in any scheme of intervention, a declaration which assured France from the outset that England would maintain an attitude of systematic neutrality, of peace at any price, 'come what may'.[2] And they revealed the further facts that in December Wellington had offered France the mediation of England and had met with a refusal; that nevertheless an English agent, a Tory and a friend of Wellington, had been sent to Madrid in January, with the approval of the French Government, to advise the Cortes to introduce into the Spanish Constitution such amendments as would satisfy and reassure the French Court, advice which had also been rejected;[3] and the public could read in the correspondence the letter addressed by Canning to A'Court on January 11: 'We wish for peace in Europe: but peace for ourselves we are determined at all events to preserve; and, should our efforts to maintain it between France and Spain prove abortive, we should have the consolation to have discharged the duty towards both of a faithful and disinterested ally; and should retire thenceforth within the limits

---

[1] H. of L., April 4, 1823, Lord Ellenborough's motion (*Parl. Deb.*, N.S., vol. viii, pp. 1175 sqq.); H. of C., April 28, 29, 30, 1823, Macdonald's motion (ibid., N.S., vol. viii, pp. 1301 sqq., 1365 sqq., 1442 sqq.).

[2] Canning to Wellington, September 27, 1822; the Duke of Montmorency to Wellington, December 26, 1822 ('Diplomatic Correspondence relative to the Relations between France and Spain', *Ann. Reg.*, 1823, Public Documents, p. 97).

[3] Canning to Wellington, December 6, 1822; the Duke of Montmorency to Wellington, December 26, 1822 (ibid., pp. 103, 106).

of a strict neutrality.'[1] Canning proceeded to urge upon A'Court the necessity of insisting upon the British determination to preserve neutrality and dissipating the hopes, entertained by the Spanish Constitutionalists, that in the last resort England would send an army to their assistance. This was not the language which Brougham, Hobhouse, and Sir Robert Wilson had attributed to the man for whom they had felt a sudden access of hero-worship.

3

Once more, therefore, Canning found himself exposed to the criticisms of the Opposition. A violent altercation, famous in the annals of the British Parliament, broke out on April 17 between Brougham and himself.[2] The subject of the dispute, however, was not the Spanish question but Catholic emancipation, and the incident was aggravated by Canning's inflammable temper. Moreover, whoever will read the lively speeches made by the Members of the Opposition, and Brougham's in particular, cannot fail to discover that, despite appearances, Canning and Brougham were still in collusion. Whenever Brougham dealt with Spanish affairs he persisted in paying tribute to the 'sentiments' expressed by Canning 'which reflected the highest honour on his character', maintained that, if in practice he had played a sorry part, 'the fault was not attributable to him but to the badness of his cause', and, after further praise for the 'liberal sentiments he had expressed', uttered the wish that 'those sentiments were common to him, and to all his colleagues and their supporters'.[3] Towards the end of April, on the eve of the day fixed for the decisive debate on the Spanish question, Dudley Ward, who enjoyed Canning's confidence, accosted Creevey in the street, represented to him the complete isolation in which Canning was placed, and entreated the Opposition to come to his succour.[4] No doubt Ward was not the only person to risk such a step, and these efforts were not fruitless. When Canning had defended the policy of the Government in a speech which was a masterpiece of oratory, Brougham replied in the name of the Opposition, and

---

[1] Canning to Sir William A'Court, January 11, 1283 ('Diplomatic Correspondence relative to the Relations between France and Spain', *Ann. Reg.*, Public Documents, p. 120).
[2] H. of C., April 17, 1823 (*Parl. Deb.*, N.S., vol. viii, pp. 1091 sqq.).
[3] H. of C., April 14, 1823 (ibid., vol. viii, pp. 897 sqq.).
[4] Creevey to Miss Ord, April 28, 1823 (*Creevey Papers*, vol. ii, p. 66).

his strictures were apparently as violent as anyone could desire. But he concluded by warning the Opposition not to attempt a vote of censure against the Government, lest 'by an unintelligible vote' they should destroy the impression of unanimity which it was essential to produce in the public mind.[1] It was Canning who insisted that the motion should be put to the vote. It was lost by the overwhelming majority of three hundred and seventy-two to twenty.

How are we to explain this persistent unanimity?—and what were the arguments with which Canning was enabled to accept so triumphantly before the bar of public opinion the responsibility for a policy of systematic neutrality? The political creed to which he, when he detached himself from the Holy Alliance, had apparently pledged his allegiance, was the traditional formula of the balance of power, 'the only safeguard of nations, the protection of the weak against the strong, the principle by which small States flourished in the vicinity of great ones'.[2] But surely the logical issue of this doctrine, so dear to Mackintosh and Lord John Russell, must be war, and particularly, as in the eighteenth century, war with France? To escape the impasse Canning now spoke in language very different from that which he had employed when he wrote to his friend Charles Bagot in January. He returned to the thesis he had developed in his Liverpool speech of August 1822. War in Europe was no longer, in the nineteenth century, what it had been in the eighteenth—war between nations: it was now a war of opinions. It was no longer a question—otherwise, a zealot for national independence, he would not have held back—of supporting Spain against France. It was a question of supporting the revolutionary against the monarchical principle: that he was not prepared to do. England, endowed with free institutions, which protected her alike against the menace of absolutism and the menace of Jacobinism, could not do otherwise than remain neutral between these two hostile principles, and offer her peaceful mediation to the parties which divided Continental opinion between them. To the Holy Alliance and to France, whose armed interventions were provoking all over Europe a war between the conflicting principles of government, England opposed a programme not of counter-intervention but

[1] H. of C., April 30, 1823 (*Parl. Deb.*, N.S., vol. viii, pp. 1345-6).
[2] H. of C., April 29, 1823, Mackintosh's speech (ibid., vol. viii, p. 1407).

of non-intervention and peace. 'We determined,' Canning declared, 'that it was our duty, in the first instance, to endeavour to preserve peace, if possible, for all the world; next to endeavour to preserve peace between the nations whose pacific relations appeared most particularly exposed to hazard; and, failing in this, to preserve at all events peace for this country.'[1]

Who, indeed, in England wanted war? Certainly not the Tories. Because they were Tories, the French declaration of war against the Cortes excited their fears for the cause of order in every country throughout the world. Like all the English they expected a long war. How, indeed, could they forget the lessons of history, and imagine that the Duke of Angoulême would succeed where Napoleon had failed? And what a prospect of endless ramifications a long war opened up! If the Russian and Prussian Armies, 'the modern Teutons and the modern Scythians',[2] came to the help of France, what would be the effect of their intervention upon French public opinion? What would be the attitude of the Army itself, infected as it was by Bonapartism and Liberalism? The Portuguese, Spanish, and Neapolitan revolutions had all begun by mutinies in the Army, and alarmist rumours were current in March as to the spirit prevalent at French headquarters, when the Army of Louis XVIII was still encamped on the right bank of the Bidassoa; and, indeed, who could be certain that even the Russian or Prussian Army would remain immune from the revolutionary plague? The war was an act of folly which might very well inaugurate, after eight years of peace, a new era of disturbances and massacres. Lord Eldon, in a letter written to a friend on March 31 to express his anxiety, deplored that men should so easily forget the misery of war, its enormous waste of treasure and blood. 'Men,' he wrote, 'delude themselves by supposing that war consists wholly in a proclamation, a battle, a victory, and a triumph. Of the soldiers' widows and the soldiers' orphans, after the fathers and husbands have fallen in the field of battle, the survivors think not.'[3]

And did even the Whigs and Liberals really desire war? The Whig aristocracy and the world of industry and commerce were alike profuse in their demonstrations of sympathy for the Spanish

[1] H. of C., April 30, 1823 (*Parl. Deb.*, N.S., vol. viii, p. 1480).
[2] H. of C., February 4, 1823, Brougham's speech (ibid., vol. viii, p. 61).
[3] Lord Eldon to Lord Encombe, March 31, 1823 (H. Twiss, *The Public and Private Life of Lord Chancellor Eldon*, vol. ii, p. 472).

Constitutionalists; were lavish with receptions, balls, and banquets. But those who were responsible for these demonstrations betrayed a constant fear lest they should be led to compromise themselves.[1] The 'Spanish ball', which had been arranged to assist the cause of Spain, degenerated into an ordinary charity ball in aid of the wounded.[2] Some Whig speakers—for example, Lord Althorp—declared themselves opposed to military intervention in any shape or form.[3] Others appeared at first sight to speak a bellicose language, but when their speeches are examined we find that they were content to blame the Government for having failed to bluff the French Government by adopting a warlike tone, and thus prevent French intervention in Spain and the consequent danger that England might find herself obliged to intervene—a contingency practically inevitable if hostilities should be prolonged. Sir Francis Burdett, the only Member of Parliament unequivocally in favour of war, was forced to admit that 'a majority of the House was in favour of peace, of peace come what may'.[4] What he said of the majority of the Commons he might have said with equal truth of the majority—the overwhelming majority—of the country, and Canning knew it. Crushed by the burden of taxation, England was obliged to replace her finances on a sound basis, and enrich herself by industry and trade, before she could indulge in the luxury of aggression abroad.[5]

The true representatives of that world of industry and commerce with which Canning, as Member for Liverpool, had been in touch for many years past, were not Mackintosh and Lord John Russell, theorists who lived on the memories of a past century,

---

[1] Diary of Thomas Moore, June 12, 1823: '. . . Had a note from Hobhouse saying it was the wish of the committee for the Spanish meeting tomorrow that I should move or second one of the resolutions to be proposed. . . . The time was too short now to prepare myself as I ought. It is not so much what one is to say as what one is *not* to say that requires consideration' (*Mem. . . . of Thomas Moore*, vol. iv, p. 81). Wilberforce wrote as follows in his Diary for March 1823: 'I gave my name yesterday as a steward to the great dinner to the Spanish and Portuguese Ministers, but did not attend because I found some violent things might be said, which I could not then contradict, yet should not like to acquiesce in, for we must not go to war' (R. I. and S. Wilberforce, *Life of William Wilberforce*, vol. v, pp. 167–8).

[2] *Quarterly Review*, January 1823, 'Affairs of Spain' (vol. xxviii, p. 538 n.).

[3] H. of C., April 16, 1823 (*Parl. Deb.*, N.S., vol. viii, p. 1019).

[4] H. of C., April 29, 1823 (ibid., vol. viii, p. 1434).

[5] See Princess Lieven to General Benckendorff, April 15, 27, 1823: 'The English public is beginning to display a little common sense; what is more to the point, an appreciation of its own interest—the first consideration with the English. They will not spend a shilling on those interesting Spaniards, the objects of their good wishes' (*Letters of Dorothea, Princess Lieven, during her Residence in London, 1821–1834*, pp. 110–11).

but Joseph Hume, the merciless critic of public expenditure, and Ricardo, who, in spite of his Radical politics, enjoyed the ear of both sides of the House whenever an economic question was under discussion. It was unthinkable that Ricardo or Hume should approve a policy of war; and their attitude provided Canning with a further argument with which to defend a policy of strict neutrality. 'Be yours,' he said with a smile to the French Ambassador, 'the glory of a victory followed by disaster and ruin, be ours the inglorious traffic of industry and an ever-increasing prosperity. *Trahit sua quemque voluptas.*'[1] When the Whigs seemed to demand, without however explaining exactly what action they would have taken, a more active intervention in the affairs of Spain, he reminded them of the contrary attitude which their party had adopted towards the Peninsular War. 'The age of chivalry,' said Mr. Burke, 'is gone; and an age of economists and calculators has succeeded.' Canning quoted these words of the statesman who in many respects had been his political teacher; but he accepted with equanimity what Burke had admitted with sorrow, and ironically expressed his surprise at witnessing the spirit of chivalry revive in Parliament on the benches formerly occupied by the economists and the calculators.[2]

4

The event of the Spanish War falsified English prognostications. It proved to be not a war but a route-march. The general insurrection which in 1807 had broken out against Napoleon's Army at the invitation of the British now broke out against the Cortes at the invitation of the Bourbon Army. The latter, which had entered Spain on April 7, reached Madrid on May 23, Seville on June 21, and by June 24 was before Cadiz, whither the Cortes had retreated, taking with them their captive monarch. On September 30 Cadiz surrendered. The British Ambassador, who had taken refuge at Gibraltar, had played an insignificant and humiliating part throughout the summer. Instinctively the entire country felt the shame of its representative, and was chagrined to see France escape, to use the language of the *Quarterly Review*, that 'species of control which for ages, with different degrees of success, we

---

[1] M. de Marcellus to M. de Chateaubriand, November 30, 1822 (Comte d'Antioche, *Chateaubriand, Ambassador à Londres*, p. 380).
[2] H. of C., April 30, 1823 (*Parl. Deb.*, N.S., vol. viii, p. 1512).

have endeavoured to exercise upon her'.[1] For the Liberals it was the discomfiture of all their hopes and the triumph of the Holy Alliance. Many financiers and private persons had subscribed to the loan opened by the Cortes; their bonds were waste paper.

Nevertheless, on mature consideration English public opinion made the best of the conditions which the French victory had brought into being. It was evident that France, and even the French Government, was deeply divided on the question of the Spanish War, and was embarrassed by its own victory. Indeed, the French were compelled to intervene at Madrid to check the excesses of Ferdinand's reaction. Nor was the British public blind to the fact that the brevity of the war had settled the question of English intervention, and, as nobody had wanted war, everybody was delighted that Canning had saved his country from compromising itself by an imprudent step. Although Canning had never expected that the war would be concluded so speedily,[2] he was not slow to proclaim that his policy had been justified by the event. He warned the public against the danger of a quixotic policy, and brought down the laughter of the entire House of Commons upon Lord Nugent and Sir Robert Wilson, who had gone to play the knight-errant at Cadiz.[3] At the same time he asked the Liberals, through private channels, to continue in sufficient numbers to vote against him, so as to produce on the Continent the belief, which would strengthen his hand, that a war party existed in England.[4] And it was not long before Canning and Sir Robert Wilson were again exchanging compliments across the floor of the House.

'You know my politics well enough,' Canning had written to a friend a few weeks after his arrival at the Foreign Office, 'to know what I mean when I say that for *Europe* I shall be desirous *now* and *then* to read *England*.'[5] This attitude of moral and diplo-

---

[1] *Quarterly Review*, January 1823, 'Affairs of Spain' (vol. xxviii, p. 537).
[2] W. H. Freemantle to the Duke of Buckingham, July 27, 1823 (Duke of Buckingham, *Memoirs of the Court of George IV*, vol. i, p. 483).
[3] H. of C., March 18, 1824 (*Parl. Deb.*, N.S., vol. x, pp. 1265 sqq., especially pp. 1273 sqq.). Cf. R. I. and S. Wilberforce, op. cit., vol. v, p. 217. 'Don Quixotism', see Canning's speech at Plymouth, October 1823 (*Speeches*, vol. vi, pp. 4-23).
[4] Sir D. le Marchant, *Memoir of Viscount Althorp*, p. 211.
[5] To Sir Charles Bagot, November 5, 1822 (A. G. Stapleton, *George Canning and his Times*, p. 364). Cf. letter to Frere, August 8, 1823: 'The Allies lament themselves heavily at our separation from them. . . . The history of all I could tell them in two words— or rather in the substitution of one word for another—for "Alliance" read "England", and you have the clue of my policy' (G. Festing, op. cit., pp. 257 sqq.).

matic isolation from the rest of the world he would never abandon. His skilful tactics secured for his policy the support not only of the humanitarian Liberals but, what was far more important, of those vast numbers whose sole wish was to sever the bond which since 1815 had united England to the Holy Alliance, and withdraw their country from the broils of the Continent. In an important speech delivered at Plymouth in October 1823, of which the peroration, an example of classic oratory, is inspired by a spirit of proud defiance which is almost a threat of war, the speaker, while paying his tribute to that modern philosophy which 'professes the perfection of our species and the amelioration of the lot of all mankind', declared that his policy had no other aim than 'the interest of England'.[1] When, a few months later, he defended against the Opposition an Alien Bill which placed every foreigner resident in England under police supervision, he spoke the same language. He refused to take into consideration 'the wishes of any other sovereign, the feelings of any other Government, or the interests of any other people, except in so far as those wishes, those feelings and those interests may, or might, concur with the just interests of England'.[2] The French success in Spain had undeniably been detrimental to English interests. But England was in a position to turn that reverse to her profit, since her commercial interest lay not in Spain, but in the Spanish colonies of South America.

'These insular shopkeepers,' wrote M. de Villèle on December 5, 1822, 'are playing a new part at Madrid. They are trying to make out that they have been the object of more bitter hostility and have been worse treated than other foreigners on account of their expedition against Cuba. But do not believe a word of it. They will profit by the expedition, and by the desperate condition of the Peninsula, to sell at a dearer rate whatever assistance they will consent to give.'[3] And, in fact, Sir William A'Court had barely arrived in Madrid before he contrived to make good use of his unique position, as the sole protector of the Government of the Cortes against the representatives of all the other Powers. In consequence of the anarchy which prevailed throughout Spanish America there had grown up in the Caribbean Sea an organized

[1] *Speeches*, vol. vi, p. 421.
[2] H. of C., April 2, 1824 (*Parl. Deb.*, N.S., vol. xi, p. 119).
[3] Chateaubriand, *Congrès de Vérone*, vol. i, p. 264.

system of piracy from which the British merchantmen suffered most heavily. Sir William demanded and obtained from the Cortes the payment to England of an indemnity of £500,000 by way of compensation for the losses already sustained and permission to land British troops in Cuba to attack the pirates in their dens.[1] And he successfully put pressure upon the Cortes to enter into negotiations with the colonial Governments with a view to recognizing their independence.[2] Pending this recognition, Canning notified the Spanish Government that the commercial independence of the Spanish States of South and Central America, which had existed *de facto* for several years past, would now be formally acknowledged by the speedy dispatch of British consuls to these States.[3] This was the price he exacted from the Cortes for the purely moral support he was prepared to accord, and the subservient attitude which the Cortes was compelled to adopt towards the British Government contributed without a doubt to its unpopularity, and thus facilitated the French victory a few months later.[4] In April he took a further step in support of the revolted colonies. England had declared her neutrality as between France and the Spanish constitutionalists, and appeared by this step to prohibit her subjects from assisting either belligerent. But Canning gave a novel interpretation to British neutrality. Though he refused to repeal the Foreign Enlistment Act, and forbade Englishmen to enlist for service in the war, he declared the traffic in munitions lawful. English traders were therefore free to make a fortune by the indiscriminate sale of arms to the Cortes and the Bourbon Govern-

---

[1] *Ann. Reg.*, 1823, p. 26. Cf. A. G. Stapleton, *The Political Life of Mr. Canning*, vol. i, pp. 166 sqq.

[2] Ibid., vol. ii, p. 17.

[3] Ibid., vol. ii, p. 10. The second and third of these instructions were suspended on January 7, 1823, when Canning at last perceived what a bad effect they had produced upon Spanish public opinion; but the news of the suspension reached Madrid too late (H. Temperley, *The Foreign Policy of Canning*, 1822–1827, pp. 76, 107).

[4] On the question of recognizing the Spanish colonies he was working with Lord Holland and Sir Robert Wilson from the first half of October 1822 (see Lord Holland's letter of October 7 and Sir Robert Wilson's of October 4, Wellington, *Despatches, Cont.*, vol. i, pp. 413, 416); and he forced the hand of Wellington, who was compelled, much against his will, to be Canning's mouthpiece at Verona (see Wellington to Canning, October 18, 1822; Canning to Wellington, October 29, 1822; Wellington to Canning, November 5, 1822; Wellington to Canning, November 10, 1822; Wellington to Canning, November 29, 1822, Wellington *Despatches, Cont.*, vol. i, pp. 384, 463, 491, 516, 616). See especially p. 516, the letter of November 10: 'I confess I should be ashamed of showing my face . . . if the piracy did not give me something to say besides the arguments of commercial advantage and the clamours of our people.'

ment, but, above all, to the Governments of the revolted colonies.[1]

Further, the dispatch of the consuls, announced in November 1822 but delayed for several months, was hurriedly effected as soon as the French victory, whose possibility had been at first doubted, seemed likely to be decisive. 'Lord Liverpool and Canning,' a politician wrote in September, 'are now running wild in speculative objects in South America; perhaps they are not wrong in this, for it is much easier to take a decision upon it now than when the Spanish King shall be restored to his throne.'[2] If France, by her declaration of war against the Cortes, had hoped to checkmate the American policy of the British Cabinet she had made a mistake, and M. de Villèle, who, though he had assumed the responsibility of declaring war, had never approved of the step, was quick to recognize the fact. But even when French statesmen perceived that the objective of the Spanish policy pursued by the English Government must be sought in America, not in Europe, they made another miscalculation, for they credited England with the design of landing an army and establishing colonies in South America. In reality the English had conceived a profound dislike for the policy of colonial expansion. When in 1816 Lord Exmouth, by bombarding Algiers, had compelled the Dey to release all his Christian slaves, neither he nor the British Government had for an instant entertained the thought of utilizing the victory to establish a permanent station on the coast of Barbary. For large numbers of Englishmen the War of American Independence was still a living memory, and now that the Spanish empire was in its turn falling to pieces, it did not seem worth while incurring fresh disasters by an attempt to seize the succession of the Spanish Crown in these distant territories. It was not colonies but markets which the English were seeking in South America.[3]

[1] *Ann. Reg.*, 1823, p. 178.

[2] Freemantle to the Duke of Buckingham, September 29, 1823 (Duke of Buckingham, *Memoirs of the Court of George IV*, vol. ii, p. 7).

[3] With the possible exception of Cuba, where the British Government considered the eventuality of a military occupation (C. W. Wynn to the Duke of Buckingham), the end of 1822 (Duke of Buckingham, op. cit., vol. i, p. 398), and even of annexation (Canning to Lord Liverpool, October 6, 1826, E. J. Stapleton, *Some Official Correspondence of Canning*, vol. ii, p. 144), to avoid at any cost the risk of annexation by the United States.

Conscious of intentions so sincerely disinterested, Canning took a bold step. He made proposals to the Government of the United States, through Rush, the American Ambassador in London, for the joint conclusion by the Governments of London and Washington of a pact guaranteeing the States of Spanish America against military intervention on the part of Spain, France, or the Holy Alliance acting in concert.[1] English public opinion had been partly prepared to accept such an agreement by a speech which Canning made at Liverpool at a banquet in honour of an American diplomat in which he had expressed his satisfaction—a satisfaction shared 'in common with the great mass of the intelligent and liberal men of both countries'—at witnessing the improved relations between two nations 'united by a common language, a common spirit of commercial enterprise, and *a common regard for well-regulated liberty*'. And he foresaw the day when old grudges would be forgotten and 'the daughter and the mother *stand together against the world*'.[2] Had he realized his design, and confronted the Holy Alliance with a hostile system of international relations based on an alliance between England and the American democracy, it may be doubted whether the Tories would have tolerated the scandal.[3] But he did not succeed in winning Rush to his views. 'It is France,' wrote Rush to his Government, 'that must not be aggrandized, not South America that must be set free.'[4] And on December 2 President Monroe promulgated his his famous doctrine.[5] For the suggested agreement by which England and the United States would unite in a joint pledge to defend Spanish America against intervention by any other Power, he substituted a declaration by which the Government of the United States assumed the sole responsibility for protecting the entire American continent against all European interference.

[1] A. G. Stapleton, *The Political Life of Mr. Canning*, vol. ii, p. 23; H. W. V. Temperley, *Life of Canning*, pp. 179, 181.

[2] See for the text of the speech *Pol. Reg.*, September 20, 1823 (vol. xlvii, pp. 711–12).

[3] See Metternich's appeal to Wellington, February 11, 1824: 'The English Government appears determined to adopt a policy of complete isolation. . . . Is it possible that England could entertain for the moment the thought of political co-operation with the United States of America? The most superficial glance at the political situation is sufficient to demonstrate the absurdity of such a notion. . . . It is our desire that America shall not by any fault of the European powers be placed in a position to dictate to Europe' (Welling, *Despatches, Cont.*, vol. ii, p. 207).

[4] H. Temperley, *The Foreign Policy of Canning*, p. 113.

[5] See the text of his message, *Ann. Reg.*, 1823, Public Documents, pp. 183 sqq.

The official Press of London received orders to represent President Monroe's message as his adhesion to Canning's policy, a victory for that policy; and the public opinion of the Continent, particularly French opinion, was deceived by the London Press. But Canning knew that he had been defeated; and it only remained for him to do his utmost to overtake the United States.[1] For already, in 1822, the United States had recognized the complete independence, political as well as commercial, of the new American States. Plenipotentiaries had been appointed by both parties in the course of 1823. Commercial treaties might therefore be concluded which would favour the commerce of the United States to the detriment of British. The United States might even be contemplating the annexation of Mexico or Cuba. It was to render these American projects innocuous to the honour and interest of Britain that Canning had attempted to reach an agreement with the Government of Washington upon a common policy. Since the attempt had failed, it was but common sense to follow the example of the United States without further delay and recognize formally the political independence which the Spanish colonies had in fact achieved. The world of industry and commerce was urgent for the recognition, organized demonstrations, and sent up petitions. The Liberal speakers in the House pleaded for it.[2] Lord Liverpool was in favour of recognition. The change would not be momentous, would, in fact, be simply a matter of sending 'ministers' where hitherto only 'consuls' had been sent. Nevertheless, it required twelve months' effort before the step which Canning desired was taken.

The delay was due to the instability of the political situation. Canning was able to control the House of Commons by the power of his oratory, his popularity in the country and his world-wide reputation. But he was not loved by the Members. Well aware of the fact, he was careful not to aggravate his unpopularity with the House by intervening in his capacity as leader in debates which did not immediately concern the Foreign Office. On such occa-

[1] See a little later, when his policy had succeeded, Canning's outburst of jubilation in his letter of December 17, 1824, to Lord Granville: 'Spanish America is free, and, if we do not mismanage our matters greatly, she is English' (A. G. Stapleton, *George Canning and his Times*, p. 411). To J. H. Frere, January 8, 1825: 'The Yankees will shout in triumph; but it is they who lose most by our decision' (G. Festing, op. cit., pp. 264 sqq.).

[2] A petition signed by 113 London business houses was presented on June 15 to the Commons by Sir James Mackintosh. The Manchester petition was presented by Mackintosh on June 21 (*Parl. Deb.*, N.S., vol. xi, pp. 1344, 1475).

sions he withdrew into the background and left the lead to Peel or Robinson.[1] It was clearly his intention to establish a dictatorship of public opinion upon the ruins of the old parties. No wonder that both parties regarded him as a schemer and a traitor, and contemplated with anxiety the possible result of Lord Liverpool's death or retirement. For at this very juncture Liverpool fell seriously ill, and for several months was unable to perform his official duties as Prime Minister. If Canning wished to succeed him as Premier,[2] as he had succeeded Castlereagh as leader of the Commons, the consent of King George was indispensable. But on the question of recognizing the South American republics the King was obdurate. He regarded the recognition as an intolerable affront to the principle of monarchy. It was only to be expected that Wellington, who had been at enmity with Canning for several months past,[3] should make use of this opportunity to prevent his being made Prime Minister. In such circumstances it it obvious that he must act with the greatest caution. When in April, accompanied by only one of his colleagues, he had attended the banquet given by the Radical Lord Mayor Waithman, who had passionately supported the cause of the Queen in 1820, a banquet at which the leaders of the Opposition and several Spanish-Americans were his fellow-guests, King George had protested against his action.[4] And he knew that the King was now plotting against him with Madame de Lieven, wife of the Russian Ambassador, a woman notorious for her political intrigues, and Prince Esterhazy, the Austrian Ambassador. It was evident that he had again lost the favour of the Court. He there-

[1] W. H. Fremantle to the Duke of Buckingham, June 25, 1823: 'Canning does nothing in the House, and I think suffers Peel to take completely the lead. . . . I think Canning loses ground greatly; he is anything but a leader of the House of Commons' (Duke of Buckingham, op. cit., vol. i, p. 469). Fremantle to the Duke, July 9, 1823: '. . . We should have done just as well without Canning as a leader as with him. He has taken upon himself no authority, either by putting down or assisting questions doubtful or difficult. Robinson and Peel have both risen much beyond him in estimation as general speakers and men of business' (ibid., vol. i, p. 475). Fremantle to the Duke, July 27, 1823: 'The complete ascendancy which both Robinson and Peel have acquired over him in the House of Commons, but more particularly the former' (ibid., vol. i, p. 481). Canning explained to Frere on August 23, 1823, the reason of his deliberate self-effacement (G. Festing, op. cit., p. 260).

[2] Or even, were such a thing possible, to act as leader of the Commons under a Prime Minister of his own choosing. When in September Canning visited Lord Wellesley at Dublin, it was rumoured that the object of his visit was to make an arrangement of this kind with Lord Wellesley (Duke of Buckingham, op. cit., vol. ii, pp. 119, 132, 156, 157).

[3] Fremantle to the Duke of Buckingham, May 31, 1823 (ibid., vol. i, pp. 457–8).

[4] C. D. Yonge, op. cit., vol. iii, pp. 278 sqq.; Duke of Buckingham, op. cit., vol. ii, p. 65; Wellington, *Despatches, Cont.*, vol. ii, pp. 261–2.

fore began to temporize, and was content to reject the proposal put forward by France, with the consent of Spain, that the South American question should be referred to a congress to be held at Paris.[1] This would have been tantamount to submitting the cause of the South American States to the decision of the Holy Alliance, and to such a solution not even President Monroe could have been more strongly opposed than was Canning. He laid before Parliament the memorandum of the interview which he had had in October, even before the *pourparlers* with Rush had been brought to an end, with the French Ambassador, M. de Polignac, in the course of which he declared that England would consider any foreign interference by force or by threats, in the dispute between Spain and her colonies, a sufficient motive for immediate recognition of the latter. From the day when this document was made public, it was no longer Monroe, it was Canning, who appeared in the eyes of the world the protector of the independence of the South American Republics. He pressed Spain to accord voluntarily the recognition of an independence which sooner or later she would be compelled to admit. When Spain was obstinate, he referred the question to the Cabinet after the prorogation of Parliament at the beginning of July.[2] Wellington carried the day, and he thought it prudent to continue his policy of delay. There was, however, one South American republic, Buenos Aires, whose actual independence was already fifteen years old, and he persuaded the Cabinet to empower the British Consul to negotiate a commercial treaty with Buenos Aires. This amounted to the implicit transition in an individual instance from commercial to political recognition.

Then the Ministers, in the words of a wit, 'packed up their differences' and went off on their holidays.[3] After the holidays the political situation had changed. Lord Liverpool, who had recovered his health, put aside all thoughts of retiring. Canning, whose position had been strengthened for the past year by the presence of Huskisson in the Cabinet, received a further accession of strength by Lord Sidmouth's retirement. Sir Charles Stuart, a Tory, who till then had been the British Ambassador in Paris, was

---

[1] A. G. Stapleton, *The Political Life of Mr. Canning*, vol. ii, pp. 26 sqq.

[2] Ibid., vol. ii, pp. 60–1; Duke of Buckingham, op. cit., vol. ii, pp. 101, 109, 113.

[3] R. P. Ward to the Duke of Buckingham, September 28, 1824: 'His Majesty's Ministers, to use the expression of one of them, *packed up* their differences for the remainder of the summer and flew off in their tangents' (ibid., vol. ii, pp. 125–6).

replaced by Lord Granville, who was in whole-hearted agreement
with Canning's views. The disposition of King George was, it is
true, as hostile as ever; he even sent a Tory member of the
Cabinet, Lord Westmoreland, to treat directly in his name with
Charles X, who had just ascended the French throne.[1] But these
royal intrigues with foreign Powers irritated British patriotism,
and when they became public proved more damaging to the
King's policy than to Canning's. Finally, even the most obstinate
members of the Cabinet realized that if there was a question upon
which the nation was unanimous, and upon which it was absurd
to attempt to thwart Canning, it was the question of South
America. As far as Buenos Aires was concerned, it had already
been practically settled; and two commissions of inquiry which
Canning had dispatched in 1823 to Colombia and Mexico
brought back favourable reports. In Mexico the execution of
Iturbide for his attempt to make himself Emperor seemed to
mark the definite establishment of the republican form of government. In Peru the last royalist army which still remained in the
field had been crushed by Bolívar in August at the battle of
Ayacucho. Lord Liverpool and Canning offered the King the
choice of accepting their resignation or consenting to recognize
the South American republics, and all the Ministers, Wellington
among them, supported their action. The King yielded, but with
such bad grace that Canning felt himself once more compelled to
resort to threats.[2] Finally, on February 3, 1825, the Speech from
the Throne announced that 'His Majesty had taken steps to secure
by treaty the commercial relations already existing between

---

[1] A. G. Stapleton, *George Canning and his Times*, p. 427. Canning even formed the
design of going himself to Paris to sound the intentions of Villèle, and thus to counter-
balance Lord Westmoreland's visit. For this incident (October 1824) see Wellington,
Despatches, Cont., vol. ii, pp. 313 sqq. See, further, Lord Liverpool's objections, October
18, 1824: 'My opinion is not so much founded on the jealousy which would be excited
in the Allies . . . as on the jealousy of the French nation of any separate understanding
between their own Government and that of Great Britain. If we are to have such understanding, it must be without *appearing* to have it, or at least to *seek* it by any *unusual
means*' (Wellington, *Despatches, Cont.*, vol. ii, pp. 315–16).

[2] For these incidents see Wellington, *Despatches, Cont.*, vol. ii, pp. 364 sqq., 368,
401–2; A. G. Stapleton, *The Political Life of Mr. Canning*, vol. ii, pp. 33–4; A. G. Stapleton,
George Canning and his Times, pp. 405–6; *Greville Memoirs*, August 9, 1827; C. D. Yonge,
op. cit., vol. iii, pp. 297 sqq.; Duke of Buckingham, op. cit., vol. ii, pp. 140, 144, 149,
163, 181–2. At the beginning of January the King, supported by Wellington, was still
raising objections to the decision of his Cabinet taken on December 14. O'Connell was
just then being prosecuted for having asked for an Irish Bolivar. 'Was that,' asked the
King, 'the moment to recognize Bolivar?' (C. S. Parker, *Sir Robert Peel*, vol. i, pp. 367–8,
and especially Wellington, *Despatches, Cont.*, vol. ii, pp. 377, 383, 384, 394).

England and those American nations who had to all appearance effected their separation from Spain'. These were Buenos Aires, Mexico and Colombia. In future not consuls but chargés d'affaires would be sent to these three States. The only complaint which the Opposition could make in the debate which followed was that so much time had been lost; but they did not blame Canning.

6

Canning was, however, faced with other problems: in the first place with the problem of the former Portuguese colonies in South America—a problem similar to that presented by the Spanish colonies. But here the problem seemed to be made easier by the fact that in Brazil not a republic but a monarchy was in question, and, moreover, the wife of the monarch was a daughter of the Austrian Emperor, a relationship which gave Canning's policy the support of one member at least of the Holy Alliance. Moreover, England, as the ally and protector of Portugal, seemed in a better position than any other Power to impose her mediation upon Portugal and Brazil. Nevertheless, long and delicate negotiations proved to be necessary, and the three Spanish republics had been recognized for more than six months before the treaty was signed by which King John recognized his son Pedro as Emperor of Brazil. By 'an empire' the Brazilians understood a democratic monarchy 'by the grace of God and the unanimous consent of the people'. But the Tory diplomatist, Sir Charles Stuart, who, as the representative of the British Government, at Lisbon first and then at Rio de Janeiro, had acted as intermediary between the two Governments, took alarm at this democratic formula. In the final text of the treaty Pedro was emperor 'by the grace of God and in accordance with the constitution of the State'.[1]

On the other side of the globe, in a corner of the Mediterranean, amid numerous vicissitudes and hideous atrocities committed by both parties the war dragged on between the Turks and the Greek rebels. But Greek independence presented a more difficult

[1] Stapleton, *The Political Life of Mr. Canning*, vol. ii, p. 358. For the title of emperor cf. ibid., vol. ii, pp. 198, 305. Canning would have preferred the adoption of a monarchical constitution by all the new States. See his letter to Sir William A'Court, December 31, 1823: 'I have no objection to monarchy in Mexico. . . . Monarchy in Mexico and monarchy in Brazil would cure the evils of universal democracy and prevent the drawing of the line of demarcation which I most dread—America *versus* Europe' (A. G. Stapleton, *George Canning and his Times*, pp. 394-5).

problem than the independence of Mexico or Brazil, since the interests of Austria and Russia were liable to be involved. Canning's Greek policy long remained ambiguous.

On the one hand, he was aware that public opinion was ardent in support of Greece. Byron had just died beneath the walls of Missolonghi, and Lord Frederick North was travelling through the Morea in the disguise of a classical Greek. In London the Greek Committee, whose membership included all the leading members of the Radical Party (Joseph Hume, John Bowring, the Ricardos, Lieutenant Blaquière and Colonel Stanhope), collected funds and offered to administer the proceeds of the loan raised in London by the Greek Government. Lord Cochrane, on his return from Peru, undertook, in 1825, in return for a large payment, to command a small squadron which had been built at the cost of the Committee and engage in the archipelago the fleets of Turkey and Egypt. Now, all these were the men with whom Canning acted unofficially in his conduct of foreign policy; therefore the British Government was the first to take action in favour of the Greeks, and, in particular, was the first Government to accord them the status of 'belligerents', and declare its neutrality in the contest between the two armies, exactly as if it were a war between the armies of two recognized States.[1]

But, on the other hand, Canning saw that the Greek rising was fomented, only too often, by Russian agents; for the Czar, Alexander, nursed the dream of adding, by the destruction of Turkey, a new Byzantine empire to his own. This made it necessary to protect the integrity of the Ottoman Empire against this threat from the north. On this point Canning shared the fears felt by every Tory; and, moreover, he was as determined as any of his colleagues not to allow himself to be drawn into a war waged 'out of reverence to Aristides or St. Paul'.[2] Moreover, the enthusiasm felt for Greece in London was less ecstatic than the corresponding sentiment in Paris,[3] possibly also less pure,

[1] A. G. Stapleton, *The Political Life of Mr. Canning*, vol. ii, pp. 408 sqq.

[2] Canning to Stratford Canning, September 5, 1826: 'Every engine short of war (which no Minister of England in his senses would dream of incurring in these times out of reverence to Aristides or St. Paul) is to be applied to beat down Turkish obstinacy' (S. L. Poole, *Life of Stratford Canning*, vol. i, p. 430). See, further, Canning to S. Canning, January 9, 1826: '. . . A new mode of speaking, *if not* of acting . . . which I confess I like the better because it has nothing to do with Epaminondas nor (with reverence be it spoken) with St. Paul' (ibid., vol. i, p. 395).

[3] Diary of Thomas Moore, June 21, 1823: '. . . Went to the Greek Committee; Hume n the chair; hardly any answers to the two thousand letters they have sent about to

and not unconnected with financial transactions of a dubious character in which the lights of the popular party were implicated.[1] It was, therefore, a comparatively easy task for Canning to place obstacles in the way of Greek emancipation at the very moment when certain of his actions appeared to support it.

He rejected every Russian proposal which involved the possibility of armed intervention, and on one occasion was even prepared, in defiance of his principles, to participate in a conference of ambassadors to be held at St. Petersburg—an undisguised conference of the Holy Alliance—if it would frustrate Russia's warlike designs.[2] And when the intervention of the Pasha of Egypt threatened the infant nationality of Greece with speedy doom, and Greek delegates came to London to request that they might be placed under British protection, he returned a harsh refusal. He pointed out that the cause of Greece was not assisted but harmed by advances of this kind, for the British Government, which was bound by a treaty of alliance with Turkey, was compelled to reply by a declaration of neutrality. And on this occasion he did not confine himself to a declaration of neutrality. Two proclamations were issued, one forbidding British subjects to serve in the war between Turkey and Greece, the other prohibiting for six months the export of munitions; and ships which left the port of London with arms on board destined for Greece were seized by the Government officials.

III TOWARDS FREE TRADE

I

Thus did Canning's diplomacy pursue its flexible, at time even tortuous, way. We must not picture him hurling defiance in the face of the great Continental Powers. If he refused to treat corporately with their Alliance, he was careful to maintain friendly relations with its members individually, settling international questions, as far as possible, by separate arrangement with the Power concerned without consulting the others or even in

solicit subscriptions; no feeling in the country on the subject' (*Memoirs of Thomas Moore,* vol. iv, p. 88).
    [1] For the Greek Committee and the scandals connected with its operations see a very detailed account in the *Ann. Reg.,* 1826, pp. 371 sqq.; also in the *Westminster Review,* July 1826, 'The Greek Committee', an article defending the Committee, but betraying embarrassment in its treatment of details (vol. vi, pp. 113 sqq.).
    [2] A. G. Stapleton, *The Political Life of Mr. Canning,* vol. ii, pp. 411 sqq.

opposition to their interests. He thus divided the Powers, and in every transaction maintained British interests and honour. This policy was dictated by circumstances: as leader of a Tory House of Commons his hands were tied. But it also suited the complexity of his natural disposition, and the approval of the country encouraged him to pursue it. For the hesitations and shifts of his foreign policy the Liberals blamed his colleagues, not himself, and the manufacturers and merchants readily pardoned vacillations which kept the country out of war. Public opinion had made Canning its hero, trusted him blindly, and presumed deep motives of statecraft whenever his motives were not apparent at first sight.

From Lord Grey and Lord Althorp among the Whigs, from Wellington and Lord Eldon among the Tories, Canning's genius could extort no homage. But being a clever courtier, as well as a great popular leader, he contrived to regain the royal favour after the quarrel of 1824. The difficult question of South America had been settled, and in the matter of Greek independence his policy was Tory. Sir William Knighton, the King's doctor and private secretary, offered him his assistance in effecting a reconciliation with his master,[1] and some months later he did the King a valuable service of a private nature: he removed Lord Ponsonby, who had formerly been the lover of the King's mistress, by sending him to Buenos Aires as the British representative.[2] Moreover, he was beloved by men of letters, who saw in him no mere politician, but a member of their fraternity. Walter Scott was his personal friend, Byron admired him from a distance. In the House of Commons he was the cynosure of every intelligent, active and ambitious spirit. Among his admirers he counted Mackintosh, Lord John Russell, Hobhouse, Sir Robert Wilson and Brougham. Over young men he exercised a fascination. When Disraeli, barely twenty years old, wrote his first novel, the ostensible hero was Vivian Grey, but the real hero was Canning; and, like Canning and Vivian Grey, Disraeli dreamed of a distant day when, unassisted by noble birth or personal wealth, he would 'make the world his oyster and open it with his knife'.

There was no doubt that Radicalism, crushed in 1819, was reviving, but it was under a new form. It was no longer Cobbett's

---

[1] See the memorandum of April 27, 1825 (A. G. Stapleton, *Canning and his Times*, pp. 439 sqq.). Cf. the note of December 21, 1825 (ibid., pp. 448 sqq.).
[2] Sir Henry Lytton Bulwer, *Historical Characters*, vol. i, p. 369.

agrarian Radicalism, at once reactionary and revolutionary. The fury of Cobbett, compelled to watch the death of that agitation of 1822 on which he had built such high hopes, and see the industrialism he detested so bitterly robed in the glory of Canning's eloquence, never relented, though from time to time an involuntary tribute was forced from him by the Minister's talents. Nor was it the Radicalism of Byron, pessimistic, romantic, and aristocratic. When Byron died in 1824 he left behind him in his native country no spiritual progeny. It was the Radicalism—respectable, middle-class, prosaic, and calculating—of Bentham and his followers. In 1823 John Stuart Mill, the son of James Mill, who united the wisdom of an old man with the simple enthusiasm proper to a youth of seventeen, gathered around him a few young men of his own age and bestowed upon himself and his fellows the new name of 'Utilitarians'. In 1824 Bentham, in collaboration with Bowring, founded the *Westminster Review* to be the organ of the Radical Party, as the *Edinburgh Review* and the *Quarterly Review* were respectively the organs of the Whig and the Tory Party. Within a few months the *Review* had reached a circulation of three thousand. In 1825 the Benthamites founded a University in London, open to members of all denominations, to provide the sons of the industrial and commercial class with an education broader and less expensive than they could obtain at Oxford or Cambridge.[1] They had also a considerable share in founding the Mechanics' Institute in London, which was controlled by a committee of which the majority were working men, and whose object was to provide the most intelligent members of the proletariat, by means of evening classes, with courses of technical and popular education. The example set by London was immediately followed by the entire country, and at the end of two or three months there were very few towns without a Mechanics' Institute.[2] Certainly this Benthamite Radicalism differed also from the new Liberalism which was making its way among the party in office. Neither the irreligion nor the republicanism nor the system of abstract dogma which marked the Benthamites was calculated to win the approval of Canning and his friends. Nevertheless, affinities and points of contact are discernible between the two groups.

[1] See Halévy, *Formation du Radicalisme philosophique*, vol. iii, pp. 311 sqq. and *passim*
[2] See Halévy, *Thomas Hodgskin*, pp. 80 sqq.

It was on the theory of the Constitution that Canning's position differed most widely from that of Bentham and his disciples. The latter wished to base the representative system on universal suffrage; the former was opposed to all parliamentary reform, even the most moderate. Consequently the first result of Canning's popularity was a weakening of the Radical pressure in this direction. During 1824 and 1825 the question of parliamentary reform was not even discussed in the House of Commons.[1] But to compensate for this check the success of Canning's foreign policy had given Radical ideas an outlet, in the language of the economists a 'market' in the European and American countries of Spanish or Portuguese tongue.

The 'patriots' of these distant countries were welcomed with equal warmth in Canning's office and at Bentham's house. At Downing Street they found a Minister who, to be sure, in the bottom of his heart, felt nothing but contempt for their raw political experiments,[2] but who, unlike Alexander or Metternich, did not regard them with fear or hatred, and was ready to seek for points of contact between the interests of these new-born democracies and those of the historic British nation. In Queen Square Place they were the guests of an old man who combined the enthusiasm of the visionary with the pedantry of the doctrinaire, and who was overjoyed to have found admirers after long years of isolation, and virgin soil where his doctrines could be tried out. At Buenos Aires, Ridavavia, a statesman who sought to base his politics upon a philosophic foundation, was Bentham's disciple and an apostle of his ideas.[3] In Guatemala, José del Vallé sought to substitute for the Spanish code of law the code devised

---

[1] The subject was mentioned in only two speeches during the session of 1824—a speech in which Hobhouse, on March 17, on the occasion of an insignificant petition, brought forward some extremely modest proposals, and a speech of Lord John Russell's, on May 17, in which he introduced a petition of the Corporation of London and promised a motion during the ensuing session. And he did not keep his promise. Moreover, the Radicals had never loved the Whigs, and preferred an independent Tory who broke through the traditional lines of party demarcation. See the curious letter from James Mill to Napier, September 18, 1819: '. . . I would undertake to make Mr. Canning a convert to the principles of good government sooner than your Lord Grey and your Sir James Mackintosh; and I have now an opportunity of speaking with some knowledge of Canning' (Bain, *James Mill*, p. 188).

[2] It is amusing to find in the *Anti-Jacobin* a satire by the youthful Canning in which he employs the name of Peru to ridicule the cosmopolitans:

'No narrow bigot he—his reasoned view
Thy interests, England! ranks with thine, Peru!'

(Charles Edmonds, *Poetry of the Anti-Jacobin*, p. 274).

[3] Bentham, *Works*, ed. Bowring, vol. x, pp. 500, 513.

by Bentham.[1] In Colombia the Treatises of Legislation were by turns accepted and rejected as school textbooks, as liberals and reactionaries succeeded each other in the government of the country.[2] Bentham's French publisher, Bossange, boasted in 1830 that he had sold in South America forty thousand copies of his works.[3] 'The name of Bentham,' wrote Hazlitt in 1824, 'is little known in England, better in Europe, best of all in the plains of Chile and the mines of Mexico. He has offered constitutions for the New World and legislated for future times.'[4]

2

But certain of Bentham's ideas were beginning to make converts even in his own country and in Government circles. Romilly first, and after his death Sir James Mackintosh, had attempted to carry through the House of Commons at least a partial reform of the law, civil and criminal, particularly the latter, and their efforts were inspired by Benthamite principles, however timidly accepted. The abuses of the Court of Chancery were the object of a particularly violent onslaught by the Whigs, for it was an attack upon the Lord Chancellor, Lord Eldon, the militant leader of the ultra-Tories, whose longevity and the stubborn determination to die in office which he seemed to display were a perpetual source of irritation and disappointment to the Opposition. But as we have already seen, Peel had scarcely entered the Home Office before he gave proof that, in this sphere at least, he was a reformer.

In 1823 and the following years he continued to pursue the task of reform which he had begun in 1822. He began with the reform of the prison system[5] and the system of deportation,[6] which it was impossible to continue in its existing form when free colonists were emigrating to New South Wales. He carried through Parliament an important statute to consolidate all the laws relating to juries.[7] He secured the appointment of a royal commission to inquire into the arrangements of the Court of Chancery and the House of Lords in its capacity as the final

---

[1] Bentham, *Works*, ed. Bowring, vol. x, pp. 558–9; vol. xi, pp. 17, 48–9, 71.
[2] Ibid., vol. x, pp. 52 sqq.; vol. xi, pp. 22, 28, 33.
[3] Ibid., vol. xi, p. 33.   [4] *Spirit of the Age*, p. 1.
[5] 3 Geo. IV, cap. 64 (Ireland), 114; 4 Geo. IV, cap. 64; 5 Geo. IV, cap. 85.
[6] 4 Geo. IV, cap. 47, 82, 96; 5 Geo. IV, cap. 19, 84.
[7] 6 Geo. IV, cap. 50.

court of appeal.[1] In 1825 he revised the entire system of remuneration for the judges of the high courts, raising their salaries, but abolishing the perquisites which they had hitherto derived from various abuses.[2] But his chief preoccupation was, as he had promised in 1822, to mitigate the penal code and reduce the frightful number of offences punishable with death. In 1823, though he continued to defend the traditional principle of a penal code of Draconian severity tempered by the discretionary power of the judge, Peel admitted that in certain specified cases the death penalty was excessive; and if Buxton protested against his extreme timidity—at the rate at which Peel was moving they would not save a life in ten years—Scarlett was applauded by the majority of the Whigs when he expressed his delight to see the day when the principles which Sir Samuel Romilly had so long advocated in vain had obtained at last the adhesion of the Government.[3] And it was not Sir James Mackintosh, but Peel himself, who introduced and carried through Parliament without debate four Bills which abolished the death penalty for no less than a hundred felonies.[4] In the following year, on the motion of a Whig member, a parliamentary committee was appointed by the Commons[5] to inquire into the advisability of amending and 'consolidating' the penal law; in 1826 Peel adopted its recommendations. The speech which he delivered on that occasion,[6] and the Bills which he introduced in the course of that and the following session, mark the commencement of the great work of legal 'consolidation' destined to transform the criminal law of England.[7] It was a work of consolidation—that is to say, the amalgamation of a group of old laws in a single statute—not a general codification on the lines advocated by Bentham. But consolidation

---

[1] H. of C., February 24, 1824 (*Parl. Deb.*, N.S., vol. x, pp. 372 sqq.). In reality the appointment of this commission, of which the composition was severely criticized, was a device to gain time—devised by Peel to shelter Lord Eldon. Without interference, indeed with ill-concealed delight, Canning watched the attack upon his most formidable adversary in the Cabinet (H. of C., March 1, 1824; ibid., N.S., vol. xvi, pp. 571 sqq.; Duke of Buckingham, op. cit., vol. ii, pp. 52–3).

[2] 6 Geo. IV, cap. 82, 83, 84, 85.

[3] H. of C., May 21, 1823 (*Parl. Deb.*, N.S., vol. ix, pp. 420 sqq.).

[4] 4 Geo. IV, cap. 48, 53, 54, 55.

[5] Motion of Dr. Lushington (H. of C., March 16, 1824; *Parl. Deb.*, N.S., vol. x, pp. 1062 sqq.); *Ann. Reg.*, 1824, p. 61.

[6] H. of C., March 9, April 17, 1826 (*Parl. Deb.*, N.S., vol. xiv, pp. 1214 sqq., 284 sqq.).

[7] 7 and 8 Geo. IV, cap. 27, 28, 29, 30 (Offences against Property); 9 Geo. IV, cap. 31 (Offences against the Person); 11 Geo. IV and 1 Will. IV, cap. 66 (Forgery); 2 Will. IV, cap. 34 (Offences relating to the Coin).

was itself a codification, however fragmentary and indirect.[1] Thus under Peel the Home Office acquired an importance it had not possessed hitherto.[2] Tierney, disheartened to see this young statesman obtain such influence at the expense of the Whigs, confided to Thomas Moore in 1824 that Peel was 'the only reformer of the day'.[3]

3

It was an excessive eulogy, and I have quoted it only to give the reader an idea of the influence wielded at this time by Peel at Westminster. Others, both in Parliament and in the Cabinet itself, deserve to be considered as before all else reformers. They were Robinson at the Exchequer and Huskisson at the Board of Trade. The master-mind of that new philosophy of commerce which they professed was the great thinker who was still a member of Parliament when the session of 1823 opened. Ricardo was a member of Bentham's group, which was in a sense governed by a duumvirate, two sovereigns reigning conjointly. They were Bentham and Ricardo, and James Mill was their secretary of state. But Ricardo was more popular with his fellow-countrymen than Bentham. When in September he was carried off by an untimely death, the Benthamites remarked with pride that his decease was mourned not by their group alone, but by Parliament —indeed, by the entire nation. His will provided for the foundation of lectures on political economy to be given annually in London, and it was a select audience which gathered to hear the first lecturer appointed, MacCulloch; for it comprised not only the leading members of the Opposition (Lord King, Sir Henry Parnell and Lord Lansdowne), but Huskisson, Canning, Peel, and Lord Liverpool.[4] The reorganization of the Cabinet

[1] H. of C., March 17, 1824. When Peel introduced his Juries Consolidation Bill Joseph Hume urged that the work of consolidation should be extended to the entire Statute Law, which would have been a codification in the fullest sense. And George Lamb made a protest from the opposite standpoint. He regarded with some jealousy these consolidation laws. They were seldom purely such. There was always some new provision which appeared so desirable that flesh and blood could not resist introducing it (*Parl. Deb.*, N.S., vol. x, p. 250).

[2] Lord Manners to Peel, April 4, 1826 (C. S. Parker, *Sir Robert Peel*, p. 400).

[3] Diary of Thomas Moore, June 16, 1824: '(Tierney) seems utterly to despair of any change in politics; remarked the success of Peel in procuring popularity for himself by this new jury measure; his name associated with it at public dinners; the only reformer of the day' (*Memoirs of Thomas Moore*, vol. iv, p. 292).

[4] *Morning Chronicle*, April 16, May 21, 1824; *Pol. Reg.*, July 16, 1825 (vol. lv, pp. 149 sqq.).

which followed Castlereagh's death had strengthened the hold of Ricardian ideas upon the Government. Robinson, who had just effected so many important reforms at the Board of Trade, replaced Vansittart as Chancellor of the Exchequer. Huskisson took his place at the Board of Trade. And although the Vice-President, Wallace, resenting Huskisson's promotion to an office to which he believed himself entitled, resigned, he continued, both as a private member and as the chairman of an important committee, to take no inconsiderable part in the task of re-modelling in a liberal sense the laws which governed commerce.

The Chancellor of the Exchequer and the President of the Board of Trade were assisted in the measures they took to apply the new policy by the extraordinary boom in trade which, after seven years of depression, set in at the very moment when the removal of Castlereagh left the field clear for Canning. For the past two years the Board of Trade had begun to apply the liberal policy. The prosperity at present enjoyed by the trade of the country was therefore attributed to the steps already taken to emancipate commerce, and taken as an encouragement to increase that prosperity by a further application of the same principles. On the other hand, Parliament still clamoured for a progressive reduction of the taxes, and it was an easy matter to satisfy the demand when the excellent condition of business produced an annual surplus.

Nevertheless, this sudden improvement in the financial position, which was so welcome to the new Ministers, must be examined more closely. It cannot be explained by a sudden increase in the production of manufactured articles at the end of 1822. When Wallace in the Commons spoke of an increase of 10 per cent in the export of cotton goods, of 17 per cent in the export of hardware, and of 13 per cent in the export of woollens, he was not comparing the figures of 1823 with the figures of 1822—his speech was delivered on February 12—but the figures of 1822 with the figures of 1821. He even carried his comparisons farther back, and remarked that the total exports for 1822 exceeded by 20 per cent the total for 1820.[1] And, in fact, it was from the latter year that the improvement dated: the total exports (official values) rose from £33,534,000 in 1819 to £38,394,000 in 1820, £40,832,000 in 1821, £44,243,000 in 1822, £43,827,000 in 1823, and £48,730,000 in 1824. That is to say, there was a fall between

[1] H. of C., February 12, 1822 (*Parl. Deb.*, N.S., vol. viii, p. 100).

1822 and 1823, and the most rapid growth took place between 1819 and 1820, and again between 1823 and 1824. If the close of 1822 was a critical date in the economic history of England, it was for quite another reason.

In December 1822 the price of cereals began to rise. The price of corn, which had scarcely exceeded 40s. a quarter, and had even fallen to 34s. at the end of November, exceeded 41s. in January, and then, rising rapidly, attained the figure of 62s. 7d. in June. It fell again after the harvest, but only to 47s. 7d., and then gradually rose till in February 1824 it stood at 67s. 7d. The following harvest lowered the price only to 54s. 6d., and finally, in May 1825, it reached the maximum figure of 69s. 2d. The Speech from the Throne of February 1823 contained no promise of assistance for the distressed farmer. The King, while deploring the distress, was content to express the hope that since the condition of trade was so prosperous, agriculture could not long continue in a state of depression. No hope could be more paradoxical. For the last thirty years the opposition between the interests of town and country had been glaring. When the price of corn rose the landlords and farmers prospered, but the artisans, on the other hand, suffered unless they secured a rise in their wages, and, even if they obtained a rise, their employers had to meet the cost, and in consequence they were soon thrown out of work. When the price of corn fell, industry prospered, but agriculture was imperilled, and this was what happened in 1822. Nevertheless, the unlikely hopes of Lord Liverpool and his colleagues were justified by the event. The price of cereals rose, and rose for the first time without damage to industry. The entire country prospered simultaneously, town and country alike. 'Even country gentlemen,' observed the *Annual Register*, 'the most querulous of all classes, the least accustomed to suffer and the most incapable of struggling with difficulties when difficulties present themselves, could no longer complain.'[1] Sir Thomas Lethbridge, who had given notice in the Commons of a motion on the agricultural distress, withdrew his motion unreservedly on June 2, to Cobbett's great annoyance.[2] The question ceased altogether to engage the attention of Parliament.

[1] *Ann Reg.*, 1824, p. 1.
[2] H. of C., February 14, June 2, 1823 (*Parl. Deb.*, N.S., vol. viii, pp. 117 sqq.; vol. ix, p. 609). *Pol. Reg.*, June 14, 1823 (vol. xlvi, pp. 641 sqq.).

4

Parliament had scarcely met when Robinson, instead of waiting for the date when the estimates and the budget must be laid before it, decided to present the House with a general sketch of the financial situation. It was excellent. The revenue for the financial year 1822 amounted to £54,414,650, the expenditure to £49,499,130. There was, therefore, a surplus of £4,915,520. For the year 1823 Robinson estimated a revenue of £57,000,000, an expenditure of £49,852,786, that is to say a surplus of £7,147,214. The Opposition seized the opportunity to demand without further delay a daring policy of tax reduction. Since England had proved her ability to pay regularly the interest on the National Debt, even in the difficult years which had followed the restoration of peace, and since it was obviously chimerical to expect even the eventual extinction of a debt of £800,000,000, of what use was it to burden the present generation in the hopeless pursuit of an impossibility? Surely it would be better to apply the entire surplus to reduce the taxes. What taxes in particular? Clearly the direct taxes which were the most unpopular and which brought in, assessed taxes and land taxes together, a revenue equal to the surplus for the present year. This attack made by the Radicals upon the direct taxes was paradoxical. But the Opposition had forced the abolition of the income tax in 1816 on the plea that it was inquisitorial, and it now condemned the assessed taxes, although they were not open to the charge, since they were levied upon the outward signs of wealth, on the pretext that their incidence was unfair, since they fell more heavily upon the poor than upon the rich. The true explanation of their attitude was, that eagerness to diminish at any cost the revenue at the disposal of the State, and to win a cheap popularity, outweighed with the Opposition care for doctrinal consistency. Maberly and Hobhouse were especially insistent in pressing for these reductions, for which they succeeded in obtaining Lord Althorp's support.[1] In the January of 1823 Robinson was not in a position to meet these demands with a complete refusal, for the agricultural

[1] See especially H. of C., February 28, 1823, Maberly's motion (*Parl. Deb.*, N.S., vol. viii, pp. 302 sqq.); March 2, 1824, Hobhouse's speech, supported by Maberly and Lord Althorp (ibid., N.S., vol. x, pp. 652 sqq.); May 10, 1824, Maberly's motion (ibid., N.S., vol. xi, pp. 617 sqq.); March 3, 1825, Maberly's motion (ibid., N.S., vol. xii, pp. 901 sqq.).

situation had not yet improved, and the landed interest clamoured for a reduction of their taxes. Though he would not go so far as to remit the assessed taxes entirely, he abolished a number of taxes on servants, gardeners, carts, and horses which hit severely people of modest means, and he also remitted all the assessed taxes levied in Ireland, and reduced by 50 per cent all the other taxes on horses, carriages, and servants. The total revenue surrendered exceeded £2,300,000. This left the sum of £5,000,000 at the disposal of the Government. Robinson applied it to redemption, of which the principle was thus maintained, but according to a novel plan which gave some satisfaction to the critics of the method hitherto pursued. William Pitt's old Sinking Fund was abolished, and a new Sinking Fund substituted for it to increase at compound interest on the same principle as the fund just abolished, but to which only £5,000,000 would henceforth be allotted from the annual budget instead of £12,000,000.[1] This was a real and not merely a nominal allocation, for Robinson expected to obtain from future budgets a surplus of at least £5,000,000.[2] In this way the reform was effected towards which, much against the grain and through a labyrinth of makeshifts, Vansittart had been moving ever since 1819.

This final measure was the target of most lively criticism. Its critics asserted that the Treasury did not really possess a surplus of £7,000,000 and the apparent surplus had been obtained by cooking the figures. But the Budgets of 1824 and 1825 justified Robinson. When the £5,000,000 had been applied to the Sinking Fund, he still disposed of a surplus of £1,052,000 the first year and £443,500 the second. What use should he make of it? In 1823 a further sum of £276,000 was taken off the assessed taxes. But agriculture had now recovered from the depression, the country gentlemen were less insistent, and the Chancellor of the Exchequer turned his attention to another quarter. When Canning expressed the wish for a further reduction of the direct taxes, Lord Liverpool, more faithful than many Liberal speakers to the doctrine of their masters, the great economists, replied in October 1824: 'If we *could* do what we *ought* to do (do not be alarmed, I am not going to propose it), we should

[1] 4 Geo. IV, cap. 19. See the debates, H. of C., February 10, March 3, 6, 11, 13, 14, 1823 (ibid., N.S., vol. viii, pp. 91, 340, 501, 534, 543, 579).
[2] H. of C., February 21, 1823, Ricardo's speech (ibid., N.S., vol. viii, pp. 219–21); March 14, 1823, speeches of Baring and Ricardo (ibid., N.S., vol. viii, pp. 587–8).

make an augmentation in our direct taxes of at least two millions; and, as a compensation, take off indirect taxes to the amount of four or five millions. By such an arrangement we should not materially reduce our revenue and we should considerably increase the wealth and resources of the country by the relief which might be afforded to commerce.'[1] Robinson and Huskisson, in complete agreement with the Prime Minister, carried out the latter part of the programme outlined by Lord Liverpool and reformed the entire system of British tariffs.

5

The prosperity of British trade was sufficient to alarm foreign nations, and they began to protect their manufactures by imposing heavy duties. How could they be persuaded to renounce this policy of economic war, if England, instead of setting the example of thoroughgoing free trade, refused to lower her own tariffs? She possessed an entire system of tariff laws of long standing and extreme complexity, which were based on no definite principle and did not correspond to the needs of the new era. And the machinery available for the enforcement of law was so inefficient that only too often the tariff laws, abominably tyrannical, had the attempt been made to execute them strictly, were a dead letter, and the smuggling carried on without any sense of shame, and almost in the open, fostered among the people a demoralizing contempt for the authority of the State. Certain duties, since they were levied on the raw material of British manufactures, paralysed instead of assisting British industries. Other tariffs were imposed, so to speak, on the void, and protected England against a non-existent competition. What sense was there, to take one example, in a duty always exceeding 50 per cent, and sometimes even amounting to 75 per cent, on foreign cotton goods? The superior methods employed in British manufacture had made the importation of foreign cotton goods impossible, and it was

---

[1] C. D. Yonge, op. cit., vol. iii, p. 311. See Canning's letter of October 19, 1824, to which the letter quoted above is an answer. 'Are you forward in your financial plans? And can you remit us any more taxes? If so, I am for *direct* taxes this season' (Wellington, *Despatches, Cont.*, vol. ii, p. 324). Lord Liverpool's opinion in the matter had never altered since he lamented, in 1816, the abolition of the income tax. See his speech, H. of L., February 21, 1821: 'Whether the present modes of taxation were the best, he would not stop to enquire. It had been his opinion that an increase of the direct taxes would have been beneficial, and therefore he was for preserving for some time the income tax' (*Parl. Deb.*, N.S., vol. iv, p. 833).

Lancashire which, by exporting cotton goods to the annual value of £30,000,000, was flooding foreign countries with its products. The Government now took in hand the task of sweeping away all this useless, ineffective or positively harmful legislation.

Robinson reformed the laws which regulated commerce in wool. The export of raw wool was forbidden, and since 1817 a duty of 6d. a pound had been levied on imported wool. He reduced the import duty to 1d. a pound and authorized its export on payment of the same duty. At the same time he reduced the import duties on raw silk, and authorized the importation of foreign silk goods, while abolishing, by way of compensation, the drawback on exports. In 1825 the entire system of tariffs was revised.[1] The duties on articles not specified in the statute were lowered from 50 per cent to 20 per cent in the case of manufactured goods, and from 20 per cent to 10 per cent on raw materials. In future, instead of 50 per cent the duty on cotton goods would only be 10 per cent, and on woollen goods 15 per cent, on linen cloth 25 per cent instead of 40 per cent to 180 per cent,[2] on glass 20 per cent instead of 80 per cent, on earthenware from 30 to 5 per cent instead of 75 per cent. Iron would now pay a duty of £1 10s. a ton instead of £6 10s., copper £27 a ton instead of £54, spelter (zinc) £24 instead of £28, tin £50 instead of £109 5s., lead 15 per cent instead of 20 per cent. A further reduction was made of the import duties on raw wool. And the duties on coffee, cocoa, wine, and spirits were also reduced. These reforms would cost a loss of revenue equal to three times the present surplus. But the loss would not be immediate, and the experience of the last two years had proved that the Government could safely rely upon an annual increase of the ordinary revenue, and that this increase would in fact be stimulated by the new policy of free trade. An optimism founded on weighty considerations justified a financial policy which might at first sight appear imprudent.

Further measures facilitated the internal trade of the kingdom. Special Acts had bestowed upon the Newcastle coalfield the

---

[1] 6 Geo. IV, cap. 104, 105, 106, 107, 108, 111 (this legislation was preceded by a statute regulating in detail the duties on wine, coffee and hemp—6 Geo. IV, cap. 13); 7 Geo. IV, cap. 56.

[2] In virtue of a statute of the previous year (5 Geo. IV, cap. 43, sec. 2) the drawback on the export of linen cloth was to be reduced by a tenth part every year, so that in ten years' time it would be completely abolished.

monopoly of the London market, a prohibitive tariff prevented the London consumer from obtaining his coal elsewhere, and for this sea-borne coal he was compelled to pay a particularly high duty. Robinson and Huskisson reduced and equalized the duties payable upon all coal whatever its place of origin.[1] Though England and Ireland had formed one nation politically since 1800, for the purposes of excise they were still separate nations. An Act passed in 1820 had been content to provide for a reduction of the tariffs every five years, until in 1840 complete free trade would be established between the two kingdoms.[2] When, however, the first of these five yearly reductions drew near, the Government decided to dispense with the further delays. Two Acts were passed in succession by which the customs barrier between England and Ireland was entirely demolished in 1825.[3]

At the same time the system which regulated economic relations between the colonies and the mother country was competely transformed. Here the new economic policy was closely connected with Canning's foreign policy. The statute of 1822, of which we have already spoken, had opened certain of the colonial ports in America to the importation from the United States of a number of specified articles. But as the Government of Washington a few months later decided to reply to Canning's advances by proclaiming the Monroe doctrine, it now replied to the Act of 1822 by refusing to permit any trade between the United States and the British colonies in America until goods from the United States were admitted into the ports of these colonies on a footing of perfect equality with the products of the other colonies. In short, the Anglo-Saxons of Europe proposed to the Anglo-Saxons of America the joint exploitation of the new world, and the Anglo-Saxons of America declined the proposal, demanding the sole right to exploit the American continent, and hoping to incorporate the West Indies and the other British possessions in America in a species of American Empire. What measures could the Anglo-Saxons of Europe oppose to this policy? They could tighten the bonds which united the West Indies and Canada to Great Britain by sweeping away the network of tariffs which sacrificed the interests of the colonists to the interests of British industry and commerce. By an Act passed in 1825[4] the

[1] 5 Geo. IV, cap. 43.
[2] 1 Geo. IV, cap. 45.
[3] 4 Geo. IV, cap. 26; 5 Geo. IV, cap. 22.
[4] 6 Geo. IV, cap. 73.

British colonies obtained unfettered liberty, not fully granted by the statute of 1822, to trade directly with every country in the world on the sole condition of submitting, like the mother country herself, to the provisions of the Navigation Acts. Foreign imports must pay moderate duties, whose amount was, moreover, to be fixed by the colonies themselves. A reduction of duty encouraged the import of Jamaica rum into England.[1] And for the sake of Canada a bolder step was taken, and the sanctity of the corn laws violated. Canadian corn was to be admitted into England, though only for a period of two years, on payment of a duty of five shillings the quarter.[2]

Some years previously the United States had begun to protect their mercantile marine, still in its infancy, by legislation copied from the English Navigation Acts, and England had been compelled, in consequence, to exempt, in return for reciprocal treatment, vessels belonging to the United States from the full operation of the Acts. Now, Prussia was threatening to follow in the footsteps of the United States. To provide against the danger, and foreseeing the day when other nations would imitate the example set by the United States and Prussia, Huskisson obtained from Parliament a statute empowering the crown to conclude treaties of commercial reciprocity with foreign States.[3] And such treaties were, in fact, concluded immediately with Prussia first and afterwards with Sweden.[4] Denmark, Hanover, the Hanseatic towns, four States of Latin America, and France, would shortly conclude treaties drawn up on the same plan.[5]

Huskisson's treaties dealt mainly with restrictions outside the scope of the Navigation Acts, but as they were calculated to make the operation of those Acts more effective and more rigorous, they might fairly be considered as belonging to an aggravated system

[1] 5 Geo. IV, cap. 34.

[2] 6 Geo. IV, cap. 64. '. . . For one year and until the end of the next session of Parliament. . . . The Government had desired a permanent measure' (H. of L., February 2, 1826, Lord King's speech, *Parl. Deb.*, N.S., vol. xiv, pp. 9–10).

[3] 4 Geo. IV, cap. 77. For the history of the measure see H. of C., May 12, 1826, Huskisson's speech (ibid., N.S., vol. xv, pp. 1144 sqq.).

[4] See the text of the Prussian treaty in the *Ann. Reg.*, 1824, p. 96; also of the Swedish, ibid., 1824, p. 98*.

[5] The Danish treaty, ibid., 1825, p. 66*; the Hanoverian, ibid., 1825, p. 69*; the Hanseatic, ibid., 1825, p. 70*. The three treaties with Brazil, Colombia, and the United Provinces of Rio and La Plata (see ibid., 1825, pp. 75*, 80*, 84*) were of a more general character; they established for the first time normal relations with the new States. See J. H. Clapham, 'The Last Years of the Navigation Acts' (*English Historical Review*, vol. xxv, pp. 480 sqq., 667 sqq.).

of navigation laws. For English free trade was, after all, in its cradle. Whatever Huskisson's sympathy for the doctrines of Ricardo and MacCulloch, he did not dream of asking England to establish by herself a system of complete free trade, leaving other nations to follow their false creed of protection. When impatient speakers demanded the reduction of the duties on imported corn, he replied that the British Government could not be deprived of its weapons in the negotiations which were proceeding with foreign Governments to secure a reduction of the duties imposed upon British manufactures: what inducement would Britain have to offer, if the duties on foreign corn were remitted immediately?[1] Nevertheless, the reforms effected by Huskisson in the commercial legislation of Britain were very considerable. Nor is our account of the progress achieved at this time yet complete. For the Board of Trade had been the scene of feverish activity ever since Huskisson had entered it.

The bonding system, already reformed by Robinson,[2] was rendered still more liberal.[3] An Act passed on the representations of the London and Liverpool merchants protected their interests by increasing the responsibility of factors or agents entrusted with the transport of goods.[4] The system of weights and measures was reformed, and although dislike of the decimal system, too Jacobin and too French for the taste of a Tory and an English Parliament, retained many complicated features of the old system, it was at least made uniform throughout the entire kingdom.[5] The system of fees payable by English merchant vessels in every foreign port, which went to swell the salaries of the officials, was now abolished. Customs officers and consuls were in future to be paid fixed salaries.[6] Moreover, a parliamentary committee was appointed, on the motion of Joseph Hume, to inquire into a number of miscellaneous questions, somewhat oddly assorted, one of which was of no slight importance.

---

[1] H. of C., April 28, 1825 (*Parl. Deb.*, N.S., vol. xiii, pp. 287–8).

[2] 1 and 2 Geo. IV, cap. 105. Cunningham, however (*Growth of English Industry and Commerce, Modern Times*, p. 830), has made a mistake on this point.

[3] 4 Geo. IV, cap 24; 6 Geo. IV, cap. 112.   [4] 4 Geo. IV, cap. 83.

[5] 5 Geo. IV, cap. 74; 6 Geo. IV, cap. 12. See H. of C., February 25, 1824. Adaptation of the Coinage to the Decimal Scale, questions asked by Sir Henry Wrottesley and Wallace's negative reply (*Parl. Deb.*, N.S., vol. x, pp. 445 sqq.). For the previous history of the measure see two articles in the *Quarterly Review*, January 1827 and June 1827 (vol. xxvi, pp. 416 sqq.; xxxvi, pp. 139 sqq.).

[6] 6 Geo. IV, cap. 87. Cf. H. of C., May 7, 1822, Joseph Hume's speech (*Parl. Deb.*, N.S., vol. vii, pp. 366 sqq.).

6

The first question submitted to the consideration of the committee was the advisability of repealing the law which prohibited the export of machinery. The object of the prohibition was to prevent continental manufacturers making use of English mechanical inventions to compete with the British manufacturer. But an entire industry had sprung up devoted to the manufacture of machines, and the manufacturers who specialized in this branch of production desired like their fellows to enrich themselves by the export trade. Moreover, the prohibition was directly opposed to the new spirit of Liberalism. Nevertheless, the attempt failed, and the tariff of 1825[1] maintained the prohibition.

In the second place, the committee had to consider whether it was advisable to repeal the law which forbade English artisans to emigrate to the Continent. French and German manufacturers were eager for English workmen who would teach their employees those technical secrets of which England at the moment possessed the monopoly. The prohibition, therefore, was like the former, a protectionist measure, but was more odious, inasmuch as it affected persons instead of things, and restrained the freedom of the British subject to go wherever he pleased. Moreover, its application was not easy, and was in fact extremely lax.[2] Its only effect was that mechanics who had once slipped out of the country by evading its provisions did not dare to return, and the nation was thus permanently deprived of their services.[3] An Act was passed repealing the law.[4]

[1] 6 Geo. IV, cap. 107 sqq. Cf. H. of C., February 24, 1825; May 5, 1826, Hume's speech, replies by Huskisson and Peel (*Parl. Deb.*, N.S., vol. xii, pp. 651 sqq.; vol. xv, pp. 908 sqq., 1118 sqq.). The prohibition, it may be added, was continued by the tariff of 1833 (3 and 4 Will. IV, cap. 52, §104). But to satisfy the complaints of the manufacturers a system of 'licences' was introduced, which the Board of Trade granted according to the following rule. When the value of the machine was held to consist wholly in the quality of the invention it embodied, its exportation was prohibited. When the materials of which the machine was composed were held to constitute the greater part of its value, a licence was granted (H. of C., December 6, 1826, Huskisson's speech, ibid., N.S., vol. xvi, p. 293). For the laxer application of this rule and the growth, in spite of the law, of the export of machinery, see H. of C., February 16, 1841 (ibid., 3rd series, vol. lvi, p. 683).

[2] Peel to Sir John Newport, July 19, 1817: 'I concur with you so entirely in the opinion you express with respect to the impolicy of preventing the emigration of mechanics and artificers, who think they can by emigration better their condition, that I have desired that the proclamations enforcing the law upon that subject be withdrawn, and that they should not be repeated' (C. S. Parker, op. cit., vol. i, p. 257).

[3] H. of C., February 12, 1824, Huskisson's speech (*Parl. Deb.*, N.S., vol. x, p. 148).

[4] 5 Geo. IV, cap. 97.

But the third and most important question submitted to the committee was the advisability of repealing the Act of 1800 which made workmen's combinations illegal. It was due to the group of Bentham's disciples that this question had been added to the others. For it had engaged their consideration ever since the period immediately following the restoration of peace.

MacCulloch, the economist, in the *Scotsman* of Edinburgh, and Wade, a journalist, in the London *Gorgon*,[1] had undertaken a campaign to secure liberty of combination. Their mouthpiece in the House of Commons was Joseph Hume. On June 23, 1819, he presented a petition signed by the artisans of London claiming the right to combine.[2] To be sure, neither MacCulloch, Wade, nor Hume believed that a combination of workmen could by any possibility exercise a lasting influence on the rate of wages. For in accordance with a law of nature, it was determined by the balance automatically constituted between two factors, the number of workmen on the one hand, and the fund available for the payment of wages on the other. The advocates of freedom of combination objected to the Act of 1800 for the same reason for which, as advocates of free trade, they objected to a tariff. The Act was, they considered, at once ineffective and mischievous. It did nothing whatever to restrain combinations of employers. And even as regards combinations of workmen, despite innumerable prosecutions, it was equally inefficacious, its only effect being that these combinations, conscious of their illegality, became secret societies, which would not shrink from acts of violence. The workmen complained that the law was unjust because it permitted the employers what it forbade to themselves. And the employers in their turn denounced the terrorism exercised by the workmen. Only a system of liberty, Hume and his friends declared, would put an end to the struggle between the two classes, at present unnaturally arrayed against each other, and leave the field to the free bargaining of individuals, peaceably contracting with each other on a business basis.

[1] *Gorgon*, August 1, 1818: '. . . We have not said anything yet as to the policy of combinations for obtaining an advance of wages. At best we consider them as rather an hazardous experiment for *journeymen*. . . . As to the *right of journeymen* to combine, we think in reason and equity they have as much right to unite to raise the price of labour as their employers have to resort to similar means to lower it.' Cf. October 3, 1818.

[2] H. of C., June 23, 1819 (*Parl. Deb.*, vol. xl, pp. 1290 sqq.). On June 29, 1820, Maxwell brought up the question again in his plea for an enquiry into the position of the cotton spinners (ibid., N.S., vol. ii, p. 118).

In June 1819 Hume admitted that, in the opinion of many, the moment was inopportune to plead the workers' claims. In saying this, he was thinking of the campaign of Radical meetings which had just begun. Neither the gentry nor the middle class would be disposed at such a juncture to repeal the legislation passed twenty years earlier to protect society against these very dangers. And from another point of view the moment was equally inopportune. England was then in the throes of a crisis, not merely political, but even more economic. The combinations which were being formed by the workmen were designed for their defence. They were engaged in an unsuccessful struggle against the persistent fall in wages. There could not be a more inauspicious moment for the growth of such organizations. But the situation changed entirely when business revived and when, after 1822, the rise in the price of foodstuffs in conjunction with a general rise in prices rendered an increase of wages an urgent necessity. Illegal combinations of labour multiplied, adopted a policy of aggression, and won victory after victory. In these circumstances, and, moreover, at a time when Liberal ideas were gaining ground in Parliament, it was not easy to maintain in force the illiberal and inefficient statute of 1800. In 1822, Hume gave notice of his intention to introduce, in the course of the following session, a Bill repealing the Act. In reply Huskisson and Wallace gave an undertaking that they would not oppose the appointment of a committee of inquiry.[1] When, however, the session opened in February 1823, the reform was delayed for several months by the conflict which broke out, in a form calculated to arrest public attention, between the old creed of a legal regulation of industry and the new creed of economic Liberalism.

One of the two members for the manufacturing town of Coventry, by name Peter Moore, who belonged to the most advanced section of the Opposition, anticipated Hume, and gave notice of his intention to introduce a Bill repealing all the existing statutes against workmen's combinations. His Bill, however, would, he claimed, make better provision for the workers' interests by setting up an entire system of boards for the regulation of wages to be composed jointly of employers and representatives of the workmen's combinations.[2] Such a scheme was far

[1] Graham Wallas, *The Life of Francis Place*, p. 207.
[2] H. of C., March 3, 1823, Peter Moore's motion (*Parl. Deb.*, N.S., vol. viii, pp. 360 sqq.).

from agreeable to Hume, Ricardo and all others who advocated freedom of combination on the principle of *laissez-faire*. The latter, therefore, supported the manufacturers in urging that the consideration of the question should be postponed at least until the following session.[1] Indeed, all their time was engaged just then by the attempt they were making in concert with the manufacturers to obtain the repeal of the statutes which placed the silk manufacture of Spitalfields under the control of the Justices of the Peace. They were as unsuccessful in this as in their attempt to secure the unconditional repeal of the Combination Acts. It was to no purpose that the London manufacturers pointed out that the Spitalfields Acts were ruining them by driving the silk industry into the provinces, where the manufacturers were not hampered by these restrictions. The alarm excited by the demonstrations which the workmen were making at the very doors of the House, together with the intrigues of certain Tories in the Commons, caused the rejection of a Bill repealing the Spitalfields Acts which had been brought in by Huskisson himself.[2]

In the following year, however, Hume and his friends turned defeat into victory. In conformity with Huskisson's wishes, and the principles of the Ricardians, the Spitalfields Acts were repealed.[3] And at the same time Hume, before Peter Moore had an opportunity to bring forward the question of free combination a second time in the form he advocated, approached Huskisson directly and obtained from him the appointment of a parliamentary committee to inquire into workmen's combination, as well as into the emigration of artisans and the export of machinery. In the choice of its members Hume had a free hand. Francis Place, the Radical tailor of Charing Cross, an intimate friend of Bentham and Hume, collected the witnesses, sixty manufacturers, and forty-four workmen, besides a number of Members of Parliament and economists, among whom were MacCulloch and Malthus.[4] An important article by MacCulloch in the

---

[1] H. of C., May 21, 1823 (*Parl. Deb.*, N.S., vol. ix, pp. 546 sqq.).
[2] For a good account of the episode see Sp. Walpole, *History of England*, vol. ii, pp. 172 sqq.
[3] 5 Geo. IV, cap. 66.
[4] For the work accomplished by the group of Westminster Radicals see S. and B. Webb, *History of Trade Unionism*, new edition, pp. 99 sqq.; J. L. and B. Hammond, *The Town Labourer*, pp. 134 sqq.; and especially Graham Wallas, op. cit., chap. vii.

January number of the *Edinburgh Review* had prepared public opinion.[1]

The committee lost no time in reaching the conclusions which Hume and his friends desired it to reach. And at the close of the session, without opposition, and almost without debate,[2] Parliament passed an Act of an extremely Liberal character.[3]

7

By the provisions of the Act of 1800 the offence of combination was punishable by imprisonment for a period not exceeding three months, but the injured employer could obtain a more severe penalty against his workmen if, instead of prosecuting them for a breach of the statute law, he had them charged with an offence which the common law vaguely described as the crime of conspiracy.[4] The new statute protected the working class against both these dangers. It admitted the right of workmen to combine to fix the rate of wages, the daily hours of work, and the amount of work to be performed; to persuade their fellow-workmen to break an existing contract or refuse to conclude a new. For the future, none of these actions would be punishable either under statute or common law. No offence would be committed unless the workmen individually or corporately had recourse to violence against persons or objects by way of threat or intimidation. And even then sentence must be pronounced by two magistrates, not as had been prescribed by the Act of 1800, by one alone, and must not exceed a maximum of two instead of three months' imprisonment.

The immediate results of the Act deceived the expectations of the Liberals. They had believed that the moment the workers ceased to feel themselves at war with the law of the land, they

---

[1] *Edinburgh Review*, January 1824, 'Combination Laws—Restraints on Emigration' (vol. xxxix, pp. 315 sqq.).

[2] See *The Times*, June 4, 1824: '. . . We were glad to see last night that the Combination Bill did excite some discussion. We regret to think that it had passed through its four previous stages without one word of observation.'

[3] 5 Geo. IV, cap. 95. All the existing statutes, including the Act of 1800, which prohibited combinations of workmen, had sought to replace them by setting up machinery for arbitration in disputes between employers and men. Now, when all the provisions of these statutes which made combination illegal were repealed, would the clauses providing for arbitration be repealed at the same time? An important consolidating Act of thirty-five articles (5 Geo. IV, cap. 46) repealed all these provisions, often inconsistent, and substituted a single method of arbitration.

[4] *The Times*, June 4, 1824.

would realize that their combinations were powerless against the operation of the laws of nature, and would therefore cease to form them. Unfortunately, economic conditions remained the same as before, and the workmen were obliged to demand a rise of wages to correspond with the continued rise in the cost of living. It was in vain that Hume addressed a public appeal to the working class, in which he attempted to lay down the precise point at which free combination degenerates into the tyranny of the trade union and to show that, admitting as a general rule that the hours of work were too long and wages too low, 'it will require time, under the operation of a free market for labour, to bring both these to their proper level'.[1] No one paid the least attention, and workmen's combinations multiplied all over the United Kingdom. They now did openly what hitherto they had done in secret, collected reserve funds, organized strikes, and sought by methods of terrorism to impose their decrees upon the mass of the workers. The middle class was horrified by the story of the cotton spinners at Glasgow, who were found guilty of having passed sentence of death upon four of their disobedient comrades and having actually carried out one murder; and of the events at Dublin, where the action of the trade unionists had resulted in the wounding of seventy persons and the murder of ten. In 1825 the entire port of London was reduced to idleness by a strike of the shipwrights.[2]

The Ministers, inundated with complaints, came to the conclusion that they had been guilty of a serious blunder when, without raising the least objection, they permitted Parliament to repeal the statute against combinations. Apparently, Huskisson was attracted by a plan suggested by the London shipbuilders, the formation of unions approved, but at the same time controlled, by the authorities. According to this scheme the previous approbation of a magistrate would be required before a union could be formed, and he was to be the *ex-officio* treasurer of the union. Huskisson sought and secured the appointment of a new committee of inquiry; but when it had concluded its labours, and the new Bill had been debated in Parliament, for this time the dis-

---

[1] Letter from Joseph Hume, Esq., M.P., to Mr. John Edmonstone, Chairman of the Committee of the Operative Weavers of Glasgow, in George White, *Combination and Arbitration Laws, Artisans, and Machinery*, 1824.

[2] H. of C., June 27, 1825, Wallace's speech (*Parl. Deb.*, N.S., vol. xiii, pp. 1400 sqq.). S. and B. Webb, *History of Trade Unionism*, new edition, p. 104.

cussion was serious, and the amendments proposed by the Opposition were considered by the Government, it was very far indeed
from satisfying the wishes of the more intransigent section of the
employers.[1] On one point, indeed, their desires were gratified.
To the offences of 'violence', 'threats', and 'intimidation' the new
statute added the more indefinite offences of 'molestation' and
'obstruction', and for all these provided a maximum penalty of
three months' imprisonment instead of the two provided by the
former Act. On the other hand, an appeal was henceforward
permitted from the sentence of the two magistrates; on payment
of £10 bail the prisoner was entitled to be tried at Quarter
Sessions.[2] Moreover, the statute of 1825 reaffirmed the repeal of all
the old legislation by which combinations were made illegal, and
to render its intention still clearer laid down in so many words
that to combine 'for the sole purpose of consulting upon and
determining the rate of wages and prices' should not constitute
an offence.

In short, freedom of combination was sanctioned as well as
restricted by the new legislation, and England maintained the
precedence which during the previous year she had attained in this
respect over all the nations of the world. It was doubtful at first
whether by taking this step she had not left the Government
defenceless in face of an agitation among the proletariat which
throughout the entire summer seemed to threaten disaster. 'The
working classes,' Cobbett wrote in August, combine to effect a
rise of wages. The masters combine against them. The different
trades combine and call their combination a *general union*. So that
here is one class of society united to oppose another class.'[3] Then
about October the agitation die down, and all the combinations
formed during 1824 seemed to be in process of dissolution.[4] This

[1] 6 Geo. IV, cap. 129.

[2] This was an amendment proposed by the Opposition. For the Opposition amendments see H. of C., June 30, 1825 (*Parl. Deb.*, N.S., vol. xiii, p. 1462; also Lord Broughton's
Recollections of a Long Life, vol. ii, p. 111. It must be added that, unlike the Act of 1824,
the Act of 1825 does not explicitly lay down that attempts by a trade union to put pressure
upon individual workmen could not be made the subject of an action at *common law*.
For an attempt to take advantage of the omission see *Ann. Reg.*, 1829, Chron., February
3rd.

[3] *Pol. Reg.*, August 27, 1825 (vol. lv, pp. 519–20). For the agitation see *The Times*,
August 2, September 1, 21, 1825; *Morning Chronicle*, August 8, September 2, October 8,
1825; *Pol. Reg.*, August 27, September 17, 1825 (vol. lv, pp. 513 sqq., 710 sqq.).

[4] *The Times*, October 11, 1825: 'The close of the shipwrights' strike in London. The
masters now require, *as it is their unquestionable right to do*, unqualified submission from
all the shipwrights who engage in their service and eat their bread; they demand, more-

was undoubtedly the result of 'natural' causes, of which we must speak later, and which had no connection with the state of the law. But the optimism of the more Liberal among the Ministers had been justified, and, to all appearance, the method had been discovered by which disorder among the working class could be suppressed without depriving the worker of the freedom to which he was legitimately entitled.[1]

IV   OTHER   REFORMS

I

Instinctively, public opinion attributed to Canning the honour of these first victories won by British Liberalism. Was he not the Leader of the Liberal group in the Cabinet? And was it not the skill with which he directed the foreign policy of the country which gave that group the prestige necessary to overcome the resistance of the ultra-Tories? In reasoning thus, public opinion judged correctly; but when we study the position more closely and attempt to determine what part Canning took in shaping the domestic policy of Lord Liverpool's Cabinet, we must confess that it was very slight indeed.

Take, for instance, the question of penal reform. We have seen that this was the work of Peel, whose position as Leader in the Commons of the orthodox Tories in opposition to Canning became more definite with every session. Any influence which Canning could possibly have exercised in this sphere was entirely indirect. By all this activity Peel was acquiring a popularity which rivalled Canning's; and if Lord Eldon, who had hitherto stoutly opposed the reform of the criminal law, now kept silence when

over, that the men shall entitle themselves to such employments, by separating themselves completely from the leaders who have made tools of them, and ceasing to act as an organized army against their masters.' *Morning Chronicle*, October 1, 1825: 'The Combinations of Mechanics throughout the country are fast approaching to their dissolution . . . from the deficiency of means to supply the wants of the numerous families of men who for months have been unemployed. . . . A great deal of nonsense had been said and written on the mischievous effects produced by the repeal of the Combination Laws. . . . The Combination Laws were mischievous, in so far as they put it into the heads of workmen that they were the cause of their not receiving higher wages.'

[1] Peel to Leonard Horner, November 29, 1825: 'I hope that we have now seen the worst of the evils of combination. . . . I think the law with regard to combination as it now stands is founded upon just principles, and I believe it will ultimately be as effectual as law can be' (C. S. Parker, op. cit., vol. i, pp. 379–80).

Bills passed by the Commons were brought up to the Lords, it was because he was Peel's political ally, and realized that in his own interest he must do nothing which might weaken his position.[1]

Or, again, consider the reforms in the economic field. The repeal of the statutes against workmen's combinations was passed almost without debate by the entire House of Commons on the initiative of a member who was a Radical and a disciple of Bentham. The only part taken by the Government was to carry, a year later, an amending Act which restricted the freedom granted by the former. Though in 1825 Robinson was in close collaboration with Canning, the alliance between them had been of gradual growth.[2] It does not appear that his promotion in January 1823 had been due to any special intervention by Canning on his behalf, and throughout the session of 1823 the Tories seem to have hesitated whether they should look to Peel or to Robinson as their leader against Canning. In regard to Huskisson, however, whose influence was increasing every year, and who after 1825 eclipsed Robinson in the Commons, the position was altogether different. With unswerving loyalty, for the past twenty years he had remained Canning's political friend, and when Canning, on becoming Foreign Secretary and Leader in the Commons, found his duties as Member for Liverpool too heavy, and exchanged the seat for a pocket borough, it was to Huskisson that he passed it on. But this close political alliance between the two men is no proof of a direct influence exercised by Canning on Huskisson's departmental policy.

The most ardent panegyrists of Canning's policy, Stapleton and Harriet Martineau,[3] are obliged to confess that he displayed no

---

[1] Lord Manvers to Peel, April 4, 1826: 'You have made the office of Secretary for the Home Department of infinitely more consequence than it has ever been in the hands of any of your predecessors. The well-managing of our foreign affairs and interests may be more striking and brilliant; it is by no means more substantial or more important' (C. S. Parker, op. cit., vol. i, p. 400).

[2] R. Plumer Ward to the Marquis of Buckingham, July 16, 1824 (Duke of Buckingham, op. cit., vol. ii, p. 105).

[3] A. G. Stapleton, *The Political Life of Mr. Canning*, vol. iii, p. 3: 'To the merit of originating these alterations (of our commercial system) or of adapting them to practice, Mr. Canning laid no claim. They were unconnected for the most part with the business of the department over which he presided, and *they related to a branch of politics the study of which was perhaps the least suited to his taste*.' H. Martineau, *History of the Thirty Years' Peace*, ed. Bohn, vol. i, p. 126: 'The Corn Bill . . . was committed to Mr. Canning's care as Leader in the Commons. He was extremely anxious about it, as it was the elaborate work of his two friends, Lord Liverpool and Mr. Huskisson, and *the subject was not one*

interest in questions of political economy, about which indeed he knew very little. He might appeal in support of his pacific policy to the teaching of those whom he called 'the economists and calculators', but he was himself neither an economist nor a calculator, and though circumstances compelled him to pursue for the time a policy of peace, he was skilful enough to clothe it with the honour attaching to a successful war. But the maintenance of national honour is necessarily expensive, and to prove that he avoided war not from lack of power to wage it but from deliberate choice, he asked for an increase in the expenditure upon the Army and Navy. In 1822 the amount spent upon the armed forces had fallen to the lowest figure reached since the restoration of peace. It rose during the following years,[1] and only the extraordinary boom in trade which took place at the same time made it possible to lighten the burden of taxation in spite of the increased expenditure necessitated by Canning's policy.

Moreover, Canning was in favour of the system of Poor Laws on which the economists and calculators waged unrelenting war.[2] In 1820, when he was not yet a member of the Cabinet, he had protested against the attempts of the Opposition to reduce the civil list on the plea that it would diminish the 'splendour' of the Crown.[3] He wanted the State to subsidize literature and art, and used his influence to prevent the dispersion of George III's library, and obtain the establishment of a National Gallery of Painting. It

---

that he felt at home in.' Cf. E. J. Stapleton, *Some Official Correspondence of Canning*, vol. i, pp. 90–1; Cabinet Memorandum of Mr. Huskisson, President of the Board of Trade, on the question of Government Support in Parliament of his Reciprocity of Shipping Dues Bill, June 24, 1823: 'On May 2 I requested a meeting at the Board of Trade of the following members of the Cabinet: Lord Liverpool, Lord Bexley, Mr. Canning, Mr. Peel, Mr. Robinson. *Mr. Canning, being prevented by other business, did not attend.*' H. of C., February 17, 1825: 'Mr. C. Wyn stated that not only was he himself friendly to the abolition of the Usury Laws, but the Chancellor of the Exchequer and the President of the Board of Trade had, on more than one occasion, defended the policy; and he was confident that all his colleagues, *with the exception perhaps of the Right Honourable Secretary for Foreign Affairs, who, to the best of his knowledge, had never taken the question into his consideration*, were strongly in favour of it' (*Parl. Deb.*, N.S., vol. xii, p. 540).

[1] 1822: Army, £7,699,000; Navy, £5,194,000; Ordnance, £1,008,000; Total, £13,901,000. 1823: Army, £7,352,000; Navy, £5,613,000; Ordnance, £1,364,000; Total, £14,329,000. 1824: Army, £7,573,000; Navy, £6,162,000; Ordnance, £1,407,000; Total, £15,142,000. 1825: Army, £7,580,000; Navy, £5,849,000; Ordnance, £1,567,000; Total, £14,996,000. 1826: Army, £8,297,000; Navy, £6,541,000; Ordnance, £1,870,000; Total, £16,708,000 (*Finance Accounts. An Account of the Public Expenditure in the Year . . .*). Cf. H. of C., March 14, 1825, March 3, 1826, Lord Palmerston's speech (*Parl. Deb.*, N.S., vol. xii, pp. 925 sqq.; vol. xiv, pp. 1083 sqq., 1011 sqq.).

[2] B. Disraeli, *Lord George Bentinck*, 1858, p. 140.

[3] H. of C., May 2, 1820 (*Parl. Deb.*, N.S., vol. i, pp. 221 sqq.).

might no doubt be argued that in this he was a disciple of the new school of economists, who allowed that their general rule of non-interference was not absolute, and that under special circumstances the State possessed the right and the duty to foster by its direct action the education of the people. But he had no wish to promote popular education,[1] what he desired was a royal or aristocratic patronage after the old style, as it had been practised by Louis XIV and the Medici. Finally, though the emancipation of the commerce of the West Indies and Canada, a reply to the declaration of economic war by the Government of Washington, possessed his considered approval, perhaps even emanated from him, in the other commercial reforms he had no share. Lord Liverpool, content in his modesty to allow Canning to play the part of Prime Minister before the public, remained in this sphere the real Premier. Ever since 1820 he had, with a considerable measure of consistency, guided the economic policy of the kingdom along a novel path; and on occasion, rather than depart from his new policy, he would refuse the suggestions of Canning, more eager than himself to acquire a cheap popularity. In short, as being at once Secretary for Foreign Affairs and Leader in the Commons, Canning had the choice between two renderings of this double part. He could be primarily a Foreign Secretary or primarily a leader in the House. From 1823 to 1825 he chose the former alternative, and the state of foreign affairs was sufficiently grave to justify him in confining himself to the administration of his department. He left to his colleagues the responsibility for their respective departments, content to profit by the popularity they acquired, as they in turn profited by his own more brilliant popularity. Nevertheless, we must not exaggerate and imagine that he could shift the entire responsibility for reforms onto his colleagues' shoulders. The moment he became Leader in the Commons he was faced with two questions for the treatment of which he must bear the responsibility—the emancipation of the slaves, and Catholic emancipation.

[1] When Brougham began his campaign on behalf of a system of elementary education, Canning collaborated in an article written by Monk, the Bishop of Gloucester, in which Brougham's speech was criticized (*Quarterly Review*, 'Mr. Brougham—Education Committee', vol. xix, pp. 492 sqq.). For Canning's share in the composition of this article see *Edinburgh Review*, July 1858, 'Canning's Literary Remains' (vol. cviii, p. 132).

2

Although in 1807 Canning had opposed a Bill against slavery introduced by the Ministry of Fox, for several years before 1822 he had interested himself in the condition of the slaves in the American plantations; for this was a question upon which a Tory could adopt a Liberal attitude without endangering the constitution of the realm. Wilberforce was his friend, and had made him Vice-President of his African Institution. The advocates of the negro hoped at the end of 1822 that the Foreign Office would in future display more determination in keeping foreign nations to their promise, and securing that they would at last imitate the example of Britain and cease to furnish America with fresh contingents of slaves from the African coast. And it was in fact in obedience to Canning's explicit instructions that Wellington's attitude at the Congress of Verona was more insistent than Castlereagh's had been at the earlier congresses.[1] Canning, however, had set himself no easy task, and his expostulations enjoyed little success. England multiplied statutes for the suppression of the slave trade, consolidated them all in a single comprehensive measure, clearer and more complete than the preceding Acts,[2] and made the slave trade piracy.[3] But her efforts were wellnigh fruitless. The Latin nations of the continent continued to enrich themselves by the traffic in slaves—Spain and Portugal without any attempt at concealment; France with greater secrecy, but on a large scale. The United States, the only nation in favour of the abolition of the slave trade, refused in 1824 to ratify a draft treaty which subjected American vessels to the control of British naval officers.[4] It cost Canning three years' struggle to obtain from Brazil a proclamation abolishing the trade.[5] However slight the success which attended his endeavours in this sphere, at least he possessed the approval of Wilberforce and his group. But, unhappily for him, at the very moment when he took office the aims of the friends of the negro took a different form; and the novel question which they brought forward was nothing less than the emancipation of the negroes, the entire abolition of slavery.

[1] H. W. V. Temperley, *Life of Canning*, pp. 194–5.
[2] 5 Geo. IV, cap. 113.   [3] 5 Geo. IV, cap. 17.
[4] *Ann. Reg.*, 1824, p. 209.
[5] See the treaty dated October 18, 1825 (ibid., 1825, pp. 72* sqq.).

3

In reality, 'emancipation' had all along been the ultimate aim of those who asked only for 'abolition'; but not to mention the inherent difficulties of the change, difficulties about which the advocates of emancipation troubled themselves very little, the constitutional position was a barrier they were unable to pass. The majority of the sugar plantation colonies were 'old colonies' which enjoyed self-government, and even if the mother country could control the Atlantic slave trade without violating the colonists' rights, it was a nice point to determine whether the control or abolition of slavery in the West Indies was or was not a purely domestic matter which belonged wholly to the jurisdiction of the local legislatures, and in which the Parliament of West-minster had no right to interfere. The abolitionists had hoped that by cutting off the supply of new slaves they would compel the planters to take more care of the lives of the slaves they already possessed, and, if not to enfranchise them, at least to treat them with greater humanity. Their hope had proved vain, and the legal position of the West Indian negro had even changed for the worse since 1807. Colombia, on the other hand, the moment she was free from the Spanish yoke, proclaimed the emancipation of her slaves.[1] How could England hesitate to follow the example set by the Spanish-Americans of Caracas? Already during the session of 1822 Wilberforce, speaking on abolition, had introduced the subject of emancipation, and secured from the Government a promise to prohibit slavery in the Cape Colony.[2] At the beginning of 1823 Wilberforce and his friends founded the 'Society for the Amelioration and Gradual Abolition of Slavery in all the Possessions of Great Britain'.

Canning was too expert a politician not to perceive the gravity of this new agitation. On many other matters the Evangelicals, whose influence was felt by both parties alike and was growing throughout the country, aroused lively opposition among the Liberals. When they founded societies for the reformation of manners or for Sunday observance their meddlesome Puritanism excited the protests of the *Edinburgh Review*, but on the question of slavery the Methodists spoke for once the language of freedom.

[1] *Ann. Reg.*, 1821, pp. 263–4.
[2] H. of C., July 25, 1822 (*Parl. Deb.*, N.S., vol. vii, pp. 1783 sqq.).

It was all very well for the John Bull of ultra-Toryism, Cobbett's *Political Register*, to denounce the emancipationists; Canning could not face undismayed the prospect of a hostile coalition of Evangelicals and Liberals if he refused to support emancipation. It was at the suggestion of the Evangelical, Zachary Macaulay, that Brougham came forward as the advocate of the new cause in the *Edinburgh Review*;[1] and it was in the same cause that Zachary's son, Thomas Babington Macaulay, a political friend of Brougham, made his first appearance as a speaker and a writer.[2]

At first Canning attempted to shirk the problem. By tricks of parliamentary procedure he twice adjourned motions against slavery.[3] But when at last on May 13, 1823, Buxton asked Parliament to effect what he termed the 'gradual' extinction of slavery by declaring all the children of slaves born after a certain date free, he decided to intervene and solve, if he could, the difficult problem. He carried three resolutions affirming the necessity of improving by degrees the moral condition of the slaves, to fit them for the day when they would participate in all the civil rights enjoyed by British subjects,[4] and the text of these resolutions was immediately transmitted by the Colonial Secretary, Lord Bathurst, to the governors of all the colonies.[5] It was, of course, impossible to impose any particular measure upon the old colonies, but it could be done in the case of the 'new' or 'Crown' colonies which were not self-governing. The island of Trinidad was chosen to be the scene of the experiment. An Order in Council issued in 1824 established an entire slave code in the island. Sunday work was forbidden, the flogging of slaves severely restricted and forbidden altogether in the case of women, a regular marriage ceremony introduced, the slave's right to his

---

[1] Z. Macaulay to Wilberforce, February 8, 1823 (R. I. and S. Wilberforce, *The Life of William Wilberforce*, vol v, p. 167); *Edinburgh Review*, February 1823, 'Negro Slavery' (vol. xxxviii, pp. 168 sqq.).

[2] See in the *Morning Chronicle*, June 26, 1824, a verbatim report of the meeting of the Anti-Slavery Society, held on the 25th, and the editorial comment: 'The able and eloquent speech of Mr. S. Macauley (*sic*), a son of Mr. Zachary Macauley (*sic*), a youth of whom high expectations have been formed which he will not disappoint, cannot fail to produce a strong impression on all who read the report of it.' In our opinion the article in the *Edinburgh Review* for January 1825, 'The West Indies', was written by Macaulay (vol. xl, pp. 464 sqq.). Cf. Macaulay to his father, October 7, 1824 (G. O. Trevelyan, *Life and Letters of Lord Macaulay*, chap. iii).

[3] R. I. and S. Wilberforce, op. cit., vol. v, pp. 170-1, also p. 176.

[4] H. of C., May 15, 1823 (*Parl. Deb.*, N.S., vol. ix, pp. 257 sqq.).

[5] See the text of Lord Bathurst's circular, May 24, 1824 (*Ann. Reg.*, 1824, p. 130 n.).

property legally recognized, and he was given the right to pur-
chase his liberty, and, with the sanction of the clergy, to give
witness in a court of law even against a white man.[1] In short, an
example was proposed for the imitation of Jamaica and the other
plantations.

Unfortunately, it was not followed. The only effect of Canning's action was to produce an extremely critical situation in the
West Indies. The report spread among the negroes that the
Government of the mother country desired to emancipate them
and that the interposition of the planters was the sole obstacle to
their freedom. In Guiana and Jamaica[2] insurrections broke out
among the slaves. They strengthened the planters' opposition.
For the planters were a handful of whites surrounded by over six
hundred thousand slaves.[3] To abandon to the latter the government of the colonies was to sweep away entirely their wealth and
civilization, and, on the other hand, their predominance could be
secured only if they kept in their hands the powers of a despotic
Government. The colonial legislatures refused to assent to the
wishes of the Parliament at Westminster, and nothing was done
to improve the condition of the slaves.[4] Missionaries—Methodists
or Baptists—who attempted to supply for the neglect of the
Established Church and evangelize the negroes were charged
with inciting them to rebellion and were subjected to persecution.
One of their number saw his chapel demolished, and was
obliged to fly for his life.[5] Another was sentenced to death by a
court-martial, and though he was, it is true, recommended to
mercy by his judges, was taken ill in gaol and died.[6] On the other
hand, the attitude of the English philanthropists became more
violent than ever. They demanded that the English Parliament
should brush aside the colonists' opposition and effect what
Buxton called the 'gradual', but what was in reality the almost
immediate, abolition of slavery; and they deplored so insistently
the blindness of the planters in leaving their slaves no other

[1] See the text of the Order in Council, *Ann. Reg.*, 1824, Public Documents, pp. 58* sqq.
[2] Ibid., 1823, pp. 134 sqq.; 1824, p. 105.
[3] P. Colquhoun (*A Treatise of the Wealth, Power and Resources of the British Empire*,
1814, p. 379) estimates the entire population of the West Indies at 64,994 whites, 33,081
free negroes, 634,096 negro slaves.
[4] H. of C., May 19, 1826, Brougham's speech (*Parl. Deb.*, N.S., vol. xv, pp. 1284 sqq.);
Edinburgh Review, December 1826, 'West Indian Slavery' (vol. xlv, pp. 174 sqq.).
[5] *Ann. Reg.*, 1823, pp. 133-4.
[6] Ibid., pp. 135-7.

escape but rebellion that they almost appeared to hope that they would rebel.[1]

To sum up, Canning undoubtedly desired in 1823 to do for the improvement of the negroes' condition what Peel was doing in his department to reform the Penal Code and Huskisson at the Board of Trade to reform the system of tariffs—namely, to take the cause of reform out of the hands of the Opposition and be the reformer himself. He failed to accomplish the task he had set himself. The two races at war in the West Indies would have none of his arbitration. What more could he do? Only preach patience to the abolitionists, urge, perhaps without much conviction, that confidence must be reposed in the prudence of the colonists, and attempt to soften the latter by a tariff favourable to their commerce—when all is said, a poor achievement, for all his noble intentions, which earned the gratitude of nobody.

4

Even poorer were the results of the policy which, during these same years, Canning pursued in regard to another question of equal gravity, and which concerned not the negro plantations of the West Indies, but that other English 'colony', Catholic Ireland. From the statesman's point of view the conditions of the latter problem were very different from those of the former. There was no alliance here between the Evangelicals and the Liberals. Instinctively, indeed from the very nature of their creed, the Evangelicals were anti-Catholic. If, from time to time, members of the 'old denominations' were prepared to approve of Catholic emancipation, it was but a half-hearted concession to the principle of toleration and made only in order to strengthen their protest against the few disabilities under which they still lay themselves. The Methodists were frankly hostile to emancipation. The Evangelical party in the Established Church, though still regarded with suspicion (in all the years during which Lord Liverpool was Premier he did not appoint a single Evangelical bishop), agreed on this point with the High Church. Nevertheless, we must not misread the situation. The theological arguments against the admission of Catholics to Parliament, still advanced in 1824 by

[1] H. of C., March 16, 1824, Wilberforce's speech: '. . . Despairing of relief from the British Parliament, they would take the matter into their own hands and endeavour to effect their own liberation' (*Parl. Deb.*, N.S., vol. x, p. 1148).

Southey in his *Book of the Church*,[1] were not those which determined public opinion; for the British public the question of Catholic emancipation was an Irish question. The English did not wish to see the House of Commons invaded by the Irish agitators.

Accordingly, in the matter of Catholic emancipation, the Tories had the good fortune to be in harmony with the feeling of the entire country. Who defended the Catholics? Men of letters such as Walter Scott, who, though a Tory, had been converted to the cause of emancipation, and Thomas Moore, an Irish Catholic by origin, who wrote his *Memoirs of Captain Rock* to plead the cause of his fellow-countrymen. Enemies of the Establishment like Hume, who every year asked Parliament to disendow at least partially the Church of Ireland,[2] and Cobbett, who published with noisy advertisement a *History of the Protestant Reformation in England and Ireland*, in which he represented the Reformation as a work of injustice and spoliation which impoverished the poorer classes and retarded the progress of culture.[3] But Hume and Cobbett damaged the cause of emancipation—Hume from mere want of address in handling the situation, Cobbett perhaps deliberately and for the mischievous pleasure of embarrassing the moderate reformers. Nor was Cobbett under any illusion as to the state of public opinion. 'The Orangemen,' he wrote, 'have for allies all the *unconquerable prejudices* of ninety-nine hundredths of the people of England.'[4]

In these circumstances Canning's sole consideration as Leader in the Commons was to bury out of sight this dangerous question on which he was opposed by an alliance of the Court and the Church with the pietist middle class and the populace who

---

[1] For the controversy which followed see Butler (Charles), *The Book of the Roman Catholic Church*, in a series of letters addressed to Robert Southey, 1825. Southey (Robert), *Vindiciae Ecclesiae Anglicanae*, letters to Charles Butler, Esq., comprising Essays on the Romish religion and vindicating *The Book of the Church*, 1826. White (the Rev. Joseph Blanco), *Practical and Internal Evidence against Catholicism*, with occasional strictures on Mr. Butler's *Book of the Roman Catholic Church*, in six letters addressed to the impartial among the Roman Catholics of Great Britain and Ireland, 1825.

[2] H. of C., May 4, 1823, May 6, 1824; June 14, 1825 (*Parl. Deb.*, N.S., vol. viii, pp. 367 sqq.; vol. xi, pp. 352 sqq.; vol. xiii, pp. 1149 sqq.).

[3] *A History of the Protestant Reformation in England and Ireland:* showing how that event has impoverished the main body of the people in those countries; and containing a list of the . . . religious foundations in England and Wales and Ireland, confiscated, seized on, or alienated by the Protestant 'Reformation' Sovereigns and Parliaments. The two volumes were published in 1829. But the 'letters' of which the work is composed were written between November 29, 1824, and March 31, 1826.

[4] *Pol. Reg.*, April 5, 1823 (vol. xlvi, p. 57).

detested the Irish. Since personally he was a convinced advocate of emancipation, the only effect of his advent to power was that the Opposition lost the support of his oratory. We have already remarked his suggestion made in August 1822, when he was a candidate for Castlereagh's inheritance, that the question should be settled by amicable arrangement, that a 'compromise' must be discovered. Was he preparing to repudiate the convictions of a lifetime? When Brougham taxed him with that intention and accused him of having entered into an agreement with Lord Eldon, he protested against the charge, and provoked a violent scene by bluntly telling Brougham that his assertion was 'false'.[1] But for all his protests, when, a year later, Lord Milton appealed to him to settle the troublesome question with the assistance of the Whigs, he excused himself from touching it, and spoke with such embarrassment that he incurred the bitter reproaches of Tierney.[2] What was the 'compromise' that he had in mind which would give some satisfaction to the Catholics without rousing the indignation of the Tories? Its nature may be conjectured from the proceedings in the House of Lords in 1824. Lord Liverpool accepted two Bills introduced by Lord Lansdowne to enable English Catholics to vote in parliamentary elections and to act as Justices of the Peace;[3] but both Bills were rejected. A few subordinate posts in the Government service were thrown open to Catholics.[4] The Catholic Duke of Norfolk was allowed to exercise the functions, which were purely honorary, attached to his hereditary office of Earl Marshal.[5] And this was all that Canning's influence did for the Catholics.

Never had the advocates of Catholic emancipation been more disheartened; they even asked themselves whether, in the impossible event of a Whig Government, the reform could be carried.[6] Even the success obtained in Ireland by the policy of

[1] H. of C., April 17, 1823 (*Parl. Deb.*, N.S., vol. viii, p. 1091).
[2] H. of C., May 11, 1824 (ibid., vol. xi, pp. 720–1).
[3] H. of L., May 24, 1824 (ibid., vol. xi, pp. 817 sqq.). Cf. W. H. Fremantle to the Duke of Buckingham, May 14, 1824 (Duke of Buckingham, *Memoirs of the Court of George IV*, vol. ii, p. 75).
[4] 5 Geo. IV, cap. 79.
[5] 5 Geo. IV, cap. 109.
[6] C. W. Wynn to the Duke of Buckingham, September 29, 1823: '. . . The Catholic Question . . . has gone back to such an incredible degree, and its supporters are now so little in earnest, that I think its opponents may now spare that assistance (Lord Eldon's, whose retirement was expected) which so long was their sheet anchor' (Duke of Buckingham, op. cit., vol. ii, p. 9). R. Plumer Ward to the Duke, July 4, 1824: 'Lord Mary-

conciliation, which, since the beginning of 1822, had been pursued by Lord Wellesley, was detrimental to their cause. Lord Wellesley was, in the parlance of the day, a 'Catholic', and did not even shrink from the scandal of a Lord-Lieutenant contracting a Catholic marriage solemnized by a bishop of the Roman Church. In the administration of the country he was careful to hold the balance even between Catholics and Protestants. The body of magistrates was purged, a constabulary established,[1] the Customs barrier between England and Ireland removed,[2] an Act passed to legalize the voluntary commutation of tithe,[3] and a series of minor reforms effected on the recommendation of a Parliamentary Committee of which Wallace was the chairman. The result of these measures seemed excellent. The year 1824 passed without farcical incidents or sanguinary riots. Though the Insurrection Act was renewed annually, the districts in which it had to be enforced were fewer every year. 'Every measure,' Lord Wellesley wrote to Lord Liverpool, 'Insurrection Act, Police, Tithe Bill, Revision of Magistracy, Petty Sessions, Better Administration of Laws, has succeeded beyond my most sanguine hopes. The general prosperity of the empire begins to reach Ireland. Prices have improved, rents and even tithes are better paid, and in the districts which had been most disturbed the people are turning their attention to pursuits of industry and honest labour instead of plotting or executing schemes of outrage and violence.'[4]

borough . . . says the Catholics themselves have so mismanaged it that it is a totally altered question, and its best supporters (he, you know, was warm for it) might abandon them. I quite think with Your Grace that perhaps Lord Grey himself, if he were Minister, would not carry it. Still more, therefore, that it ought not to prevent men who have no other source of difference from uniting to keep the vessel steady' (ibid., vol. ii, p. 100). *Edinburgh Review*, October 24, 'Memoirs of Captain Rock': 'Looking at the facts and the persons by which we are now surrounded, we are constrained to say that we greatly fear that these incapacities' (the Catholic disabilities) 'never will be removed till they are removed by fear. What else, indeed, can we expect when we see them opposed by such enlightened men as Mr. Peel—faintly assisted by men of such admirable genius as Mr. Canning—when men act ignominiously and contemptibly on this question who do so on no other question—when almost the only persons zealously opposed to this general baseness and fatuity are a few Whigs and reviewers, or here and there a virtuous poet like Mr. Moore? We repeat again that the measure never will be effected but by fear. In the midst of one of our just and necessary wars the Irish Catholics will compel the country to grant them a great deal more than they at present require, or even contemplate' (vol. xli, pp. 151–2).

[1] 3 Geo. IV, cap. 103. [2] 5 Geo. IV, cap. 22.
[3] 4 Geo. IV, cap. 99.
[4] Lord Wellesley to Lord Liverpool, November 22, 1824 (C. D. Yonge, op. cit., vol. iii, pp. 312–13).

5

'In short,' concluded Lord Wellesley, 'I should have been able to present the gratifying tribute of *Ireland tranquillized* to His Majesty were not the general prosperity and happiness disturbed by the noisy fury of the Catholic Association.'[1] What was this Association? It was an association which O'Connell and other Irish barristers had formed in 1823 to present petitions on behalf of emancipation and generally to take whatever action seemed likely to further the cause.[2] Within a few months it had assumed gigantic proportions. It comprised the entire Catholic population of Ireland, levied what was nothing less than a tax upon its members (the Catholic Rent, collected by agents it appointed in every parish and who were usually the parish priests), and held sessions in Dublin at which the government of Ireland was discussed, and which presented the aspect of a Parliament assembled in opposition to the Parliament of Great Britain. According to O'Connell, the cessation of disorder in the country districts was due to the Catholic Association, not to the measures taken by the Government. The Association, he claimed, subjected the masses to discipline, gave them a taste for peaceful methods of propaganda, diverted them from agrarian outrages, and interested them once more in questions of a strictly political character. This was possibly true, but it did not alter the fact that the Catholic Association was nothing less than a State within the State, and was in a position to renew at any time the civil or, more correctly, the religious war between the Catholics and the Protestants. The ultra-Tories, therefore, at the beginning of 1825, judged the opportunity favourable to make use of the Catholic Association to embarrass Canning and his supporters, thus taking their revenge for the victory he had won in December when he obtained the recognition of the South American republics. In 1823 they had reluctantly accepted an Act which declared the Orange societies illegal. Now they demanded and obtained the introduction of a Bill suppressing the Catholic Association, and Canning found himself obliged to take sides with them against the Catholics.

The Whigs put up a stiff fight against the Bill, but from the

[1] Lord Wellesley to Lord Liverpool, November 22, 1824 (C. D. Yonge, op. cit., vol. iii, pp. 312–13).
[2] Wyse (Thomas), *Historical Sketch of the late Catholic Association of Ireland*, 2 vols., 1829.

outset they knew they were beaten. No sooner was the Bill carried,[1] when they turned their forces in another direction and replied to the Tory attack by a counter-offensive. Granted that the Catholic Association was dangerous to public order, it had nevertheless an excuse for its formation, the inferior civil status to which the Catholics of the United Kingdom were reduced by law. The Government ought, therefore, to seize this opportunity to deprive the association of all reason for existence by emancipating the Catholics. Through his success in December on the question of the South American colonies, Canning had acquired very wide influence throughout the country; he would be a coward if he did not make use of it to obtain from Parliament the reform which, as everyone knew, he had had at heart for so many years. Moreover, since in 1824 he had accepted Lord Lansdowne's two Bills, it was currently believed that Lord Liverpool was no longer an obstinate opponent of the Catholic claims. On February 28, 1825, Sir Francis Burdett introduced a Catholic petition and carried the verbatim adoption of his motion by a majority of 247 to 230 votes.[2] Thus did 'Catholics' and 'Protestants' unite, though for opposite motives, to compel Canning to declare himself. Despite all his efforts to prevent it, the battle had been joined.

The supporters of emancipation sought to reassure public opinion by adding to the Emancipation Bill two supplementary measures which were termed the wings of the Bill. The first of these restricted the franchise in the Irish counties. Henceforward the voters must possess a freehold of the annual value of £10 instead of 40s.[3] By the provisions of the second, the Government would pay the Irish Catholic clergy: when the bishops and parish priests became State officials, they would, it was hoped, cease to

---

[1] 6 Geo. IV, cap. 4.

[2] H. of C., February 28, 1825 (*Parl. Deb.*, N.S., vol. xii, pp. 757 sqq.).

[3] An Act (4 Geo. IV, cap. 26) had already been passed which attempted to limit the scandal of sham 40s. freeholds by demanding, in the case of joint tenancy (see vol. i, pp. 107, 186 sqq.), a freehold of the annual value of £20. The two auxiliary measures would seem to have been suggested for the first time in committee by an Irishman named Blake (C. Wynn to the Duke of Buckingham, February 26, 1825, Duke of Buckingham, op. cit., vol. ii, p. 218). It should also be noticed that, although the Emancipation Bill preserved the veto of the Crown, the consultative committee to whose advice the exercise of the veto was subordinated would be composed entirely of Irish Catholic bishops. B. Ward (*Eve of Catholic Emancipation*, p. 124) remarks that in the process of drafting the Bill the existence of English Catholics seems never even to have been remembered; its promoters were thinking only of Ireland.

be revolutionaries.[1] In an interview with Plunket, the Irish Attorney-General, and, like Lord Wellesley, a 'Catholic', O'Connell gave his approbation to the two supplementary measures.[2] Every step was taken in concert with O'Connell, and he helped to draft the oath which would be exacted from Catholics on taking their seats in Parliament; and, on the other side, Canning was in favour of the proposal to pay the Catholic clergy. But it was with great reluctance that he accepted the reform of the franchise.[3] On this point he shared the dislike felt by certain influential Whigs, by Lord Grey in particular, though his motives were not theirs. Lord Grey objected to what he considered a measure of counter-reform. And from his opposite standpoint, as an inflexible defender of the present system, Canning was anxious that the political institutions of the kingdom should appear unalterable.

But not one of these measures was destined to succeed. The supporters of emancipation seem to have been encouraged at first by the fact that George IV, in his capacity as King of Hanover, had just concluded a species of concordat with the Holy See.[4] Might not this be an indication that the opposition of the Court was beginning to yield? But on April 27 the Duke of York, the King's brother and heir-apparent, delivered a speech in the House of Lords. He repeated the stock arguments against emancipation and ended by declaring that whatever position he might one day occupy, he would always consider the King of England bound by his oath to defend the Established Church. The speech warned the Members of Parliament, and Canning in the first place, that the Court would continue to oppose an obstinate resistance to emancipation; and it was impossible to believe that in these circumstances the House of Lords would change the attitude it had followed hitherto and for the first time record a favourable vote. The Bill, which passed its third reading in the Commons on May 10 by a majority of 248 to 227, was thrown out

---

[1] See the text of the Bill (*Parl. Deb.*, N.S., vol. xii, pp. 1151 sqq.), and for the two supplementary measures the debate of March 28, 1825 (ibid., vol. xii, pp. 1246 sqq.).

[2] *Ann. Reg.*, 1825, p. 54 n. Cf. H. of C., March 28, 1825, speeches of Sir F. Burdett and Tierney (*Parl. Deb.*, N.S., vol. xii, pp. 1254, 1255); Lord Broughton's *Recollections of a Long Life*, March 9, 1825 (vol. ii, p. 93); George Ensor, *Irish Affairs at the Close of 1825–26*, pp. 7 sqq.).

[3] Fremantle to the Duke of Buckingham, April 21, 1825 (Duke of Buckingham, op. cit., vol. ii, pp. 238–9).

[4] Wellington, *Despatches, Cont.*, vol. ii. pp. 413, 592 sqq.

by the Lords on the 17th by 170 votes to 130. What would Canning do? As soon as the Bill had been rejected by the Lords he called a Cabinet Council, at which he claimed freedom to introduce at his own time and on his personal responsibility a new Emancipation Bill.[1] Many people—among them the entire Grenville clan[2]—wished him to go farther and commit himself unreservedly and immediately on the question. But he had not forgotten the defeat which had been inflicted upon those who had risked an attempt of this kind in 1807. The Tory party, then supported by himself, had held its ground successfully. Was it credible that Peel would fail in 1825 to hold a position which even a politician so insignificant as Perceval had held successfully?[3] Would he, then, allow both parties to contest the General Election, fixed for the autumn, under the impression left by the parliamentary battle in which the Protestants had been victorious? All his personal influence would be unable to prevent the Tories winning seats on the cry of No Popery. In September it was evident that he had adopted a more prudent course. He persuaded Lord Liverpool to postpone the General Election until the autumn of 1826,[4] the Opposition not to raise the Catholic question during the following session. When the memories of the session of 1825 had been thus extinguished the election would be fought, he hoped, under conditions less unfavourable to the advocates of emancipation. Cautious folk, chary of awkward questions, were relieved to learn that his clever management had postponed for two years the troublesome Catholic problem.

[1] Canning to Lord Liverpool, May 18, 1825 (E. J. Stapleton, *Some Official Correspondence of Canning*, vol. i, p. 269); Diary of J. C. Hobhouse, May 27, 1825 (Lord Broughton, op. cit., vol. iii, p. 103).

[2] C. W. Wynn to the Duke of Buckingham, June 11, 1825 (Duke of Buckingham, op. cit., vol. ii, p. 260).

[3] C. W. Wynn to the Duke of Buckingham, June 20, 1825 (ibid., vol. ii, p. 260).

[4] This postponement of the election until 1826 was so great a departure from custom that it may be regarded as a constitutional *coup d'état* on a small scale; for the first time for many a long year Parliament lived out its full six sessions and was not dissolved. On this point see Wellington to Lord Liverpool, June 22, 1825; Lord Liverpool to Wellington, June 23, 1825 (Wellington, *Despatches, Cont.*, vol. ii, pp. 463 sqq.); Canning to Lord Grenville, June 3, 1825 (E. J. Stapleton, op. cit., vol. i, pp. 271-2); Canning to Lord Liverpool, September 5, 1825 (id., ibid., vol. i, pp. 289-91); Wellington to Lord Eldon, September 7, 1825; to Lord Liverpool, September 19, 1825; to the Duke of York, September 22, 1825 (Wellington, *Despatches, Cont.*, vol ii, pp. 482-3, 499-500, 501-2); C. W. Wynn to the Duke of Buckingham, September 18, 1825; Lord Grenville to the Duke of Buckingham, September 27, 1825 (Duke of Buckingham, op. cit., vol. ii, pp. 281 sqq.).

V THE CRISIS OF 1825

I

Scarcely had this serious difficulty been settled, or at least shelved, when suddenly and without warning another arose. The marvellous prosperity which the nation had enjoyed for the past three years, and which was credited to the new policy adopted by Lord Liverpool's colleagues, Canning and Huskisson, received a check. An economic crisis broke out, similar to those of 1816 and 1819. Would this new crisis, like its predecessors, lead the country, at least apparently, to the brink of revolution?

To say the truth, although the panic did not break out until December, for nearly a year past the economic situation had shown disquieting symptoms. It was not only that the price of cereals had risen, compelling the House of Commons to reconsider the system of duties on corn set up in 1815, and by provoking widespread unrest and secret plotting among the working class had forced the Government to amend in haste the statute of the preceding session legalizing the workmen's trade unions; at the very moment when the price of cereals reached its maximum, the price of manufactured articles began to fall. And there was a simultaneous fall in the price of shares which, issued indiscriminately by innumerable companies, had been the object of wild speculation, and complaints began to be heard of the dubious methods by which these companies obtained parliamentary sanction for their formation. Only a few weeks after he had composed a royal speech overflowing with optimism, Lord Liverpool thought it advisable to warn the public against the consequence of its folly, and make it known that in the event of a crisis arising as the result of such speculations, the Government disclaimed in advance all responsibility; undertakings threatened with ruin must not look to the State for assistance.[1] In May the Bank of England, which hitherto had freely issued notes to meet the demand for discount, and had even lowered in 1823 the rate of discount from 5 to 4 per cent, began to refuse to discount bills.

Premonitory signs of the crash appeared towards the end of August and during the early days of September. There was a

---

[1] H. of L., March 25, 1825 (*Parl. Deb.*, N.S., vol. xii, pp. 1194–5).

panic on the London Stock Exchange,[1] and a sudden collapse in the price of cotton in Lancashire after the final failure of an attempt to corner the crop which had lasted more than a year.[2] Then, on September 27, a long-established and respected banking house at Plymouth suspended payment, and the panic which ensued in the neighbourhood led to the failure of another bank on October 1. On November 25 a third Plymouth bank failed, but this time the panic was not confined to the locality. A large bank in Yorkshire failed, and its failure was followed on December 3 by the failure of one of the leading banks in the City, after the Bank of England had in vain attempted to tide it over the crisis by a loan of £300,000. The disaster reached its climax in the course of the same week: three London banks and sixty-three banks in the provinces suspended payment. Would the Bank of England itself share their ruin? Fortunately, the disease which for six months had afflicted the economic system of England showed a tendency to cure itself. As a result of the appreciation in the value of money, the exchange, which until September had been adverse, became favourable, and the situation was further improved when French money came into the bank at the very moment when the demands upon its reserve were becoming less urgent. Thus the supreme catastrophe had been avoided. Nevertheless, provincial banks continued to fail, and the situation throughout the country was still far from satisfactory when on February 2 Parliament began what must be the last session before a General Election. Would the Tories, who a year earlier had consented with such bad grace to recognize the South American republics, take their revenge now? For the infatuation for South America was obviously the cause of the crisis through which England was passing. The manufacturers had dumped in South America their entire surplus production, the capitalists had lent money to the new Governments,[3] and had floated companies to exploit the

[1] *The Times*, August 27, 30, 1825. See also an article which had already appeared on July 30, which attempted to explain the fall in Consols as merely the effect of the conversion of the French Government stock.

[2] Ibid., September 3, 1825. For previous corners see ibid., April 26, 27, 1825.

[3] Brazilian loan (1824, Wilson), £3,200,000; (1825, Rothschild), £2,000,000. To Buenos Aires (1824, Baring), £1,000,000. Chilean (1822, Hollett), £1,000,000. Colombian (1822, Baring), £2,000,000; (1824, Goldschmidt) £4,750,000. To Guatemala (1825, Powles), £1,428,571. To Guadalajara (1825, Elland), £600,000; Mexican (1824, Goldschmidt), £3,200,000; (1825, Barclay), £3,300,000. Peruvian (1822, Frys), £450,000; (1824, Frys) £750,000; (1825, Frys), £616,000 (Doubleday, *Life of Sir Robert Peel*, 1856, vol. i, p. 326). Cf. H. of C., February 20, 1826, Joseph Hume's speech (*Parl. Deb.*, N.S., vol. xiv, p. 591).

mineral wealth of Mexico and Peru.[1] It was calculated that in this way no less than £150,000,000 had crossed the Atlantic.[2] What had happened in 1825 was that the absurdity of the hopes recently built upon the future of the South American Republics had at last been perceived. The new Governments were insolvent, the mining companies failed, the exports found no purchasers. English exporters must even count themselves lucky, if a portion of the goods they had dispatched to the other side of the Atlantic were bought with a portion of the money exported simultaneously by the English capitalist! If there were Liberals so simple that the victories gained by republicanism in the New World still aroused their enthusiasm, after the recent financial catastrophe they might justly be regarded as dupes—dupes of the bankers and stock-brokers, who had drawn them into partnership in their specula-tions; and dupes of Canning, who had played upon their enthusi-asm to win popularity for himself.

2

Public opinion, however, persisted in supporting Canning's South American policy. A Bill to facilitate, in spite of the pro-visions of the Navigation Act to the contrary, the construction of a mercantile fleet by the Republic of La Plata and by Colombia was introduced by Huskisson and readily passed by Parliament.[3] Liberal enthusiasm was too strong to be destroyed by its dis-appointment, and, moreover, the English capitalist was too much of a gambler, the English manufacturer too self-confident, to lose heart at the first failure. If they had not obtained all the profit they had expected from one market, they must find others. 'As well might it be argued,' Brougham urged, 'that we ought not to open a new market, or discover a new colony with which to trade, as that we were not to adopt sound and wise and en-lightened principles of commerce, because the one as well as the other might give rise to overtrading on the part of certain indi-viduals.'[4]

---

[1] For the fluctuations of South American securities (Government bonds and mining shares) see the figures given in the *Ann. Reg.*, 1825, p. 3. According to H. English, twenty-nine companies were floated to work foreign mines between February 1824 and September 1825 (*A General Guide to the Companies formed for Working Foreign Mines . . .* 1826).
[2] H. D. Macleod, *Theory and Practice of Banking*, vol. ii, p. 241.
[3] 7 Geo. IV, cap. 5. H. of C., February 14, 1826 (*Parl. Deb.*, N.S., vol. xiv, pp. 359 sqq.).
[4] H. of C., February 2, 1826 (ibid., vol. xiv, p. 36).

To be sure, the voice of complaint was not silent. Many private interests had suffered from the new commercial policy inaugurated by Huskisson, and when those on whom it had borne heavily were among the victims of the crisis, it was natural that they should blame his policy for their losses. The grievances of the silk manufacturers and the shipbuilders were brought to the notice of Parliament, but no attention was paid to their protests. It was clearly impossible to attribute their sufferings to particular causes when the crisis was universal and affected every branch of British trade without exception. And the advocates of Free Trade were not content to defend their position against these attacks; they contended that the industrial depression was a proof that the only valid criticism of Huskisson's policy was that it had been too timid. England, they urged, could not hope to remain the great exporting country which she had become since the beginning of the century, if she persisted in closing her frontiers against the importation of corn from the Continent. The workmen, who suffered far more severely than the masters, and saw their wages reduced by half, demanded cheap bread. Petitions against the Corn Laws began to pour in. At first the Ministers shirked the difficulty by a policy of delay, pleaded the inopportunity of provoking on the eve of a General Election a debate which could have no result, and pledged themselves to deal with the question during the first session of the new Parliament;[1] but the popular agitation became more intense, and produced in Lancashire what was nothing short of a revolt among the workers. The Cabinet then ventured on a step of no slight importance, and, in spite of the hostility of the country gentlemen, carried through Parliament a Bill which for a limited period, a little over two months, authorized the sale of a quantity of corn already in bond on payment of a trifling duty;[2] and a second Bill bestowed upon the Government during the approaching recess discretionary powers to admit foreign corn for two months and to an amount not exceeding 500,000 quarters.[3]

These two measures cannot be regarded as remedies for the industrial crisis. Their sole object was to alleviate the distress of the working class, without the necessity of asking Parliament to

[1] H. of C., April 18, 1826, Huskisson's speech (*Parl. Deb.*, N.S., vol. xv, pp. 342–3, 346, 347–8).
[2] 7 Geo. IV, cap. 70.   [3] 7 Geo. IV, cap. 71.

make a grant for that purpose. It was in the same spirit that the Government, when pressed to come to the assistance of trade, finally persuaded the Bank to make advances on the security of bills or goods to the amount of £3,000,000.[1] If Canning had had his way the Treasury would have been empowered to make direct advances to merchants; a loan for a short period would have furnished the necessary credits; but he was faced by the inflexible opposition of Lord Liverpool, who, to a greater degree than himself, was under the influence of the new political economy and regarded every kind of State intervention as likely to do more harm than good.[2] 'Some of the causes to which this evil must be attributed,' ran the words of the King's Speech, 'lie without the reach of direct parliamentary interposition; nor can security against the recurrence of them be found, unless in the experience of the sufferings which they occasioned.' Nevertheless, the following words appealed to the wisdom of Parliament: 'To devise such measures as may tend to protect both *private and public* interests against the like sudden and violent fluctuations, by placing on a more firm foundation the currency and circulating credit of the country.' In other words, the Cabinet proposed to reform the banking system.

3

As we have already had occasion to notice, it would seem that a development may be distinctly traced during the first quarter of the century of the doctrine held upon these matters by the Liberal economists who now inspired Huskisson's policy. So long as the war lasted the bullionists had held the Bank responsible for the economic distress of the country, due, they maintained, to an excessive issue of notes, and had declared that in this over-issue the Bank was the accomplice of a Government which required paper money to defray the current expenditure on the war and meet the arrears of the debt. Since the restoration of peace, and, above all, since the return to specie payment, the criticisms of Ricardo and his disciples had taken another turn. The issue of notes was, they alleged, only another form of coining money. It was, therefore, a function of the State, which was betraying the

[1] 7 Geo. IV., cap. 7. H. of C., February 28, March 8, 1826 (*Parl. Deb.*, N.S., vol. xiv, pp. 920 sqq., 1148 sqq.).
[2] Peel to Wellington, March 3, 1826; Canning to Wellington, March 4, 1826; Croker to Wellington, March 20, 1826 (Wellington, *Despatches, Cont.*, vol. iii, pp. 143, 147, 200).

interests of the nation when it divested itself of this right in favour of one or more banks. It was because the State had surrendered this right that still, after, as before, the return to specie payment, too much paper money was issued.

They maintained that the Bank of England, before it suddenly restricted its currency in May 1825 and by the alarm which its action gave precipitated the crisis, had produced that crisis by an excessive increase for the past three years of the paper currency. The latter had been increased by £3,000,000 during the two years preceding the crisis, in spite of the serious decrease during the same period of the cash reserve; and the provincial banks had contributed to the inflation. In 1823 their note issues amounted to £4,657,000, in 1824 to £6,098,000, in 1825 to £8,532,000.[1] That is to say, they had almost doubled; hence the exodus of coin, the depreciation of the pound sterling, the rise in the rate of foreign exchange. It was the bankers, not the manufacturers or the merchants, who were responsible for the crisis.

How, then, could the disaster be remedied? On this point clearly logic demanded that the new school should depart from its principles and call for a policy of restraint instead of freedom. Should the bankers, whether companies or private persons, be deprived of the right to issue notes, and the right reserved for the future to a State Bank which would not discount commercial assets, but confine itself to the issue of paper money? No one, either in the Cabinet or in Parliament, seriously contemplated such a step. The monopoly of the Bank of England did not expire until 1833, and whatever its previous mistakes, the level-headed prudence it had displayed in tiding over the crisis in December was universally recognized. Or would, at any rate, the provincial banks be subjected to the conditions imposed upon the Bank of England, and forbidden to issue notes which were not guaranteed, according to a proportion legally fixed, by a prescribed amount of bullion? The Government had no thought of adopting a measure of this kind, and hardly a voice was raised to blame their attitude. Two measures were taken which, from the strictly logical standpoint, may be regarded as in mutual contradiction: a measure of restraint, the principle of which was debatable, but its adoption easily explicable under the circumstances, and a measure of emancipation.

[1] *Edinburgh Review*, June 1826, 'Commercial Revulsions' (vol. xliv, p. 86).

4

In 1822 the English banking houses had obtained the right to issue, until the year 1833, when the expiration of the monopoly of the Bank of England would necessitate a revision of the entire banking system, notes for small sums not exceeding £5. The country banks had hastened to avail themselves on a very large scale of the permission then granted, and, in the majority of English counties, pound notes had almost entirely replaced the gold sovereign. Presumably this issue of notes for petty sums had assisted the inflation of the paper currency. The Government introduced and carried a Bill by which the banks were immediately deprived of the right to issue small notes, and providing that the notes already issued should go out of circulation before 1829.[1] But it is most unlikely that the issue of these notes by the provincial banks had in fact contributed to the crisis to the extent alleged; for it began in Lancashire, where these small notes were unknown. On the other hand, the banks had weathered the storm more successfully in Scotland than anywhere else, and in Scotland paper money had for a long time past entirely driven out the gold coinage: indeed, the Government could only avoid antagonizing Scottish public opinion by a pledge that the new statute should not be applied north of the Tweed. But the Act of 1822 had been passed to satisfy the complaints of the agriculturalists, who ascribed their distress to the restriction of the currency due, in their belief, to the restoration of specie payment. Ever since, Cobbett had not ceased to boast of the victory then achieved, and to depict the Act of 1822 as the first step towards the repeal of the statute of 1819: and, when at last the crisis came, he predicted that the Bank of England would shortly suspend payment. But not only had the Bank successfully proved its solvency; the authors of 'Peel's Bill' seized the opportunity afforded by the crisis to obtain the repeal of the Act of 1822 and a return to the rigid enforcement of the Act of 1819.

The other measure proposed by the Government, and passed by Parliament, presented a different character. As the law then stood, the Bank of England was the sole company in England consisting of more than six members which enjoyed the right to conduct banking operations. In 1822 Lord Liverpool had at-

[1] 7 Geo. IV, cap. 6.

tempted unsuccessfully to abolish the monopoly; but in 1825 the Royal Bank of Ireland, which enjoyed the same right, was deprived of its privilege;[1] and the same year the powerful Scottish banking companies obtained legal recognition.[2] The time, therefore, seemed ripe to vanquish at last the opposition of the Bank of England, and the crisis, which was ascribed to the insufficient capital in the hands of the private banks, furnished the desirable opportunity. The monopoly of the Bank was confined to a radius of sixty-five miles from London; outside this limit capitalists in any number were empowered to combine to establish banks for deposit and issue. By way of compensation, the Bank of England received the right to establish branches outside London.[3] In this way a very considerable step was taken towards a system of free banking.

The step was the more significant because it was taken at the very moment when joint-stock companies were being made the object of violent attack. About six hundred had been formed within the last three years, and the capital subscribed was estimated to amount to nearly £500,000,000.[4] They were not only companies for the exploitation of the real or imaginary wealth of the New World, but insurance companies, water companies, gas companies, mining companies, and companies for the construction of canals, bridges, and already even of railways. The legal position of these anonymous companies, which lacked a charter of incorporation, appeared highly dubious to the lawyer.[5] Was the financial responsibility of the shareholders confined to the amount of their investment? Were they entitled to sell their shares to a third party, at a profit sometimes enormous, and thereby free themselves from all future responsibility? To return

---

[1] 6 Geo. IV, cap. 42. The Act sanctioned outside the radius of fifty miles from Dublin the formation of a society or co-partnership for the purpose of granting credit with a membership of more than six persons. An earlier Act (4 and 5 Geo. IV, cap. 73) had initiated for Ireland the work of emancipation.

[2] 6 Geo. IV, cap. 67.   [3] 7 Geo. IV, cap. 46.

[4] The *Annual Register* for 1825 contains a list, taken from a French publication, of 276 companies arranged in groups and representing a total capital of £174,114,050, all of which had been formed during 1824 or at the beginning of 1825. Doubleday (*Life of Sir Robert Peel*, vol. i, p. 327 n.) gives a list of 532 companies also arranged in groups and representing a total capital of £441,649,000. English (Henry), *A Complete View of the Joint-Stock Companies formed during the Years 1824 and 1825 . . . 1827*, enumerates 624 companies with a capital of £372,173,000.

[5] For their difficulties, and the uncertain state of the law, see Ellis T. Powell, *The Evolution of the Money Market* (1385–1915), 1915, chap. vi; also C. T. Carr, *The General Principles of the Law of Corporations*, 1905, chap. vii.

an affirmative answer to these questions would be to authorize the risky speculations, all too common during the last three years, in which the promoters had profited by the ruin of their dupes. Since 1824 Lord Eldon had been the declared enemy of joint-stock companies, and had urged that they should be subjected to a more rigorous control. The names of the shareholders should be formally registered; every shareholder who wished to sell his shares should be obliged to give notice of his intention to leave the company, and, unless the notification had been given, should be held responsible if the undertaking failed; and, moreover, persons injured by the failure should have a remedy, not only against the entire body of shareholders, but also against any two individual shareholders chosen at their pleasure.[1] Thus at the very time when Huskisson's one consideration was to establish a system of unfettered commercial freedom, a Tory was denouncing the abuses which it would entail, and several Radicals, Hobhouse among them, echoed his protest.[2] Nevertheless, it passed unheeded.

When, in 1825, Lord Liverpool warned the public against speculators and company promoters, he had taken care to make it plain that in no circumstances would the State interfere to save the public from the consequences of its own folly; and during the same session, at the request of the Government, Parliament repealed the obsolete Bubble Act of 1720, in virtue of which all joint-stock companies were still theoretically illegal.[3] There were a large number of undertakings, Huskisson pleaded, which it was altogether beyond the power of any individual capitalist to carry out. Who, then, could provide the necessary resources? Either public bodies, as on the Continent, or joint-stock companies. This being the alternative, the choice could not be in doubt.[4] There could not however be a stronger proof of the favour which, in spite of so many failures, the joint-stock companies still enjoyed, than the alteration which Huskisson introduced into the English banking system. So far was the crisis of 1825

[1] H. of L., May 21, 1824 (*Parl. Deb.*, N.S., vol. xi, pp. 791–2); February 3, 7, 1825 (ibid., vol. xii, pp. 13, 127).
[2] H. of C., March 16, 1825 (ibid., vol. xii, pp. 1048 sqq.); February 21, 1826 (ibid., vol. xiv, pp. 644 sqq.).
[3] 6 Geo. IV, cap. 91.
[4] The speech in which Huskisson explained his entire position in regard to joint-stock companies belongs in reality to a slightly later date (H. of C., December 5, 1826, *Parl. Deb.*, N.S., vol. xvi, pp. 275 sqq.).

from causing even a temporary setback to the system of joint-stock companies that it actually hastened the decline of the private bank. The number of private banks fell from eight hundred to about seven hundred, and they never regained the ground lost, while, in imitation of the system which had long obtained in Scotland, joint-stock banks began to get the control of the banking system of the country into their hands.[1]

5

The discussion of these measures occupied the greater part of the session of 1826. Canning threw himself into the fray with his characteristic ardour, spoke a language not usually heard from the lips of a Tory Minister, and compared himself with Turgot victimized by the intrigues of the nobility and Galileo persecuted by the Inquisition.[2] He found himself compelled at last to discuss those problems of practical economics which he had avoided so long. He spoke on the question of restricting the monopoly of the Bank. He spoke on the Corn Law. Before delivering his speeches, he was careful to obtain the necessary information from his more proficient colleagues, Robinson and Huskisson, especially the latter; for Robinson, after cutting for a session or two such a brilliant figure that he had all the appearance of a great parliamentary leader, was now being reduced by public opinion to the position he deserved, and receding into the background. In 1825, when alarmists were already predicting an imminent crisis, he had made the disastrous mistake of asserting in the most emphatic terms that the national prosperity rested on a solid and secure foundation. When the crisis actually came, Cobbett called him Prosperity Robinson, and the nickname stuck to him.[3] Huskisson's influence, on the contrary, was growing steadily, and it was to him that public opinion ascribed all the

[1] Three were formed in 1826, four in 1827, none in 1828, seven in 1829, one in 1830, nine in 1831, seven in 1832, nine in 1833, ten in 1834, nine in 1835, twenty-seven in 1836 (*Appendix to Report from Committee on Joint-Stock Banks*, 1836, pp. 246 sqq.). See *Morning Chronicle*, April 12, 1827, for an interesting account of a public meeting held in Huddersfield for the formation of a joint-stock bank. Its object was to render impossible for the future crises in speculation such as that which the country had just experienced. The bank was formed amid a veritable outburst of public enthusiasm.

[2] H. of C., February 24, 1826 (*Parl. Deb.*, N.S., vol xiv, p. 854).

[3] H. of C., February 28, 1825 (ibid., vol. xii, p. 750); *Pol. Reg.*, December 3, 1825 (vol. lvi, p. 580)

financial measures adopted by the Government to tide over the existing crisis and prevent future crises.

The situation improved, and fortunately for the Government the crisis had reached its height in December, two months before Parliament met. Naturally, its effects still continued to be felt, and when it was known that wages had fallen by half in some branches of industry, the knowledge could not but give rise to fears of a new upheaval among the labouring class. 'I fear,' wrote Lord John Russell to Thomas Moore on February 23, 'the summer may resemble that of 1819—and then for the Six Acts again—it is woeful.'[1] But the apprehensions expressed by Lord John were not verified by the event.

There were strikes and riots at Whitehaven, Norwich, Bradford, Trowbridge, Carlisle, Dudley, and, above all, in Lancashire, where the weavers broke the machines recently introduced: it was calculated that a thousand frames were broken, to the value of £30,000;[2] but these disorders were sporadic, and the contemporary evidence bears unanimous witness to the remarkably peaceable spirit displayed by the working class.[3] There were no comprehensive plans to concentrate the forces of the proletariat, such as had been formed at the end of 1824; the fall of wages had broken the trade unions.[4] Even the rioting which did occur was merely the instinctive effect of hunger, like the first Luddite outbreak in 1812. There were no Radical agitators to assume the leadership of the masses, as in 1816 and 1819, and impose upon them a programme of political revolution, and the conquest of civil power.[5] The Tories had, therefore, no occasion to demand

---

[1] Lord John Russell to Thomas Moore, February 23, 1826 (*Early Correspondence of Lord John Russell*, vol. i, p. 246).

[2] *Ann. Reg.*, 1826, Chron., February 3, 13; May 3, 8, 13; July 29; April 24; May 3; July 15, 16. A. Prentice, *Historical Sketches of Manchester*, pp. 273 sqq.

[3] *Ann. Reg.*, 1826, p. 2; H. of C., May 19, 1826, Canning's speech (*Parl. Deb.*, N.S., vol. xv, p. 1283); also the charitable appeal made on April 5 in the *Blackburn Mail*, quoted by J. L. and B. Hammond, *The Skilled Labourer*, p. 127.

[4] H. of L., February 2, 1826: 'Lord Sheffield . . . congratulated their lordships that in all the manufacturing districts the spirit of combination among the working classes had entirely disappeared.' H. of C., February 2, 1826, J. S. Wortley's speech: 'The combination among the workmen, which had reached so alarming an extent, had now happily subsided' (*Parl. Deb.*, N.S., vol. xiv, pp. 6, 25).

[5] During his speech (Mr. Huskisson) spoke of the manufacturing distress of 1819 and 1820, and he took occasion to say that the poor suffering manufacturers were *not now* misled by *designing men* (*Pol. Reg.*, March 4, 1826, vol. lvii, p. 616). Also the letter written from Manchester by Eckersley, which is quoted by J. L. and B. Hammond, op. cit., p. 126: '. . . It is certainly very different now (for the better) from 1819 and 1820, when politics were mixed up with the distresses of the people.'

the re-enactment of the Seditious Meetings Act of 1819, which had expired, unnoticed, two years earlier. Private charity was organized on a large scale to relieve the sufferings of the masses and seal the reconciliation of classes: in Yorkshire Wilberforce directed the organization and recovered his former popularity, which had been several times endangered since 1815. While Lord John Russell was predicting insurrection, Greville made a truer diagnosis of the situation. 'So great and so absorbing,' he wrote, 'is the interest which the present discussions excite that all men are become political economists and financiers.'[1] The difference between the attitude of the public during the present crisis and their attitude during the crises which had occurred during the first six or seven years after the restoration of peace was very striking; nobody now talked politics, men talked of nothing but banks, paper money, Free Trade, and the abolition of the Corn Law.

After three years' silence Lord John brought up again in the Commons the question of parliamentary reform. The approach of the General Election obliged him to take up a definite position on the subject, if only as a matter of form. He introduced a Bill to disfranchise every borough convicted of corruption, and transfer its franchise to a new constituency possessed of a larger population and with better claims to a representative. He also brought forward a motion in favour of parliamentary reform which he prefaced by a long and carefully studied speech. Nevertheless, he acknowledged that the policy lately pursued by the Government was in accordance with the wishes of the people, and was content to urge the danger that under the existing franchise the more intransigent Tories might find themselves in a majority in the next Parliament. Lord Althorp, who supported him in a short speech, disclaimed the suggestion that the country was badly governed under the present system. Hobhouse, the author of the celebrated attack of 1821, delivered a detailed panegyric of the policy of reform pursued by Peel, Huskisson, and Canning;[2] and, indeed, the same speaker, eight days earlier, had assured Canning of the 'gratitude' and 'affection' of the country for what he had accomplished, and had promised him her 'veneration' if he would but take one further step and yield on this vital question

[1] *Greville Memoirs*, February 20, 1826 (vol. i, p. 83).
[2] H. of C., April 27, 1826 (*Parl. Deb.*, N.S., vol. xv, pp. 651 sqq.).

of parliamentary reform.[1] Canning did not even trouble to intervene in the debate opened by Lord John Russell. Every Liberal speaker confirmed his opinion that reform of Parliament was superfluous, since all necessary reforms could be obtained by a clever leader from a House of Commons elected like the present under a system which had undergone no reform whatsoever. Evidently the crisis of 1825, far from shaking Canning's position in the country, had strengthened it. It was nothing less than a triumph for his policy that the nation had passed through an economic crisis similar to the crises of 1816 and 1819, and that it had not, as under Castlereagh's Government, been accompanied by agitation of a Radical and revolutionary character. Canning, therefore, on the eve of the election, could claim that, with the support of Lord Liverpool and the assistance of Huskisson, he had reconciled Parliament and people.

[3] Creevey to Miss Ord, April 14, 1820 (*Creevey Papers*, vol. ii, p. 98). See the modified text of the speech, H. of C., April 13, 1826 (*Parl. Deb.*, N.S., vol. xv, p. 188).

Catholic Emancipation

I   CANNING'S FINAL PERIOD

I

CANNING'S policy had triumphed, and the fashion in which the extremely grave crisis of December had been surmounted without political troubles had set the seal upon his victory; but the questions which were contested in June, during the General Election which immediately followed the dissolution of Parliament, showed how precarious, after all, that victory was. The elections were riotous, the issues before the electorate confused, and the questions raised precisely those which Canning and his friends had been shirking for the last four years. At no cheaper rate than this had they purchased their success.

There was, first of all, the question of the Corn Law. Robinson and Huskisson had given the financial and commercial policy of the country the orientation desired by the political economists, the advocates of Free Trade; but their adherence to the principle of Free Trade was glaringly imperfect so long as they were satisfied with lowering the import duties upon the manufactured articles and raw materials required by the industries of the nation, and a Parliament, which contained an overwhelming majority of landowners, persisted in keeping foreign corn out of the country by a tariff wellnigh prohibitive. Already, in 1825, preferential treatment had been temporarily accorded to Canadian cereals, and, in 1826, to alleviate the distress of the poorer classes a certain amount of corn in bond had been released; but these were very feeble concessions to the doctrine of the economists and the pressure exerted with increasing force by the inhabitants of the great urban centres. On April 28, 1825, Huskisson, in a speech which betrayed no little embarrassment, had declared himself favourable in principle to a fixed tariff, had pleaded that the prohibitive system at present in operation might prove a useful weapon in the hands of the President of the Board of Trade, when negotiating a commercial treaty with a foreign Power, but had ended with the admission 'that it would be necessary to enter at a future time upon the revision of the Corn Laws'.[1] During the elections the candidates in every constituency where there was a broad franchise made a bid for popularity by promising to demand this reform.

Catholic emancipation was another dangerous question. It was to give time for the excitement aroused in the public mind by the debates of the previous session to fade that Canning had obtained the postponement of the election from 1825 until 1826; and since the economic crisis through which England had passed in the interval had distracted the attention of the public to other problems, there was reason to hope that anti-Catholic feeling had grown less violent. The hope proved false. In Ireland, where the Catholics, though ineligible for election, possessed the franchise, the party in favour of emancipation gained a very considerable number of seats. O'Connell organized the revolt of the free tenants against their Protestant landlords, and Lord George Beresford lost to two of his supporters the representation of the County of Waterford, which he had been accustomed to regard as his hereditary appanage.[2] In England there was a reaction, and the elections were fought to the old tune of No Popery. It was not merely that the anti-Catholic candidates enjoyed the support of the Prime Minister, for his influence with the electorate was after all very slight; they had behind them the mass of the gentry, the middle class, and even the labourers. It was with the greatest difficulty that Lord Palmerston, who was still unknown, and in the Cabinet played a very minor part among Canning's followers, secured his re-election for the University of Cambridge with the help of Whig votes.[3] On the other hand, their favourable attitude to the Catholic claims cost the Whigs many a defeat. The Protestant Dissenters, traditional supporters of the Whigs, voted in many constituencies, out of hatred for the Church of Rome, for the Tory candidate who was opposed to emancipation.[4] The

[1] H. of C., April 28, 1825 (*Parl. Deb.*, N.S., vol. xiii, pp. 273 sqq.).

[2] B. Ward, *Eve of Catholic Emancipation*, p. 171.

[3] Sir H. L. Bulwer, *Life of Viscount Palmerston*, Book III (ed. 1870, vol. i, pp. 168–70).

[4] H. of C., March 23, 1827, D. W. Harvey's speech: 'It had been said that the Dissenters were generally unfavourable to the Catholic claims. He believed they were; and he had generally found that those amongst them who best understood the subject, and were the most deeply imbued with the spirit of religious liberty, were the most alive in their apprehensions on the subject.' See also Sir Robert Wilson's speech, delivered later at the same sitting: 'The main body of the Dissenters were certainly more opposed to the Catholic claims than even the members of the Established Church' (*Parl. Deb.*, N.S., vol. xvii, pp. 14, 15). For the attitude of the Evangelicals, who united with the High

large county of Yorkshire, which, for the first time, returned four members to Parliament, witnessed a bitter contest between the 'Catholics' and the 'Protestants', in which Sydney Smith took part and published an open letter to the electors dealing with the Catholic question.[1] The result was indecisive, two 'Protestants' being returned and two 'Catholics'—Lord Milton, the eldest son of Lord Fitzwilliam, and a manufacturer named John Marshall.[2] In Bedfordshire the Marquis of Tavistock, the Duke of Bedford's eldest son, obtained only the second place, an anti-Catholic Tory receiving a greater number of votes. In Huntingdonshire Lord John Russell was defeated. When the seats won in Ireland and the seats lost in England had been balanced against each other, it was not easy at a juncture when the condition of party politics was so chaotic to forecast what would be the vote of the recently elected Parliament, which contained one hundred and fifty new members, when the Catholic question was again brought forward.[3] Nevertheless, even before Parliament met, it seemed certain that the Protestant party had strengthened its position.

But the real effect of the election was to place in a clearer light than ever the paradox of the political situation. The outstanding figure in Parliament, the real leader of the nation, was Canning; and he was, moreover, the official head of the Tory party in the House of Commons. Nevertheless, every defeat suffered by the Tories in an urban constituency upon the question of the Corn Law was the victory of his principles, and every victory won by the Tories from the 'Catholics' the defeat of his policy. Hobhouse had described the situation a few months previously when he had drawn attention to the spectacle of the two parties seated on opposite sides of the House—His Majesty's Government engaged in the task of filling the Government offices and drawing large salaries, and 'His Majesty's Opposition' engaged in the task of

Church against the Catholics, see, further, H. of L., March 9, 1826, Lord Darnley's speech (ibid., vol xiv, pp. 1200–1).

[1] *A Letter to the Electors upon the Catholic Question*, 1826. *The Electors' True Guide*: a Review of the Rev. Sydney Smith's *Letter to Electors upon the Roman Catholic Question*, by an East Riding Freeholder, 1826. *The Catholic Claims Rejected*: being an Answer to the letters of an 'English Catholic', 'The Reverend Sydney Smith', and 'Mr. Charles Butler', and Thirty-two Thousand other Popish Productions recently circulated in this Kingdom. By an English Protestant. York, 1826.

[2] *Life of Edward Baines*, by his son, pp. 139–40.

[3] Lord Palmerston to W. Temple, July 17, 1826 (Sir H. L. Bulwer, op. cit., Book III, ed. 1870, vol. i, p. 171). It should be noticed that in this letter Lord Palmerston expresses the opinion that the elections had been a defeat for the opponents of emancipation: '. . . The No Popery cry has been tried in many places and has failed everywhere.'

formulating the policy of the Cabinet.[1] In other words, if we would not stop at appearances, we must agree with Lord Palmerston that 'the real Opposition of the present days is behind the Treasury Bench'.[2] How long could this unstable balance be maintained?

2

Parliament met in extraordinary session on November 14. The Cabinet asked Parliament to approve the action it had taken on September 1, when to avert a threatened famine the Government had authorized by Order in Council[3] the importation, on payment of a slight duty, of certain cereals, oats, barley, peas, and beans. The sanction for which they asked was accorded without difficulty; but an important diplomatic incident occupied the attention of the Commons during this brief session. It possessed no little significance, for although, taken in itself, it was a further triumph for Canning's policy, it revealed the difficulties which sooner or later his policy must inevitably face. In September he had visited Paris. He thus realized the design he had formed in 1825 when Charles X had just ascended the throne, but which the Tories had prevented him from carrying out. He had been entertained by everyone outside the ill-humoured group on the extreme right. The King had received him with the honours due to the man who was practically, if not officially, the Prime Minister of George IV. For the first and the last time, in the person of Canning, a commoner had the honour of dining with Charles X;[4] and the Liberals paid their homage to the only statesman who had dared to oppose openly the powerful monarchs of the Continent. Canning, thus for several weeks his own ambassador at Paris, had attempted to reach an agreement with M. de Villèle on the various questions affecting the balance of power in Europe. The aspect of the Eastern question had changed during the past year. The Czar Alexander had died on December 1 at a time when Canning

[1] H. of C., April 10, 1826 (*Parl. Deb.*, N.S., vol. xv, p. 135). See Lord Broughton. op. cit., vol. iii, pp. 129–31. The description was ascribed later to Tierney. See J. C. Hobhouse's Diary, May 5, 1827 (ibid., p. 191).

[2] Lord Palmerston to William Temple, July 17, 1826 (Sir H. L. Bulwer, op. cit., ed. 1870, vol. i, p. 171).

[3] The order was illegal, for the statute passed during the last session empowering the Government to authorize the importation of a certain quality of foreign corn mentioned only wheat.

[4] A. G. Stapleton, *George Canning and his Times*, p. 516.

was aware that it was becoming more and more difficult to prevent him from using force in the Near East. But his successor Nicholas might, so at least Canning hoped, prove easier to manage. Threatened on the morrow of his accession by a military plot, he would perhaps be less ready to encourage, even in Greece, the intrigues of a revolutionary government. Since he was not, like Alexander, the father of the Holy Alliance, he was unlikely to share the late Czar's dream of leading, as the representative of all the sovereigns of Europe, a nineteenth-century crusade against the Turk. Wellington, with whom, in everything that concerned the Eastern question, Canning was in entire agreement,[1] had been sent in the spring of 1826 on an extraordinary mission to St. Petersburg to tender the congratulations of the British Government to the Czar and attempt a settlement of outstanding questions on a new basis. A protocol had been signed on April 4 by which Russia and England would bring joint pressure to bear upon the Sultan to recognize the autonomy of Greece under Turkish suzerainty, and in the event of his refusal recognize the absolute independence of Greece and declare war upon Turkey; and, on the other hand, Russia was given a free hand to settle with Turkey various matters which had long been in dispute between the two Powers on the Danube. By the treaty concluded at Ackermann on September 4, the Emperor of Russia's demands had received full satisfaction. The French Government, to whom, as to the other members of the Holy Alliance, the text of the Protocol had been submitted, had expressed approval, and offered support. Charles X, in the interviews which he held with Canning in September and October, renewed the offer in a more definite form. He offered to send a French fleet to the Levant and place it under the command of a British admiral. Certainly the new policy thus inaugurated by Canning was sufficiently impressive, but it was also risky. What exactly did it signify? Did he consider that Turkey was pursuing, with Metternich's support, an imprudent course, and gratuitously provoking Russia by the refusal to make any concession to her rebellious subjects in Greece? By this ostensible understanding with Russia he put sufficient pressure upon the Porte to compel a more conciliatory attitude, and at the same time paralysed the action of Russia herself, obliged hence-

---

[1] Canning to Lord Granville, January 10, 1825 (E. J. Stapleton, *Some Official Correspondence of Canning*, vol. i, p. 231).

forward to act in concert with England, and prevented her from entering upon that war with Turkey which the British Foreign Office and public opinion dreaded above any other contingency? His design, in fact, went farther than this, for he was laying the foundations of an understanding not with Russia alone, but with Russia and France. Did he calculate that an entente between France and Russia, the bugbear of English statecraft, would lose all its terrors, if it were effected under the patronage of England?

Nevertheless, the Eastern question was not the subject of the most lengthy conversations between Canning, Charles X, and M. de Villèle. It was still in the Peninsula that friction between England and France seemed inevitable. How was it possible, in spite of these disagreements, to maintain between the two Governments that good understanding which Canning had always professed to desire and de Villèle did undoubtedly desire?

Ever since 1822 the affairs of Portugal had been a source of incessant anxiety to Canning. When he entered the Foreign Office the 'Constitutionalists' were in power at Lisbon; but the 'Constitutionalists', the Portuguese 'Jacobins', were bitterly hostile to England—in revolt against an alliance which wore the aspect of a protectorate. He had, therefore, adopted towards them the attitude of an orthodox Tory, had prevented them from making common cause with the Liberals of Cadiz, and had supported the *coup d'état* by which in the spring of 1823 King John abolished the Constitution of 1822. But within King John's Government itself there had sprung up, as by some fatal necessity, two rival groups—the one in favour of England, the other in favour of France; and it was only by intrigues extending over months that Canning's diplomacy had finally secured the victory of the 'English' party. Then the King's death had produced a situation more favourable from one point of view to the unfettered development of Canning's policy. His legitimate heir, the Emperor of Brazil, Dom Pedro, abdicated in favour of his daughter, the little Infanta Maria, a child of seven, at the same time granting a Constitution. Pedro's younger brother, Dom Miguel, the leader of the Absolutist party, intrigued against Maria. The Constitutional party was supported by England, and Dom Miguel's party made a powerful appeal to the sympathies of the people by the very fact that it was now, as the Constitutional party had been in 1822, the anti-English party. Dom

Miguel had behind him a section of the Army, which mutinied, and the Absolutist Government of Madrid, just restored by a French Army which had not yet quitted Spain. Portuguese deserters who had taken refuge in Spanish territory were conspiring against the Government of Donna Maria. Canning, during his visit to Paris, prevailed upon M. de Villèle to instruct the French Ambassador at Madrid to demand from Ferdinand the formal recognition of the new Portuguese Government, and an active repudiation of any conspiracy to overthrow it.

But de Villèle's instructions were fruitless. On December 3 the news reached Paris and London that two Portuguese armies had crossed the frontier and were marching upon Lisbon to establish Miguel upon the throne; and the same day an official note was received in London from the Portuguese Prime Minister imploring the British Government to send an army to his assistance. Twice already since he had been Foreign Secretary had Canning been faced with the same request. On the first occasion he had replied by the dispatch of a squadron, on which King John had finally taken refuge from the threats of the contending factions;[1] the second time he had offered Hanoverian troops;[2] and now for the third time the party at Lisbon friendly to England begged for the dispatch of an army. Was it possible to evade the demand any longer?—and if it were not to be evaded, must not his policy undergo a marked change? It was no longer a question of opposing to the policy of the Holy Alliance a policy of systematic non-intervention. Intervention must be met by counterintervention, a return must be made to the old principle which had inspired England's wars in the past, and her armed forces must oppose the Bourbons, if for their advantage they upset the Balance of Power.

[1] A. G. Stapleton, *The Political Life of Mr. Canning*, vol. ii, p. 205.

[2] Ibid., vol. ii, p. 234. Cf. C. W. Wynn to the Duke of Buckingham, August 8, 1824: 'The justification of our sending a military force to support our ancient ally the King of Portugal in a struggle against another party in the interior of his dominions rests, in my opinion, exactly on the same grounds on which we armed in concert with the King of Prussia to restore the Stadtholder in 1787, and to put down a party which, acting under the protection of France and with a hostile disposition to the British interest, had deposed him. On that question, when Fox declared his entire concurrence in the system on which Pitt acted, he deprecated any discussion of the justice of the cause of either party. That, he said, was not the question a British Minister was bound to look to, but which of them was most likely to promote the interests of Great Britain' (Duke of Buckingham, op. cit., vol. ii, p. 100). Cf. Canning to Lord Granville, January 21, 1825: '. . . Portugal has been and always *must* be English, so long as Europe and the world remain in anything like their present state . . .' (A. G. Stapleton, *Canning and his Times*, p. 509).

3

Canning was ill, and it was not until December 12 that he addressed the Commons in defence of his policy. The opening of his speech was flat.[1] He explained that old treaties, dating from the seventeenth and eighteenth centuries, obliged England to assist Portugal against a foreign attack and in particular against a Spanish or a French attack; but he soon caught fire as he showed how he had not delayed for a single hour the fulfilment of that obligation. Full information had not been received in London until the 8th, and at that very moment when he was speaking 'the troops were on the march for embarkation'. He then adopted a wider point of view. While giving due credit to the French Government for its action in recalling its Ambassador from Spain on the news of the invasion, he let it be understood that in his opinion France could have taken 'a more efficient course'. Even now he desired peace; but it was not because he believed that England was too weak to make war, or her finances too impoverished. It was because he knew that at the present juncture any war was liable to degenerate into a universal war and, moreover, into a 'conflict of opinions'. He foresaw, and, if they would believe him, feared the day when his country 'could not avoid seeing ranked under her banners all the restless and dissatisfied of any nation with which she might come in conflict'. Modern England was Æolus, Master of the Winds, free at her pleasure to let loose the tempest. Let the Continental Powers beware of exciting the wrath of the god. 'We go to plant the standard of England on the well-known heights of Lisbon. Where that standard is planted foreign dominion shall not come.'

The debate proceeded. Certain speakers attempted to draw a contrast between the active policy which Canning was pursuing in regard to Portugal and the policy of non-intervention he had adopted three years earlier towards the Government of Cadiz. Canning intervened a second time to justify his action. England, he said, was not bound by treaty to Spain as she was bound to Portugal. He was far from blaming the jealousy, in harmony with the great traditions of the eighteenth century, with which the British

[1] Sir H. L. Bulwer, *Historical Characters*, vol. ii, pp. 351-2: '. . . I was talking the other day with a friend who, then being a Westminster boy, was present at the debate; and he told me . . . that with the exception of one or two passages . . . there was a want of the elasticity and flow which distinguished Mr. Canning's happier effects.'

Parliament watched the Spanish policy of the Bourbons; but he desired to reassure his hearers as to the effects of the French intervention. The French Army of Occupation served a useful purpose in the Peninsula—a purpose which the French extremists had assuredly never foreseen, for it protected the Spanish Liberals against the excesses of the Absolutist reaction; and moreover he claimed credit for having skilfully launched a counter-stroke to the French invasion without letting loose upon Europe the horrors of war. As he approached his peroration his excitement grew more intense—he no longer spoke, he screamed. 'I sought materials of compensation in another hemisphere. Contemplating Spain, such as our ancestors had known her, I resolved that, if France had Spain, it should not be Spain "with the Indies". I called the New World into existence to redress the balance of the Old.'[1]

Exhausted, almost fainting[2] he sat down, amid the applause of the House. Since Pitt's death, over twenty years before, no English statesman had addressed such language to Europe, and to France. This sitting of December 12, 1826, may be regarded as the culmination of Canning's career. Nevertheless, amid the enthusiasm of a nation wellnigh unanimous, the voice of criticism was not wholly silent. There were those who thought the tone he had adopted towards France unnecessarily provocative—indeed, if we may believe some who were present at the debate, it was more provocative than we could gather from reading the printed report of his speech, in which his language had been softened.[3] Moreover, he annoyed several of his colleagues by a behaviour which was increasingly dictatorial. Wellington complained that he had taken all his decisions in regard to Portugal without even troubling to consult the Cabinet. He declared that the English intervention would inevitably involve the intervention on the side of Spain, first of France and then of the United States, for every Englishman of that generation seems to have believed that a war with the latter was imminent. He threatened to resign.[4] In

[1] Diary of Thomas Moore, December 21, 22: 'When he said, "I thought of Spain and the Indies" it was in a sort of scream' (*Memoirs of Thomas Moore*, vol. v, p. 135).

[2] Ibid.: 'Nearly fainted after he had done.'

[3] Lord Broughton, op. cit., vol. ii, pp. 159–60. Cf. *Pol. Reg.*, December 30, 1826, postscript to Mr. Canning, pp. 1 sqq.

[4] Wellington to Canning, August 11, 1826; Lord Liverpool to Wellington, August 16, 1826; Wellington to Lord Liverpool, August 18, 1826; to Planter, October 9, 1826; to Lord Liverpool, October 11, 1826; to the same, October 12, 1826; to Canning, October 13, 1826 (Wellington, *Despatches, Cont.*, vol. iii, pp. 375, 381, 381–3, 414–15, 417, 419, 419–21). C. Arbuthnot to Lord Liverpool, September 5, 1826 (C. D. Yonge, op. cit.,

the House of Commons Hume had the courage to move an amendment to the address proposed by Canning, in which he asserted in so many words that England, ruined by the great war, could not afford the expense of another military adventure.[1] This unconcerted agreement of a group of Tories and a group of Radicals to censure Canning's policy the moment it was plainly degenerating into a policy of war was a most significant fact.

But Wellington was appeased by Lord Liverpool and did not resign. Hume could scarcely make himself heard by a hostile assembly[2] and drew down upon himself the sarcasms, not only of Canning, but of Brougham.[3] Moreover, the pessimistic forecasts of Canning's critics were not fulfilled. Before the end of January the mere presence of English troops in Portugal had enabled the Portuguese Army to rout the Miguelist forces, and the Spanish Government at last yielded and accredited an ambassador to Donna Maria. By a display of oratory, and a military parade, Canning had imposed his will upon Western Europe. Therefore, when on February 8 the Government again met Parliament, his position appeared for the moment firmer than ever, strengthened by the success of his diplomatic *coup de main* of December. He had, however, still to face the difficult domestic problems, the Corn Law and Catholic emancipation.

4

Lord Liverpool suggested at first that it would be wise not to raise both questions simultaneously. He yielded, however, to Canning's argument, when he urged that the discussion of the Catholic question would excite public feeling less if it were, so to

vol. iii, p. 394). Canning to Lord Liverpool, October 16, 1826 (A. G. Stapleton, *Canning and his Times*, pp. 526–8). Canning shared these fears of the rivalry of the United States as a sea Power. See his Memorandum on our relations with the Spanish American Provinces communicated to Wellington on November 30, 1824 (*Despatches, Cont.*, vol. ii, pp. 354 sqq.). And at this very moment James published a new edition of his *Naval History of Great Britain*, brought up to date with the object of reassuring the British public, too fearful, in his opinion, of the imaginary naval power of the United States (W. James to Canning, January 9, 1827, E. J. Stapleton, *Some Official Correspondence of Canning*, vol. ii, pp. 340 sqq.).

[1] H. of C., December 12, 1826 (*Parl. Deb.*, N.S., vol. xvi, p. 371).

[2] Lord Broughton, op. cit., vol. ii, p. 159. Styles (*Memoirs of Canning*, vol. ii, pp. 412–13) quotes the Diary of a contemporary present at the sitting: 'Even the reiterated laughter he occasioned did not atone for his folly; the very people in the gallery, reporters and all, disguised their contempt for him as little as their admiration of Mr. Canning.'

[3] Lord Broughton, op. cit., vol. ii, pp. 159–60. The allusion to the Greek Committee, which, Hobhouse informs us, excited the laughter of the House (there was a great tittering), is not to be found in *Parl. Deb.*, N.S., vol. xvi, p. 381.

speak, swamped by the discussion of the Corn Law, with which a Parliament of country landlords had a far more immediate concern;[1] and to give effect to his opinion, on March 1 Canning, who for the past year had accustomed himself to deal not only with questions of foreign policy but also with questions of political economy, proposed in the House of Commons that the sliding scale of 1822, which had never come into operation, should be replaced by a new sliding scale, which would be a step in the direction of Free Trade. The price of 60s. a quarter should be taken as the 'pivot' on which the entire scale would depend. When that price had been reached in the home market, foreign corn would be admitted on payment of a duty of 20s. For every fall of 1s. in the price there would be a corresponding increase of 2s. on the import duty; for every rise of 1s., 2s. would be taken off the duty—so that above 70s. foreign corn would be admitted free of duty. Other sliding scales were provided for the other cereals. Finally, after protracted debates, the Bill, with a few concessions of detail to the Protectionists in the cases of barley and oats, passed the Commons. What welcome it would receive from the Lords remained to be seen.

In the interval the question of Catholic emancipation had been raised on March 5 by Sir Francis Burdett. The House was not called upon to vote for or against a Bill, but merely to affirm in principle the expediency of taking into consideration the disqualifying statutes to which Catholics were subject. The debates lasted two days, and on the second day Peel, in a lengthy and impressive speech, expounded the reasons which led him to oppose emancipation. Of the 548 votes recorded, 272 were in favour of Burdett's motion, and 276 against it. Two years earlier, when for the first time Burdett had made a motion, couched in terms practically identical, it had obtained 247 votes as against 234 out of 421 votes recorded. In the late Parliament the 'Catholics' had secured a majority of thirteen. In the present Parliament the 'Protestants' had a majority of four. The question debated since July had at length been answered; the 'Protestant' gains at the last election in the English constituencies had more than compensated for the 'Catholic' gains in the Irish.[2]

[1] Lord Liverpool to Canning, February 13, 1827 (Wellington, *Despatches, Cont.*, vol. iii, p. 588).

[2] A precarious victory nevertheless. The 'Protestants' had counted upon a majority of twenty to thirty votes (Peel to the Bishop of Oxford, August 21, 1827; C. S. Parker,

Indeed, the circumstances in which the debate took place were awkward for Canning. From one point of view they were favourable to the speedy solution of the Catholic question. The Duke of York, an active leader of the Tories, and the man who, in 1815, had been responsible for the defeat of the Catholic Bill in the Lords, had died on January 5. Lord Liverpool, who, in spite of the many points in which he agreed with Canning, had always opposed in the Cabinet Catholic emancipation, had been seized with a fit of apoplexy on February 18. He was now Prime Minister only in name, and it would soon be necessary to find a successor. The obstacles which had prevented Canning from emancipating the Catholics seemed now to have been removed from his path; but it was in the very fact that he must now officially occupy the first place in the Government that his danger lay. Hitherto public opinion had credited the great man of the party with every Liberal measure adopted by the Ministry even when it emanated from Huskisson or Peel. If, on the other hand, on any matter of home or foreign politics the attitude of the Government was timid or reactionary, Liberal opinion blamed those who in the Cabinet thwarted Canning's will. The balance of opinion in the Ministerial ranks so fortunate for Canning, the benefit of which he had reaped for the past four years and a half, was now destroyed by the disappearance of Lord Liverpool.

After some hesitation the King decided to make Canning Prime Minister. After the stormy days of 1824 he had contrived to regain the royal favour. He had convinced the King that through his policy the British monarchy had regained all the prestige which it had lost in the days of Castlereagh and the Holy Alliance, and, further, that it was owing to him that the danger of revolution, so threatening when he ascended the throne, had completely disappeared. As regards the Catholic question Canning, while reserving complete freedom of action, had given the King to understand that he would spare him the necessity of any unpleasant decision or humiliating surrender. Nor did the question seem urgent, since, unlike the former, the newly elected Parliament contained a 'Protestant' majority. Possibly Canning,

op. cit., vol. ii, p. 14). If we are to believe Greville (March 13, 1827), the defeat of the 'Catholics' was in reality due to accident. 'Several pro-Catholics were suddenly taken ill or arrived too late for the division, and the election petitions went all against them.' Cf. *The Times*, March 8, 1827. 'The number of votes, as well for as against emancipation, was greater than it had ever been before.' (*The Times*, March 7, 1827).

so well versed in the arts of the courtier, hoped that his diplomacy would succeed in persuading the King to take a step which hitherto he had failed to persuade the Lords or even the Commons to take.

5

But the Royal favour did not suffice to secure for Canning the favour of the Tories. Already Peel had warned him that, although in agreement with him on other matters, he could not, by accepting the post of Home Secretary in his administration and thus making himself responsible in many respects for the government of Ireland, give what might seem an implicit consent to his Catholic policy. What was the reason of his obstinacy on this point, for which his political career would suffer for many years to come? Was it the result of anti-Catholic convictions which he had formed when he governed Ireland and of which he was unable to rid himself? Or was it his regard for the wishes which his constituents, the members of the University of Oxford, had formally expressed when ten years ago they had elected him precisely on the score of his opposition to the Catholic claims? Or was it a mere pretext, to justify in his own eyes and in the eyes of the world a determination not to serve under Canning, who inspired him, as he inspired many others, with an invincible distrust? Or was it perhaps the effect of all these motives together, and he was unwilling to make clear even to himself which of them was predominant in his mind?

Then it was Wellington's turn. After an acrimonious correspondence he refused to serve under Canning. Indeed, he went further. Since the Duke of York's death he had been Commander-in-Chief of the British Army; he now resigned the position rather than work in any capacity with Canning. Five other members of the Cabinet—among them a 'Catholic', Lord Melville—followed the example of Wellington and Peel.[1] This wholesale secession of the Tories might have been expected to alarm the King. But when Canning cleverly put his own complexion upon it and represented it as disloyalty, not to himself but to the sove-

[1] (Lady Charlotte Bury), *Diary Illustrative of the Times of George the Fourth*, vol. iv, pp. 359–60. No sooner was it known that a new administration must be formed than six members of the Cabinet resigned. This, in the familiar language of the day, was called a *strike*, and it certainly was not regarded with so much solemnity as it ought to have been.

reign, whom the Tories were seeking to deprive of the right to choose his own Prime Minister, its only effect was to tighten the bonds of friendship between himself and his sovereign. George had never loved Wellington, whom he found too haughty in his demeanour, too disposed to regard himself, both in England and on the Continent, in the light of an uncrowned king. It was against the grain that in January he had appointed him Commander-in-Chief. He brushed aside his opposition, and persisted in entrusting to Canning the task of forming an administration.

For himself Canning chose the Exchequer and became First Lord of the Treasury, handed over the Foreign Office to his friend and confidant Lord Dudley, and sent Robinson to the Lords with the title of Lord Goderich, to administer the Colonial Office in place of Lord Bathurst, who had resigned, and defend the policy of the Government in the Upper House. Another of Canning's friends, Sturges Bourne, received the Home Office, which Peel had vacated. Lord Anglesey took Wellington's place at the Ordnance, and the Duke of Portland succeeded Lord Westmoreland as Lord Privy Seal. W. Lamb, a supporter of Catholic emancipation, replaced Goulburn as Chief Secretary for Ireland. Lord Eldon having at last resigned the post of Lord Chancellor, his place was taken by Sir John Copley, an opponent of emancipation, who became Lord Lyndhurst. It was not necessary to find a successor to Lord Bexley as Chancellor of the Duchy of Lancaster, for he withdrew his resignation; nor to Lord Melville as first Lord of the Admiralty, for the office was suppressed. To ingratiate himself still further with King George, Canning revived, for the benefit of the Duke of Clarence, the King's brother and heir-apparent to the Crown, the office of Lord High Admiral. If since the Duke of York's death there was no longer a prince of the blood in command of the Army, the Navy would now be commanded by a prince.

The Cabinet thus reconstituted was still a Tory Cabinet, and still professed neutrality on the question of Catholic emancipation, although, as a result of the resignation of Wellington, Peel, and their followers, the 'Catholics' had strengthened their position at the expense of the 'Protestants'. Therefore it was only to be expected that hostility to Canning should persist among the Radicals, and that he should even find opponents in the ranks of the Whig aristocracy. We need not be told that Cobbett, the political

Ishmael, continued to abuse Canning, whose policy in regard to Spain and Portugal he attacked with such violence that he was suspected of being in the pay of the Bourbons.[1] Walter Savage Landor never forgave him for betraying the causes of Spanish Liberalism and Greek Independence. He was unwearied in denouncing his cynicism and Machiavellianism.[2] On May 7 in the House of Lords Lord Grey pronounced a long diatribe against the Premier's policy. In the Commons neither Hume the Radical, nor Lord Spencer's son, Lord Althorp, the most respected of all the Whig leaders, would desert the Opposition benches. But, notwithstanding these exceptions, the Liberals, as a body, supported Canning. He could count on the unreserved support of Sir Francis Burdett, the advocate of universal suffrage, of Lord John Russell and Brougham. The *Edinburgh Review*, the organ of Holland House, drew arguments in his favour from the memories of the French revolution which for many were still living. By treating him as the French aristocracy had treated Turgot, the British aristocracy, the *Review* pleaded, would expose itself, and along with itself the entire nation, to the disasters which had befallen the French nobility, and one day perhaps tread the same path of exile.[3] The alliance was sealed when Lord Lansdowne actually entered the Cabinet and Tierney was placed in charge of the Mint. The alliance cost the Whigs many concessions. They undertook not to raise the question of parliamentary reform of which Canning still declared himself the unyielding opponent. Not to embarrass him they refrained from raising afresh the question of Catholic emancipation, and preached patience to the Irish Catholics. When Hume moved the amendment of one of the Six Acts of 1817—the Acts which had at the time been contested so fiercely by the Liberals and defended so warmly by Canning—the Liberals did not vote upon the motion, and to escape the difficulty in which Hume sought to place them

---

[1] Canning to Robert Peel, December 28, 1826 (C. S. Parker, op. cit., vol. i, pp. 407–8). There is no doubt that Cobbett was in communication with the French Government. See his letter to Chateaubriand, March 1, 1823 (Chateaubriand, *Congrés de Vèrone*, vol. i, pp. 331 sqq.).

[2] Fonblanque, in the *Examiner*, hostile at first, rapidly became favourable; but it is interesting to note how carefully worded was his approval of Canning as a Prime Minister. 'We must fairly *try* him, not implicitly *trust* him' (May 13). 'The true policy of Mr. Canning's Whig supporters is to present in their principles a true resistance to his Tory propensities' (June 17). 'He will do us no more harm than is absolutely essential to the consistency of the dark sides of his character' (July 29).

[3] *Edinburgh Review*, June 1827, 'The Present Administration' (vol. xlvi, pp. 264 sqq.).

quitted the House in a body. Was this attitude of conciliation a mistake? The violence with which the Tory Press attacked Canning sufficiently proves the wisdom shown by the Whigs when they allied themselves with the Premier without even binding him to a definite programme of reform. Pitt's old party was breaking up. Tories were now leading the official Opposition, and the Whigs re-entering the Government in alliance with the most popular man in the country.

Canning introduced and carried the Budget. He abandoned the Corn Bill, into which Wellington in the Lords had introduced a clause which, in his opinion, stultified the principle on which the measure was based, and obtained in its place a temporary statute which enabled him to postpone the final settlement of the question until the following session. But his heart was still in his foreign policy. The Eastern Question continued to be grave. With Egyptian aid the Turks had defeated the insurgents, and the capture of Athens was a far more serious blow to the Greek cause than the capture of Missolonghi had been in 1826. At Constantinople British prestige was at a lower ebb than ever before, and Stratford Canning sent piteous dispatches to London.[1] Then Canning struck the mighty blow he had been contemplating for months.[2] On July 6, four days after the Prorogation of Parliament, he completed the St. Petersburg protocol by a formal treaty, the parties to which were no longer England and Russia alone, but England, Russia and France. By this treaty the three signatories pledged themselves to take joint action to compel the Sultan and the Greek insurgents to accept their arbitration, and to carry the treaty into effect the three fleets in the Levant—the English, the French and the Russian—were placed under the command of the English admiral, Sir Edward Codrington. The admiral's commission was to impose peace, not to make war. But the fatality which haunted Canning's policy, the danger that it might degenerate into a policy of war, presented itself here in a particularly threatening form. Could Admiral Codrington, who was free to give his own interpretation to the instructions he had

[1] S. L. Poole, *Life of Stratford Canning*, vol. i, pp. 446–7.
[2] Wellington to Phillpotts, August 15, 1830: '. . . I did everything I could to prevail upon Mr. Canning not to enter into the treaty; and he certainly negotiated it as far as the negotiations went, before the illness and secession of Lord Liverpool, without the knowledge of any of his colleagues except myself. But they and we all are highly blameable for having suffered the negotiations to move at all after we had, and particularly I had, a knowledge of it' (Wellington, *Despatches, Cont.*, vol. vii, p. 170).

received from the Government, restrain for long, not only the bellicose ardour of the Egyptian, Ibrahim Pasha, but his own desire to give battle?

The political outlook was uncertain. The parliamentary majority on which the Cabinet rested was heterogeneous and fragile. 'If Canning lasts, the Ministry will last', Lord John Russell wrote on July 10 to Thomas Moore.[1] He did not last. He was already fifty-two when he first assumed the burden of government, and his vitality had rapidly declined. The overwhelming mass of work involved in the administration of his department, the long hours which his position as Leader obliged him to spend at Westminster when Parliament was sitting had multiplied and aggravated the attacks of gout to which he was liable, and seriously undermined his health.[2] Already in January he had passed through a severe illness, and it was in vain that in August he sought a holiday at the Duke of Devonshire's house at Chiswick. He fell ill a second time, and died on August 8 in the very house in which Fox had died twenty years earlier. Perhaps he died at the right moment for his reputation. Had he died a little sooner his breach with the Tories would not have been complete, and therefore the Liberal aspects of his policy would not have been displayed so impressively. Had he died a little later, there can be no doubt that he would have found it impossible to maintain the delicate balance so characteristic of his policy, and avoid committing himself to the democratic party farther than he wished. An enemy of democracy, he believed that England's traditional institutions left nothing to be desired; and because they were so perfect she could in turn teach democratic Governments respect for tradition, and despotic Governments the principles of Liberalism, as best suited her interest at the moment. No statesman could be more alien to the spirit of crusade and the propaganda of ideas. Nevertheless, the circumstances of the time, which he had skilfully exploited, had clothed him with the garb of a cosmopolitan. His death was not mourned by the English people alone; it was felt as a bitter loss by Liberals and democrats throughout the world, for in Canning they honoured the man who broke the Holy Alliance.

[1] *Early Correspondence of Lord John Russell*, vol. i, p. 249.
[2] For a long while past he had complained of ill-health. See his letters to Frere, August 23, 1823, January 8, 1825 (G. Festing, op. cit., pp. 261, 264).

6

A reconstruction of the Cabinet had again become necessary. Now Canning was out of the way, would the King recall Wellington and Peel? He had not forgiven their secession the previous April. It is true that on the royal invitation Wellington reassumed the command of the army. But his return to the Horse Guards was in fact a victory for Canning's friends. In April he had refused not only to occupy a seat in the Cabinet, but even to hold a military command so long as Canning was Prime Minister. He now made amends for that refusal, though the political situation remained the same. It was Lord Goderich, Canning's political ally, whom the King designated to succeed him as Premier. Certainly, so far as his private convictions were concerned, the King was still a Tory. He energetically opposed any addition to the Whig element in the Ministry and forced the new Prime Minister to replace Canning at the Exchequer by Herries, a Tory who at the beginning of the year had been under-secretary to the Treasury, but who had since withdrawn, after considerable hesitation, from Canning's Cabinet on the plea of ill-health.[1] King George, whose head had been turned by four months of Canning's flattery, disliked only those Tories sufficiently important to keep him in his place and pursue their own policy in his name. The old fop, grown corpulent almost to deformity, whose bodily and mental health were decaying, indulged the dream of restoring the power of the Crown, by appointing weak Ministers, prepared to gratify all his whims.

Parliament would not reassemble in the regular course until the opening weeks of 1828, but in the meanwhile the condition of foreign affairs was a source of anxiety to the Cabinet. In the Levant the new system which Canning had inaugurated a year earlier was producing the fruits that might have been expected. Admiral Codrington, in command of the allied squadrons, surrounded the Turkish-Egyptian fleet in the Bay of Navarino, and, without fighting, succeeded in preventing it from moving freely along the Greek coast. He could not, however, prevent the fleet from serving as a base to the Egyptian army which devastated

[1] *Memoir of John Charles Herries*, vol. i, pp. 122 sqq. For his appointment as Chancellor of the Exchequer, ibid., pp. 155 sqq., 'Narrative of Events from August 6 to September 3, 1827', by Mr. Herries.

the Morea with fire and sword. To put a stop to these outrages the admiral decided to intimidate the enemy by a demonstration. The demonstration, undertaken on October 20, became a battle on a large scale, or, to speak more accurately, a disorderly bombardment. The allied fleet did not lose a single ship, and their total losses did not exceed 140 killed and 300 wounded. The Sultan's was practically annihilated. The battle has remained famous in the history of modern Europe, and at first sight the student might be tempted to regard it as the crowning victory of that policy of national liberation to which Canning had willingly seen his name attached. In reality it was a defeat of the policy which Canning had secretly pursued—the policy of the Balance of Power—for it provoked that Russian war which, ever since 1822, he had endeavoured to prevent by every means at his disposal.

What attitude did Canning's friends in the Cabinet adopt towards the Battle of Navarino? Apparently they continued to take an optimistic outlook, maintained their belief that peace would be preserved, but faced without alarm the possibility of war.[1] And among the Whigs, men such as Lord Holland, Lord John Russell and Brougham boasted that by joining battle at Navarino their country had hastened the emancipation of the Greeks. But both groups alike were isolated amid a public obviously disquieted and gloomy.[2] If the *Courier*, as the organ of the Government, was obliged to defend its policy, *The Times*, which represented independent opinion, spoke a less confident language and considered the Battle of Navarino 'an event to be looked at with mingled admiration and regret'.[3] And in the opinion of the organ of the Whigs, the *Morning Chronicle*, there was only one European Power whose Eastern policy was deserving of praise,

[1] Lord Palmerston to William Temple, November 27, 1827, December 4, 1827, January 18, 1828, March 25, 1828, May 8, 1828 (Sir H. L. Bulwer, *Life of Viscount Palmerston*, Books IV, V).

[2] Lord Grey to Creevey, December 15, 1827: '. . . Holland is the only person of whom I have heard that goes the whole length of defending the business of Navarino in all its parts, and that with a degree of violence that really surprises me.' Creevey to Miss Ord, December 14, 1827: 'Punch (Charles Greville) writes there is not an individual in the city who does not consider our attack upon the Turkish fleet as the greatest outrage ever committed by any Government or country, and above all by ours' (*Creevey Papers*, vol. ii, pp. 141, 142). Cf. Lord Palmerston to William Temple, May 8, 1828: '. . . The French Government say they must send money, and wish to send troops, and propose that six thousand English and an equal number of French should go. That was always my plan, and I proposed it to Goderich in November, when it was determined to evacuate Portugal; but nobody else approved it, and it is not more in favour now, and will not be done' (Sir H. L. Bulwer, op. cit., Book V, ed. 1870, vol i, p. 227).

[3] *The Times*, November 12, 1827.

and that Power was the Austria of Metternich.[1] Had it not been for the 'unfortunate' Battle of Navarino Austria would probably have restored peace between the Porte and the Allies.[2] 'Great apprehensions are entertained for the durability of the Alliance under the present very critical circumstances, on which some of those did not calculate who entered into the treaty more with a view to gain time with Russia than to come to a rupture with Turkey, which would have the effect of delivering over the latter Power to the former. The affair of Navarino has, however, committed our Government. But if we were to say that the result has been one of satisfaction, or that it has not given rise to very unpleasant forebodings, we should only be misleading our readers.'[3]

By December the danger of an immediate outbreak of war had been averted, and the Ministers considered it unnecessary to summon Parliament before the normal date, as they had for a moment contemplated, to discuss Eastern affairs. But even before Parliament met it was already plain how precarious the position of the Cabinet was. The Whigs were dissatisfied with the principles which had governed the reconstruction of the preceding August, and demanded that their party should possess a stronger representation in the ministry. They asked that a place in the Cabinet should be found, not indeed for Lord Grey, who even after Canning's death had maintained his attitude of uncompromising hostility to the policy of coalition, but for Lord Holland, whose claim since April had been constantly under discussion. Lord Wellesley, who was weary of his position as Viceroy of Ireland, also demanded a seat in the Cabinet. When the King met these demands with a decided refusal, Lord Goderich, at the beginning of December, offered his resignation for the first time, pleading his wife's ill-health. But if the Whigs could not force their way into the Cabinet, they might perhaps increase their influence indirectly. In the course of the last session Canning had announced his intention to move the appointment of a Finance Committee to review the Budget as a whole, draw up a statement of the expenditure and the revenue, and suggest whatever economies could in their opinion be effected. In November Tierney obtained from Lord Althorp a promise to

---

[1] *Morning Chronicle*, December 4, 6, 8, 14, 1827; January 5, 1828.
[2] Ibid., December 6, 1827. [3] Ibid., December 4, 1827.

accept the chairmanship of this committee. In this way Herries, the Tory whose presence at the Exchequer had been forced upon them by the King's determination and Lord Goderich's weakness, would himself be placed under the control of the most typical representative of the Whig aristocracy. When Herries was informed of this arrangement, after all the negotiations had been concluded between Tierney, Huskisson, Lord Althorp, and Lord Goderich, he revolted. Finally, Lord Goderich found himself faced with the choice between Huskisson and Herries. He wanted to keep Huskisson, but he knew that Herries was the King's favourite. He attempted to escape from the difficulty by throwing upon King George the onus of settling the dispute. He settled it by dismissing Lord Goderich.

II   WELLINGTON PRIME MINISTER

I

In September the King would not appoint an energetic Premier capable, if necessary, of overriding his wishes. In January he was disgusted with a weak Premier who threw upon the Crown the responsibility for his decisions. He sent for Wellington, thus forgiving him his 'treason' of 1827. Wellington, who gladly accepted the task of forming a Government, would appear to have entertained for a moment the thought of combining the duties of Commander-in-Chief with those of a Prime Minister.[1] But immediately a general outcry was raised against the attempted 'dictatorship',[2] and he resigned the command of the army. He got rid of the Whigs who, under cover of their alliance with Canning and his followers, had begun to invade the Government. He dared not, however, dismiss immediately all the members of the Canning group; he kept Huskisson at the Colonial Office, Lord Dudley at the Foreign Office, Grant at the Board of Trade, Palmerston at the War Office, and Lamb as Irish Secretary. Since Huskisson remained, he was compelled, in spite of his Toryism, to sacrifice Herries. He had recourse to the double device of replacing Herries at the Exchequer by Goulburn, another Tory, and finding Herries another place in the Cabinet, as successor to

[1] Lord Ellenborough's *Diary*, January 24 and 25, 1828.
[2] H. of C., January 29, 1828, Brougham's speech (*Parl. Deb.*, N.S., vol. xviii, pp. 55 sqq.).

the Whig Tierney at the Mint. Lord Ellenborough, who had distinguished himself by the violence of his attacks upon the Canningites, succeeded Lord Carlisle as Lord Privy Seal. Lord Lansdowne left the Home Office, to which Peel returned. In short, the Government had returned to the complexion of Lord Liverpool's Cabinet, a blend of orthodox and liberal Tories. Nevertheless, it might fairly be maintained that the orthodox Tories had strengthened their position, for in Lord Liverpool's Cabinet it was the Prime Minister himself who played the part of mediator between the two groups, and the head of the Liberal group all but occupied the position of Premier. Now it was the leader of the orthodox party who presided at Cabinet Councils, and the leader of the Liberals, Huskisson, did not possess, to balance the power of Wellington and his followers, a tithe of Canning's influence. It was Peel, Leader in the Commons, who attempted to mediate between Wellington as Prime Minister and Huskisson, as Lord Liverpool had mediated between Wellington and Canning.[1]

Abroad the Government was compelled to witness the bankruptcy of Canning's system. This was due in Portugal to a national reaction against it. The Regent Dom Miguel landed at Lisbon in February and was endeavouring to overthrow the Constitution. His task was enormously facilitated by the unpopularity of the British Army, which had been dispatched the previous year with the alleged purpose of protecting Portugal against a Spanish invasion, and had already begun to evacuate the country. In Turkey the system was destroyed by its own operation. In May Russia declared war against Turkey. Undoubtedly the war was the inevitable result of what the Royal Speech had designated the 'untoward' Battle of Navarino? If Canning had lived, he might possibly have prevented Miguel establishing himself at Lisbon, but it is very difficult to see how he could have prevented the outbreak of war in the Levant; and in any case, the most important Government departments, and among them the Foreign Office, were occupied in February and also in May by his disciples, and they were powerless to hinder either event.

---

[1] Lord Palmerston to William Temple, March 25, 1828: 'Our Government consists of some discordant elements, but still I think it will go on. Peel is so right-headed and liberal, and so up to the opinions and feelings of the times, that he smoothes difficulties which might otherwise be insurmountable' (Sir H. L. Bulwer, op. cit., Book V, ed. 1870, vol. i, p. 223).

At home the Cabinet began its life with a reverse. The Whig Opposition, Lord Althorp's group and the group of Lord John Russell compelled the Government to assent to the repeal of the Test and Corporation Acts, which made the legal position of the Nonconformists, theoretically at least, inferior to that of the Anglicans. To be sure, orthodox Tories and Canningites shared a common defeat. Nevertheless, it was the disagreement within the Government ranks which rendered the existence of the Cabinet precarious from day to day.

How should Wellington and Huskisson agree on the question of the Corn Bill, which had been provisionally shelved but must now be definitely settled? The latter wished to reintroduce without alteration the Corn Bill of 1827. The former wished to embody the amendment he had carried in the House of Lords, which had temporarily hung up the Bill. Feeling ran high between the contending parties. Grant, the President of the Board of Trade, threatened to resign. Finally an agreement was reached, and a Corn Bill was introduced and carried[1] identical in principle with the Bill which had failed in 1827, but with modifications of a Protectionist character. At 54s. the quarter the duty was that which had been prescribed by the former Bill. Above this figure, for every rise of 1s. in the price of corn, the duty would be lowered, not by 2s., as then provided, but only by 1s., until the price of 66s. had been reached; then the duty was remitted on a more rapid scale, and at 73s., instead of 70s., corn would for all practical purposes be admitted free of duty.

The Ministers had overcome the difficulty of the Corn Bill. They were not so successful in grappling with the difficulties of parliamentary reform. Two boroughs—Penryn in Cornwall and East Retford in Nottinghamshire—had been convicted of corruption. What punishment would Parliament inflict? It was the same problem which had already presented itself in 1819. The borough could be absorbed in the smallest territorial division to which it belonged, the local hundred, in which case all the free-holders would become voters, or the franchise might be transferred to some large urban district unjustly disfranchised by the present system. Huskisson and his supporters, forsaking the principle of rigid conservatism which Canning had consistently maintained in the matter of parliamentary reform, declared in

[1] 9 Geo. IV, cap. 60.

favour of the latter method. Finally a compromise was reached. The franchise of Penryn was to be transferred to Manchester; the borough of East Retford to be absorbed in the hundred. But when the House of Lords refused to establish a new constituency at Manchester, Huskisson and his friends considered themselves released from their engagement in regard to East Retford. They voted against the Government, and Huskisson resigned or offered to resign. Wellington immediately accepted his resignation. He attempted to withdraw it, and denied that it had been formally tendered. Wellington stood firm. All the Canningites left the Cabinet, dismissed rather than resigning of their free choice.

2

The Canningites were replaced by obscure Tories, and the discontented complained that there were too many soldiers in a Cabinet in which the Prime Minister was a field-marshal.[1] Lord Aberdeen, who replaced Lord Dudley at the Foreign Office, had been ambassador at Vienna, and the friendship he had then made with Metternich was probably, in conjunction with Peel's recommendation, his chief claim to Wellington's favour. The latter might well believe that he had now accomplished his mission and delivered English politics from the anarchy in which they had been involved since Lord Liverpool's death. The 'Protestant' party imagined that at last it possessed the ideal Cabinet. At the dinner held annually to celebrate the anniversary of Pitt's birth the hopes entertained by the ultra-Tories were evident in the exultant tone of their speeches.[2] Their hopes? No, their illusions; for Wellington was destined to effect as Prime Minister, scarcely two years after Canning's death, a reform for which Canning had possessed neither the courage nor the power: he was to emancipate the Catholics.

[1] Sir George Murray at the Colonial Office; Sir Henry Hardinge at the War Office. See Thomas Grenville to the Duke of Buckingham, September 9, 1828: 'My original objections to the formation of a Government concocted out of the Army List and the ultra-Tories are quite insuperable on constitutional principles alone; neither is there any instance since the Revolution of any Government so adverse in its formation to all the free principles and practice of our constitution' (Duke of Buckingham, op. cit., vol. ii, p. 380). Cf. Lord Palmerston, December 1828: 'Somebody' (in the House of Commons) 'said that, considering the military character of the present Government, Courtenay should have likened their minds to cartridge paper at least' (Sir H. L. Bulwer, op. cit., Book VI, ed. 1870, vol. i, p. 286).
[2] The Times, May 30, 1828.

To understand the state of this grave question we must go back to the moment when the newly elected Parliament had declared by a slight majority against emancipation, and Canning had pledged his word to the King that he would not compel him to take any distasteful action in the matter. The progress of the 'Catholic' party had thus, it appeared, received a slight and temporary check. It was, however, mere appearance, and everybody was well aware of it. No doubt the vast majority of the English people was still hostile to emancipation; but that majority was plainly diminishing. All the young men were in favour of emancipation, and the *Morning Chronicle* might well remark that the opposition to the Catholic claims would one day be defeated 'not by the march of improvement, but by the march of death'.[1] The 'Catholics' moreover could claim that irrespective of age the flower alike of the thinkers and the practical politicians was on their side. Whatever the composition of the Government, and even at a time like the present, when ministerial changes were frequent, it was impossible to form a Cabinet from which the partisans of emancipation were excluded, or even in which they were not a majority. In the House of Commons Peel was the only 'Protestant' on the Government bench.

The Liberals, secure of final success, but perceiving that the anti-Catholics were too strong to be overthrown by a frontal attack, attempted to turn their position. The Catholics were not the only Englishmen legally disqualified for public offices. If Catholics were subject to the 'penal laws', the Dissenters were subject to the Test and Corporation Acts. It is true that the latter statutes had become a dead letter. As we have already seen, Parliament accorded an annual amnesty to Dissenters who had infringed the Acts.[2] Nevertheless, this method of yearly amnesty wore a humiliating aspect. Were the Dissenters in any respect worse citizens than the members of the Establishment? Had they not earned the praises of the Tories at the last election by their anti-Catholic vote? If, therefore, after twenty years of acquiescence in their present position, they were now to demand the repeal of the Test and Corporation Acts it would be difficult for the Tories to refuse. On the other hand, when the Test and Corporation Acts had once been repealed, it would be harder to

[1] Quoted by the *Examiner*, June 15, 1828.
[2] See vol. i, p. 403.

oppose Catholic emancipation, for it was a favourite argument
with the anti-Catholics that, so long as the Test and Corporation
Acts remained on the Statute Book, the emancipated Catholics,
unless they were made subject to them, would be placed in a
better position than the Protestant Dissenters.[1] At the beginning
of 1827 the Unitarians, the most liberal of the sects (two years
earlier, to give the Congregationalists and Baptists a lesson in
toleration, they had passed a formal resolution in favour of
Catholic emancipation),[2] concerted measures with Lord Holland
and Lord John Russell to bring forward in Parliament the repeal
of the Test and Corporation Acts.

On March 9, 1827, the old Committee of the Three Denominations decided, at the request of the Unitarians, to hold a meeting
on March 17 in concert with the Board of Congregationalist
Ministers, the Protestant Society for the protection of religious
liberty, and the Unitarian Association to determine upon a common line of action. At this meeting arrangements were made to
hold a further consultation with certain of their parliamentary
patrons. The consultation took place on April 6, and Lord John
was commissioned to move in the Commons the repeal of the
Test and Corporation Acts.[3] Suddenly an unforeseen obstacle
arose. Canning became Prime Minster, and expressed himself
unconditionally opposed to repeal.[4] The reason he gave for his
attitude was that he considered the proposal likely to prejudice
the cause of Catholic emancipation; but was this not perhaps a
mere pretext, and his real motive the perception that repeal
would pave the way for Catholic emancipation, and his fear of
being brought face to face with that formidable question? Some
Unitarians, among them the Rev. Robert Aspland[5] and a few
Liberal leaders, for example, Lord John,[6] apparently desired to
go forward in spite of Canning's opposition; but the moderates,

---

[1] H. of C., February 26, 1828, Robert Peel's speech (*Parl. Deb.*, N.S., vol. xviii,
pp. 753–4). Cf. Sydney Smith, 'A Letter to the Electors upon the Catholic Question'
(*Works*, 1859, vol. ii, pp. 225–6); *The Catholic Question in 1828*, by an Elector of the
University of Oxford, 1828, pp. 20–1; *Reasons for Not Taking the Test*, by John, Earl of
Shrewsbury, 1828, pp. xcvii sqq.

[2] In May 1825, B. Ward, *Eve of Catholic Emancipation*, vol. iii, p. 168.

[3] *The Test Act Reporter, or Report of Proceedings in the late Application to Parliament for
the Repeal of the Corporation and Test Acts*, 1829, pp. 2 sqq.

[4] H. of C., May 3, 1827 (*Parl. Deb.*, N.S., vol. xvii, p. 591).

[5] The Rev. Robert Aspland to Rev. R. Brook Aspland, May 17, 1827 (R. Brook
Aspland, *Memoirs of the Rev. Robert Aspland*, p. 969).

[6] H. of C., May 11, June 7, 1827 (*Parl. Deb.*, N.S., vol. xvii, pp. 744, 1146).

who wished to place no obstacles in the way of his policy, carried the day, and on June 7 Lord John withdrew his motion.

But, in the meantime, the Dissenters had organized their propaganda, and circulated all over the country at great expense a *Statement of the Case of the Protestant Dissenters*, in which their grievances were clearly explained; and they agreed to Lord John's withdrawal of the motion only on the express understanding that the matter should be brought before Parliament the following year, and again at every succeeding session until their claims were satisfied. When Parliament met in January 1828, Canning's death had smoothed their path. The special committee for propaganda, which had been formed in the spring of 1827, issued periodical reports, collected petitions, put forth an address to the public, and persuaded the Court of Common Council of the City of London to pass for the second time, and on this occasion with only two dissentient votes, a resolution demanding the repeal of the Test and Corporation Acts.[1] When, on February 26, Lord John introduced a motion calling upon the House to go into committee to examine the question he obtained a majority of forty-four, in spite of the opposition of Peel, and of Huskisson and Lord Palmerston, who were still in office. When the debate was reopened on the 28th, Peel moved an adjournment; but he immediately perceived that his motion would fail, and withdrew from the House, leaving the debate to be continued in his absence.[2]

That very evening the Ministers held a council to decide what course of action to adopt, and they determined to yield. Public opinion either supported the Dissenter's claim or was obviously indifferent. The Bishop of Oxford assured Peel that the Church and University were 'by a very large majority' in favour of repealing the Test which far too often, in the opinion of many High Churchmen, involved a profanation of the Sacrament.[3] At Oxford the heads of colleges and fellows expressly refused to countenance a demonstration against repeal.[4] There was nothing left for the Ministers to do but to cover their retreat by inserting

[1] *Test Act Reporter*, pp. 45, 64.
[2] H. of C., February 28 (*Parl. Deb.*, N.S., vol. xviii, pp. 827 sqq.).
[3] The Bishop of Oxford to Robert Peel, March 23 and 26, 1828 (Peel, *Memoirs*, vol. i, p. 92).
[4] Wellington to the Duke of Montrose, April 30, 1818 (*Despatches, Cont.*, vol. iv, p. 411).

in Lord John's measure a clause to protect the Established Church against eventual attacks by the Nonconformists. Every Dissenter who was elected into a Corporation would be obliged to 'solemnly declare' that he would not make use of his civic authority 'to injure or weaken the Protestant Church as it is by law established in *England*, or to disturb the said Church . . . in the possession of any Rights or Privileges to which it is, or may be, by law entitled'; and the Bishop of Llandaff, to exclude deists, atheists, and Jews, obtained the addition of the words 'on the true faith of a Christian'.[1]

The Catholics had followed this campaign with keen interest, had petitioned for the repeal of the Test and Corporation Acts, and had made proposals to the Protestant Dissenters for the joint organization of meetings. It was the Protestants who refused the alliance; and Lord John himself advised the Catholics not to alarm their opponents by making themselves too prominent.[2] But the victory once secure, 'his delight knew no bounds'. 'It is really a gratifying thing,' he wrote to Thomas Moore, on March 31, 'to force the enemy to give up his first line, that none but Churchmen are worthy to serve the State, and I trust we shall soon make him give up the second, that none but Protestants are. Peel is a very pretty hand at hauling down his colours.'[3]

3

On May 8 Sir Francis Burdett brought forward the identical motion in favour of the Catholic claims which, in 1827, had been rejected by a majority of four, and this time it was carried by a majority of six.[4] When it was taken to the Lords it was thrown out by a majority of fifty-four, 181 against 127. But Wellington's language was moderate: he disclaimed hostility to the principle of emancipation, and was content to urge that it could not be conceded unless guarantees had been previously secured to safeguard the National Church and to plead that the question should

---

[1] H. of L., April 21, 1828 (*Parl. Deb.*, N.S., vol. xviii, pp. 1591 sqq.).

[2] *Test Act Reporter*, p. 442.

[3] *Early Correspondence of Lord John Russell*, vol. i, p. 272.

[4] H. of C., May 8, 1828 (*Parl. Deb.*, N.S., vol. xix, pp. 375 sqq.). Moreover, Wellington estimated that the real majority amounted to twenty or thirty votes, 'many of its warmest friends having been . . . under the necessity of staying away in consequence of the exercise over them of some local or personal influence' (Memorandum of August 1, 1828, *Despatches, Cont.*, vol. iv, p. 569).

be postponed until conditions were more peaceful (would that day ever come!), and a settlement could be effected to the satisfaction of all parties.[1] The great Irish Catholic agitator, O'Connell, had become convinced for the last two months that Wellington could be relied upon to effect Catholic emancipation after the emancipation of the Protestant Dissenters.[2] Though the speech of June 9 did not prove his forecast mistaken, it showed that Wellington still wished to temporize. By tactics of a revolutionary character O'Connell vanquished the final resistance of the Protestant party and the Premier.

If in England the General Election of 1826 had momentarily revived the hopes of the Protestant party, in Ireland it had left them more disheartened than before. The great landowners had witnessed the ready response of the small landlords to the appeal of O'Connell's Catholic Association. To evade the statute of 1825 the Association had been reorganized, and the reorganization had been effected so skilfully that prosecution was impossible. It constituted a theocracy which exercised a far-reaching sway, and in every parish in Ireland continued to elect its delegates, levy its taxes, and act as if the regular government were non-existent. Against an organization so powerful, the attempts made about this time by the evangelicals to protestantize the Irish country districts by a missionary campaign were necessarily fruitless.[3] Equally ineffective was the opposition of an England divided against itself in which the Protestant' party was too weak to

[1] H. of L., June 19, 1828 (Parl. Deb., N.S., vol. xix, pp. 1286 sqq.). Cf. Greville, June 18 (?), 1828: 'The Duke of Wellington's speech on the Catholic question is considered by many to have been so moderate as to indicate a disposition on his part to concede emancipation, and bets have been laid that Catholics will sit in Parliament next year.'

[2] Princess Lieven to General Alexander Benckendorff, June 18–30, 1828: 'Wellington, although thoroughly mediocre, is not without guile. He fools the Ultras; he fools the Liberals still more, on the Catholic question—the latter are as completely satisfied that he will bring about their emancipation as the others are convinced of his unalterable intolerance' (Letters of Dorothea, Princess Lieven, during her Residence in London, p. 137).

[3] The mission received the name of the New Reformation. Even a thoroughgoing sceptic like Lord Palmerston seems to have taken it seriously (Letter to William Temple, October 21, 1826, Book III, ed. 1870, vol. i, p. 177). Cf. a letter written in 1863 by Darby, founder of the Plymouth Brethren: 'I may mention that just at that time' (about 1825) 'the Roman Catholics were becoming Protestants at the rate of six hundred or eight hundred a week. The Archbishop (Magee) imposed, within the limits of his jurisdiction, the oaths of allegiance and supremacy; and the work everywhere instantly ceased' (W. B. Neatby, A History of the Plymouth Brethren, p. 16). For a very different view of the movement see the caustic criticisms of George Ensor, Letters Showing the Inutility and Exhibiting the Absurdity of what is rather fantastically termed 'the New Reformation', 1828. Peel reluctantly admitted the futility of the propaganda (H. of C., March 6, 1827, Parl. Deb., N.S., vol. xvi, p. 967).

secure a rigorous and consistent repression of the Irish disorders, and the 'Catholic' party too weak to satisfy O'Connell's demands. It is true that O'Connell's authority, as head of the Association, was not altogether unopposed. It was rumoured that the elder priests and the Catholic bishops disapproved of his methods as too extreme, and that, on the other hand, his leading subordinates in the associations, Sheil among their number, often thought him too timid;[1] but his influence over the mass of the people remained enormous, and he continued to apply his equivocal method, careful to avoid any revolutionary action, while employing a revolutionary organization as a means to extort concessions from the British Government by threats.[2]

When, in May, Wellington reconstituted his Cabinet he placed at the Board of Trade one of the two members for the Irish County of Clare, Vesey Fitzgerald. His appointment compelled him to seek re-election, and, as he was a partisan of emancipation, his return seemed certain; but, as he had consented to enter a Cabinet which as a body refused to pledge itself to emancipation, the Association declared war upon him, and determined to set up a rival candidate, no longer, as in County Waterford in 1826, a Protestant who supported emancipation, but an actual Catholic. To render the demonstration more imposing, and its success more certain, O'Connell himself was the candidate chosen. The people marched in regular squadrons to the polls, their priests at their head. On the fifth day of the election Fitzgerald abandoned the contest. What was the sheriff to do? As a Catholic O'Connell was ineligible. A declaration that he had not been returned would have caused a rebellion throughout the entire county, perhaps throughout the whole of Southern Ireland. The sheriff evaded the difficulty by issuing a simple statement that O'Connell had received the majority of votes.

The effect of this manœuvre was to render the Government, not of Ireland only, but of the entire United Kingdom, impossible. Henceforward Wellington could not appoint to an office in the Cabinet or raise to the peerage any representative of an Irish constituency without risking its repetition. Neither could he dissolve Parliament whenever he might desire to do so; for even

[1] Lord F. Gower to Peel, December 2, 1828 (Peel, *Memoirs*, vol. i, p. 253).
[2] Lord Anglesey to Lord F. L. Gower, July 2, 1828 (ibid., p. 147); Goulburn to Peel, July 25, 1826 (C. S. Parker, op. cit., vol. i, p. 417).

if the subsequent election increased the Protestant majority in England, in Ireland, on the other hand, all the counties with the exception of two or three, all the large towns, and all the boroughs with a popular franchise would return Catholics. After June a settlement of the Catholic question could no longer be avoided.

In July and the following months the Irish situation grew worse. On July 1 the Act of 1825, which proscribed the Catholic Association, expired, and the Association, abandoning the legal subterfuges of the past three years, returned to its original form and its original programme, or rather it adopted a programme even more ambitious. The Orangemen, now also freed from legal restraint, formed 'Brunswick Clubs' in imitation of the Catholic organizations. The North-East of Ireland was covered by them. The Catholics then decided to carry the war into the North where the Protestants were in the majority, and one of their agents visited Ulster on a campaign of propaganda. Ireland, therefore, seemed in September to be on the brink of a civil and religious war. O'Connell, however, did not want a civil war. He forbade his supporters to hold illegal meetings, posed as an upholder of order, and offered the Lord-Lieutenant the protection of the Catholic Association against the seditious plots of the Brunswick Clubs. He knew that the attitude of the Protestant gentry could not be judged by the language of the clubs. They understood that they could hold out no longer. A brother-in-law of Peel, George Dawson, who represented an Irish constituency, and often embarrassed the Government by the violence of his anti-Catholic speeches, in August 1828 dismayed Peel by a speech in which he frankly pleaded for a policy of concession.[1]

A policy of concession the Marquis of Anglesey, who in January had succeeded Lord Wellesley as Lord-Lieutenant, had, in fact, never ceased to demand. He undertook to maintain order until the end of the current year; but he warned the Government that, if Parliament failed to deal with the Catholic question when the next session opened in January, the result would be a rebellion which not even O'Connell could prevent.[2] However, neither Wellington nor Peel informed Lord Anglesey of his intentions; they were content to insist that he should repress all disorders

---

[1] *Ann. Reg.*, 1828, p. 131 (Wellington, *Despatches, Cont.*, vol. iv, pp. 5, 604 sqq.).
[2] Lord Anglesey to Peel, July 26 and the end of August 1828 (C. S. Parker, op. cit., vol. ii, pp. 61–2).

with a stern hand, and appeared to interpret O'Connell's moderation as a sign that he was afraid and wished to retreat.[1] The
Marquis was obliged on October 1 to issue a proclamation forbidding all public meetings which he followed up by the arrest
of a conspirator; but he took these steps with visible reluctance,
and on December 31 was recalled, and replaced by the Duke of
Northumberland, whose anti-Catholic views were notorious.
Thus for the first time since the accession of George IV the
government of Ireland was not in the hands of a 'Catholic'.
Moreover, Wellington had just compelled the Duke of Clarence,
the King's brother and a supporter of emancipation, to resign his
position as Lord High Admiral, since his conduct in that capacity
had become insufferable to his subordinates. Never for many a
long year had the English Government seemed more Protestant.

4

It was therefore with a shock of dismay that the public read the
Speech from the Throne in which, on February 5, the King
invited Parliament to 'review' with a view to their reform 'the
laws which impose civil disabilities on His Majesty's Roman
Catholic subjects'. How was the sudden *volte-face* to be explained?
Was it after all so sudden as it appeared? In reality the Cabinet
had been convinced for the last six months that Catholic emancipation must be granted, and only the opposition of the King had
prevented it from taking action.

Wellington's opposition to emancipation had never been
violent, and even before O'Connell's election he had been of the
opinion that the settlement of the question could not be long
delayed. The election had removed his final hesitations, and on
August 1 he presented a memorandum to King George in which
he asked permission to examine the question in concert with Peel
and the Lord Chancellor, and submit their conclusions to him.
He reported on August 7. Then the difficulties and delays began.
The old fool, sometimes tormented by the gout, at others stupe-
fied by laudanum,[2] would not come to any decision; instead, he
demanded the recall of Lord Anglesey.[3] Wellington, as we have

---

[1] Peel to Wellington, November 28, 1828 (Wellington, *Despatches, Cont.*, vol. v,
p. 294).
[2] Wellington, ibid., vol. v, pp. 292, 419, 2786.
[3] Wellington to the King, October 14, 1828 (Wellington, ibid., vol. v, pp. 131-2).

seen, yielded the point, but Lord Anglesey's successor, the Duke of Northumberland, though believed by the public to be an anti-Catholic, had in reality been converted to the policy of emancipation.[1] On November 16, in the hope of bringing a more powerful influence to bear on the King, Wellington asked permission to consult the Archbishop of Canterbury and five other bishops. Unfortunately the majority of these prelates, though they had voted the year before for the repeal of the Test and Corporation Acts, were opposed to further concessions.[2] Then Wellington, seeking in despair support from the last possible quarter, turned to Peel.

For months past Peel had been convinced that the hour of emancipation was at hand. He had said as much to Wellington and the King;[3] but he felt that, if the Cabinet should decide to emancipate the Catholics, he could not, after his repeated declarations, remain Leader of the Commons and introduce himself the Bill he had hitherto fought so unremittingly. He therefore proposed to Wellington that he should resign; he would undertake to be content with a silent vote against the Bill, and would not embarrass the Government by his presence in the Cabinet; but in December Wellington perceived that he could never overcome the King's reluctance, unless Peel remained in the Cabinet, and gave him his entire support.[4] After some hesitation Peel gave way, continued in office, and joined his entreaties to Wellington's. On the very eve of the day when the Speech from the Throne must be drawn up the King yielded for the first time. At the beginning of March, at the very moment when Peel introduced the Emancipation Bill in the Commons, he retracted his assent, and for several hours the Cabinet was out of office. Then he again capitulated. While Canning was alive, he could fall back upon Wellington and Peel. Against Wellington and Peel he had no recourse. At a pinch he might have found in the House of Lords the material from which to piece together a patchwork Cabinet—

[1] The Duke of Northumberland to Wellington, January 18, 1829 (Wellington, *Despatches, Cont.*, vol. v, p. 453).
[2] 'Only the Bishop of Winchester and the Bishop of Chester pronounced in favour of emancipation. The Bishop of Chester was particularly outspoken in this sense' (Wellington, ibid., vol. v, pp. 324–6).
[3] Palmerston, *Journal*, June 12, 1828 (Sir H. L. Bulwer, op. cit., Book VI, ed. 1870, vol. i, pp. 284–5); Peel, *Memoirs*, vol. i, pp. 127–8, 187; Wellington, *Despatches, Cont.*, vol. v, pp. 435 sqq.
[4] Wellington to Peel, January 17, 1828 (Wellington, *Despatches, Cont.*, vol. v, p. 452).

Lord Eldon, Lord Sidmouth, Lord Bexley; but whom could he place on the Government bench in the Commons? Sir Richard Wetherell, and Sir Thomas Lethbridge? The Protestant party had no leaders.

Three Bills were introduced in succession. The first suppressed the Catholic Association. It was a mere formality, intended to give satisfaction to the upholders of order and offended nobody, since once the Act of Emancipation had been passed, the Association would no longer have any reason for existence. The second repealed all the penal laws which subjected Catholics to civil disabilities. The third, copied from the Bill of 1825, raised the freehold qualification for the franchise in the Irish counties from forty shillings to ten pounds sterling. The new franchise would protect Westminster against invasion by the Irish demagogues. It was calculated that under the existing system the number of Catholic representatives would have been sixty.[1] By raising the property qualification not only would the number of Catholic members be diminished, but those who were elected would not belong to the lower classes. They would be Catholic gentlemen, and the social status of Parliament would not be lowered by the change. The first and the third Bills[2] were passed without serious debate. The Liberals were prepared to accept them as the price of the second Bill which alone mattered, and which effected the reform they had desired so long, the unconditional emancipation of the Catholics of Great Britain and Ireland.

5

The Protestant party made one last desperate effort to save the privileges of the Church of England. They had opened their campaign in the previous October with a mass meeting held on Penenden Heath, in Kent, at which it was claimed that over forty thousand were present.[3] The 'party' counted on the support not only of the 'Protestants', who were members of the Church of England, but of a large number of Dissenters; for although the

[1] Wellington to the Duke of Westmoreland, October 16, 1828 (Wellington, *Despatches, Cont.*, vol. iv, p. 142).

[2] 10 Geo. IV, cap. 1; 10 Geo. IV, cap. 8.

[3] *The Times*, October 25, 1828: 'The two parties faced each other at the meeting under the respective appellations of the High Court party and the Liberal party, and Sheil, Cobbett, and Hunt had the courage to defend the Liberal position.' Cf. Charles Butler, *A Memoir of the Catholic Relief, passed in 1829*, p. 38.

alliance concluded the previous winter between the Liberals and the Dissenters to obtain the repeal of the Test and Corporation Acts had weakened Nonconformist opposition to the Catholic claims, and the Committee of the Three Denominations had passed in January a motion in favour of emancipation,[1] the Methodists, who had even refused to participate in the agitation of 1827, remained obdurate, and their point of view was shared by all those among the older sects who had been imbued with the spirit of the evangelical revival.[2] There was many a prejudice—powerful instincts deep-rooted in the national past—hatred of Ireland, hatred of France, hatred of Roman interference—upon which the opponents of emancipation could play at will. As soon as the intentions of the Government were known, anti-Catholic petitions flooded the table of the Commons. They amounted to over nine hundred. The orthodox Tories could therefore indulge the belief that their revolt against the Prime Minister was supported, if not by the majority of a servile Parliament, at least by the majority of the nation. They fought against Wellington with the violence of despair. Peel, who had felt himself bound in honour to resign his seat for the University of Oxford, whose anti-Catholic convictions he had represented in Parliament for ten years, was not re-elected, and it was only through the kindness of a friend that he was enabled to find a seat at the last moment as member for the Borough of Westbury. At Court the Duke of Cumberland had returned from Germany to occupy the place left vacant since the Duke of York's death two years before. He was a loathsome brute, about whom the vilest rumours were current, with or without foundation. Twenty years before report had charged him with murder; now the Press publicly accused him of incest.[3] An amalgam of the English Tory and the Continental reactionary, he impressed upon his brother that, if he made the least concession to Liberalism, he would share the fate of

[1] Dr. William's Library, and the debate on the Roman Catholic claims; a letter addressed to the Trinitarian Members of the General Body of Dissenting Ministers of the Three Denominations on the above subject by Joseph Ivimey, 1829.

[2] *The Roman Catholic Claims:* an address to the Protestant Dissenters of Great Britain, assigning reasons why (in reference to that subject) they should maintain the most strict neutrality by Joseph Ivimey, 1828. *England's Liberties Defended*. By William Thorp, Dissenting Minister of Bristol, 1829.

[3] *Examiner*, June 14, 1829. Also at the beginning of 1830 for the second time of murder, though without the least warrant. See the letter from Princess Lieven to General Beckendorff, February 10–22, 1830 (*Letters of Dorothea, Princess Lieven, during her Residence in London*, pp. 212–3).

Louis XVI. Such was the violence of the ultra-Tory Press that Wellington lost his self-control. When a letter from Lord Winchilsea to himself, in which his policy was severely censured, appeared in the papers, he took the matter as a personal insult, sent Lord Winchilsea a challenge, and the quarrel was settled by a duel.

Such was the heated atmosphere in which the debates began and pursued their weary course. Is it worth while even to summarize the arguments of both sides, the old stock arguments worn threadbare by constant repetition, and merely adapted to the circumstances of the moment? The Catholic danger, urged the diehards, is more serious now than it has ever been; for Spain has restored the Inquisition, and the Jesuits have returned to France and dictate the policy of the Bourbons. Your fears, replied the advocates of emancipation, are ridiculous at a time when even Charles X has been compelled to accept M. de Martignac's Liberal Cabinet, and your objections sound very strange on the lips of ultra-Tories who sympathize so warmly with the policy of those who have restored the Inquisition in Spain and recalled the Jesuits to France. To believe, the diehards argued, that Catholic emancipation will solve the Irish question, is to nurse a delusion. The Catholics will scarcely have received their liberty before they demand the confiscation of the property of the Church and refuse to pay tithes. Even if this forecast is correct, replied the supporters of the Bill, the penal legislation must be swept away nevertheless. If the Irish should then persist in rebellion, England, conscious that she, at any rate, has done her duty, will unanimously approve a policy of stern repression, and the Government in consequence will be in a stronger position to adopt it. Emancipation is no longer a matter of choice, it has become a necessity. Out of the thirty thousand soldiers which compose the forces stationed in the United Kingdom, the Government is obliged to employ twenty-five thousand to police Ireland.[1] What will happen on the day, near or distant, when England is once more at war with a foreign power?

The great difficulty attached to the problem of emancipation was to discover the securities which would defend the State against the interference of an international Church. For the

[1] Memorial presented by Peel to the King in January 1829 (Wellington, *Despatches, Cont.*, vol. v, p. 439).

274

objection of the Protestants to Catholic emancipation was not so much theological as political, or, rather perhaps, national. They were afraid of the Catholic Church because they regarded her as a State within the State, whose members owed allegiance to a foreign monarch; and the danger presented by the admission of Catholics into Parliament appeared all the more serious because the Church of England was so strictly bound to the State and unconditionally subject to the authority of Parliament. Should Catholic members, as Wilmot Horton, one of the Canning group, proposed, be excluded from the House every time a question was debated which directly or indirectly concerned the Church?[1] The suggestion was too complicated to be considered by a practical statesman. More promising was the solution adopted by the House of Commons in 1825, to pay the Catholic clergy and thus place them under the control of the State, while withdrawing them from the control of the Pope and the demagogues. Wellington was in favour of it; and as there had never been any question of paying Catholic priests in England itself, he had in view a system of licences to be granted by the State without which no Catholic priest, paid or unpaid, would have the right to exercise his sacerdotal functions:[2] But this plan also had its difficulties. It had obviously failed to obtain the unanimous support either of the Protestants or the Catholics.

In England itself the Catholics, who since 1823 had been organized in an Association distinct from the Irish, had shewn themselves willing to accept emancipation accompanied by securities. In November the secretary of the Association, Edward Blunt, the highly respected representative of an old Catholic family, had made a pronouncement to that effect;[3] but among the Catholics of the United Kingdom those of Great Britain caused the Protestant party the least anxiety. The declaration, signed in 1826 by the English hierarchy, abounded in protestations of respect for liberty of conscience, and the integrity of the British constitution, both political and religious.[4] The Irish Catholics, on

[1] H. of C., March 18, 1829 (*Parl. Deb.*, N.S., vol. xx, pp. 1190 sqq.), 'Protestant, safety compatible with the remission of the civil disabilities of Roman Catholics; being a Vindication of the Security suggested by the Right Honourable R. Wilmot Horton, 1829.'

[2] Memorandum of August 9, 1828 (Wellington, *Despatches, Cont.*, vol. v, pp. 254 sqq.).

[3] B. Ward, *Eve of Catholic Emancipation*, vol. iii, pp. 243 sqq. On May 12 O'Connell was blackballed at the Cisalpine Club in London (ibid., p. 267).

[4] Declaration of the Catholic Bishops, the Vicars Apostolic, and their Coadjutors in

the contrary, under the leadership of O'Connell, at once ultra-montane and politically discontented, categorically opposed any species of State control over the Catholic clergy. On this point they were at open war with their English co-religionists, but numerically they alone counted.

Among the Protestants the plan of Government licences for the Catholic clergy attracted considerable support. It had apparently been suggested to Wellington by Phillpotts, an ecclesiastic of the High Church party, who was soon to make himself notorious by his vehement intransigeance.[1] But unless the State granted a salary which it could pay or withhold, what sanctions could it employ against the unlicensed priest who persisted in acting as such? And if the Government returned to the plan of making the Catholic Church in Ireland a Church of State officials, would not negotiations with Rome, an agreement with the Pope about the appointment of Bishops, in short a concordat, be unavoidable? But here the Protestant conscience and national feeling rose in revolt. It was not to be tolerated that the court of Saint James, by entering into regular relations with the Holy See, should accord legal recognition to the latter.

It was clear that to raise the question would open a prospect of interminable debates; but at a crisis when the question of emancipation clamoured for immediate settlement the first essential was haste. Peel persuaded Wellington that the securities must be abandoned,[2] and the matter was then dispatched without further delay. On February 5 the Speech from the Throne had announced the intentions of the Government. On March 30 the Emancipation Bill passed its third reading in the Commons by a majority of 320 to 142. On April 10 it passed the Lords by a majority of 111 to 109. On April 13 it received the Royal Assent and became law.[3] Wellington received the credit for the truly military speed with which the reform had been carried through, but in fact he had followed the advice of his civilian colleague.

Great Britain, 1826. All these bishops were bishops *in partibus* and all the signatures English. For the circumstances under which the Declaration originated see C. Butler, *A Memoir of the Catholic Relief Bill*, 1829; B. Ward, op. cit., vol. iii, p. 168.

[1] Thoughts on Communications with Rome, and on Concession of Equal Civil Rights to Roman Catholics (Wellington, *Despatches, Cont.*, vol. iv, pp. 324 sqq.). Sketch of Securities proposed to accompany concession to the Roman Catholics, September 12, 1828 (Wellington, *Despatches, Cont.*, vol. v, pp. 48–50).

[2] Peel, *Memoirs*, vol. i, p. 306.

[3] 10 Geo. IV, cap. 7.

The Bill introduced by Peel, and passed without amendment, was content to prohibit Catholic bishops from taking titles already held by Anglican prelates, to make it illegal to found any new religious house in England, to exclude the Jesuits by name from the United Kingdom, and to provide that whenever any control over the administration of the Anglican Church attached to an office held by a Catholic, it should be dissociated from the office in question. With the reservation of these trifling securities the Bill bestowed upon the Catholics of the three Kingdoms in return for an oath denying the Pope any power to interfere in the domestic affairs of the realm, recognizing the Protestant succession, and repudiating every intention to upset the Established Church, the right of suffrage, and the right to sit in Parliament, and threw open to them every post in the Administration, except those of Lord Chancellor of England and Lord-Lieutenant of Ireland. Moreover, Catholics were still excluded from the Universities and certain establishments for secondary education which by law were exclusively Anglican.

III DIVERSE QUESTIONS

I

What was the practical effect of the reform just accomplished? Irish Catholics, who already possessed the vote, were henceforward capable of election to Parliament, British Catholics received both the suffrage and the right to be elected. Further, Catholics, who already could be appointed to any position in the Army and Navy, might in future occupy any administrative or judicial post. The surprising, but also the significant, aspect of the reform is the strength of the anti-Catholic opposition, the violence of the Protestant feeling it provoked. It was this feeling which had enabled the Court to resist for so many years a reform desired by the majority in Parliament. Now, just because the delay had been so protracted, a Tory Government found itself compelled to rush Catholic emancipation through under the threat of revolution in Ireland; and the chaotic condition of parties, already so strikingly in evidence since Lord Liverpool's death, was further aggravated by the circumstances under which Catholic emancipation had been effected.

The Opposition was divided into four groups. There were the members of the old Opposition who had never joined the coalition with Canning. There were the dissident members of this Opposition who had formed part of Canning's Government, and were slow to be reconciled with Lord Grey and Lord Althorp. There were Huskisson and his friends who were disliked by both Whig groups, by the former because they had been Canningites, by the latter because they had remained in office, when, on the resignation of Lord Goderich, their Whig colleagues had been dismissed;[1] and, lastly, there were the ultra-Tories, the most violent of the four groups. They had broken with Wellington when he decided to grant emancipation, but had practically nothing in common with Huskisson, Brougham, or Lord Althorp. The anarchy might have been expected to weaken Wellington's position considerably. This, however, does not appear to have been the case. Many Whigs and Liberals were disposed to accord their confidence to the Prime Minister so long as he continued to resist the ultra-Tories and carry out a policy at once prudent and energetic. 'Here am I,' Bentham wrote to Wellington in a letter of remonstrance which he addressed to the Premier on the occasion of his duel with Lord Winchilsea, 'leader of the Radicals, more solicitous for the life of the leader of the Absolutists than he himself is !'[2] 'A greater than Cæsar is here,' wrote the *Edinburgh Review*, 'one who has not destroyed in peace the country he had saved by his sword'.[3] Catholic emancipation was followed by long months of disquiet and tension, but not by revolution. We must now attempt to obtain a bird's-eye view of the position.

2

Catholic emancipation is commonly believed to have been the signal for an energetic movement hostile to the Established Church. The opponents of emancipation had foretold that when Parliament had once ceased to be exclusively Anglican disestablishment was inevitable. Now that emancipation had actually been effected the Church was undoubtedly weakened and lost credit

[1] See the list of the members of this group drawn up in June 1828 by Lord Palmerston: eleven peers and twenty-seven members of the Lower House (Sir H. L. Bulwer, *Life of Viscount Palmerston*, Book V, ed. 1870, vol. i, p. 378).

[2] Bentham to Wellington, March 22, 1829 (Wellington, *Despatches, Cont.*, vol. v, pp. 546–7).

[3] *Edinburgh Review*, March 1829, 'The Last of the Catholic Question' (vol. xlix, p. 221).

from the mere effect of these gloomy forebodings. It was re-marked that some of her most distinguished adherents forsook the Establishment and joined either the Catholic Church or one or other of the Protestant sects.[1] The powerful Methodist body, a second national church by the side of the first, and the centre of British evangelicalism, was forced to register, if not, as in 1820, an actual decline in numbers, at least a marked diminution in its growth.[2] Catholic emancipation had been a victory of Liberalism over Evangelicalism, and Evangelicalism suffered from the defeat. Many among the friends of the Church were asking themselves whether the danger, lest the disestablishment of the Church which was inscribed upon the Radical programme might possibly be accomplished, should not be averted before it became a popular political cry, by reforming the Church, re-distributing, possibly even reducing her revenue, and improving the system on which the tithes were collected.

The movement began in Ireland, where ecclesiastical abuses were the most glaring. An important meeting was held at Cork, with Lord Mountcashel in the chair, to organize what was termed 'the Third Reformation'.[3] But, in the opinion of the more prudent, it was dangerous to attempt to deal separately with the abuses of the Irish Church, as though it were distinct from the Church of England; the conclusion might very well be drawn that the Irish Church could be disestablished without touching the Church of England. Wellington accordingly suggested to the Archbishop of Canterbury that it would be advisable to include England in the terms of reference of the important committee which had just been appointed to examine the constitution of the Church.[4] And the rumour was current in the autumn of 1829 that he was about to submit to Parliament a plan for the reform of

[1] Morley, *Reminiscences*, vol. i, p. 175.

[2] *Minutes of Methodist Conferences.* '1829, increase for Great Britain and Ireland, 2,743; 1830, 1,063. In 1829 the report ascribes the disappointingly small increase to the distress of the times . . . and to various other causes which have been in active and injurious operation.' This guarded language refers to the disputes occasioned by the question of emancipation, on which the report preserves absolute silence.

[3] No doubt in opposition to the New Reformation of which we spoke above (p. 267–8). *Examiner*, September 27; *Morning Chronicle*, September 28; *The Times*, December 19, 1829.

[4] Wellington to the Duke of Northumberland, October 27, 1829 (*Despatches, Cont.*, vol. vi, p. 263). Cf. Lord Rolle's letter to Wellington, November 2, and his reply, November 3, 1829 (ibid., vol. vi, pp. 279, 283). See, further, *A Letter to the Duke of Wellington on the Reasonableness of a Church Reform and its Peculiar Fitness to the Present Times*, 3rd edition, with considerable additions, by a Minister of the Establishment, 1830.

ecclesiastical abuses.[1] No such plan was forthcoming. He was disgusted to find civil strife continue in Ireland and would do nothing more for such an ungrateful nation; but there is no evidence that public opinion was aroused by his inaction. Beyond dispute the condition of the Church was unsatisfactory in the extreme; and in the spring of 1829 she became conscious of her weakness. If ever in future she should have to face a popular attack, she would meet it with diminished confidence. It is, nevertheless, equally true that emancipation had not in England been in any measure a victory of the people over the governing classes. On the contrary, it had been a victory of a Liberal aristocracy and middle class over the Conservative prejudice of the nation. Neither at the close of 1829 nor during the first half of 1830 did the situation augur the approach of an acute conflict between public opinion and the Church.

It is also held—and with a greater show of probability—that the question of parliamentary reform, dormant since 1822, had been suddenly revived by Catholic emancipation. Even the Act which disfranchised the forty-shilling freeholders had proved, as in 1825 Canning had feared it would prove, that the franchise was not sacrosanct, and when O'Connell once more presented himself as candidate to the electors of County Clare, he was not satisfied with demanding the repeal of the statute, but placed parliamentary reform upon his programme side by side with the repeal of the Act of Union. Moreover, he had shown that a political reform could be forced through by organizing a popular agitation on a large scale. Surely the agitator would not be wanting in England to imitate these Irish methods and apply them to the question of parliamentary reform; and in fact, during the second half of 1829, we hear of attempts to found societies for democratic propaganda on the model of O'Connell's Association.[2] The

---

[1] *Morning Chronicle*, September 2; *The Times*, December 19, 1829. Wellington denies the rumour in his letter of November 3, 1829, to Lord Rolle (*Despatches, Cont.*, vol. vi, p. 233).

[2] *Examiner*, August 26, 1829. A correspondent who signs himself 'A Reformer' suggests an agitation conducted on the lines of the Catholic Association: members would pay a subscription, a 'rent' of one shilling. 'Mr. Otway Cave is setting an example which ought to be followed by other well-disposed public men. The country is to be moved in every quarter. We have the example of the Irish Roman Catholics before us and should profit by it.' For the plans of Mr. Otway Cave see *Morning Chronicle*, August 11, 1829 (report of the meeting at Leicester). Cf. ibid., December 18, 1829: '. . . We have seen what one man has done in Ireland, for we presume there can be little doubt that but for Mr. O'Connell the Catholics would yet have been unrelieved. Who knows but parliamentary reform may yet find in England a man capable of rousing the great body of the people

Examiner, which even during the reign of Canning had never ceased its campaign on behalf of a radical reform of the franchise, noticed meetings held in Sussex, Hampshire, Leicestershire, Yorkshire, and Lancashire.[1] In London a 'Society to effect a Reform of Parliament' met once a month at the Mechanics' Institution.[2]

Nevertheless, the agitation lacked much that was necessary to render it formidable.

In the first place it lacked popular support. About this time important strikes occurred in London and the provinces, but there is no evidence that they were diverted into instruments of political agitation. Cobbett and Hunt, who, in September, amused the public with the spectacle of one of their numerous quarrels,[3] had lost every shred of influence over the masses. Thomas Hodgskin and William Thompson, starting from the principles of the Utilitarian philosophy, and even accepting certain postulates of Ricardo's political economy, had failed to discover in this system of economics either a scientific explanation of the capitalist's profit or a moral justification for it, and had begun to elaborate the doctrine, not slow to find adherents among the working class, which maintains that the worker has a right to the entire capital produced by his labour;[4] but their disciples among the proletariat did not connect their economic claims with the old Radical claim to political rights. It was not from the institution of universal suffrage that they expected the advent of social justice. Indifferent to the political question, they looked to Robert Owen to solve the social problem by the foundation of trading unions, or, to use the term which finally prevailed, of co-operative societies. The first co-operative society was founded at Brighton at the end of 1828. Owen, who had returned from America, took the movement under his patronage, and within a short time almost five hundred

to a sense of the vital importance of the question—a man possessed of commanding talents, great energy and enthusiasm, and a restless perseverance equal to that displayed by Mr. O'Connell?' Cf. Bentham to O'Connell, August 25, 1829: 'Colonel Jones (late of the Guards), a zealous Radical and pro-Catholic, who is *agitating* against the Aristocratical Sélect Vestry System, has adopted the word *rents*, and projected rents for the purpose of buying seats in Parliament. He has got already between £1,100 to £1,200, he tells me' (*Works*, ed. Bowring, vol. xi, p. 20).

[1] *Examiner*, June 14, September 13, 14; *Morning Chronicle*, August 11, October 20, 1829.
[2] *Examiner*, September 13, 14, October 25, 1829.
[3] Ibid., September 20, 1829.
[4] Karl Menger, *Das Recht auf den vollen Arbeitsertrag*, pp. 51 sqq.; M. Beer, *Geschichte des Sozialismus in England*, pp. 213 sqq.; also Halévy, *Thomas Hodgskin*.

little societies had come into existence, whose scope, confined at first to co-operative sale, was presently extended to co-operative production, and which vaguely aspired by their free development to gain possession automatically of the entire capital of the country.[1]

In the second place the newborn agitation on behalf of parliamentary reform lacked the support of the Whig or Liberal party leaders. Far from seeking to discover a formula of agreement between themselves and the Radicals the Liberals seemed more anxious than ever to insist upon the differences which separated them from the latter. The *Edinburgh Review*, in its issue of June 1829, published two long articles—one written by the youthful Macaulay, the other by the youthful Carlyle—refuting the Utilitarian creed.[2] Neither *The Times* nor the *Morning Chronicle* gave the least approval to the agitation for reform. If, declared the latter, so many who call themselves supporters of parliamentary reform, display such anxiety to dissociate themselves from Hunt and Cobbett, it is because they are delighted to find an excuse for their lukewarmness.[3] Nor was it enough for the *Chronicle* to condemn categorically the doctrine of universal suffrage. It even expressed the opinion that it might perhaps be advisable to raise the pecuniary qualification for the franchise. The measure would render the electors independent and secure them from the pressure to which they were at present exposed from noblemen and men of wealth.[4] The misgivings with which the Liberal Press regarded parliamentary reform towards the end of 1829 are to be explained by the political situation. Wellington was the object of the attacks of the extreme Tories. The Liberal Press desired to keep him in office. Hence *The Times* and the

[1] William Lovett, *Life and Struggles*, ed. 1876, pp. 40 sqq.; Helene Simon, *Robert Owen*, pp. 153 sqq., 208 sqq.; B. Potter, *The Co-operative Movement in Great Britain*, pp. 44 sqq. See, further, the excellent article in sympathy with the movement in the *Quarterly Review* for November 1829, 'The Co-operatives' (vol. xli, pp. 359 sqq.); also the appreciation by Robert Southey in his *Colloquies*, 1829, Colloquy VI: 'Walla Crag—Owen of Lanark' (vol. i, pp. 116 sqq.).

[2] *Edinburgh Review*, June 1829, 'Utilitarian System of Philosophy', 'Signs of the Times' (vol. xlix, pp. 273 sqq., 439 sqq.)

[3] *Morning Chronicle*, September 26, 1829, after quoting from the *Leeds Mercury* the following sentence: 'The cause of reform never was at a lower ebb than at this moment; and it is more indebted to Cobbett and Hunt than anybody else for its fallen condition.'

[4] *Morning Chronicle*, September 10, 1829: 'The small number of voters in France protects French Liberalism against the *la canaille*, the rabble which is at the mercy of the priests.' October 10, 1829: '. . . the best mode of destroying the influence of the high Aristocracy is to raise the qualification.'

Morning Chronicle had become organs of the government rather than of the opposition;[1] and ever since Catholic emancipation it was the ultra-Tories who had taken up the programme of parliamentary reform as a weapon against the Government.

3

In March and April the ultra-Tories had witnessed, with astonishment, the Cabinet extort from the Commons the act of emancipation against the evident will of the majority of the English people. The spectacle had inspired them with the belief that they were the natural representatives of the people against the majority in Parliament. Some, like Michael Thomas Sadler, of whom we shall hear more later on, professed, in opposition to the individualism of the Free Traders, a sort of Tory socialism; the aged poet, Southey, was among their number.[2] Others, like Lord Winchilsea in the Lords,[3] and in the Commons the Marquis of Blandford, the Duke of Marlborough's eldest son, adopted the programme of parliamentary reform. They believed that the Tory aristocracy and gentry could best serve their interests by an alliance with the people against the combination of the great Whig families and the financiers. On June 2, 1829, the Marquis of Blandford submitted to the House of Commons a series of propositions declaring the system of borough representation venal and corrupt. His motion secured forty votes, chiefly radical.[4]

The town of Birmingham was just then in the throes of a crisis, prices and wages alike were falling. This was obviously the right moment for the Tory Attwood to put forward his old remedy, the raising of prices by the repeal of Peel's Bill and the return to an artificial currency; and when the House of Commons turned a deaf ear and continued to accord its confidence to Peel, it was not surprising that he should demand parliamentary reform. On February 28, 1830, Attwood, who had founded a 'Union of the middle and lower classes for the attainment of Parliamentary

[1] For the attitude of *The Times* see its leader of September 3, 1829. See, further, the defence of Wellington against the attacks of the French Liberal Press in the *Morning Chronicle*, September 21, 1829.

[2] Robert Southey, *Thomas More: or Colloquies on the Progress and Prospects of Society*, 2 vols., 1829.

[3] H. of L., April 6, 1829 (*Parl. Deb.*, N.S., vol. xxi, p. 424).

[4] H. of C., June 2, 1829 (ibid., vol. xxi, pp. 1672 sqq.).

Reform', held his first public meeting: 'the largest meeting ever assembled in this kingdom within the walls of a building.'[1] Its object was the foundation in Birmingham first of all, then throughout the rest of the country, of union clubs to spread the doctrine of radical reform. The democrats present approved in principle of Attwood's programme but expressed their doubts as to the advisability of taking action at the present juncture. One of them avowed his misgivings in regard to the movement and expressed his belief 'that the cry for Parliamentary Reform was a mere varnish for some other design'. Another, Joseph Parkes, who was soon to play an important part in the history of English democracy, warned his hearers against the danger of provoking a reaction, as in 1817 and 1819, by the foundation of revolutionary 'clubs', protested against the project of returning to an artificial currency and refused to associate himself with the attacks made upon Wellington in the course of the meeting. Indeed, neither Attwood nor the other organizers of the meeting attempted to conceal the fact that they were Tories.[2] The Marquis of Blandford did not delay to give his adhesion to the movement.[3]

We are now in a better position to estimate the real importance of the debates on parliamentary reform which took place in the House of Commons during the session of 1830. No doubt they occupied more time than had been the case for years past. The Marquis of Blandford introduced a Bill suppressing boroughs which should be found undeserving of a representative, extending to all the boroughs the old scot and lot franchise, and providing for the payment of members.[4] The question of the borough of East Retford was again raised.[5] The attention of the House was drawn to the scandalous conduct of the Duke of Newcastle, who

---

[1] *The Times*, January 27, 1830.

[2] See the full report of the meeting in the *Examiner*, January 31, 1830; also its comment upon the report: 'The project of the Birmingham meeting—an Union of the Middle and Lower Classes for the attainment of Parliamentary Reform—is excellent, and, whatever questionable objects may be aimed at under the pretence of the better purpose, we are persuaded that the effect will, in the mass, be beneficial. Those who think that they can *finesse* with the popular power, and drawing it forth with one design, purpose to wield it for another, will find themselves egregiously in error, and will have the ultimate mortification of forwarding good where they intended to compass mischief. . . . If Birmingham should have its counterfeit, Manchester, Liverpool and other great towns may imitate the scheme of combination and, by putting forward sounder men, correct the error of the other places.' Cf. *Morning Chronicle*, January 28, 1830.

[3] *The Times*, February 10, 1830.

[4] H. of C., February 18, 1830 (*Parl. Deb.*, N.S., vol. xxii, pp. 678 sqq.).

[5] H. of C., February 11, 1830 (ibid., vol. xxii, pp. 334 sqq.); March 5, 1830 (ibid., vol. xxii, pp. 1319 sqq.); March 8, 1830 (ibid., vol. xxii, pp. 1393 sqq.).

had turned out some of his tenants for voting against his wishes, and on this occasion the question of voting by ballot was discussed.[1] Lord John Russell asked that the franchise should be given to the three towns of Leeds, Manchester, and Birmingham,[2] O'Connell for universal suffrage, the ballot, and biennial parliaments. O'Connell's motion barely obtained thirteen votes and its rejection appeared to Lord John the right moment to introduce a detailed scheme of reform. He proposed an increase in the membership of the House of Commons, additional representatives for the large towns and densely populated counties, and one representative, in place of two, for boroughs whose population was less than 2,500. The list of those who voted for his motion contains Radicals, Whigs of Lord Grey's group and of Lord Lansdowne's, members of Huskisson's group and ultra-Tories. Nevertheless, they only mustered 117 votes against 223.[3] For the moment public opinion was indifferent to the disputes which divided the political parties.

In the course of the debate O'Connell and Peel had agreed that the country was 'in a state of perfect tranquillity'.[4] Thus they confirmed the *Examiner's* complaints, when about the same time it lamented the 'torpor', the 'apathy', the 'incurable lethargy' of the English public.[5] And Lord John explained this indifference by the discredit which had attached for several years past to the agitators for universal suffrage.[6] Only fourteen petitions were sent up to Parliament. In 1823 twenty-nine had been received. Evidently the agitation begun in Birmingham had awakened little response in the country at large.[7] This was Wellington's opportunity to follow the advice which Croker gave him in the *Quarterly Review* and satisfy, even exceed, the wishes of the nation,

[1] H. of C., March 1, 1830 (*Parl. Deb.*, N.S., vol. xxii, pp. 1077 sqq.).
[2] H. of C., February 23, 1830 (ibid., vol. xxii, pp. 858 sqq.).
[3] H. of C., May 28, 1830 (ibid., vol. xxiv, pp. 1204 sqq.).
[4] H. of C., May 28, 1830 (ibid., vol. xxiv, pp. 1215).
[5] *Examiner*, January 10, 17, 1830.
[6] H. of C., May 28, 1830 (*Parl. Deb.*, N.S., vol. xxiv, p. 1223).
[7] H. of C., March 9, 1831 (ibid., vol. iii, p. 87); Nottingham Political Union, *Examiner*, April 11, 1830; Coventry Petition, H. of C., March 11, 1830 (*Parl. Deb.*, N.S., vol. xxiii, p. 176). The agitation, however, was continued in London by a mass meeting held in March (*Life and Struggles of William Lovett*, pp. 56–7). According to O'Connell, thirty thousand were present at this meeting, March 11, 1830 (*Parl. Deb.*, N.S., vol. xxiii, p. 182); but O'Connell was obliged to admit that the petition signed at the close of the meeting and placed by himself upon the table of the House bore only ten signatures. An article in the *Morning Chronicle* of July 25 complains in characteristic language of the scanty progress made by the reform movement in the provinces.

by an extremely modest measure of reform.[1] 'It is sad,' wrote Croker, 'to witness how little confidence is reposed in our statesmen, with the exception of the Duke of Wellington. All eyes are fixed upon him as though he were the umpire on whose decision depends the lot of every class in the nation.' Throughout the entire session the 'umpire' did not utter a syllable which could encourage the hope of even the very slightest reform of the representative system. Nevertheless, the bewildered public would not renounce their trust in his leadership. The Whigs refrained from pressing him. They saw him in bad odour with the Court, as a result of Catholic emancipation, and his position threatened by the intrigues of the ultra-Tories. Adopting tactics exactly the opposite of those they had adopted between 1820 and 1822, they were unwilling to take any action which might appear to favour their intrigues.

4

Did not Wellington display, in the circumstances, excessive prudence? Would he not have acted more wisely, if he had acted more boldly, and followed up his exploit of 1829 by some further measure of reform, calculated to impress the popular imagination? This, at least, is certain: public opinion was evidently satisfied, for the moment, to see the Cabinet continue the policy of moderate reform which the party in office, while refusing to touch the question of parliamentary reform, had inaugurated in 1820. It possessed the advantage of satisfying, on certain vital issues, the needs of the middle class, while leaving untouched the political and, with the exception of the Emancipation Act, the ecclesiastical institutions of the realm.

Peel was once more Home Secretary, and still harnessed to the task of reform on which he had been engaged since 1822. When O'Connell, himself a lawyer, offered Bentham his services to act as his lieutenant,[2] and when Bentham dreamed of founding a Law Reform Association, to do for the reform of the law what the

---

[1] *Quarterly Review*, January 1830, 'Internal Policy' (vol. xlii, p. 273). It was in this article that Croker proposed, for the first time, that the Tory party should adopt the new name of Conservative party.

[2] O'Connell to Bentham, July 31, 1829 (Bentham, *Works*, ed. Bowring, vol. xi, p. 20). Cf. H. of C., July 8, 1830; O'Connell's motion demanding 'measures to have drafts or plans of a Code of Laws and Procedure', either in the whole or in parts, to be laid before that House (*Parl. Deb.*, N.S., vol. xxv, pp. 1114 sqq.).

Catholic Association had done for emancipation,[1] and bombarded Wellington with letters pressing him to undertake the reform of the law and of judicial procedure,[2] they were both aware that the Government departments would not offer any systematic opposition to their wishes. Two royal commissions had been appointed on Brougham's motion to inquire, the one into the procedure of the Courts of Common Law, the other into the laws affecting real estate.[3] An Act passed in 1830 reduced considerably the number of cases in which forgery was a capital offence;[4] and it was at this time that Peel gave his name to a reform which cost him more trouble than any of those to which his name was already attached. It had engaged his attention since he first entered the Home Office. In 1822 he had obtained the appointment of a parliamentary committee to advise how best to provide for the prevention and repression of crime in London by efficient measures of police; but he had found his path blocked by deep-rooted and tenacious prejudices inherited from the past. 'It is difficult,' declared the report of the committee, 'to reconcile an effective system of police with that perfect freedom of action and exemption from interference which are the great privileges and blessings of society in this country.'[5] In Ireland, he had encouraged the formation of a constabulary with the most satisfactory results; and later, when in 1826, as a result of the crisis which was then at its height, disturbances broke out in the manufacturing districts, he regretted the absence of some 'local force', like the Irish constabulary, which could protect private property without the necessity of calling out the yeomanry or the regular troops.[6] We might have expected him, therefore, to have tackled the problem of policing England as a whole. On the contrary, he

[1] Bentham to O'Connell, August 25, 1829; O'Connell to Bentham, October 22, 1829 (Bentham, *Works*, ed. Bowring, vol. xi, pp. 21 sqq.).

[2] Bentham to O'Connell, December 8, 1829 (ibid., ed. Bowring, vol. xi, p. 28).

[3] H. of C., February 7, 1828, Brougham's speech (*Parl. Deb.*, N.S., vol. xviii, pp. 127 sqq.). See First Report of Commissioners appointed to inquire into the Practice and Proceedings of the Courts of Common Law, 1829; Second Report, 1830; also First Report of Commissioners appointed to inquire into the Law of England respecting Real Property, 1829; Second Report, 1830.

[4] 1 Will. IV, cap. 66. The King's speech of February 4, 1830, promised measures 'calculated . . . to facilitate and expedite the course of justice in different parts of the United Kingdom, and other necessary preliminaries to a revision of the practice and proceedings of the superior courts'. Cf. Bentham to Brougham, March 30, 1830 (Bentham, *Works*, ed. Bowring, vol. xi, pp. 36–7).

[5] Report from the Select Committee on the Police of the Metropolis, 1822, p. 11.

[6] Peel to Mr. Hobhouse, July 9, 1826 (C. S. Parker, *Sir Robert Peel*, vol. i, p. 405).

again concentrated his efforts upon the metropolis where the number of crimes was steadily increasing.[1] In 1828 a second parliamentary committee appointed to investigate the question, with Peel as chairman, did not take long to formulate definite recommendations,[2] and in 1829 there came into existence the New Police which was under the immediate control of the Home Department. At first it was composed of five divisions, each division being subdivided into eight sections, and each section, in turn, into eight beats. In each division there was a company consisting of a superintendent, four inspectors, sixteen sergeants and 144 constables.[3] The force could be extended indefinitely and was intended by Peel to grow into a little army of three thousand men. Was there, at the back of his mind, the intention to furnish the Government with the means of defence against a possible 'Jacobin' rising in the capital?[4] He does not seem to have entertained any such thought. The 'prevention of crime' was apparently his sole consideration. Never had the possibility of an insurrection in England seemed more remote than at the time when the New Police Bill was carried. It is significant that the only opposition to the Bill came from the ultra-Tories. They protested against this attempt to inflict upon England a 'body of spies', a 'gendarmérie' after the French pattern; and, on the other hand, the new system had the approval of the Liberals and Radicals, of Fonblanque and Francis Place.[5]

But the reforms which public opinion demanded most insistently were economic. When the session of 1830 opened England was still, as she had been ever since the accession of George IV, indifferent to purely political questions. Public opinion was mainly concerned with industrial development, with possible economies in the Government departments, and with taxation. 'The people of England,' wrote the *Morning Chronicle* when Canning was

[1] Peel to Mr. Hobhouse, December 8, 1826 (C. S. Parker, op. cit., vol. i, p. 432).

[2] Report from the Select Committee appointed to inquire into the cause of the increase of the number of Commitments and Convictions in London and Middlesex, and into the state of the Police of the Metropolis and of the districts adjoining thereto, 1828.

[3] 10 Geo. IV, cap. 49. Cf. Peel to Mr. Hobhouse, December 12, 1828, May 29, 1829 (ibid., vol. ii, pp. 39, 111).

[4] The thought had undoubtedly been in Wellington's mind when, in June 1820, he drew up his Memorandum to the Earl of Liverpool respecting the state of the Guards. The existence of a police force would render a mutiny of the regular army less dangerous. Indeed, the rivalry between the two bodies would make it impossible (Wellington, *Despatches, Cont.*, vol. i, pp. 127-9).

[5] *Examiner*, September 27, October 4, 1829; Graham Wallas, *Life of Francis Place*, p. 248 n.

Prime Minister, 'are making a wonderful progress in intellectual improvement; and one of the first objects on which men exercise their intellect is the belly.'[1] Just then the Englishman's belly was feeling the pinch of hunger.

5

The violence of the sudden outburst of complaint which is heard at this time is disconcerting; for, as we listen to it, it is impossible at time to resist the impression that England was passing through a crisis as grave as that of December 1825. But in 1826 not a single politician denied the reality or the gravity of the distress which afflicted the country. In 1830, on the contrary, the Ministers, and many Members of Parliament also, denied the existence of a crisis, and affirmed their conviction, which they supported by the official statistics of the Treasury and the Board of Trade, that England was prosperous and her prosperity was increasing. The historian, therefore, is confronted by an obscure situation—an enigma to which, however, the copious debates in the House of Lords and the House of Commons provide the key.[2]

Take manufacture first. The level of prices continued to be low, and apparently a further fall took place during 1829. The price of labour followed the price of manufactured articles. Hence the complaints of the manufacturers and their men. The causes of this fall in prices differed in different cases. For instance, there was a glut of sugar and coffee and the West India interest suffered accordingly; but this glut was obviously unconnected with the industrial situation at home.[3] Almost at the doors of Parliament the position of the Spitalfields silk manufacture was still critical, and the highly respected merchant drapers of Gloucestershire and Somersetshire, who were strongly represented in the House of Commons, wearied Parliament with their complaints. Nevertheless, we should be mistaken if we saw anything in these cases of a purely local distress more than a result of the

[1] *Morning Chronicle*, June 15, 1827.
[2] See especially the long debates on the State of the Nation which arose out of a motion by a Tory member, Edward D. Davenport, H. of C., March 16, 18, 19, 23, 1830 (*Parl. Deb.*, N.S., vol. xxiii, pp. 391 sqq., 548 sqq., 624 sqq., 789 sqq.). All the prominent statesmen took part in the debate. See also the interesting speech by Slaney, H. of C., May 13, 1830 (ibid., vol. xxiv, pp. 682 sqq.); also Report from the Select Committee appointed to consider the Means of Lessening the Evils arising from the Fluctuation of Employment in Manufacturing Districts, July 2, 1830.
[3] T. Tooke, *History of Prices*, vol. ii, p. 211.

northward migration of industry from London to Warwickshire and Lancashire, and from Gloucestershire to Yorkshire. While certain districts of England were being impoverished, others were growing rich.[1] The distress prevalent among the hand-loom weavers was more general; serious disturbances, rioting against the introduction of machinery, occurred towards the end of 1829 at Coventry, Bedworth, Nuneaton, Macclesfield, and Barnsley;[2] but these troubles also were only the growing-pains of modern industrialism. A dying class was rising in vain against the new system of production which had condemned it to death.

We have still to explain the great strike which for six months paralysed the cotton mills of Manchester, when John Doherty united every spinner in the Kingdom in a single trade union;[3] and we have also to explain the distress which prevailed at Birmingham when Attwood embraced in his Political Union representatives of the employers and the workmen, fellow-sufferers from a trade depression. It must be admitted that the country had not yet completely recovered from the crisis of 1825, that it was suffering generally from chronic over-production, and that the manufacturers, finding a difficulty in disposing of their enormous stocks, attempted to improve their profits by reducing wages. But the persistence with which the manufacturers had continued since 1826 to produce, even at a marginal profit, was already reaping its reward.[4] By the cheapness of their goods they successfully overcame the new tariffs which were being introduced in Germany and America to exclude their products.[5] During the years immediately preceding 1830 two phenomena were witnessed, the co-existence of which presents a curious paradox. On the one hand, the number of English emigrants steadily increased —a sign of distress among the working class; and, on the other hand, exports increased simultaneously—a sign of the prosperous condition of trade, which in the long run was bound to react

---

[1] H. of C., March 16, 1830, Irving's speech (*Parl. Deb.*, N.S., vol. xxiii, pp. 385–404).

[2] *Ann. Reg.*, 1829, pp. 131–3. Cf. *The Times*, October 2, 1829. For the abject poverty to which the weavers were reduced about this date see the curious correspondence between the Rev. Humphrey Price and Bentham (Bentham, *Works*, ed. Bowring, vol. lxxxi, pp. 43 sqq.).

[3] *The Times*, October 2, 1829; *Morning Chronicle*, October 13, 1829. Cf. S. and B. Webb, *History of Trade Unionism*, ed. 1920, pp. 117–18.

[4] T. Tooke, op. cit., vol. ii, pp. 211–12, 213. Cf. *Edinburgh Review*, April 1832, 'Supply and Consumption of the Precious Metals' (vol. lv, pp. 43 sqq.); also N. Chater to Wellington, February 8, 1830 (Wellington, *Despatches, Cont.*, vol. vi, pp. 486–7).

[5] H. of C., March 16, 1830, Irving's speech (*Parl. Deb.*, N.S., vol. xxiii, p. 405).

favourably upon the position of the workers.[1] Western, in the House of Commons, expressed his astonishment at the situation. 'There was an increased activity in commerce, increased exports and imports, increased production, increased energy throughout the country; and yet there were difficulties and distresses such as could not be contemplated without commiseration.'[2]

Even harder to understand are the complaints heard at the same time from the agriculturalists. Hitherto agriculturalists and manufacturers had not usually suffered at the same time; the prosperity of the former had caused the distress of the latter and vice versa; but now their complaints were simultaneous. What was the reason? Since the Corn Bill of 1828 had been passed, the price of cereals, very low at first, had rapidly risen, until wheat had twice stood above 80s. the quarter and had once even attained 90s. Then the price of corn had once more fallen until at the end of 1829 and the beginning of 1830 it appeared to be stabilized at about 73s. From the point of view of those who had obtained the Corn Bill this was a satisfactory result, for as they had permitted the import of foreign corn free of duty as soon as this figure had been reached, they evidently considered 73s. a remunerative price for the farmer.[3] But the manufacturers and the working class as a whole found bread still too dear; and the farmers remarked that the last fall in price had actually followed a bad harvest, and foresaw a further fall after the first good harvest. Moreover, they were not only corn-growers but breeders of sheep; and they saw that, as a result of the reforms effected by Huskisson, the amount of foreign wool which had entered the English market had considerably lowered the price of wool; while the value of cattle had decreased by 25 per cent, the price of cheese by 30 per cent, and the value of pigs and poultry in the same proportion.[4] They

---

[1] Emigrants in 1824 (minimum figure), 14,805; in 1825, 14,891; in 1826, 20,900; in 1827, 28,003; in 1828, 26,092; in 1829, 31,198; in 1830, 56,907 (W. Page, *Commerce and Industry*, vol. ii, p. 30). Exports in 1826 (minimum figure), £40,966,000; in 1827, £52,222,000; in 1828, £52,788,000; in 1829, £56,218,000; in 1830, £61,152,000 (ibid., p. 73).

[2] H. of C., March 23, 1830 (*Parl. Deb.*, N.S., vol. xxiii, p. 821).

[3] H. of L., March 29, 1830, Wellington's speech (ibid., vol. xxiii, pp. 981 sqq.).

[4] H. of C., March 16, 1830, Edward D. Davenport's speech (ibid., vol. xxiii, pp. 391 sqq.); March 16, 1830, Heathcote's speech introducing a petition from Boston (Lincolnshire); April 6, 1830, Lord Nugent's speech introducing a petition from Buckinghamshire (ibid., vol. xxiii, pp. 382, 1406). For a statement of the opposite point of view see *The Times*, January 28, 1830; A. Stevenson to Wellington, January 28, 1830; G. Conwen to Wellington, February 12, 1830; and D. Gunning to Wellington, February 13, 1830 (Wellington, *Despatches, Cont.*, vol. vi, pp. 451, 502–3, 507).

were not even inclined to regard the price of 73s. for wheat as remunerative when they had to bear such heavy taxation. The burden of the poor rates, especially in the southern counties, was becoming every day more intolerable. When Lord Stanhope presented a petition from Kent to the House of Lords, he quoted the case of an estate whose rental was £2,500 which paid £2,900 in poor rates, and a farm which paid a rent of only £50 but rates and taxes to the amount of £112.[1] The condition of the cultivators resembled, of course on a very different scale, the condition of the hand-loom weavers of the same period. They were a class which was steadily declining, while the position of those, whether masters or men, who were engaged in wholesale manufacture with the help of steam was improving every year. Only by selling his produce at famine prices could the farmer hope to maintain his former standard of living, and employ as much labour as formerly.

6

If the grumblers were correct, and there had really been a general fall in prices, inflation could not fail to recover its attraction. The general fall of prices was, according to the inflationist, due to the restriction of the currency; and that restriction was itself the consequence of Peel's Act of 1819 and the return to specie payment. The disastrous effects of this statute had been delayed by the permission granted to the banks to issue notes for low values; but this permission had again been rescinded and all these notes withdrawn from circulation at the beginning of 1829. Hence the present depression. And the crisis had been aggravated, added the ultra-Tories, by the liberation of the Spanish Colonies; for the anarchy which had prevailed in Spanish America ever since had suspended the working of the gold and silver mines and consequently diminished the number of coins available in Europe. Accordingly the agricultural interest renewed its campaign.

The agriculturalists complained that, since they were obliged to pay the same taxes as before with a currency whose value had increased, they were in fact subject to a burden of taxation which grew continually heavier. They therefore demanded a reduction of the taxes, and in particular the abolition of the taxes on malt

[1] H. of L., March 25, 1830 (*Parl. Deb.*, N.S., vol. xxiii, p. 837).

and beer, which hampered agriculture. They remarked that the salaries of officials did not merely remain the same, although profits from every source, rents and wages, were falling, but actually rose from year to year, since they were paid with a currency whose purchasing power was constantly increasing. Sir James Graham, a young and rising member, who, during the session of 1830, figured in the front rank of the speakers of the Whig Opposition, demanded a general reduction of salaries, proportionate to the rise in the value of money. And finally the agriculturalists demanded, if not the immediate repeal of Peel's Act, at least the adoption of measures which, if less radical, would nevertheless enlarge the currency—namely, that the bimetallism discontinued in 1797 should be restored, and the banks once more permitted to issue notes for low values. Crowded meetings were held in a large number of counties, at which the banking policy associated with the name of Peel was denounced with greater vehemence than ever. We have already noticed Attwood's attempt to interest the working class of the towns in his propaganda by combining with his attack upon Peel's Act the demand for universal suffrage. It was noticed that the petitions signed at these meetings were addressed not to the House of Commons, in accordance with constitutional custom, but to Wellington. Possibly the Tories hoped by this device to compromise the man whom they depicted as a dictator, a mayor of the palace, and whom they charged with imposing his will upon Court, Parliament, and people. But it was not only the Tories who took part in this insurrection of the landowners. Neither Sir James Graham, nor Western, nor Burdett was a Tory.[1] About this time Creevey paid a visit to Lord and Lady Holland. He found them ill, distracted by financial difficulties. Creevey prophesied a return to

---

[1] See Sir Francis Burdett's speech, *Morning Chronicle*, March 25, 1830; also the letter addressed by Charles Western 'to the gentry, clergy, freeholders, and inhabitants of the county of Essex' (*The Times*, December 2, 1829); and the speech delivered by Sir James Graham to the county meeting of Cumberland containing a characteristic appeal to Wellington: 'I trust he will see the necessity of emancipating himself from the obstinacy of colleagues who are wedded to certain theories and opinions which time has shown to be impracticable; and that he will consent to revise those measures relative to the currency which have produced greater changes in property than the Revolution of 1688, or even the great civil war. The continuance of the Duke's Government rests upon public opinion. The Court, there is no longer any doubt, is inimical to him; the aristocracy of the country stand aloof from him; he must therefore be the Minister of the people or cease to be a Minister at all. His continuance in office depends upon the public voice' (*Morning Chronicle*, February 1, 1830).

the days of paper money. 'I wish to God,' exclaimed Lady Holland, 'the time was come, or anything else, to save us.'[1]

7

But the political economists had remedies of their own to propose. Unlike the agriculturalists they did not behave as demagogues, but as men of science, as befitted desciples of Ricardo and friends of James Mill. They were not disposed like the agriculturalists to exaggerate the gravity of a crisis which at first sight appeared to disprove the Liberal doctrines. They refused to take alarm, and promised that the financial situation would rapdily recover if only the State did nothing to hamper the expansion of industry and commerce. At the beginning of February 1830 a little book was published which made a great stir and was destined to remain a classic of English finance. Its subject was 'Financial Reform'. Its author, Sir Henry Parnell, whom Wellington, on becoming Prime Minister, had made the Chairman of the Finance Committee instead of Lord Althorp, discussed in a more concrete and practical form the questions which Ricardo had raised in his great work of 1817.[2] Estimating the national revenue at the round sum of £50,000,000, Sir Henry calculated that out of that £50,000,000, £39,000,000 represented the produce of luxury taxes, paid only by taxpayers in easy circumstances and to an amount determined by themselves. Here the only question for consideration was the advisability of reducing the burden of these taxes in order to encourage the consumption of the articles taxed, and thus increase the revenue received by the State. But there remained £11,000,000 derived from taxes on raw materials and manufactured articles, and from duties imposed to protect agriculture and industry, which cost the nation more than they brought into the Treasury, and therefore in the long run were bound to impoverish the State by diminishing the wealth in private hands. Sir Henry's object was to convince his fellow-countrymen—and in support of his contention he appealed to the facts collected by the committee over which he had presided—that it was to the interest of the State to diminish the number of taxes in order, by stimulating the national production, to increase

---

[1] Creevey to Miss Ord, March 11, 1830 (*Creevey Papers*, vol. ii, pp. 209–10).
[2] Ricardo had himself recognized how useful a book on the lines now followed by Sir Henry Parnell would be (to Trower, October 4, 1821).

the revenue from the remaining taxes; and to make provision against a temporary deficit he proposed a radical reform of the system of redemption, which, in spite of the improvements which had gradually been effected, was still too costly, and the re-imposition of the income tax at the rate of $1\frac{1}{2}$ or 2 per cent.

A young merchant, Poulett Thomson, who had represented Dover in Parliament since the election of 1826, and, like Parnell, was in communication with the Benthamite group, brought Parnell's ideas before the House of Commons on March 25 in an important speech, in which he expounded his economic principles. He demanded the total or partial abolition of a large number of duties levied upon raw materials, especially the duties on timber and on coal brought to London by sea, the entire abolition of the duties on certain manufactured articles (glass, paper and printed calicoes), and a reduction of the duties on tea, tobacco, wine and spirits, with a view to increasing their consumption. He did not dare to raise the question of imposing new taxes as substitutes for those remitted; an ambiguous expression in his speech betrayed the difficulty he felt on this point.[1] The reason of his embarrassment was that the Opposition to which he belonged was not unanimous in support of an income tax. Huskisson favoured the proposal,[2] also Lord Althorp.[3] But there were too many Whigs, and Brougham was among their number, who in 1816 had won a cheap popularity by compelling the Government to abolish the income tax imposed during the war, and who were therefore not in the least disposed to alter their attitude now.

IV RETRENCHMENT

I

Both parties, however, agriculturalists and political economists, were agreed upon one point at least: to demand a policy of retrenchment, even of cheese-paring economies; and their demands were pressed so insistently upon the House of Commons that we might have expected them to have occasioned the Government the same difficulties as in the period immediately following

[1] H. of C., March 25, 1830 (*Parl. Deb.*, N.S., vol. xxiii, pp. 857 sqq., especially p. 893).
[2] H. of C., March 18, 1830 (ibid., vol. xxiii, pp. 599, 604-5).
[3] Le Marchant, *Memoir of Viscount Althorp*, pp. 238-9. The *Edinburgh Review* declared against the tax. It distinguished between a property and an income tax, only to condemn both (April 1830, 'Finance: The Budget', vol. li, pp. 223-4).

1815. But on the one hand, the Opposition, though stronger numerically than it had been fifteen years earlier, was also more heterogeneous; so that if the ultra-Tories and the Canningites waged a relentless war against the Cabinet, the Whigs, on the contrary, were disposed to treat it with consideration and defend it against the ultra-Tories; and, on the other hand, Wellington and his colleagues had the wisdom, by adopting an energetic financial policy, to assume the control and monopolize the credit of the programme of reform.

In fact, for the past ten years there had been a *rapprochement* between the Tory Government and the group of political economists. Before Canning, Lord Liverpool and Robinson had taken a decisive part in guiding the policy of the Government along the path which approved itself to the economists, and although Canning had given whole-hearted support to Huskisson's tariff experiments, it is by no means certain that in other respects his general policy had been such as to satisfy the school of Ricardo. For a policy of retrenchment necessitates a policy of peace, and for all its pacific appearance Canning's foreign policy had been almost, if not entirely, a policy of war. Hence the gradual increase during his hegemony of the expenditure upon the Army and Navy. Nothing speaks more eloquently of this aspect of his policy than the budget of 1827, the only budget for which he was solely responsible, as at once Prime Minister and Chancellor of the Exchequer. He asked Parliament to sanction an expenditure which exceeded by £800,000 the estimates for 1826, and the expedition to Portugal was the cause of this additional burden. He proceeded to promise for the future a policy of retrenchment; the return to an expenditure which should be even less than that of 1826. He concluded his speech with a long panegyric of Adam Smith's philosophy, borrowed from Pitt, and announced the forthcoming appointment of a Finance Committee to review the entire system of revenue and expenditure. If, however, he had lived to decide British policy in the Levant after the battle of Navarino, would he have been content to practise the unassuming diplomacy which alone could make a reduction of the naval and military expenditure possible? There can be no doubt that Wellington, Peel, and Goulburn, just because they had been Canning's political adversaries, were better able to fulfil his promise than Canning himself.

Nobody could have better represented the principles which animated the political economists than Sir Henry Parnell, who, as we have seen, owed his position as Chairman of the Finance Committee to Wellington's appointment. In conformity with the Committee's recommendations, Goulburn drew up the budgets of 1828 and 1829 in a spirit of rigid economy. For the financial year 1828 he estimated an expenditure less by £500,000 than the expenditure for which the previous budget had made provision, and the estimated expenditure for the financial year 1829 was £200,000 less than the estimate of 1828. On the other hand, the estimated surplus for the financial year 1828 did not exceed £3,000,000. Goulburn, here also obedient to the recommendations of Sir Henry Parnell and his committee, decided that it would be ridiculous to borrow £2,000,000 to complete the £5,000,000 regularly allocated to the redemption of debt. In future only £3,000,000 instead of £5,000,000 would be devoted to this purpose. A portion of this sum of £3,000,000 would consist of the interest on the capital, which since 1823 had once more begun to accumulate in the hands of the Commissioners of the National Debt according to the modified system then inaugurated. The remainder would be a first charge upon the annual surplus.[1] The principle established by Pitt of a sinking fund to increase at compound interest was, therefore, still respected. It ceased to be respected in 1829. A further statute then prescribed that the sum devoted to the redemption of the Debt should be taken solely from the actual surplus and no longer need be maintained at the figure of £3,000,000, and, further, that the loan redeemed must be immediately cancelled, as also retrospectively all loans redeemed since 1823.[2] Possibly it was a rash step, and England was saved from the consequences of this imprudence only by the abnormal growth of her production and the abnormal increase of the national wealth which was its result. In any case, it had been inevitable since the day when a combination of the Opposition, the business community, and the country gentlemen had deprived the Exchequer of the revenue derived from the income tax, and, under whatever aspect it is considered, was a victory for the Liberals, who for so many years had pursued the old system of Pitt and the Tories with their implacable hate. When Parliament met in February 1830 and heard the Govern-

[1] 9 Geo. IV, cap. 90. [2] 10 Geo. IV, cap. 27.

ment's financial proposals, it knew that the Treasury had accepted the views of the political economists.

The Cabinet saved no less than £452,000 on the Army estimates, £29,000 on the Artillery, and on the Naval estimates £273,000. Further economies were effected in other departments —economies so extensive that the total reduction in expenditure was £1,300,000. But it was plain that public opinion would not be satisfied with the abandonment of £1,000,000 to £1,500,000 of revenue. Goulburn, with the assent of all his colleagues, proposed the entire remission of the Excise duty on beer—a loss of £3,500,000. But the agriculturalists gave little sign of satisfaction—they would have preferred the abolition of the duty on malt, which hit them directly; and the large brewers were equally dissatisfied. For the remission of the tax was accompanied by the grant to anyone who wished of permission to sell beer for the trifling cost of a licence: they therefore lost their monopoly of sale to the profit of the small retailer. The Tories denounced a measure which encouraged drunkenness among the lower classes. Sir Henry Parnell and the other supporters of what they called 'financial reform' called attention to the fact that of all the taxes the tax on beer was precisely the one whose remission was least calculated to increase production. The only satisfaction they received from the Government, apart from a few trifling decreases in the duties which protected West Indian sugar and the English silk manufacture, was the abolition, as a sign of the Government's attitude, of the tax on leather. But the abolition of the tax on beer delighted the masses; and it was warmly approved by the speakers of the Liberal party, which had not yet become the Temperance party.

How would the Government supply the loss of revenue thus entailed? They might, if they chose, adopt Sir Henry Parnell's proposal and restore the income tax. The Cabinet considered the advisability of doing so. Goulburn submitted to his colleagues a plan for an income tax to be imposed on rent, interest, salaries and wages, and exempting only profits from trade. He was warmly supported by Peel, and by almost all the Ministers who were members of the House of Commons; but Wellington opposed the tax, and after discussions, which lasted almost a fortnight, his opinion finally prevailed.[1] To balance the budget

[1] Lord Ellenborough's *Diary*, March 1, 6, 13, 14, 19, 24, 1830. Cf. the ambiguous speech by Peel, H. of C., March 25, 1830 (*Parl. Deb.*, N.S., vol. xxi, pp. 911 sqq.).

Goulburn contented himself with converting the 4 per cent stock, which had reached par, into 3½ per cent—an estimated saving of £750,000—and postponing until October the remission of the duty on beer. The postponement would lighten the difficulty of providing for the financial year 1830-31, and he counted upon an increase in the receipts from the malt duty as a consequence of the increased consumption of beer. Finally, he promised in the near future to effect further economies in the Government services, and reform the system of retiring pensions.

2

Thus, to give immediate satisfaction to the demands of public opinion, the Cabinet overstepped the recommendations of the Finance Committee, passed a budget without a surplus, and therefore renounced the attempt to redeem the National Debt. But this policy of parsimonious economy—£1,500,000 saved in four financial years on the Army and £1,000,000 on the Navy[1]—obliged the Government to adopt an attitude wellnigh more pacific than the pacifism, already so marked, of Sir Henry Parnell and his friends. Under Wellington and his Foreign Secretary, Lord Aberdeen, England became accustomed to play a subordinate instead of a leading part in international politics; for, unlike Canning, they practised the policy of non-intervention, instead of merely professing it. In Portugal Dom Miguel restored despotism, and the British Government adopted an attitude of strict neutrality between the Absolutists and the Constitutionalists: when a Portuguese expedition sailed from an English port to carry reinforcements to the Constitutional party, a British fleet prevented it from landing at Madeira. In the Levant Russia declared war upon Turkey, and, though defeated in the first campaign, finally dictated the peace of Adrianople on October 15, 1829, and a French army, with English connivance or assist-

---

[1] 1826: Army, £8,297,000; Navy, £6,541,000; Ordnance, £1,870,000; Total, £16,708,000. 1827: Army, £7,877,000; Navy, £6,451,000; Ordnance, £1,914,000; Total, £16,242,000. 1828: Army, £8,084,000; Navy, £5,668,000; Ordnance, £1,447,000; Total, £15,199,000. 1829: Army, £7,709,000; Navy, £5,902,000; Ordnance, £1,569,000; Total, £15,180,000. 1830: Army, £6,991,000; Navy, £5,310,000; Ordnance, £1,613,000; Total, £13,914,000 (*An Account of the Public Expenditure of the United Kingdom, exclusive of the Sums applied to the Reduction of the National Debt in the Year*, the yearly official publication). The same authority gives the following figures for the civil expenditure voted annually by Parliament: 1826, £2,567,000; 1827, £2,863,000; 1828, £2,012,000; 1829, £2,486,000; 1830, £1,950,000.

299

ance,[1] expelled the Egyptian army from the Morea. The day seemed at hand 'when Russia' would 'be mistress of Constantinople, France of Athens, and England, in her new livery of a satellite kingdom, left to stand behind the chair of either, a laughing-stock to both'.[2]

How did public opinion receive this sudden reversal of Canning's policy, so popular two years before? Lady Canning, the widow of the great man, who had been granted a peerage after her husband's death in recognition of his services to the nation, went so far as to address protests and threats to the Ministry, and entrusted all her private papers to Stapleton to serve as material for a defence of Canning's policy. She inspired and even wrote pamphlets attacking the foreign policy of Wellington and Lord Aberdeen.[3] In the House of Commons Canning's system was defended by Huskisson and Lord Palmerston. With them voted a certain number of ultra-Tories and the Liberals, Sir James Mackintosh and Lord John Russell, who were devotees of the Balance of Power. But when they ceased to criticize and made proposals of a positive nature, their language was hesitating and undecided. Did they want England to attack Turkey to save Greece, or, on the contrary, to protect Turkey against Russia? And in either case did they want war? They disclaimed any such desire, and argued that, if Canning had lived, he would, by speaking a language more warlike than the present Government dared employ, have intimidated the foreign Powers and prevented the outbreak of war between Russia and Turkey in the Levant, and between the Absolutists and the Constitutionalists in Portugal.[4] Possibly they were right. Their opponents might, however, well be pardoned for their belief that, if England was to be kept out of war, the method pursued by Wellington and Lord Aberdeen was more honourable and more certain.

England never ceased to be obsessed by fear of the Russian

[1] Croker to Wellington, July 25, 1828: 'I submit that it would be desirable that all the measures should be taken in the Mediterranean, and that the matter should not get wind in England, which would be the case if we were to send any transports hence' (Wellington, *Despatches, Cont.*, vol. iv, p. 557).

[2] *The Times*, July 29, 1828.

[3] *A Letter addressed to the Earl of Aberdeen, Secretary of State for Foreign Affairs*, by Henry Gally Knight, 1829. *An Authentic Account of Mr. Canning's Policy towards Portugal*, 1829, by Lady Canning. A brief exposition of the foreign policy of Mr. Canning contrasted with that of the existing administration, 1830.

[4] H. of C., February 5, 1830, Lord Palmerston's speech (*Parl. Deb.*, N.S., vol. xii, p. 139).

Empire, of the danger which it might one day constitute in Asia
to her Indian possessions, and in Europe to the Balance of Power;
but in 1828 the first campaign of the Russian Army failed, and
England enjoyed for a moment the pleasure of finding Russia less
dangerous than she had believed. Then in 1829 the question of
Catholic emancipation absorbed public attention, and questions of
foreign politics fell into the background.[1] Moreover, it was out
of the question for a naval Power like England to check the growth
of the Russian Empire by force. All that could possibly be done
was to prevent Russia from strengthening her position in Europe
by an alliance with some other nation which possessed a powerful
army. The possibility of a Franco-Russian alliance was a subject
of constant anxiety to English statesmen, and the desire to detach
France from Russia impelled them to seek more earnestly than
ever to lay the foundations of a 'good understanding' with France.
When in August 1829 Charles X dismissed his Liberal Ministers
and replaced Martignac by Polignac, the English Press and even
the Liberal organs welcomed the change; for in Paris the Liberals
were bellicose and anti-English, and when they were succeeded
by the extreme reactionaries *The Times* and the *Morning Chronicle*
considered their delight justified by the fact that Polignac left the
French Embassy in London with the intention of restoring
friendly relations between France and England.[2]

In short, England's great desire was for peace at any price.
Feeling the burden of a Debt which remained constant at a level
in the neighbourhood of £800,000,000, she was convinced that it
would be impossible to finance another war. But the English
recognized that it was unreasonable to hope that peace could be
prolonged indefinitely. It was, indeed, wellnigh a miracle that
England had preserved peace with all her neighbours for fifteen

[1] Lord Palmerston to William Temple, March 30, June 4, 1827 (Sir H. L. Bulwer,
Life of Viscount Palmerston, Book VI, ed. 1870, vol. i, pp. 327 sqq., 333 sqq.).

[2] *Morning Chronicle*, August 12, 1829: 'We speak advisedly when we say that we have
the assurance of those who have the best personal opportunities of ascertaining the fact,
that the recent appointments are the subject of unmixed congratulation, that they are
considered as a guarantee for the continuance of the good understanding on foreign policy
which has for some time existed, and the harbinger of advantages of another description,
less showy but infinitely more substantial' (a commercial treaty, an increase in the trade
between the two countries). Cf. ibid., August 13, 1825; also *The Times*, August 11, 12,
1829. The *Examiner*, August 23, September 13, criticizes this attitude; also the *Edinburgh
Review*, October 1829, 'New French Ministry' (vol. l, pp. 277 sqq.). But it is significant
that the *Edinburgh Review* disclaims any intention of holding Wellington responsible for
the choice of Polignac. Cf. Lord Grey to Lord John Russell, December 13, 1829 (*Early
Correspondence of Lord John Russell*, vol. i, p. 298).

years. And since Wellington was working with an obvious sincerity, all the more meritorious in a soldier, to make the miracle continue, he had a right to the confidence of the nation. From the moment he became Premier his foreign policy received the uninterrupted support of the *Morning Chronicle*, the organ of the group of Lord Grey and Lord Althorp.[1] It approved his recognition of Dom Miguel and his refusal to allow the Portuguese Constitutionalists to make British ports the base of their operations.[2] Possibly there were occasions when it was even more Wellingtonian than Wellington himself. One of these was when it derided the fears felt in England of Russia's aggressive imperialism,[3] and another, when a little later commenting upon the expedition sent by Polignac to Algiers, it praised the natural aptitude of the French for colonizing and encouraged France to establish herself on the African coast—even, if she wished, in Egypt.[4] But one thing, at any rate, was certain: Wellington's policy would never be blamed in this quarter for its weakness, but would continue to be praised for its consistent pacifism.

3

In the spring of 1830 Wellington was master of the political situation. No doubt the French activity in the Mediterranean aroused much ill-feeling, but in the present state of public opinion love of peace was decidedly more powerful than the desire to oppose Russian or French expansion at the risk of war. The budget was the object of universal praise, the position of industry was improving every day, and by remitting the tax on beer Wellington had earned a popularity which, if not altogether of

[1] *Morning Chronicle*, March 27, 1828: 'We have often heard old men express satisfaction that they could not, if they would, continue the follies of their youth. We are in this happy state—forced to be wise and prudent, whether we will or not.' August 18, 1828: 'England seems to be viewed on the Continent somewhat in the light in which a prodigal who has spent his fortune in electioneering is viewed by his quondam constituents, when he has no longer the wherewithal. We can no longer afford to throw money about the Continent, and, as we attached great consequence to the idea of being thought the general paymasters, the reproach of poverty is thought to be one which we severely feel.'

[2] Ibid., July 22, 23, 1828; April 28, June 2, 13, 1829.

[3] See especially, ibid., August 23, 1828; September 26, October 15, 16, 1829.

[4] Ibid., July 23, 24, 1830. Only on a single point did the *Morning Chronicle* find fault with the foreign policy of the Government. That was when Wellington prevented Mexico from dispatching an expedition to assist the insurgents in Cuba (May 21, 1830). The Ministers' reply to their critics was that by preserving Cuba for Spain they were not preventing the island from achieving independence, but from being annexed by the United States (H. of C., February 5, 1830, *Parl. Deb.*, N.S., vol. xxii, p. 151).

the highest quality, was none the less genuine. His majority, no doubt, would have proved very weak if the fragments which constituted the Opposition had opposed a solid front to the Government. But they were far from doing this; only once during a protracted session was the Government defeated, and that was upon a point of detail. If the ultra-Tories on the one hand, and Huskisson's group on the other, had declared against Wellington a war apparently unrelenting, the opposition of the Whigs—the followers of Lord Grey and Lord Althorp, and even those who had formerly co-operated with Canning—was by no means so decided. They assisted the Ministers to defeat the motions made by the ultra-Tories, and on critical occasions absented themselves from the House in sufficient numbers to enable the Government to avoid defeat. Was this attitude merely political tactics due to a desire to compromise and humiliate the Cabinet by an ostentatious patronage? One member of the Opposition ironically expressed his pleasure at seeing 'a Tory administration governing on Whig principles';[1] another congratulated himself that he had found at last his ideal administration, 'a good weak Government'.[2] But neither speaker was a Whig, and the possibility of strengthening the Government by a coalition with the Whigs was openly discussed.

It had been discussed ever since the day when, by passing Catholic emancipation, Wellington and Peel saw themselves faced by a Tory opposition. Brougham's entrance into the Cabinet had been mentioned:[3] when, indeed, during the past ten years had it not been rumoured that he was on the verge of taking office? A reconciliation with Huskisson had also been suggested.[4] The Colonial Secretary, Sir George Murray, and the Secretary for War, Sir Henry Hardinge, maintained friendly relations with the Whigs. A Whig, Sir James Scarlett, had been chosen to succeed Sir Charles Wetherell as Attorney-General, another Whig, the Earl of Rosslyn, to succeed Lord Carlisle as Lord Privy Seal; and it was remarked that in filling a number of less important positions Wellington seemed desirous to conciliate Liberal opinion.[5] For

[1] H. of C., February 11, 1830, Huskisson's speech (*Parl. Deb.*, N.S., vol. xxii, p. 344).
[2] H. of C., February 19, 1830, Hobhouse's speech (ibid., vol. xxii, p. 784).
[3] *Examiner*, June 7, 1829. Brougham was counsel 'for the Crown' when Wellington instructed the Attorney-General to prosecute two ultra-Tory journals (ibid., January 3, 1830).
[4] *Morning Chronicle*, February 4, 1830.
[5] *The Times*, February 16, 1830.

the last three years Lord Grey had been brought closer to Wellington by a common hatred for the political dreams of Canning,
which both cherished with equal intensity. He now kept silence,
and was universally believed to be holding himself in readiness to
collaborate with Wellington, if invited to do so. When in June
Lord Althorp began to gather around him the leading members
of the Opposition, and to put himself forward in Parliament as
official leader of an organized Opposition, his object was not so
much to open a campaign against Wellington as to compel him
to come to a decision. Either open war, or preferably an open
alliance.[1]

When Lord Althorp adopted this attitude, the political situation was on the eve of a sudden change, due to the death of King
George IV, which had been expected for two months. He quitted
the scene on June 26, followed to his grave by the contempt of the
nation, and his death delivered the Prime Minister from a grave
source of anxiety. Since the passage of Catholic emancipation the
Duke of Cumberland had sent for his wife from Germany, and
definitely taken up his abode in England in the neighbourhood
of the King, with the intention of doing everything in his power
to thwart Wellington's influence. When in the previous winter
Wellington had decided to prosecute two organs of the ultra-
Tory party, it was because he attributed the offensive articles to
the direct inspiration of the Duke; and when he had insisted that
General King, one of the Grooms of the Bedchamber who had
voted against the Government after the debate upon the Address,
should be dismissed from the Royal Household, he wished to
prove that he and not the Duke of Cumberland was master of
the Court. By the death of George IV the Duke of Cumberland
lost all his influence.

It was, indeed, uncertain for several hours what attitude the
Duke of Clarence, who now became King under the title of
William IV, would adopt towards Wellington; for Wellington,

[1] Le Marchant, op. cit., pp. 243 sqq. Cf. Lord Broughton's *Recollections of a Long Life*,
vol. iv, pp. 36–7. July 4, 1830: '. . . Morpeth and Sir James Graham said that the reason
they had not attended these meetings before was that they did not think they were sufficiently hostile to Ministers.' Cf. Lord Grey to Princess Lieven, June 25, 1830: 'Nothing
has happened with respect to myself except some further demonstrations of a disposition
to act with me from the different parties who are not satisfied with the present Government, to which I have made a civil return, without entering into any engagement or
any concerted system of operations' (*Correspondence of Princess Lieven and Earl Grey*,
vol. ii, p. 11).

an old soldier and a strict disciplinarian, had refused to tolerate
the extravagant behaviour which the Duke of Clarence had
displayed in the exercise of his functions as Lord High Admiral,
and had compelled him to resign. For months together the matter
had caused him almost as much annoyance as Catholic emancipation itself.[1] Fortunately for him the new sovereign was quick to
show that he bore him no grudge, and immediately invited him
to continue in office. He was an old fool like his brother, and very
soon shocked the nobility by his eccentric behaviour and interminable rambling speeches. But he was an honest, good-hearted fool,
who won the sympathy of the general public by the bourgeois
simplicity of his habits. The rumour got abroad that a Tory
king had been succeeded by a Liberal. Therefore, since William
IV gave his confidence to Wellington, he would not raise any
objection, as his brother would have done, to a coalition between
Wellington and the Whigs. In particular George had always
refused to consent to Lord Grey's admission to the Cabinet. He
would not forgive the attitude he had adopted at the Queen's trial.
It was whispered also that an old love affair, in which Lord Grey
had been the King's rival, was the cause of this irreconcilable
hate.[2] Wellington could therefore let it be believed that, if he did
not invite Lord Grey to join his Cabinet, the King's attitude was
the sole reason. Now this excuse was no longer available. The
change of monarch offered an excellent opportunity to recon-
stitute his administration upon a broader basis. Would he invite
Lord Grey?

He did nothing of the sort. Was it because he regarded himself
as an uncrowned dictator, called to rule outside and above the
parties, and was unwilling to diminish his authority by admitting
into his Cabinet any politician sufficiently powerful to dispute it?
So it was said, and so it was believed. But the misunderstanding
between Wellington and the public went far deeper. The Prime
Minister always remained a convinced Tory in the strictest sense
of the term. When he judged it expedient to emancipate the
Catholics, he took the step, as much in the interest of his party

[1] See Wellington, *Despatches, Cont.*, vol. iv, pp. 512 sqq., 530–9, 573–4, 578–9, 581–2,
588 sqq., 615, 625.
[2] Sir Henry Hardinge to Wellington, August 9, 1827: '. . . Croker remarked . . .
that Lord Lansdowne . . . (should be) more manageable than Lord Grey, exclusive of the
King's dislike of the latter so far back as when they crossed in each other's way with
the Duchess of Devonshire . . .' (ibid., vol. iv, p. 75).

as of his country. He acted in the same spirit as when in his Peninsula campaigns he had often led a retreat, but a section of his army had refused to carry out his orders and had persisted in fighting. He regarded these ultra-Tories as mutinous soldiers, almost liable to court-martial. He could not forgive them for compelling him by their desertion to endure the patronage of the Whigs.[1] He became extremely despondent, entertained the idea of resignation, and offered his succession to Peel: it would perhaps be better, he thought, in the existing circumstances, if the Prime Minister were a member of the Commons.[2] But Peel—since his father's death two months before, Sir Robert Peel—declined Wellington's offer. He was aware that, although his industry, his skill as an administrator, his business capacity, his ability as a reformer, and the talent displayed by his speeches in the House were universally recognized, nevertheless he was credited with only second-rate qualities.[3] Canning had been a genius. The conqueror of Vittoria and Waterloo was in his own way a great man. Peel was afraid to follow Canning and Wellington. Moreover, he was no cynic, and his retractation of 1829 on the question of Catholic emancipation sat heavy on his conscience. He was convinced that he had acted as an honourable man, but he must

[1] Wellington to Maurice Fitzgerald, December 26, 1825: 'They' (the Whigs) 'wanted to be admitted to power as a party. They forgot that I was, as I am still, at the head of the most numerous and powerful party in the State. That this party (putting the King out of the question) would not hear of any junction with the Whigs as a party, however they might submit to their introduction into office as individuals; and that the attempt would have ended, as that of Mr. Canning did, and would, even if he had lived, be a total failure' (Wellington, *Despatches, Cont.*, vol. vii, p. 383).

[2] Memorandum of a letter from the Duke of Wellington to Sir Robert Peel, 1830 (ibid., vol. vii, pp. 106–8). Cf. also, three years earlier, Arbuthnot's letter to Peel, March 18, 1827 (C. S. Parker, *Sir Robert Peel*, vol. i, pp. 452–3).

[3] *Edinburgh Review*, July 1830, 'The Ministry and the State of Parties' (vol. li, pp. 574–5): 'He is a man of respectable talents, but far, very far certainly, from being a first-rate man. . . . For the stormy times we live in, for questions involving the fate of Cabinets and even of dynasties—for the real tug-of-war, and to meet such antagonists as he sees ranged against him, it must be admitted that he is wholly unfit.' Three years before (June 6, 1827) *The Times* had written in exactly the same strain: '. . . In Parliament he was a speaker of that tribe which fluctuates between the third rate and the second. He never produced one burst of eloquence since he was born. We never heard a sentence or expression from Mr. Peel which found a place in the memory after the debate was over. His mind is of thin staple, carefully yet not finely cultivated. The soil is slight and dry—not rich nor deep: no brilliant flowers—no costly fruits of delicious flavour—no exuberant vintage—nothing beautiful by which society is adorned—nothing generous or noble by which true greatness is commemorated—has ever sprung from, or ever been connected with, this specimen of commonplace nature. . . . To talk of this person as a statesman or chief is merely an idle abuse of words.' Lord Brougham, two months afterwards, complained, on the other hand, that Peel lacked 'firmness' and 'nerve', and that he seemed not to have sufficiently realized his own importance (*The Country without a Government*, p. 5).

needs rehearse to others and even to himself the grounds of his
conviction. For a long time past he had irritated a large number of
people by this constant anxiety to produce a moral justification
for his actions. The anxiety was wholly sincere, but it had the
appearance of insincerity. Blifil, said those who remembered their
Fielding; Joseph Surface, those who remembered their Sheridan.
He suffered, therefore, under a reputation for hypocrisy which
dogged his steps for many years to come.

The change of sovereign made the little Princess Victoria,
daughter of the Duke of Kent, who had died ten years before,
heir-apparent. It became necessary, therefore, to make provision
for a Regency should William IV die before she attained her
majority. Should the Government keep Parliament in session to
pass a Regency Bill, or dissolve immediately and postpone the
discussion of the question until the next Parliament? Wellington
was anxious to get rid as soon as possible of a House of Commons
where his majority was so uncertain, and the Cabinet decided
upon the second course. Their decision was violently attacked by
the Whig Opposition in both Houses. Lord Grey in the Lords
declared war upon the Prime Minister.[1] Brougham caused a
scene in the Commons by denouncing the Duke's 'flatterers, his
mean fawning parasites'.[2] The *Edinburgh Review*, which since
April 1829 had not permitted itself any allusion to current politics,
demanded a change of administration, and suggested a coalition
between the Whigs and the ultra-Tories, between Lord Grey and
the Duke of Richmond. Now that Catholic emancipation was a
fait accompli, on what question were they divided?[3]

But when the House of Lords, after Lord Grey's speech, proceeded to vote, Lord Grey saw himself deserted by many of his
political allies, the Duke of Bedford at their head. Six days after
his violent outburst, Brougham began once more to sing
Wellington's praises.[4] The very article in the *Edinburgh Review*,
which at the opening appears to be a declaration of war against
the Government, ends with a final appeal to Wellington, from
whom, it expressly states, it is most reluctant to differ;[5] and Lord

[1] H. of L., June 30, 1830 (*Parl. Deb.*, N.S., vol. xxv, pp. 726 sqq.).
[2] H. of C., June 30, 1830 (ibid., vol. xxv, p. 825).
[3] *Edinburgh Review*, July 1830, 'The Ministry and the State of Parties' (vol. li,
pp. 564 sqq.). See especially pp. 580-1.
[4] H. of C., July 6, 1830 (*Parl. Deb.*, N.S., vol. xxv, pp. 1064-5).
[5] The same article, *sub finem*: 'Let it not for a moment be supposed that we regard
the services, even the political services, of the Duke of Wellington as desirous to under-

Grey, who was still expecting to receive from him before the end of the summer an invitation to join his administration, let it be understood that to any further advances he would not return a decided refusal.[1] When Parliament was dissolved on July 23, and the country was faced with the preparations for another election, it was still in the same muddled and apathetic condition which had prevailed for the past year. *The Times* congratulated the Government's candidates on the fact that the only violent attacks they had to face came from the ultra-Tories.[2] The *Morning Chronicle* called attention to the tranquillity which prevailed universally and the small number of seats contested either in the counties or the boroughs,[3] and prophesied that party politics would very soon be a thing of the past. 'If a Minister,' added the great Liberal organ, 'lets it be seen that he is really desirous of reducing the expenditure of the country, he will have little to fear from cabals.'[4]

In many respects the situation resembled that which had existed exactly eight years before, in the June and July of 1822. No doubt the defection of the Canningites had seriously weakened the Tory party, and Catholic emancipation effected under the conditions we have described had hastened its disruption. But, on the other hand, the Whigs were less eager to defeat Wellington now than they had been in 1822 to defeat Castlereagh, and a considerable section of the Liberals persisted in trusting the Prime Minister, however inflexibly he might reject their advances. The economic position was, no doubt, less favourable than it had been in 1822. Nevertheless, business was improving every month, and even during the previous winter the outlook had not been so dark—far from it—as it had been on many occasions since the restoration of peace; for example, in 1816, in 1819, and at the

value them. . . . To the supposition on which we have proceeded we have been slowly and most reluctantly driven by the late conduct of the Duke of Wellington himself. . . .'

[1] Lord Grey to Princess Lieven, July 2, 1830: 'Some things have come to me in the course of the last twenty-four hours which induce me to believe that some attempt may be made to conciliate me during the recess. This, however, is now more difficult, and, to tell you the truth, in what I have done I had it in view to put myself in a situation in which it would be impossible to make me anything less than a fair offer, and to place myself on good ground for rejecting anything of a contrary description' (*Correspondence of Princess Lieven and Earl Grey*, vol. ii, p. 18).

[2] *The Times*, July 14, 1830.

[3] *Morning Chronicle*, July 1830: '. . . Many persons are exceedingly puzzled to understand the phenomena peculiar to the present elections. Counties may be said to be everywhere going a-begging. The popular venal boroughs, too, find some difficulty in obtaining third candidates to prevent the two from walking over the course' (cf. July 28, 1830).

[4] Ibid., July 12, 1830.

end of 1825. And when we take a comprehensive view of the position, we find, in 1830 and in 1822 alike, the same weariness of party strife united with the same absence of revolutionary feeling, the same discontent among the Tory gentry, the same predominance of economic over political questions, and the same confusion in the mind of a public which was looking in vain for a leader. The problem which the situation had presented in 1822 had been solved by the suicide of Castlereagh and the unexpected advent of Canning. This time the solution was of a different character. At the very moment when the first elections were about to be held in the boroughs, the news reached London of the serious events which had taken place in France. These events were destined to have their repercussion in England, and to carry into office a combination of the Opposition groups under circumstances which were almost revolutionary.

Index

INDEX

Colonies freedom of trade, 201; reforms and unifies weights and measures, 202; appoints committee to investigate workmen's combinations, and passes Act to regulate them, 208–9; suppresses Catholic Association, 223; Commons pass, Lords reject, Catholic Emancipation Bill, 224–5; General Election postponed, 225. *Session 1826*, opened February 2, 1826, 227; chiefly occupied with banking system, 234–5; partial consolidation of penal laws, 192–3; Act to facilitate construction of South American merchant fleets, 228; two temporary Acts mitigating Corn Law, 229; supports Government during economic crisis, 229; two banking laws, 232–3; rejects Bill for parliamentary reform, 237–8
4. 1826–30, General Election, June 26, 239–41, 249. *Extraordinary Session, November, December* 1826, 242, 246–8; illegal measure of Government permitting cereal imports approved, 242 *and n.*; supports Canning's intervention in Portugal, 246–8. *Session 1827*, opened February 1827, 248; Canning's strength in, 248; further consolidation of penal laws, 192–3; rejects Burdett's motion for Catholic emancipation, 249–50; his Corn Bill, 249; Canning Premier, 250 *et seq.*; dropped, 254; Lord Goderich Premier, 256; Wellington Premier, 259; Lord John Russell introduces and withdraws motion to repeal Test and Corporation Acts, 264–5. *Session 1828*, Test and Corporation Acts repealed, 261; Lords refuse to enfranchise Manchester, 262; Commons accept, Lords reject, motion for Catholic emancipation, 266; committee appointed to inquire into London police, 288. *Session 1829*, opened February 5, 1829, 270; Catholic emancipation, 270–2; Committee on Church Reform, 279; rejects motion for parliamentary reform, 282; institution of 'New Police', 288; system of redemption altered, 297. *Session 1830*, debates on parliamentary reform, three proposals rejected, 284–5; capital cases of forgery reduced, 287; death of George IV, 304; Whig attack on Cabinet fails, 307; dissolved, 307; General Election, 1830, 308
Parliamentary reform, 11 *et seq.*, 34–5, 54, 56, 59–60, 61, 77–9, 145–9, 151, 190, 237–8, 253, 261–2, 280, 283–5
Parnell, Sir Henry, 193, 294–5, 297–8, 299
Pedro, Dom, Emperor of Brazil, 185, 244
Peel, Robert (later Sir Robert), relations with Ireland, 20, 138–9; opposes Catholic emancipation, 52, 141, 142–3, 144–5, 225, 249, 251, 263, 271; Chairman of Currency

Committee, introduces Bill to restore specie payment, 52–3; resigns from the Cabinet, 1818, 54; Home Secretary, 108, 114–15, 142–3; reforms penal code, 108–9, 192–3, 210; an economic Liberal, 142; attitude towards parliamentary reform, 145–6; refuses leadership of Commons, 158–9; influence, 193, 210–11; leaves Cabinet, 1827, 251; returns to Home Office, 260; Leader in Commons, 260; mediates between Wellington and Huskisson, 260; unsuccessfully opposes repeal of Test and Corporation Acts, 265; introduces Catholic emancipation Bill, 1829, 271–7; resigns seat for Oxford, 273; institutes police force, 288; supports income tax, 298; refuses to replace Wellington as Premier, 306; character and abilities, 306–7; mentioned, 21, 45, 150, 168–9, 218, 237, 250, 252, 267n., 276, 285, 287, 293, 303
Penal laws, reform of, 107–9, 191–3, 210, 287
Penenden Heath, 272
Penryn disfranchised, 261–2
Pensions system reformed, 119
Perceval, Spencer, 225
Perry, newspaper proprietor, 24, 25n., 62
Peru, 184, 186, 228
Peterloo, 64–5, 66, 83, 103; *see also* Agitation, popular, democratic agitation in textile districts
Phillpotts, Henry, Bishop of Exeter, 276
Piedmont, 128, 136, 166
Pino, General, 96
Place, Francis, 13, 21, 206, 288
Plata, La, *see* Buenos Aires
Plunket, William Conyngham, Baron, 143–4, 224
Plymouth, 177, 227
Police, 109, 221, 287–8
Polignac, M. de, 183, 301, 302
Political Litany, 32
Political Protestants, 59–60
Political Register, 15, 19, 26, 71, 103, 216
Ponsonby, Lord, 8, 188
Poor Law and Poor Rate, 40–6, 110–11, 292; Poor Rate statistics, 1815–18, 40; 1819–24, 43
Pope, the, of Rome, 142
Portland, Duke of, 252
Portugal, 127, 145, 185, 214, 244–6, 247, 253, 260, 296, 299, 300
Portuguese Colonies, 185; *see also* Brazil
Pozzo di Borgo, C. A., Count, 72
Press, Whig, 24–5, 282–3; revolutionary, 66; Radical, 94; its circulation declines, 103 *and n.*; favourable to Queen Caroline, 97, 101–2; attacks upon Canning, 160–1; explains away Monroe Doctrine, 181;

321

Reprinted by Lithography in Great Britain
by Jarrold & Sons Ltd, Norwich